THE
HEALTH
CENTURY

Books by Edward Shorter

THE MAKING OF THE MODERN FAMILY

THE HISTORY OF WOMEN'S BODIES

BEDSIDE MANNERS:
THE TROUBLED HISTORY OF DOCTORS AND PATIENTS

THE
HEALTH
CENTURY

Edward Shorter, Ph.D.

Doubleday

NEW YORK

1987

Library of Congress Cataloging-in-Publication Data

Shorter, Edward.
The health century.

Companion v. to PBS television series.
Includes index.
1. Medical innovations—United States—History.
2. Medical innovations—History. I. Health century
(television program) II. National Institutes of Health
(U.S.) III. Title. [DNLM: 1. Medicine—trends.
2. History of Medicine, 20th Cent.—United States.
WZ 70 AA1 S42h]
RA418.5.M4S56   1987   610'.9'04   87–13439
ISBN: 0-385-24236-0

For my dearest Anne Marie

Acknowledgments

I should like to thank The Blackwell Corporation for making possible the research that has led to this book. It was the insight of Neal Freeman, and the gracious, invariably good-humored management skills of David Roland that gave rise to the project.

This book is much in the debt of Kaia Toop, my splendid research assistant. Linda Distad provided transcripts of many of the interviews on which the book is based, and tapes of the interviews have been deposited in the History of Medicine Division of the National Library of Medicine.

Archivist Peter Hirtle of that library and Victoria Harden, "museologist" of the National Institutes of Health, have been kind in supplying advice. I always learn from editors, and it is a pleasure to say I have learned a great deal from the painstaking editorial work of David Gernert of Doubleday.

I must thank Dr. Peter Carlen, M.D.; Professor Jack Hay; Dr. John Parascandola; Dr. Anne Marie Shorter, M.D.; and Dr. John K. Wilson, M.D., for offering criticism of earlier drafts.

CONTENTS

PREFACE

As he lay dying, Hezekiah turned his face to the wall and prayed to God to grant him fifteen more years. He had been a good man, and it came to pass that the Lord fulfilled his prayer. Hezekiah got fifteen more years. But for a thousand years and more after that biblical story, it did not occur to most people that fifteen more years might be possible, outside of a miracle. They lived in the midst of plague, filth, and death.

We are the modern Hezekiahs. Only in the last century has it become possible for us to seize more time. Although the *idea* that science could help medicine goes back a long ways, the results were yet to be born. Today we have them in hand. The practical means of extending our life span and granting ourselves years free from chronic disease lie now before us as a result of the advances in research and therapy of the Health Century.

Before the middle of the last century, doctors could set broken bones, lance boils, and treat symptoms, but they could not cure disease. Today, if we fall ill with most of the common diseases, we have a good chance of getting Hezekiah's fifteen years and many more. This book tells the story of that progress.

The story is an international one, of scientists and bedside doctors from throughout the world—especially Europe and North America—making contributions in research that cumulate sooner or later in better health. This book concentrates on American contributions to that larger tale, for two reasons. One is that, after 1945, it really was the American locomotive that led the train; other engines pulled along, but the strongest by far was that of the United States. And this world predominance of American medical research was made possible by a historically unique combination of circumstances: a triangle of cooperation among academic medicine, research in the private sector, and the American government's National Institutes of Health, the world's largest organization for medical research. Some countries, such as Germany, had great traditions of academic medicine. Others, such as Switzerland, had energetic drug companies doing research. But only in the United States did these three spheres—academe, industry, and government—come together for a surge in knowledge about the body that is comparable to the surge of understanding of art and culture in the Renaissance.

There is a second reason for concentrating on the United States. The publication of this book marks the hundredth anniversary of the "jewel in the crown" of the federal government's research effort, the National Institutes of Health (NIH). This is not a history of the NIH. But it is a history of the Health Century that began in 1887 with the foundation of a one-room laboratory in the Marine Hospital on New York's Staten Island from which the NIH later grew.

While there are many players in the game, among them universities like Harvard and Yale or companies like Merck and Pfizer, the NIH has dominated the field in the years after World War II, either financing or being directly involved in most of the major medical advances we have seen. So it is not puffery to feature its contribution to the Health Century.

We shall move in the book from youth through old age. Or, as Dr. Edward Schneider of the National Institute on Aging—one of the twelve NIH institutes—says, "Only after scientists had conquered the diseases of infancy and childhood could they afford the luxury of investigating the diseases of old age." We begin with the triumphs over infectious diseases, maladies that once struck children with special force. We will look at a new conception of the body and its processes—molecular knowledge—and then at several specific areas where fundamental medical research has produced important clinical payoffs: the brain (which is the organ of the mind), cancer, and the immune system. We describe the real advances over heart disease and the melioration of the aches and pains of aging which have occurred. And finally, we will explore the manipulation of genetic material, the very stuff of life itself, for a future of research that would have seemed unimaginable twenty years ago.

Twenty years ago! At that time John Kennedy had already been dead for four years. The changes have been breathtaking. This book will let us catch our breath a bit by putting these changes in historical perspective.

EDWARD SHORTER

Toronto, Canada
April 1987

THE
HEALTH
CENTURY

ONE

The Health Century

Begins

Two Sick People, a Hundred Years Apart

Our first story concerns two sisters from Long Island. In 1887, in their world of grand homes and carriages to take them to the doctor, the sisters swam in disease. Five of their eight brothers and sisters had perished in infancy. Their mother "had died of some nervous trouble after child-birth."

At age nineteen one of the sisters went to see Dr. F. I. Knight with a cough of some nine months' duration. Dr. Knight diagnosed tuberculosis in her lungs, but there was nothing he could do about it; he had neither drugs nor therapy for tuberculosis. Nor did any other doctor. "The patient gradually declined," Dr. Knight wrote, "and died April 15, 1887."

But then her sister fell ill as well, and it is the case of this sister that interested Dr. Knight, for he was trying to demonstrate that tuberculosis was contagious. The sister had occupied the same bedroom as the first victim. "She had continued to attend closely upon the invalid all winter, and had disregarded all my advice. She had even slept with her sister. . . .

She was with her night and day." The second sister then developed a dry, hacking cough, a fever, and began breathing quickly. After listening to her lungs, Dr. Knight diagnosed tuberculosis. She was now so weak that she had to be supported from the carriage to Dr. Knight's house, where he saw his patients. She started coughing up blood, and died two months after her sister.

In the world of disease of 1887, the beginning of the Health Century, doctors could diagnose disease but not cure it. Medicine had been placed on a sufficiently scientific basis that doctors were starting to understand what underlying physical lesions in the body produced what symptoms.[1] But there science stopped. Tuberculosis was the number one cause of death in those days, and doctors had few drugs that worked. For pain they could inject morphine; for malaria there was quinine; smallpox vaccination was becoming routine; and digitalis was available though seldom used for heart failure. And that was it. There were no other vaccines; no specific remedies against any particular disease; no antibiotics; nothing. Not even aspirin was available.

A hundred years later another New York woman, Professor Elaine Brody, a sixty-three-year-old musicologist at New York University, lay ill. This time it was not tuberculosis, which has been curable since the 1950s. It was breast cancer. Her doctors at New York's St. Vincent's Hospital had treated the actual cancer in the breast well enough, but it had spread to her liver and abdomen. "Her liver was massively enlarged and it was failing. She was a few days from death," said Dr. William Grace, chief of the hospital's cancer program. Professor Brody knew she was dying. "I was making funeral arrangements. I knew I would never finish my book. My family and I would never take our barge trip through France."

But medicine now has resources, even against as awesome a disease as breast cancer. Radiologist Richard Neff, watching what he was doing with a computerized X ray system that produces an enhanced image, was able to insert a thin tube into the patient's liver. "With this system," Dr. Neff said, "we can put a catheter in some very hard-to-reach places. Without secondary organ damage, and with much less discomfort for the patient." Cancer drugs could now be infused directly into the liver, at concentrations that wouldn't be possible if they were injected into the blood or swallowed. And after six days of treatment, Professor Brody's liver had gone back to its normal size. "All evidence of cancer on physical examination," the hospital tells us, "had disappeared. Within two weeks, she was back at work on her book. And soon thereafter she and her family were floating down a French canal."[2]

In the hundred years between these two typical illnesses, many diseases have miraculously been cured, and our life expectancy increased. In 1887 a baby girl could expect to have forty-four years of life, today she can expect to live for seventy-eight years. That is a 77 percent increase in life expectancy at birth in this Health Century. If you were a woman of twenty in 1887, you could expect to live another forty-two years; today a woman of twenty can expect to live another fifty-nine years. Today's young woman has thus won a 40 percent greater life expectancy.[3]

Not all these extra years are owing solely to medical research and drugs. Before the Second World War, great strides in the life expectancy of children, for example, had resulted from the public health movement, from clean water and flushing away sewage in cast-iron pipes, from washing one's clothes and body regularly, and from laws stipulating that food and drink no longer be adulterated. It is really after the Second World War that the drug revolution begins to take hold, making a major contribution to life expectancy and to the relief of such chronic problems as arthritis and infertility. Since 1950, for example, death rates from heart disease have been dropping by an astonishing 4 percent a year; over that period deaths from stroke have declined almost 2 percent annually.[4] Both declines are due in large part to the development of drugs against high blood pressure.

Because so much of this book will be about distinctively American contributions to health after the 1930s, it shouldn't be forgotten that all was not blackest night before that time. In the millennia of previous history, some substances had been unearthed that helped fight some illnesses.

Take malaria, for instance, a disease that James Shannon, one of the coming cast of characters, helped push back. In the sixteenth century it was discovered that the bark of a certain tree, when taken medicinally, helped fight the disease. Quinine was isolated from that bark as early as 1820.

Parents have always been hypnotized by the epidemic killers of childhood, although historically many more children have died of simple dehydration from diarrhea than from such notorious maladies as scarlet fever. It was not with antibiotics but with vaccines that these diseases were vanquished. The first vaccine, against smallpox, came in 1798. Then there was a bit of a pause, and an antiserum against the toxin of diphtheria appeared early in the 1890s. Thus, even before the beginning of the Health Century, the health of children had begun to improve significantly.

And what of the health of middle-aged men? After reaching an age when they could look back in dismay upon their student days and drunken trips to bordellos, men would begin to obsess about syphilis. Of course, people had long known of a general connection between venery and syphilis, but doctors also thought that loose living and staying up late at night could cause it. Not until the first decade of the twentieth century was it established that syphilis was transmitted through a venerally acquired organism. And a successful therapy for it came several years later, when in 1910 Paul Ehrlich announced the discovery of a compound that really did stop the causative organism from multiplying in the body. The Bayer chemical company produced it at works in Hoechst, Germany, under the proprietary name Salvarsan.

Before 1935 there were a few other drugs for specific maladies: insulin for diabetes, discovered in 1922 at the University of Toronto; a liver extract developed by several American scientists for pernicious anemia; and several vaccines for other diseases of childhood.[5] But although diabetes and pernicious anemia were tragic diseases, they did not reach into the life of every household.

What reached into every household were bacterial infections, and against these doctors were totally helpless. "As I look back over the old casebooks," wrote Arthur Hertzler, a Kansas country doctor, in 1938, "I wonder now just how much real good I did. Certainly the medicines I dispensed were merely symbols of good intentions."[6] William Osler, probably the most distinguished physician of the day and then at Johns Hopkins Medical School, wrote of scarlet fever, "Many specifics have been vaunted . . . but they are all useless." Of therapies for rheumatic fever, a bacterial infection that affects the heart valves in particular, Osler said, "Medicines have little or no control over the duration or course of the disease, which, like other self-limited affections, practically takes its own time to disappear."[7] Osler was like many doctors before 1935, when the first wonder drugs were announced—a therapeutic nihilist. He was dubious about the ability of drugs to cure disease.

Although earlier vaccines had caused many historic killers such as smallpox to recede, children in particular in the Roaring Twenties were still exposed to infections that could be life-threatening. A random survey of illness in 1928–31 among nine thousand white families living in eighteen different states found that, for children under five, each year one child in thirteen had had measles; one child in twelve had had whooping cough; one child in a hundred caught scarlet fever.[8] These figures may not sound enormous. But they mean that, in any given year, if a child had twelve friends, one of them would have whooping cough; if there were a hundred children in the first grade, one of them would come down annually with scarlet fever. You can die very easily from either disease, and there was nothing that medicine could do to help, save ease the symptoms.

The true medical revolution of our times begins in 1927, when Gerhard Domagk was appointed chief of animal research in a German drug and chemical firm, the I. G. Farben company, a firm later to become notorious for its exploitation of slave labor under the Nazis. He had been experimenting with the kind of dyes the German organic chemical industry had been so successful in developing. In 1931 he hit paydirt when some of the dyes with a sulfur-nitrogen side chain (sulfonamide) began to cure mice without side effects. The researchers were jubilant, and a year later, on Christmas Day, 1932, they submitted a patent application for a particularly promising red dye. They called it Streptozon.

Weeks later the head of I. G. Farben's medical division approached Domagk, asking him if he had anything that might help a ten-month-old boy dying of blood poisoning. "Treatment began at once, the baby receiving half a tablet twice daily by mouth. To everyone's astonishment, the baby did not die." Instead the infant was cured and was discharged from hospital three weeks later. Two years now pass; the drug is tested on patients locally, and in February 1935 Domagk announces his discovery to the world. He has invented sulfa drugs.

Domagk's own daughter pricks her finger, develops severe blood poisoning, and is saved by the new drug. In January 1936 samples are given to doctors at the Queen Charlotte's Maternity Hospital in London for women with postdelivery and postabortion infections. There is success on every front with a drug that I. G. Farben is at this point calling Prontosil.

In the meantime the scene switches to France. In the spring of 1935 doctors at the Pasteur Institute—the French equivalent of the National Institutes of Health (NIH)—had synthesized some Prontosil on their own. Then they analyzed the urine of the patients to whom the drug had been given. They found, not leftover Prontosil, but a much simpler substance long known in the literature as sulfanilamide. The complex dye had been broken down in the body to its essential active ingredient, and now since the patent protecting it had just expired, French chemists proceeded to make sulfanilamide on their own.[9]

These sulfa drugs mark the beginning of the end of *bacterial* infection. There are other kinds of infections, which as yet remained untouched, but this first step in conquering bacteria was revolutionary. And the sulfa drugs were just the beginning. By 1941 penicillin was on the horizon. Then after the war new drugs were discovered for tuberculosis, for chronic inflammation, for ulcers. And the list goes on. The current edition of *Goodman and Gilman,* which is the Bible of drug therapy, has 1839 pages, and these are not pages about the healing power of chamomile tea, like the old pharmacopoeias, but about heavy-duty, scientifically proven drugs that work.[10] In the hundred years that constitute the Health Century, drugs have become important only in the last fifty. Precisely in these last fifty years the baton of medical research has passed from Europe to the United States.

Microbe Hunters

Not far away from Long Island, where in 1887 the two sisters lay ill, young Dr. Joseph Kinyoun was installing at the same time a Zeiss microscope in his Hygienic Laboratory. This laboratory, at the Marine Hospital at Stapleton, Staten Island, had materialized in 1887 rather magically. The country had been undergoing terrible epidemics of cholera and yellow fever that periodically swept the South, in particular. A few years previously, Congress had established a National Board of Health to investigate these epidemics; the vice chairman of the board was one of those great dynamos in the history of American public health, John Shaw Billings.

But Billings had a rival. The surgeon general of another service, the Marine Hospital Service, hated Billings and his pretensions in the public health area. The Marine Hospital Service itself, established by Congress in 1798 to provide medical care to sick merchant seamen, was intending to fight epidemics. John Brown Hamilton was the surgeon general of this service, and as in 1888 he battled in congressional hearings against the claims of his rival Billings, he was able to play a trump card: The National Board of Health wanted to move into laboratory studies of cholera, did it? Well, the Marine Hospital Service was already doing the same thing. "Relative to what Dr. Billings says about cholera germs, I desire to invite the attention of the Committee . . . to the diagnosis of cholera [which] was made of the cases that occurred in New York, by an officer of my service by the name of Kinyoun, who has spent nearly five years in the study of bacteriology. We have spent several hundred dollars in forming a laboratory in New York . . ."[11] This was the first anyone had heard of a Hygienic Laboratory with Kinyoun as its director. The story permitted Hamilton to defeat his rival Billings. And the Hygienic Laboratory went on to become the National Institutes of Health.

So we have young Dr. Kinyoun. Although legend has it—doubtless encouraged by John Brown Hamilton for political reasons—that Kinyoun arrived in New York after studying bacteriology in Europe with the masters, in fact, Kinyoun seems to have come as a twenty-seven-year-old fresh from a country practice. A North Carolina boy, he studied medicine first under the preceptorship of his physician father, then took a course of

lectures at the St. Louis Medical College. He then attended for another
year the famous Bellevue Hospital Medical College in New York, receiving
his M.D. in the spring of 1882. Those were the days when it was not
difficult to get an American medical degree: the schools were crying out
for students and the examinations were perfunctory. Neither Kinyoun nor
most other American graduates received any kind of hospital training.

But in his scientific curiosity Kinyoun was quite untypical of his medical
counterparts. For after graduating he continued to study, taking in 1882
special instruction in surgery and gynecology with various New York doctors. In 1883 it was microscopy, the gateway to understanding how infectious disease changes the tissues of the body. "In 1885," he continued in
his curriculum vitae, "I took a course of instruction in the Carnegie Laboratory, New York, under Dr. Hermann M. Biggs, investigating cholera
asiatica, cholera morbus, and the different germs. I have since that time
made experiments with the micrococcus of erysipelas and osteomyelitis
from a surgical standpoint." (Erysipelas is a kind of strep infection that
produces a red rash; osteomyelitis is an infection of the bone marrow.) So
at Bellevue's Carnegie Laboratory, Kinyoun was swept along by the lead
locomotives of American science. Only in 1882 had Robert Koch in Germany announced his discovery that tuberculosis (TB) was caused by a
germ. All over the world these young sciences of bacteriology, microscopy, and histology (the microscopic study of tissue) were springing into
life.

Why Kinyoun left New York after 1885 is unclear. But he joined his
father in practice in Johnson County, Missouri, for a year. In April 1886 he
went to Washington and took the examination for a civil service appointment in the Marine Hospital Service. He passed, was commissioned as an
assistant surgeon in October of that year, and in August 1887 established
this tiny microbiology laboratory on Staten Island.[12]

The Marine Hospital Service became the Public Health Service in
1902.[13] In order to understand the importance of the Public Health Service's later swing to basic science, we must remember that the men of
Kinyoun's generation thought of themselves as "microbe hunters." Although they had medical rather than military training, they constituted a
corps of federal officers, selected after 1873 by a civil service exam. They
fought epidemics and ran the Marine Hospital system rather than doing
surgery. Indeed in 1878 one of the surgeon officers designed for the corps
a special uniform, with the letters "M.D." on the blouse in old English
script. A formal commissioned corps was established by Congress in
1889.[14] To this very day, commissioned Public Health Service employees
wear their uniforms on ceremonial occasions.

Officers of the Public Health Service in their first uniforms, 1878.

Why officers, why uniforms rather than white coats? The health experiences of the Civil War had demonstrated how useful it was to have a disciplined, professional corps of M.D.s who could be directed about as the need arose to investigate epidemics. The states were constantly calling upon the Marine Hospital Service for aid in outbreaks of smallpox, yellow fever, and cholera. Quarantines, in particular, required an authoritative hand for their direction. And it was actually because the merchants of San Francisco resisted Kinyoun's efforts to quarantine Chinatown in a bubonic plague epidemic in 1901 that he left the Marine Hospital Service.[15]

Now that the public has become so cynical about the public spirit of the medical profession, it is difficult for us to imagine the real personal courage these men displayed as they waded into epidemics. Bubonic plague (black death) and yellow fever are, after all, very nasty diseases. They look terribly brave and military, these small bands of officer M.D.s in their high leather boots and peaked caps, as they assemble for photographs whose captions read: "Bubonic Plague Campaign, San Francisco, California, 1907–1908," or "Plague Campaign in New Orleans, 1914."

Public Health Service officers on the bubonic plague campaign, New Orleans, 1914.

As in any military campaign, there were casualties. By 1951, 271 service doctors had contracted major infections from the diseases they were studying, and 24 had died, among them, for example, Assistant Surgeon Roswell H. Waldo, dead of yellow fever in 1878 in Cairo, Illinois; Past Assistant Surgeon Thomas Richardson, dead of typhoid fever in 1906 in New Orleans; Junior Bacteriologist Anna Pabst, dead of meningitis in 1935 in Washington, D.C.[16] Thus, for many years the Marine Health Service directed its activities at the practical suppression of epidemics.

When Congress reshaped the Public Health Service in 1912, it expanded considerably the organization's mandate, authorizing the investigation of the "diseases of man," as they were known in those days.[17] In 1912 Joseph Goldberger, the man who conquered pellagra, was thirty-eight years old.

A Tireless Man Who Paid Attention

Aside from their dedication to field work for the Public Health Service, it would be hard to imagine two types more dissimilar than Joseph Kinyoun and Joseph Goldberger. Kinyoun was a doctor's son from rural North Carolina. Goldberger had been born in Hungary, his parents emigrating to the East Side of Manhattan in 1881 when Joseph was seven. They ran a grocery store and he worked as a delivery boy. Goldberger, being extremely bright, entered the City College of New York at age sixteen to study engineering, and stood fifth in a class of six hundred by the end of his second year. He dropped in on a lecture at Bellevue Hospital Medical College one day, became entranced, and switched to medicine. After two dull years of private practice in Wilkes Barre, Pennsylvania, he took the competitive exams for the Marine Hospital Service, got the highest score, and in 1899 became a microbe hunter.[18] Thus, for the next fourteen years Goldberger spent a highly active life fighting yellow fever, dengue fever, typhus, typhoid, and so forth all over the United States and the Gulf of Mexico. Because he was such an experienced, energetic hand at infectious disease, it was to Goldberger that Surgeon General Rupert Blue turned in February 1914 to fight a disease called pellagra.

That few people today have even heard of pellagra is a measure of the success of Goldberger's efforts. Contrary to what was assumed at the time, pellagra is not an infectious disease on the model of typhoid or yellow fever, but a disease resulting from a deficiency in the B vitamin niacin. Where do we get niacin? From our diets, or from the body's own synthesis of it—from the amino acid tryptophan. Thus, pellagra will ensue if the body is short either of dietary niacin or tryptophan. Now, if you get your niacin from indian corn, or maize, you're in trouble: maize binds niacin so that the intestines can't absorb it unless the maize is specially treated first.

Poor people in the South were heavy cornbread (maize) eaters, but in normal times they got their niacin and tryptophan requirements from meat, milk, and vegetables. In times of scarcity, however, they were obliged to cut back on these substances and rely on cornbread alone, plus molasses and hog back, the fatty parts of the pig around its spine. Rich enough in calories, this diet was lacking both in tryptophan and in niacin and would lead to pellagra.

An endemic problem in the South for years, only around the time of the First World War did pellagra begin to become *epidemic,* as economic circumstances drove down wages of the field hands, tenant farmers, miners, and sawmill workers. The pellagra diet became normal upon the Southern table. That was why Surgeon General Blue called upon Goldberger.

In full-blown pellagra the skin turns swollen, crusted, and bright red, the victim is plagued by diarrhea, and if niacin is not added in time to reverse the changes, dementia ensues as well. The mental asylums of the Deep South thus had an ample share of pellagrins, irreversibly impaired by the disease. Lesser degrees of pellagra were so common as to be considered a normal developmental phase in children, especially in orphanages where cornbread and molasses were served three times daily. Thus, as Goldberger wrote in his diary, Superintendent Carter of the Baptist orphanage near Jackson, Mississippi, told him in August 1915 that "every spring since he took charge some 12 years ago (1903), some of the

children would 'break out' on hands and feet, face and neck. Also many of
the children would have sore mouths [a common early complaint in pella-
gra].

   "Nothing much was thought about all this," Goldberger continued in

Dr. Joseph Goldberger.

his diary, "it being explained as due to 'bad blood.' . . . [Carter] had
observed that the children, after 2 or 3 years of such attacks, would tend to
get over it. As [Carter] sees it now, this 'getting over it' was associated with
the fact that as they grew older and began to do work, their diet was
modified by the addition of 'meat.' "[19]

   Of particular interest to us is how Goldberger figured out that the cause
of pellagra was dietary and not infectious. He simply observed very carefully who in a given community had the disease, who did not, and then
tried to see how the two groups differed. In his first Southern trip, in the
spring of 1914, it took him about three weeks to come up with the answer.
His biographer explains, "Everywhere, he just looked and listened. He
carried no monkeys or rabbits with him. He set up no laboratories; he
carried no microscope. Unencumbered by equipment and preconceived
ideas, he brought to the two-centuries-old pellagra problem a fresh perspective."[20]

Goldberger made these observations mainly in asylums. If pellagra was an infectious disease, why didn't staff members ever catch it? Goldberger ascribed it to differences in their rations. "Although the nurses and attendants may apparently receive the same food," he wrote, "there is nevertheless a difference in that the nurses have the privilege—which they exercise—of selecting the best and greatest variety for themselves."[21] Thus he slowly concluded pellagra must be a question of diet.

In the field Goldberger was tireless. Virtually every night he was in a different community, talking with this local doctor or that asylum supervisor, quizzing the locals about what they ate and whether their privies were screened (just in case pellagra turned out after all to be spread by flies). What particular deficiency in the diet could possibly be causing pellagra? In June 1915 he found himself in the hinterland of Shreveport, Louisiana. "Dr. Eddie stated . . . that so far this spring they have had about 175 cases of pellagra, a number vastly in excess of what had been met with in preceding years." Another doctor had already treated three hundred cases, up from about twelve a year previously. He quizzed the merchants as well, "all of whom stated as did also the doctors that last winter they had a 'famine' in this region. That on account of the cotton failure the merchants were obliged to reduce the cost of the ration to the lowest possible point and consequently they [the field hands] had not been allowed meat nor flour [corn meal] and so had largely subsisted on bread and molasses, a so-called 'black-strap' about 2 gals. a week for the average family of 5 members." What struck Goldberger was that in areas around Shreveport where the destitution had been greatest, pellagra was most common. But in communities where "many of the negroes had winter employment making ties, and consequently were in a position to live better than otherwise would have been possible," there had been less pellagra.

This particular observation had no earthshaking consequences; Goldberger recorded many others which he found equally interesting. But the stories in Goldberger's notebook are important for two reasons. First, they are typical of this generation of public health officers and the fierce energy with which they drove themselves. It was only at the end of this marathon that Goldberger's energy began to flag: "In the evening [I] left for Macon intending to go to Savannah but on arrival in Macon found myself so tired and worn that I felt obliged to go to the hotel."

Second, the initial technique he employed was epidemiological: seeing what distinguishes two groups of people, one healthy, the other ill. Later he would experimentally induce black tongue in dogs to make his discovery in 1923 of a pellagra-preventive factor in brewer's yeast. Progress in fighting pellagra did not come about at the biochemical, much less the molecular level, until much later. Only in 1937 did Conrad Elvehjem of the University of Wisconsin identify the pellagra-preventive factor as nicotinic acid, or niacin. And only after other discoveries in the 1940s and '50s did it become apparent that niacin, like the other B-complex vitamins, works in the body as a coenzyme in absolutely fundamental processes: niacin forms part of something called NAD, or *n*icotinamide *a*denine *d*inucleotide, which permits the cell to utilize oxygen.[22] As this process is basic to life, people deficient in niacin suffer from a potentially fatal disease. Tens of thousands of Southerners, above all black people, had died of pellagra. That pellagra virtually vanished from the South was owing to the sharp eyes and tireless energy of Joseph Goldberger, the grocer's son from the Lower East Side.

"Putting Things in Bottles"

The other players in the game, besides the Public Health Service officers, were the universities and the drug companies. At the point of departure, the American pharmaceutical industry lay far behind Europe. Part of the story of the Health Century is how it grew up to do first-rank science.

The big drug companies are not household names. Most of them have a familiar ring, but few who are not medical scientists and observers of the pharmaceutical industry are able to make specific connections. The reason nobody has heard of these enormous firms, whose annual sales run into the billions of dollars today, is that they don't advertise to the public. Making what are called ethical specialties—meaning that the drugs are sold by prescription, not that they're specially moral—these firms advertise only in medical journals. References in medical circles to MSD for Merck Sharp & Dohme or SK&F for Smith Kline & French are self-understood.

The fact that there weren't many effective drugs in times past doesn't mean there weren't any drugs. But most of the drugs that people took were either innocuous teas that affected mainly the imagination, or laxatives, or out-and-out poisons containing substances such as mercury. Before the germ theory of disease late in the nineteenth century, medical ideas about how disease affected the body were often completely wrong. Therapies based on these ideas did more harm than good. Thus, for many years it was held that one could regain health again only by "getting those poisons out of there." This entailed swallowing a powerful purgative and becoming dehydrated through successive bowel movements, in addition to losing important minerals in the stool. Samuel Gross, a well-known Philadelphia surgeon of the nineteenth century, remembered something

Most early medicines (as shown here and on facing page) were either purgatives or poisons, many containing mercury. The first effective medicines—sleeping drugs (hypnotics) and painkillers—were synthesized from coal-tar products in the 1880s.

called the R.A.C. pill, consisting of *r*hubarb (a purgative), *a*loe (also a purgative), and *c*alomel (mercurous chloride, a toxic purgative that would cause bowels, kidneys, and many other body parts to act up). "The R.A.C. pill slew its thousands of victims, and caused the destruction of innumerable lips, cheeks, teeth, and jaw-bones, the result of the horrible ptyalism [mercury poisoning] so common in those days."[23] Such purgatives were usually compounded from scratch by local pharmacists, as nationwide drug companies did not yet exist.

The German organic chemical industry changed all this in the 1880s by synthesizing from coal-tar products a slew of new drugs which, although not specific for given diseases, did relieve pain, reduce fever, and calm the mind. Discovered in laboratories, these drugs were manufactured in big plants and sold to drugstores prepackaged, eventually putting an end to the pharmacist's role of making up prescriptions from raw ingredients.

Chief among these German firms was the Friedrich Bayer Company of Elberfeld, which launched in 1888 two products whose success would change dramatically the pharmaceutical industry: a sleeping drug (hypnotic) called sulphonal, and a minor painkiller named phenacetin, the ancestor of Tylenol. A decade later Bayer brought aspirin to the market.[24] As the formula for aspirin had been long known in chemistry, Bayer was unable to patent it, but patented a process for making lots of it instead, becoming thereby a household word.

The Bayer star—now transformed into the great chemical trust I. G. Farben—continued to rise. From another basic coal-tar structure named barbituric acid, German chemists synthesized in 1903 the powerful hypnotic Veronal, then eight years later another, phenobarbital (Luminal), still in use today.[25] As many people, both then and now, suffered from "nerves" and insomnia, the market for these preparations was immense. Bayer, with its eighty international branches, became a model for the pharmaceutical multinational corporations of today. By 1938 the company library had accumulated seventy-five thousand volumes and thirty thousand doctoral dissertations. A company history commemorating the fiftieth anniversary shows a company plane overflying the works at Leverkusen. The plane, of course, bears a swastika.[26]

American drug companies before the First World War made virtually no synthetic drugs of their own, importing sulphonal, phenobarbital, and the like in bulk from Germany, or purchasing the license to manufacture them under American labels.[27] The First World War changed all this. American firms began copying many German drugs, once Congress had suspended the patents. And as the British blockade interrupted shipments from Germany of such basic chemicals as acetone and phenol, local manufacturers stepped in. A huge domestic surplus of bulk chemicals was accumulated. Then, as peace came in 1918 and prices collapsed again, all these bulk chemicals—the building blocks of pharmaceuticals—could be purchased by drug companies for a song.

Only at this point does the American pharmaceutical industry begin synthesizing its own products. Abbott Laboratories, for example, started making a local anesthetic similar to the German drug Novocain, simply because the price drop of the raw chemicals had made it so appealing. The sedatives and hypnotics from barbituric acid all became big American winners in the 1920s. For example, Hoffmann-La Roche marketed Allonal in 1921, Lilly Amytal in 1923, Abbot Nembutal in 1929, and so forth. Family doctors greatly loved these drugs because they could now give prescriptions to patients whose symptoms were owing to stress and anxiety.

The American drug houses thus started from humble origins indeed. Here is Elmer Bobst's description of Roche's New York office on Fulton Street in 1911: "When I first entered . . . the windows of its small medicinal 'mixing' room were open to all of the dust and grime of the city. Hygienic standards were rudimentary. . . . Delicate pharmaceutical manufacture took place above ancient wooden floors from which dust rose with every vibration. Rats and mice infested the walls and crawl spaces of the building. Some of our production involved volatile chemicals that presented a constant danger of explosion and fire."[28]

Another big name is Merck. In the same way that Roche-New York had been established by a Swiss parent company, in 1885 Merck and Company in Darmstadt, Germany, entrusted young Theodore Weicker to establish for them an American branch, which he did in New York. Then in 1900 at a garden party in Stamford, Connecticut, Theodore Weicker met the nineteen-year-old daughter of Lewis Palmer, a highly successful Brooklyn industrialist. After marrying the daughter, Weicker severed his Merck connection, and persuaded his father-in-law to buy a small chemical company owned by a Dr. Squibb. It mainly produced ether. Thus, for Palmer's investment of $1 million—and his son-in-law's added $100,000—yet another industry giant was born.[29]

World War I gave the American drug industry its start by weaning it from the German parents. But it was research plus aggressive marketing that turned these little chemical companies into pharmaceutical giants. In 1921 the American drug industry was still a pretty punk affair. Sharp & Dohme in Philadelphia, long before its 1953 merger with Merck, employed fifteen chemists of various kinds and two pharmacologists, specialists in how drugs affect the body. The Gibraltars of the day were Eli Lilly in Indianapolis and Parke-Davis in Detroit, each having a research staff of more than forty, with a goodly share of those workers devoted to ferreting out new drugs.[30] In 1902 Parke-Davis had opened its research offices, the first in the United States. Lilly followed in 1911, establishing a separate research building. Roche built its new facility at Nutley, New Jersey, in 1929, and Squibb founded the Squibb Institute for research in 1938.

The Abbott company began its great boom during World War I by duplicating German drugs whose patents had been canceled. In 1922 it built a new $2 million plant, covering twenty-four acres and including twenty-seven buildings, in North Chicago.[31] Abbott now had big research labs, and hired Ernest Volwiler, a first-rate chemist from the University of Illinois, to direct them. Merck then snared Vienna's Hans Molitor. These men were good scientists, interested in something more than getting toothpaste smiles brighter than white. Research chemists employed by the five major companies increased in number from 26 in 1920 to 147 in 1940.[32]

What were these labs all doing research on? Vitamins, for one thing. It was ironically at the beginning of the Depression decade that the drug companies really began to rise, lifted by the tide of vitamins. Elmer Bobst wrote later, "While an international bear market dragged down the economies and living standards of every country on earth, a bull market in pharmaceuticals . . . began to revitalize mankind."[33] It was vitamins that provided the profits that would make the drug industry a major player in the science game. First came the vitamins that abound in liver: A and D had been discovered in the 1920s. Who can forget cod-liver oil, the source of vitamin D! Then Abbott and Parke-Davis formed a consortium, establishing in 1929 a huge extraction plant in Seattle for Pacific Coast halibut, whose livers were even richer than cod in these fat-soluble vitamins. Thus Haliver Oil replaced cod-liver oil. In 1934 these busy researchers determined that the livers of the tuna family, including the mackerel, were richer still in vitamins, and Abbott marketed Tunliver Oil. (Vitamin A is essential for good vision, D to prevent infantile rickets. Whether one needs store-bought supplements for either vitamin is another story, however.)

Brewer's yeast had been known as a source of niacin since the mid-1920s. But the thirties saw the birth of other members of the great B vitamin family. Vitamin B_1, which protects against beriberi, was first isolated in 1926. Ten years later Robert Williams, the chemical director of the Bell Telephone Laboratories, figured out in his spare time a commercially feasible way of producing vitamin B_1, or thiamine, and marketed it to the Merck company.[34] The public's appetite for vitamins, then as now, was insatiable. Such products as Abbott's Vita-Kaps, a mixture of A, B_1, C, D, and "G" (riboflavin, now called vitamin B_2), brought to market in 1936, made great profits.[35]

But what made the biggest difference in the contribution of the private sector to the Health Century was the discovery of the sulfa drugs in 1935. It was only at this point that the drug companies realized that good science and profits went hand in hand. After 1935 the drug houses rushed over five thousand different sulfa drugs onto the market, their chemists all bent upon improvements. Elmer Bobst, manager of the Swiss firm Hoffmann-La Roche's American branch and an important figure in the modern pharmaceutical story, recalled the frenzy into which the arrival of sulfanilamide thrust the American drug industry. "Suddenly, sulfanilamide became the most valuable pharmaceutical on earth. Since it was in the public domain, every pharmaceutical house . . . jumped into the race to produce it.

"Overnight, every penny that the pharmaceutical industry had invested in their painstaking vaccine cures for pneumonia washed down the drain; a new product that not only cured pneumonia but many other diseases as well took its place."[36]

But money does not necessarily buy happiness, or legitimacy. Even though the drug houses were becoming substantial corporate citizens, an odor of commerce still clung to their scientific activities, causing academic researchers to look down on them. Going to work for a drug company was grounds for losing one's membership in at least one professional society. Arnold Welch, later a leading American pharmacologist, had to give up his membership in the American Society for Pharmacology and Experimental Therapeutics in 1940 when he took a job with Sharp & Dohme.[37] In 1943 Francis Boyer, a vice president of Smith Kline & French who was trying to encourage cooperation between the drug industry and academe, referred in embarrassed tones to the "scrimmage era" of drug making that he hoped was now past.[38] But some odium clung well into the 1950s. When a friend asked James Shannon, whom we later meet as the architect of today's NIH, why he had terminated his association with an important pharmaceutical manufacturer, he said with a gesture of distaste that it was because they "put things into bottles."[39]

The National Institute of Health Is Founded

Even though Joseph Kinyoun himself had left the little Hygienic Laboratory in 1899, it continued to grow. In 1902 Congress decided to regulate the production of vaccines and other biologicals, making more work for the laboratory. The microbe hunters' tasks of administering quarantines, checking immigrants for disease, and so forth became more rather than less pressing. So in 1891 the laboratory moved from Staten Island to Washington, and then in 1904 inhabited a handsome new building in downtown Washington of which old hands, even in the 1980s, would speak with fondness. Bernice Eddy, the microbiologist who will later play an important role in our tale, described it as "wonderful. Only about two hundred people. It was down at Twenty-fifth and E. You knew everybody." By the 1980s this Hygienic Lab had expanded into the National Institutes of Health, with 15,000 employees.[40]

But microbe hunting wasn't enough in an era when people were starting to see the importance of science. "The practice of medicine leads to a good income, undoubtedly, but it does not lead to the control of disease," Joseph Bloodgood of the Johns Hopkins Medical School told a congressional hearing in 1929. "The cure for diseases is found in research laboratories."[41] The nation was aware that science in Britain and Germany was bounding ahead with government support. The United States too needed some government science, although Congress was careful to specify that it be "in the problems of the diseases of man," as opposed to basic research.

So in 1930 Congress passed a law renaming the Hygienic Laboratory the National Institute of Health. It was now possible for "professors" to accept civil service appointments without donning the uniform of the Public Health Service, and for them to receive salaries somewhat higher than those of other health bureaucrats.[42]

The laboratory's move from downtown Washington to Bethesda, a Maryland suburb, became possible in 1935, when Helen and Luke Wilson donated forty-five acres of land to the government, having an estimated value of $75,000. It was a district of pleasant woods and rolling hills and even today—in the middle of a sprawling bedroom community—retains a leafy kind of charm. Thus, in December 1938 the NIH consisted of three handsome brick buildings, designed in the gracious prewar style of much federal architecture. By the mid-1980s there would be sixty-four buildings on three hundred acres.[43] The distinctively American contribution to the Health Century revolves heavily about these buildings.

TWO

America, the Can-Do Country

Erwin Chargaff was the bad boy of biochemistry. At loose ends in Vienna in 1928, he was learning Danish, just in case something opened up in Denmark. Then he heard of a research post available at Yale, sent off an application, and got the job. "As the time of departure grew nearer," he said, "so grew my fears. I was afraid of going to a country that was younger than most of Vienna's toilets."[1]

Chargaff, who helped discover the chemical basis of DNA, represents the deep roots of Old World science. James Shannon, who built the NIH to what it is today, embodies the science of a budding New World. The American part of the Health Century occurred when these two worlds were grafted together.

Although it is an exaggeration to think of European science before the Second World War as the brain, and American science as the body and muscle, it is not much of an exaggeration. Until the 1940s, what the Americans excelled at was getting jobs done, rather than coming up with brilliant ideas. This was the can-do spirit, the spirit of the Seabees driving bulldozers under machine gun fire on Pacific islands during World War II. This spirit created the revenues that made America the scientific center of the world in the 1950s and after.

"Science Could Have Died in This Country"

It was not by accident that a Johnny-come-lately pioneer culture found itself behind the Europeans. The Germans, for example, had a superb high school system in which the pupils would study not science but Latin, Greek, and history. Although these subjects were not useful for scientific investigation, they imparted to young minds rigor and system. American schools, on the other hand, were highly uneven. Many of the people we shall read about came from elite high schools in New York City. But other entire regions might remain silent.

German culture placed high esteem upon science—*Wissenschaft*—and the credentials of an academic researcher would open doors in Berlin and Vienna that, by contrast, a business card might pry apart here. A major landmark in Sigmund Freud's life, for example, was his elevation in 1902 to the title of professor, which exerted upon the minds of his fellow Viennese a powerful effect. Even his otherwise snooty English followers, such as James and Alix Strachey, referred to him as "the Professor." In America, on the other hand, academic accomplishment has traditionally won little social status.

In Germany all twenty-one universities were state-financed, and each had its science chairs and laboratories. As early as 1891 there were more than three hundred German scientists doing research in biology and medicine.[2] In America the number was negligible, for American colleges were largely private, dependent on tuition fees and on faculty that taught for a living rather than doing research. Unlike the Germans, the federal government confined its science funding to the microbe-slaying efforts of the Public Health Service, an organization which, however fine, did not have basic science as a mission.

Thus, the few American laboratories for basic science contrasted feebly with the great chemistry and pathology institutes of Paris and Berlin. What did we have? In 1871 Henry Bowditch, fresh home from studying with the German greats, founded at Harvard the country's first physiology laboratory. Physiology, the study of how the body functions, is completely fundamental to any kind of medical research. A hospital laboratory for research was founded in Philadelphia in 1894, another at the Johns Hopkins Medical School in 1905; the New York City Health Department had a lab, as did the Public Health Service; the list is not much longer.[3]

In those days such biological courses as existed were usually taught in medical schools rather than science faculties. So it was mainly medical students who contemplated scientific careers. Consider the raw material. Here is Columbia physiologist John Curtis writing in 1897 to Seth Low, the university's president: "We are accepting students in numbers who are unfit to study medicine, and who are dropped by examination at the end of the first year, but who pay $200 each, which, obviously, we can ill afford to do without. This situation retards our headway as a first-class institution, like a sail towing behind a yacht."[4]

Gifted individuals existed, to be sure. But generally speaking, a science with such unpromising recruits would remain internationally unrecognized. Chargaff said of his Vienna student days that, "Not a single American journal was kept in the Chemistry Library; and when I once inquired about the *Journal of the American Chemical Society,* I was informed that nothing worthwhile was being published there."[5] Although by the 1930s much had changed, the young James Shannon—considered something of a comer—found himself in 1939 still at a loss for a post. He had finished a training program in kidney physiology at New York University, only to discover that "there was not a single job in the United States" in his field. "There was one professor who had adequate resources and there [were] a lot of people who had marginal resources and that was it." He later declared with exasperation, "Science could have died in this country in the 1930s."[6]

In this sea of American scientific mediocrity an island of excellence— indeed brilliance—stood out: the Rockefeller Institute for Medical Research, which opened in 1901. Frederick Taylor Gates, the Baptist minister who was John D. Rockefeller's adviser in charity matters, had read William Osler's famous textbook *The Principles and Practice of Medicine.* It was, he said, "one of the very few scientific books that I have ever read possessed of literary charm." As he pressed through it, he discovered how few diseases medicine could treat. "It was nature, and not the doctor, and in most cases nature practically unassisted, that performed the cures." When he put the book down, he realized that, especially in the United States, "medicine could hardly hope to become a science until medicine should be endowed and qualified men could give themselves to uninterrupted study and investigation, on ample salary, entirely independent of practice."[7]

Gates had put his finger upon a main cause of America's lag. It was not that Americans were dumber than Europeans, but that American doctors were too busy with practice to do research. Research in this country has historically meant invention rather than investigation of mechanisms, which is what basic science is all about.

John D. Rockefeller became the more receptive to founding a research institute when his first grandchild, John Rockefeller McCormick, died of scarlet fever in 1901 at the age of three. "Mr. Rockefeller was shocked to learn from the doctors that the cause of scarlet fever was unknown," wrote René Dubos, "and that there was no method of treatment for the disease."[8]

The original Board of Scientific Directors of the Rockefeller Institute. Left to right: Theobald Smith, Hermann M. Biggs, Simon Flexner, William H. Welch, T. Mitchell Prudden, L. Emmett Holt, Christian A. Herter. These were among the most distinguished men in American medical science in the early 1900s.

To set up a research institute, Gates needed an advisory board, people who could help create on these shores a counterpart of the Pasteur Institute in Paris or the Koch Institute in Berlin. He recruited the most distinguished men he could find in American medical science—for indeed up to that point medicine had been considered largely an art. Thus, William H. Welch, the dean of the Johns Hopkins Medical School, came on board. Hopkins, considered the most scientific of all the faculties of medicine, had opened in 1893 and was organized specifically along German lines. From the world of public health Gates got Theobald Smith, the director of the antitoxin laboratory of the famous Massachusetts State Board of

Health. If the application of the budding science of vaccines could be said to have a cutting edge, Smith's lab was it. From Yale, Gates signed on T. Mitchell Prudden, who introduced the science of pathology to this country, learning about disease by matching the patient's symptoms to what you see under the microscope. Among other board members was Hermann Biggs, whom we have already met as director of Bellevue's microbiology laboratory; young Joseph Kinyoun had acquired his own scientific education under Biggs.

There were others as well.[9] The point is that Reverend Gates gathered about him the best men available to establish the Rockefeller Institute. Just as perhaps a third of all American elite physicians had studied in Germany before World War I, the members of the Rockefeller board had been there too.[10] The institute they established equaled the best the Germans had to offer. In 1911 the Germans themselves created a series of research institutes, the Kaiser Wilhelm Institutes, modeled after the Rockefeller Institute.

The Great Immigration

Perhaps no historical event contributed more to American medical progress than the Nazis' rise to power in Germany. The exciting German scientific world was transplanted after 1933 into such places as the pathology department of New York University or Columbia's biochemistry department, providing the branch from which many American scientific buds would stem. By the First World War it was Berlin, rather than Paris, London, or Vienna, that had become the world's most important city for studying biochemistry and organic chemistry. Biochemistry, a phrase which started to acquire currency only at this time, is the chemistry of events in the body, and is based upon organic chemistry, the chemistry of the substances of which the body is composed.

In 1924, his medical education just behind him, David Nachmansohn arrived in the biochemistry lab of Berlin University. The lab, typically, was situated in the pathology department, and run by an influential chemist named Peter Rona. Young Nachmansohn had studied Latin, Greek, and history in high school, had never touched the sciences, and in fact wanted to be a philosopher. But clouds were already darkening for German Jews in 1918, who were being blamed for the loss of the war. His parents advised him that he should study medicine to have something to fall back on.

"My first experience in the medical school was very discouraging," Nachmansohn remembers. "I found the lectures on anatomy, which at that time still dominated the preclinical training, extremely dull and boring." But by the time he graduated his whole outlook had changed; he had discovered biochemistry. It had "opened to me an entirely new and exciting world full of challenging and interesting problems." Hence he drifted to Rona's lab, and from there to the Kaiser Wilhelm institute in a middle-class suburb of Berlin called Dahlem. He studied in Dahlem with Otto Meyerhof, whose name every science student knows today as the discoverer of the basic chemical pathway by which the cell turns sugar into a fuel it can burn. Two flights up was the lab of the nasty, arrogant, brilliant Otto Warburg. Remember Joseph Goldberger's discovery of the pellagra-preventive factor in the previous chapter? It was Warburg who figured out why niacin (the factor) is important. Minutes away by foot were the labs of other great scientists such as Carl Neuberg and Fritz Haber. The concentration of talent in Dahlem was dazzling.[11]

Around the same time, the young Severo Ochoa was also arriving in Berlin, a medical degree from the University of Madrid tucked into his pocket. He too came to Meyerhof's lab and found himself beside Nachmansohn, and beside Fritz Lipmann, who would get a Nobel prize in 1953 for his discovery of how the cell actually burns fuel (oxidation).[12] In a 1929 photo from Dahlem, Lipmann, Nachmansohn, and Ochoa stare out at us, along with other insouciant young men in lab coats who later would be famous as well. Three of the group are smoking.[13] We do not know who took the picture; perhaps it was Hans Krebs, who shared the 1953 Nobel prize with Lipmann, because Krebs was also in Meyerhof's laboratory in those years. Krebs later described the laboratory, and to those accustomed to the sprawling scale of medical research today, what is striking about these early facilities is their modesty. Meyerhof had only four or five small rooms at his disposal, and never more than a few collaborators at any time, plus a lab technician (a *Diener,* as they are called in German) and a part-time typist. (Warburg had no secretarial help and everybody had to type his own letters.) Working hours were from eight in the morning to six at night. Meyerhof was constantly in attendance. "There were no committee meetings and hardly any academic tourism."[14] This enchanted little world dissolved in 1933.

Although the international epicenter of research in the basic medical sciences ultimately shifted from a suburb of Berlin to a suburb of Washington, this peregrinating epicenter stopped off first in New York City. Why New York and not Cambridge, England, in which brilliant work in biochemistry was then being done? Or Paris? Or any of a number of other places? It helps us keep things in perspective to recall that by 1930 the United States had become the wealthiest country in the world. Even

Scientists in Berlin-Dahlem, Germany, 1929. Left to right: Fritz Lipmann, David Nachmansohn, Severo Ochoa, Francis O. Schmitt, Ken Iwasaki, Paul Rothschild. "The concentration of talent in Dahlem was dazzling."

though foundation spending had plunged during the Depression, there was still far more money in the system than elsewhere. It needed merely to be mobilized, and the can-do spirit of the Americans made that task relatively simple: compared to other countries, money has never really been a problem in medical research here.

Second, the Americans looked up to these brilliant European refugees in a way that just isn't possible in the prideful scientific cultures of England and France. Erwin Chargaff commented on the "good-humored lack of ambition" that he found among his American colleagues. "This was actually not due to the low caliber of the individuals who constituted the departments, but to the feeling on their part that nothing they could do counted on the scientific stage, which was occupied by the loud-mouthed and conceited European heavyweights."[15] In addition, the many Jews among the refugees found the climate of New York more congenial than that of Oxford or Cambridge, where a haughty variety of anti-Semitism was often not far from the surface.

Sooner or later almost all the German biochemists wound up in New

York.[16] Later in the book the reader will learn why these individuals are important. Here we need to establish their role in making the United States a world center of science in the late 1930s. Max Bergmann, for example, landed at the Rockefeller Institute to continue his work on the lock-and-key theory of enzymes. Thus, at a stroke the United States acquired a great enzyme scientist. Chargaff recalls going to visit Bergmann's lab, the air thick with German and the smell of the "peace pipe," as Bergmann called the cigarettes he kept in a large glass jar.[17]

Fritz Lipmann initially fled Germany for Copenhagen, coming in 1939 to the Cornell Medical College in New York City. The Spaniard Severo Ochoa went first to Washington University in St. Louis, Missouri, to be with Carl and Gerty Cori, one of the most distinguished scientific couples of the twentieth century. They discovered together the Cori cycle, which explains how sugar (glucose) goes in and out of the liver via the blood to provide energy to the muscles. Then in 1942 Ochoa went to New York, as a research associate in the biochemistry department at New York University. Under Ochoa's guidance at NYU a whole generation of American biochemists and immunologists after the war would enter the "molecular mainline." Thus, the immigrants found safety in New York.

The other New York institution that produced so many important scientists after World War II was the biochemistry department of Columbia's medical school, rather quaintly named the College of Physicians and Surgeons, or P and S. Why Columbia? And why a medical school, for men who were basic scientists and who, in Chargaff's phrase, viewed clinicians as the "delivery boys of the health care system?" The story goes back to 1928, when an industrial chemist named Hans T. Clarke, who previously had worked for Eastman Kodak at Rochester, became chairman of the biochemistry department. Columbia had originally wanted Harvard's professor of organic chemistry (after 1934, president), James Bryant Conant. But Conant turned down the job and recommended Clarke, for even though Clarke didn't know much about the "bio" side of things, he knew how to recognize good people.[18] He would sit and talk with candidates for a few minutes and ask them something like how to make aspirin, a standard beginner's exercise in organic chemistry. His choices were usually excellent. Although Clarke's parents were Americans, he had grown up and studied in England. And he had spent two years before World War I in Berlin, learning to speak German fluently and becoming fond of German culture and music.

Thus, Clarke, the right man in the right place for culling the immigrants, drew the best of them to his department. That was how he got the brilliant and irrepressible Chargaff, who arrived at the end of 1934 from Paris.

That was how David Nachmansohn was taken on. After spending 1933 to 1939 in Paris as an independent investigator, Nachmansohn landed first at Yale, then came down to New York in 1942. Oskar Wintersteiner, Karl Meyer, Erwin Brand, Zacharias Dische—these men had been among the top biologists in the world and now they formed a great scientific nucleus in New York.

Talk about rootless cosmopolitans! "We had to have a speaking knowledge of German and French in order to get a Ph.D. in Clarke's department," DeWitt ("Hans") Stetten recalled years later. "Hans Clarke would personally administer the examinations. He'd give you an article out of the French [scientific] literature and tell you to translate it and tell me what it says. Many of the young men and women coming through today simply do not look at the French and German literature because they can't translate it."[19] Chargaff remembered the babble of tongues. "Most doors were open, and a rich mixture of Brooklynese, Bostonese, but mostly Hamburg-American, filled the air."[20]

The graduate students all shared space in one big room. In addition to keeping track of each other's work, they came into constant contact with the faculty. Sarah Ratner, who was later to make important discoveries at NYU, remembered how people like Chargaff might drift into their graduate lab groups.[21] This story of NYU and the P and S conveys how important a critical mass is in scientific discovery: you bring bright people together in the expectation that something will happen that wouldn't if they were dispersed on their own. This would later become a model for the NIH in Bethesda.

Something did happen when a young man whom we haven't mentioned yet arrived among these refugees. Rudolph Schoenheimer was thirty-four when, teaching biochemistry in Freiburg, he read the handwriting on the wall. DeWitt Stetten, then a grad student at Columbia, had come over to work in Schoenheimer's lab. And after the two of them observed one of Hitler's mass rallies, Schoenheimer realized it was time to get out. In December 1932 he left for New York on a Josiah Macy Foundation fellowship. Money for science in the United States again becomes critical: there were no Pasteur fellowships to bring panicky refugees to Paris.

Schoenheimer joined the biochemistry department at Columbia. Unfortunately, he suffered from a manic-depressive illness, and although in his manic phase he would be a fire wheel of ideas, in his depressed phase he was impossible. Stetten recalled that, "on one occasion he was unable to find a particular spatula which he wanted at that moment in the laboratory. He exploded with some violence, charged all of us with stealing his favorite spatula, and stormed out of the laboratory. He was not seen again for three days, after which he arrived unshaved and disheveled. He had spent much of the intervening time sitting in a movie theater."[22]

One day Hans Clarke introduced Schoenheimer to a chemist named Harold Urey at the Rockefeller Institute. Urey had just determined how to make "heavy water," which is the same as regular water except that the hydrogen atom in the H_2O is twice as heavy as a normal hydrogen atom. Schoenheimer immediately realized that by injecting such distinctive liquids into experimental animals, one could follow their course about the body. After Urey had succeeded in making a similar isotope of nitrogen, Schoenheimer established that the proteins in our bodies, which contain nitrogen, are constantly turning over. This discovery exemplifies the kind of finding that would change greatly our whole conception of body chemistry.

One of DeWitt Stetten's fellow grad students in the biochemistry lab at P and S was a young man named David Rittenberg, and Rittenberg helped Schoenheimer with some crucial experiments. All these people would probably not have gotten together for this striking development had they not been bumping into one another in the corridors.

Schoenheimer's brilliance ended in tragedy. Depressed about the breakup of his marriage and his sister's disappearance in Germany at the hands of the Nazis—and suffering from severe mental illness—he committed suicide in 1941.

The German scientists were important for one other reason. "The European-born scientists who have made the greatest impact on American biology are the atomic physicists," said biochemist Herbert Anker of the University of Chicago to Laura Fermi. "They have shown that basic science when sufficiently supported can yield extremely practical results." The chemist Eugene Rabinowitch added to this analysis: "The greatest role of the European-born scientist was to change the American concept of science—it used to mean invention; it seemed impossible to convince the congressmen that basic science is important. [But] after the atomic bomb, even biological research . . ." had become politically acceptable. After the war, the National Institutes of Health would find themselves the direct beneficiaries of this new faith.[23]

The Can-Do Country Does

What the Americans did well was putting ideas into practice. A huge gulf separates the drug designer's computer images from a safely tested product on the market. There are miles between new insights into how viruses capture cells and the introduction of effective vaccines. German scientists had once successfully filled in these wide open spaces, but the German biological sciences fell apart after 1933. In the 1930s and after, applying science to health would become a distinctively American success because of collaboration between the federal government, academic researchers, and the drug industry.

Elmer Bobst was in Paris in 1936. As the manager of Roche's American branch, he was meeting his boss, Emil Barell, director of Roche's parent firm in Basel. They had just finished a splendid going-away dinner at Bobst's hotel, the Crillon, when Barell said in his heavily accented English: "Mr. Bobst, I want you to come with me to the men's room."

"The men's room?"

"Yes, I'll tell you why when we get there."

Bobst followed Barell to the empty men's room. "Barrell looked furtively around as if expecting to be attacked. He opened the door of one of the toilet stalls. Then he entered and motioned for me to follow." Bobst, suppressing a desire to laugh, followed Barell into the booth.

"Barell carefully closed the door. Sighing with relief, he reached carefully into a vest pocket and extracted a small sealed bottle." Barell held it carefully in both hands. It was a fermentation culture of bacteria for making vitamin C.

To explain what these men are doing in the men's room of the Hotel Crillon we have to go back to a disease called scurvy. It happens to people who don't get enough vitamin C, such as the crew exploring the St. Lawrence River in 1534 with Jacques Cartier:

"The sickness began among us in a marvelous and most unknown manner, for some lost weight, and their legs became large and swollen, and their muscles shrank and grew black as coal, and with some all besprinkled with spots of blood almost purple. Then the sickness mounted to the hips, thighs, and shoulders . . . and the mouth became so infected and the gums so putrid that all the flesh fell away from them, even to the roots of the teeth, which almost all fell out."[24]

The underlying problem from which these men suffered was the inability of their bodies to make properly a protein called collagen. Collagen is essential in the walls of blood vessels. Without it little hemorrhages take place all over the body, the gums bleed, the teeth fall out, and wounds don't heal. Collagen itself consists of several smaller strands of protein that are held together with little chemical bonds of hydrogen. In order to make those bonds form, vitamin C (ascorbic acid) is needed. Thus, like niacin in pellagra, ascorbic acid figures in some of the body's most fundamental reactions. And like pellagra, scurvy can be a fatal disease. Far many more British sailors died of it—because they didn't take lemon juice or lime juice on board—than died in all Her Majesty's naval wars. Hence the American slang term "limey" arose, short for lime-juicer, after the British sailors finally started eating limes (mainly lemons) to ward off scurvy.[25]

In 1933 the Birmingham chemist W. Norman Haworth described the structure of vitamin C. From that point the question became: Who would be first to synthesize it and start factory production? Because extracting vitamin C from lemons, vegetables, and potatoes where it occurs naturally was too expensive. The Roche drug company in Basel had given a grant to the chemist Tadeus Reichstein at the University of Basel, and in 1936 Reichstein had come up with the answer: a process using bacteria to produce a kind of sugar called sorbose. Vitamin C itself could then be produced from the sorbose. The vial that Barell handed Bobst contained a culture of those bacteria. When Bobst got back to Roche's plant in Nutley, New Jersey, his production people would work out the practical side of making vast amounts of vitamin C from this tiny bottle.[26]

Can-do spirit? It was the British who in 1933 had first described the chemical structure of vitamin C. But producing the first crystals had actually occurred in 1932 at the University of Pittsburgh.[27] The Swiss had figured out the theory of making vitamin C with a system of bacteria. But implementing the theory happened in the big fermentation vats of Roche at Nutley, New Jersey. (The Pfizer company, however, went on to become the major producer of vitamin C in the 1930s.)[28]

The Cortisone Story

A far more terrible menace than scurvy was—and still is—rheumatoid arthritis. By the 1930s most Americans had diets sufficient to ward off scurvy. But rheumatoid arthritis even today afflicts around three million Americans, and hits women two to three times more often than men. The disease has a special poignancy, in that it occurs most commonly in young people between twenty-five and fifty.[29] In this variety of arthritis the joints become inflamed, swollen, and locked in position. Why this happens is still unclear, but an inflammatory process causes the membrane lining the inside of the joint to proliferate, and as it grows it envelops the other contents of the joint—such as ligaments, cartilage, and bone—and destroys them. Inflammation seizes the entire joint and the victim becomes immobilized. The disease is also very painful. Accordingly, it has been called "one of the most intractable, obstinate, and crippling diseases that can befall the human body." William Osler said in 1892, "There are cases in which pain of an agonizing character is an almost constant symptom, requiring for years the use of morphia." He continued, "In extreme cases

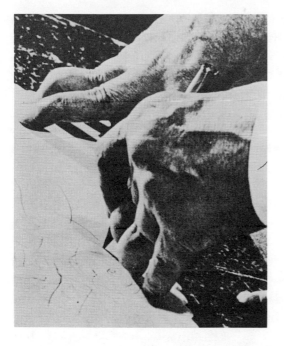

Hands of the famous French painter Raoul Dufy, badly crippled with rheumatoid arthritis. He was later treated with Merck's newly developed Cortone (cortisone).

the patient is completely helpless, and lies on one side with the legs drawn up, the arms fixed, and all the articulations [joints] of the extremities locked."[30]

The invention of aspirin at the turn of the century brought some relief, and aspirin today is still the first line of defense in arthritis treatment. But those patients whom aspirin couldn't help endured years of pain. Philip Hench had been fascinated by arthritis ever since he came to the joint disease department of the Mayo Clinic in Rochester, Minnesota, in 1923. He noticed that under some circumstances patients got remissions from their arthritis, such as during pregnancy or in the presence of a liver infection (hepatitis). This suggested to him that a kind of chemical called a steroid might be involved in arthritis.

Now, simultaneously at the Mayo Clinic, a biochemist named Edward Kendall was interested in a small gland that sits on top of the kidneys called the adrenal gland. Its outer layer (cortex) produces hormones made out of steroids: hence the phrase corticosteroids. Nobody knew, however, exactly what these various adrenal steroids did.

The scene changes to the late 1930s. Kendall has succeeded in isolating from the adrenal cortex four different steroids that seem to have some activity on the body. He calls them A, B, E, and F. Nobody at this point is thinking about arthritis. This is just basic science: Here's what we've found but we don't know what it does. In 1938 Kendall and Hench start working together. The joint disease man Hench is hunting for substance X, which he knows to be produced somewhere in the body and naturally fights arthritis. The chemist Kendall has isolated the four mysterious lettered substances from the adrenals. Nobody yet has any idea that Kendall's substance E and Hench's substance X are in fact the same thing: cortisone. Hench goes off to war. Everything is put on hold.

The scene will shift in a minute to 1948. But in the meantime several things have happened. The U.S. National Research Council became very interested in the adrenal gland's steroids during the war and launched a big cooperative project among industry and universities to make compound A, the simplest of the four. All efforts fail. Finally in 1944 Kendall himself devises a procedure which yields quite a bit of compound A, shows it to the Merck company in Rahway, New Jersey, and their chemist Lewis Hastings Sarett produces some substance A (and a tiny bit of E) after much toil. Substance A turns out to be virtually inactive in the body. They don't have enough E even to test. Now, at this point, reasonable people would probably have given up on E and all the other adrenal substances because chemically they differ so little from A. They too would probably cure nothing.

Sarett, however, continues his efforts to make enough E for testing. Although it involved just sticking one more oxygen atom onto the molecule, in practical terms the synthesis was quite difficult. He succeeds in 1947 and in 1948 determines a method for making a few grams at a time.

The scene shifts from Merck back to the Mayo Clinic. Hench and Kendall remember their 1941 resolution to test substance E on arthritic patients. In 1941 none was available, but now they write to Sarett and ask for a shipment of E. On September 21, 1948, they inject it into the first of fourteen patients, a twenty-nine-year-old woman crippled for four years by severe arthritis. Result: "marked improvement." One patient, "a farmer's wife, came in a wheelchair, improved markedly after injection of the hormone, and was soon walking well. . . . She maintained practically all her improvement for twenty-three more days in the hospital and for at least five weeks since returning to the farm and housework."

Was the improvement in these fourteen patients owing to the power of suggestion rather than to the effects of the drug? "Unknown to the patients, injection of the hormone was abruptly replaced by injection of a [placebo]. In eight of the nine cases symptoms began to return or to increase promptly, generally within two to four days." Thus, even though they had not obtained a cure for arthritis, they had found a means of relieving the symptoms of this disabling disease as long as patients took the drug.

In the spring of 1949 the results of their six-month trial were announced

Dr. Lewis H. Sarett made the first synthesis of cortisone.

to the press. The news created a media sensation. Because some reporters had confused substance E with vitamin E, making a reputation for this vitamin as a miracle drug, Hench and Kendall decided to rename the substance cortisone. But no supplies of cortisone were available.

At this point the Merck company had a tough decision to make. Considering that research by other companies and scientists had already muddied the patent waters, should Merck go ahead and set up a full-scale plant for cortisone? Could the process even be reproduced for large amounts? The progression from making drugs in test tubes to huge industrial vats is not always a smooth one, as we shall see in the case of the polio vaccine. "No compound as complex as cortisone had ever been made on a factory scale. The venture would be without precedent," said Kendall in his Nobel prize acceptance speech in 1950, thus giving credit where it was due. Merck, to its credit, went ahead.[31]

But so did other companies. It is, after all, the spirit of capitalism that fueled many of these can-do accomplishments. The Upjohn Company in Kalamazoo, Michigan, assigned half of its three-hundred-person research staff to find a way of synthesizing cortisone cheaper than Merck's. A six-month expedition of Upjohn botanists, for example, criss-crossed Africa, looking for a vine whose chemistry resembled that of cortisone. "The trip,

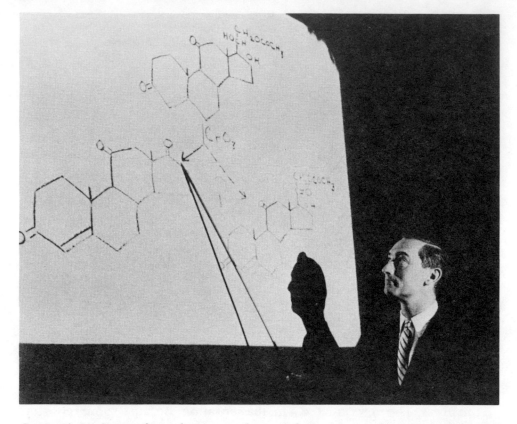

Dr. Lewis H. Sarett of Merck points to the crucial experiment in his initial synthesis of cortisone.

considered an expensive waste of time by some Upjohn researchers, resulted in little useful information for the company." Then Upjohn biochemist Durey Peterson hit upon the idea of letting a fruit mold act as a factory—in the way that Roche had let bacteria function as a factory for vitamin C. This collapsed the former thirty-six manufacturing steps into a single process, and in June 1952 Upjohn introduced an inexpensive mass market cortisone.[32]

But one sees how precarious any supposedly secure market position is in the drug industry. In 1955 the Schering company figured out how to make from its mold cultures a version of cortisone that was five times more powerful than the old variety, while causing little more salt retention (one of the many side effects of cortisone; retaining sodium drives up the blood pressure). Schering thus pulled the rug from under the competition and sold $20 million of prednisone (Meticorten) in the first year alone. By 1957, due largely to Meticorten, Schering's annual sales had passed the

$80 million mark.[33] It is not a critique of the system that the chance to do great good is often accompanied by the chance to make great profits.

The Greatest Can-Do Story: Penicillin

The problem with the sulfa drugs of the previous chapter was that although they were wonderful, they were not adequate. They did not actually kill bacteria in the body, but just slowed their growth enough for the body's own immune system to finish off the germs. Some germs also became quickly immune to the sulfonamides, and in other kinds of bacterial infections they were entirely ineffective.

Long before any of these problems surfaced, we find Alexander Fleming at work in his germ lab at St. Mary's Hospital in London. The year is 1928. "No one who knew Fleming would call him a tidy bacteriologist," wrote Ernst Chain years later.[34] Fleming should have kept those flat little plates called Petri dishes—in which scientists try to grow cultures of germs—washed up. But he didn't. He went out of town for a bit and left his laboratory window open to the cold. When he returned, in one of the dishes lying on the table in which he was trying to grow staph germ cultures, he noticed "a contaminating colony." According to the Fleming legend, it had found its way there by accident. The colony, a mold from the genus *Penicillium,* had clearly killed the staph germs. This was a finding of great interest: a substance that kills an important family of deadly bacteria. So Fleming investigated it as best he could. He discovered, for example, that only certain strains of penicillium seemed to kill the germs. But he didn't really pursue the question resolutely; he certainly never tried giving any of the mold juice—which the following year he named penicillin—to sick patients or to sick mice. After publishing his discovery that mold juice worked against germs in lab cultures in 1929, he turned his attention elsewhere and the minor finding was forgotten.[35]

Enter Ernst Chain, a young Berlin Jew fleeing the Nazis in 1933. Chain landed at Cambridge University in England, studied with the important school of biochemists there, and two years later found himself on the job market. Oxford's Howard Florey hired Chain. Florey, who had just become professor of pathology, was trying to bring the university's science program abreast of the times. This bright young German was perfect, and as Florey had already begun research on substances that might kill germs, Chain joined the search. He and Florey went through the literature, encountering references to Fleming's work, among others.

Then one day in 1938 Chain saw a co-worker, Miss Campbell-Renton, carrying germ culture bottles on the surface of which a mold had grown. "I

"In the Fall of 1928, a single mold spore floated through a window into the London laboratory of Dr. Alexander Fleming, and settled into a culture dish that contained staphylococci. Fleming, seeing his culture had been contaminated, was about to wash it away when he hesitated. Something remarkable was happening."

asked her what the mold was . . . and for which purpose she used it. She explained to me that it was the mold Fleming had described, in 1929, producing penicillin . . . I asked Miss Campbell-Renton for a sample of the mold and started experiments with it straight away." Chain and Professor Florey thus resumed the penicillin narrative, supported by a Rockefeller Foundation grant, as there was little money in England at the time for such purposes.[36]

Florey and Chain started out by curing infected animals, reporting the results in 1940 in the British medical weekly *The Lancet*. Then they tried the small amounts of penicillin they were able to fabricate on five sick

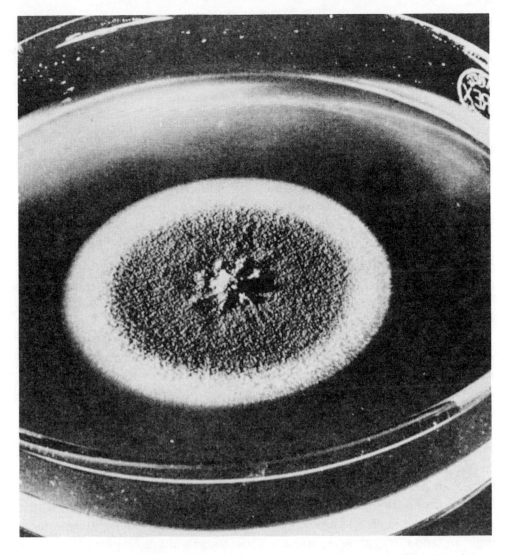

"What had formerly been a well-grown colony was now a faint shadow of its former self. Something was dissolving the microbes. Fleming isolated the excretion the mold gave off. It destroyed staphylococci, pneumococci, gonococci, and meningococci without damaging the blood leucocytes." This was the most powerful microbe killer he'd ever seen. He called it penicillin, after **Pencillium**, *the genus to which the mold belonged.*

patients, reporting these findings in August 1941. Britain had now entered the Second World War.

Penicillin up to this point had been clearly a British story. But a problem existed: producing the drug. The mold grows only in the presence of oxygen. Large surface areas seemed essential so that every bit of mold would come into contact with the air. But the yield from these huge expanses of growing culture was tiny, and half of the penicillin might be lost to the action of destructive contaminants before it was even harvested. Florey was reaping about 1,000 units of penicillin per liter of culture. How much was a unit? A patient with a severe infection might require 100,000 units per day. Thus 100 liters of culture would be needed for each patient daily! "Every case of severe sepsis," Florey wrote, "might need the brewing and processing of as much as 2000 litres of medium. It appeared, therefore, that the cost would be high and the number of cases that could be treated by parenteral injection [hypodermic needle] would be few."[37]

The British drug industry must not be excoriated for failing to produce the can-do spirit at this point because the country was plunged in war. France had fallen in June 1940, and the Battle of Britain began two weeks after Florey and Chain's first article appeared in *The Lancet*. Other priorities were simply more pressing than this highly experimental drug. To seek help producing penicillin Florey and his associate, the microbiologist Norman Heatley, traveled by air Clipper to New York on July 2, 1941. The Rockefeller Foundation had paid for the trip.

Now we have to back up for a second. The American drug industry was not run by idiots. The firms had been avid for other bacteria-killing drugs ever since the sulfonamides erupted in 1935. Florey and Chain's 1940 *Lancet* paper had circulated, and considerably before Florey's arrival American drug houses—Merck and Squibb, in particular—had been trying to produce penicillin.[38] A group of scientists at Columbia's College of Physicians and Surgeons, led by Martin H. Dawson, were also attempting to make penicillin on their own. In May 1941 at a meeting of a medical society in Atlantic City, Dawson reported the results of giving this penicillin to twelve patients. Two members of the scientific staff of Charles Pfizer and Company, a small chemical manufacturer in Brooklyn, attended the meeting and went home resolved to see if they could make penicillin. They had some reason to be optimistic because, of all chemical companies, Pfizer was especially skilled in fermentation techniques (used, of course, for vitamin C).

Pfizer started making up big carboys of penicillin fermentation "liquor" and sending them off by cab to the team at Columbia. So fragile was the substance that half of it might vanish during the cab ride.[39] A Pfizer employee later recalled, "It was a very difficult fermentation. It was easily contaminated and the content of penicillin wasn't very much more than that of gold in seawater. A few parts per million were extremely dilute and it was a very involved recovery process to get an impure product which no one knew how to analyze."[40]

Meanwhile Florey and Heatley had landed. The day of their arrival

Florey phoned his old friend physiologist John Fulton at the Yale medical school. They had known each other since being Rhodes scholars together at Oxford (Florey was an Australian). The following day Florey and Heatley went up to New Haven, where Yale is, and their friend Fulton introduced them to an official on the National Research Council. The NRC was handling America's science mobilization, for even though the country was still at peace, people were beginning to realize it might not be for long. The NRC man steered the two Britons to Peoria, Illinois.

Why Peoria? A federal agricultural research service in Peoria had acquired considerable experience in fermentation, which is why Florey and Heatley went there. But by chance this experience had been with corn fermentation liquor, a by-product of corn starch. Unknown in advance, penicillin grew far better in corn liquor than in what Florey had previously been using. Britain had no field corn, although what we call wheat they call corn. But there was plenty around Peoria. After considerable experimenting, the Peoria people realized that adding corn steep liquor to the broth increased the yields twentyfold. Using deep flasks rather than shallow trays increased output another fivefold. And finding more productive strains of *Penicillium*—indeed the most productive had been isolated from a rotten canteloupe in a Peoria market—stepped up the yield by severalfold again. Thus they started getting yields of 900 units per milliliter of brew, whereas Florey had gotten yields of 2.[41]

By now it is December and the United States is in the Second World War. The country's scientific mobilization is being run by the Office of Scientific Research and Development. Ten days after Pearl Harbor the medical branch of that office organized a meeting between doctor-administrators and drug companies to get penicillin production going. Initially only Merck and Squibb showed any interest in joining forces, but by September 1942 the Pfizer company came on board as well. By using modified surface culture techniques (because they couldn't figure out how to supply oxygen to the mold in deep vats, nor how to keep the penicillin free of destroying enzymes from other organisms), they produced enough to test the drug on a few patients.

The first of these patients to be injected with penicillin was Mrs. Ogden Miller, the thirty-three-year-old wife of Yale's athletic director. The family doctor had implored Yale's Professor Fulton to get some penicillin for Mrs. Miller, who had a major infection after a miscarriage. Fulton got on the telephone to Merck and Company. Merck said that the chairman of the OSRD's medical committee had the little bit Merck had produced. Fulton got hold of the chairman on a Thursday evening in Washington, and was told that some other administrator had the precious supply. More phoning, with the result that a small packet arrived in New Haven by airmail that Saturday morning.

It was Dr. Herbert Tabor, whom we later meet as a key scientist but then was an intern at the Yale medical center, who injected the penicillin into Mrs. Miller.

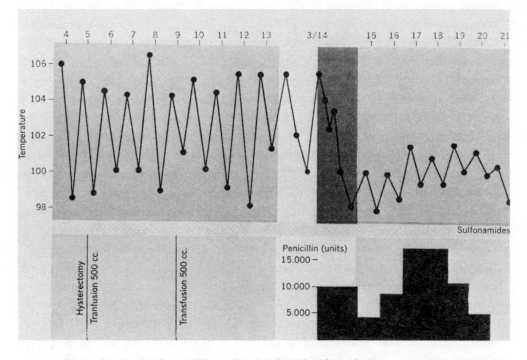

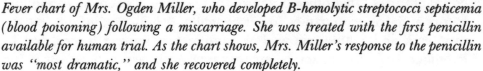

Fever chart of Mrs. Ogden Miller, who developed B-hemolytic streptococci septicemia (blood poisoning) following a miscarriage. She was treated with the first penicillin available for human trial. As the chart shows, Mrs. Miller's response to the penicillin was "most dramatic," and she recovered completely.

"Why did they give that valuable drug to you, a junior intern, to inject?" Dr. Tabor was asked years later.

"The junior intern is the one who knows how to inject things," Tabor replied. "You wouldn't let the professor of medicine do it!"[42]

Mrs. Miller's fever came "right down," Tabor remembers. Fulton noted in his diary a week later, "The case of Mrs. Ogden Miller, who for four weeks had been going downhill with what appeared, on the basis of all previous experience, to be a fatal hemolytic streptococcus septicemia. She had had a temperature ranging from 103° to 106.5° steadily for four weeks despite liberal administration of the sulfa drugs. . . . [Today, a week after the injections] the blood culture is still sterile. It is still too soon to say she is cured, but the response has been most dramatic."[43] In fact, Mrs. Miller recovered completely.

As similar dramatic recoveries became known, many drug companies faced a difficult choice. The Pfizer company ended up producing a majority of the nation's penicillin supply, and its records show what went through the minds of company chiefs, who were pulled by patriotism and human concern on the one hand, by fear on the other of colossal losses if their own (inevitably costly) processes were outmoded by a competitor's artificial synthesis of penicillin. Jasper Kane, a Pfizer chemist, went to John L. Smith, then vice president of the company: "We're getting nowhere with the flasks. Even if we boost production considerably, we can't hope to make enough."

"What are you suggesting?" Smith asked.

"I'm suggesting we try deep-tank fermentation. [We] did it with gluconic acid. I think we can do it with penicillin." Gluconic acid had been the company's prewar mainstay.

Smith thought about it. "You know what you're up against, don't you? The mold is as temperamental as an opera singer, the yields are low, the isolation is difficult, the extraction is murder, the purification invites disaster, and the assay is unsatisfactory. Think of the risks, and then think of the expensive investment in big tanks—think of what it means if you lose a two-thousand-gallon tank as against what you lose if a flask goes bad. Is it worth it?"

Kane urged him to take the gamble. So Smith called a meeting of all the plant management people. He told them what Kane had said. "You are all owners of the business. Are you willing to risk the money necessary to put up a penicillin plant with the little we know so far about this drug?" The vote was an overwhelming yes. Pfizer went ahead.[44]

By 1943 word of penicillin is getting out. People know it can save dying relatives and call desperately for it. Yet the government has reserved the supply for research on civilians and for military needs. What, therefore, was Pfizer executive John Smith supposed to do when Dr. Leo Loewe, a physician at the Brooklyn Jewish Hospital, came to him and pleaded for penicillin to "save the life of a doctor's small daughter" dying of an infection of the valves of the heart? Penicillin was thought useless for such cases, and in any event little was available. Smith said he'd come and see the little girl. His heart melted.

"For three days Dr. Loewe administered penicillin to the dying child by intravenous infusion, dripping it into a vein from a hanging bottle twenty-four hours a day. Her condition improved." They continued giving her enormous amounts. "During those days, as the color came back to her face, Smith . . . came, day after day, to watch a miracle—the first human being to be snatched from death's sure grip by his company's own penicillin." Smith continued to give Loewe penicillin free of cost for these patients, even after the government ruled such donations strictly illegal. He thus acted at some risk to himself and to his firm.[45]

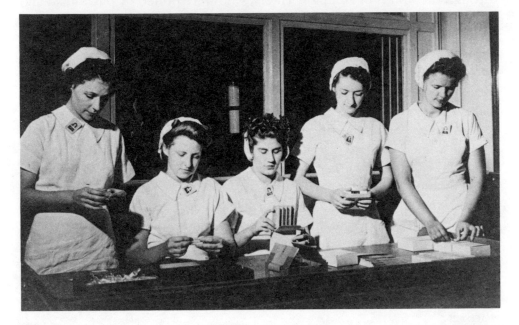

Early days of penicillin production shows girls in the packaging department at Merck and Company, Inc., Rahway, New Jersey, in 1943 labeling and packing ampoules of penicillin to be shipped to the U.S. Armed Forces in all parts of the world.

Saying no became difficult for anyone with access to penicillin in these wartime years, as the list of diseases that penicillin would cure—not just ameliorate but actually and definitively cure—became longer and longer: gonorrhea, meningitis, syphilitic infections of the central nervous system. Diseases that had plagued humankind for hundreds of years suddenly, with the stroke of a clock, became curable. The demand for penicillin leapt. In the summer of 1943 the War Production Board recruited another twenty-one drug houses, in addition to Merck, Squibb, Pfizer, Abbott, and Winthrop, to begin making penicillin. Huge vats of submerged growth culture now came on-line. In the first five months of 1943 only 400 million units of penicillin had been made; in the last seven months, 21 billion units. In March 1945 commercial sales began. By the time of Japan's surrender in August 1945, the U.S. drug industry was making 650 billion units of penicillin per month.[46]

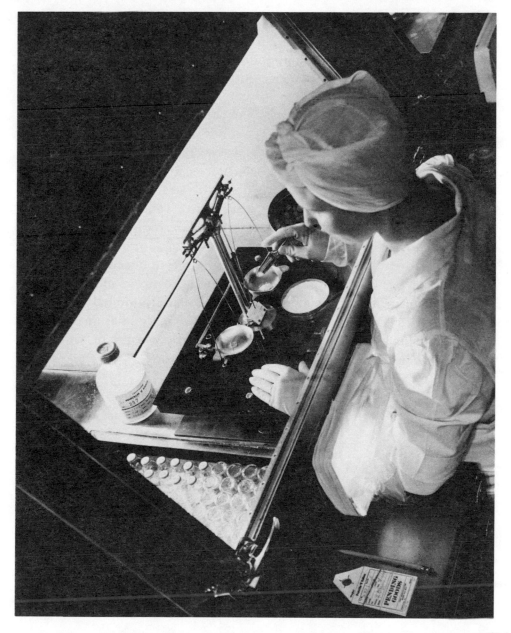

In 1948, in the sterile techniques building of Merck's Rahway plant, operators filled and weighed vials of penicillin using built-in rubber gloves in a sealed cubicle.

Between 1945 and 1955 in the United States, mortality from influenza and pneumonia fell by 47 percent; deaths from syphilis dropped 78 percent. Deaths from diphtheria—for not all children had been vaccinated—virtually vanished, the mortality from that disease falling by 92 percent.[47]

Thanks to drugs from the penicillin family and to the waves of other antibiotics following behind, dying from bacterial infection would become a rarity in Western society, something which happened only to people already debilitated from other diseases or whose immune systems were depressed. Infectious diseases, of course, had once caused the great majority of all deaths.

In the United States today, eighteen times more people will die of lung cancer, a lifestyle disease caused mainly by smoking, than of rheumatic fever and rheumatic heart disease, which are caused by bacteria and are largely avoidable with antibiotics. Rheumatic fever was once a terrible killer; lung cancer virtually did not exist before 1900.[48]

The story of penicillin is a spectacular early example of how well government, industry, and academic research can collaborate, once they put their minds to it. We shall shortly leap to more recent decades to see other examples of this cooperation in fighting polio, cancer, and AIDS. The point to be made, though, is that this kind of collaboration has taken place in the American scientific environment. No other nation has displayed the unique combination of resources involving the government, university, and private sectors.

THREE

Adolescent Growth Pains

Young sciences can suffer pangs as they grow. So can scientific institutions. These kinds of aches and pains sharpened when the National Institutes of Health grappled with vaccines after World War II. Both were young, and both got into trouble while passing through the turbulence of adolescence.

The adolescence of the Health Century features the rise of James A. Shannon, the man who became America's science baron. Under his leadership the Bethesda campus was transformed from a small gaggle of specialists in bacteria and cancer to a great research center.

The Logic of Vaccines

Readers' eyes often glaze over when they read about vaccines. The subject seems so unlike the classical medical drama: Rex Morgan, M.D., rushing in to save the feverish child with a pill. Vaccines have the advantage of immunizing people against getting the disease in the first place, so instead of drama, we have only the tedious task of hauling small children to the pediatrician for yet another round of shots. But these vaccines have saved far more lives than all the magic bullets—all the sulfa drugs and antibiotics —put together. Remember that in the eighteenth century up to 20 percent *of all deaths* resulted directly from smallpox, a viral disease for which Edward Jenner devised the first vaccine in 1798.[1]

The logic of a vaccine is straightforward: the white cells that circulate in the bloodstream protect us from invading viruses and bacteria. Because they mobilize against anything foreign, they protect us as well from transplanted kidneys and transplanted skin, and thus sometimes have to be turned off. When the white cells detect an invader, called an antigen, those particular white cells that are programmed for that particular invader go into action. Some of them pour a kind of protein called antibody into the bloodstream. The antibody attaches itself to the invading antigen and delivers it tidily to another kind of white cell called the big eaters (macrophages) to be eaten up. While the first of the antigen is being eaten up, the particular white cells that make these specific antibodies are proliferating furiously. More and more antibody pours into the bloodstream. The antigen is gobbled up by macrophages. The sick child feels better and goes back to school.

But after Billy has returned to school he will have, on a permanent basis, many more of the specific white cells that fought the antigen than before. And the antibodies made by those cells will circulate plentifully in his blood, on the lookout for the next assault. Now, let us say that Billy's first illness was caused by a flu virus. If that very same flu virus returns a second time: *Blam!* The circulating antibodies and already mobilized white cells (for that specific flu virus) leap on the antigen now so rapidly that Billy will probably not even have symptoms. He will not even know that he's been sick, even though in his bloodstream a second major battle has been fought and easily won. Billy has acquired immunity to that particular flu virus.

But let us say that Billy is assailed with something horrible: not flu but yellow fever. When that yellow fever virus initially reaches his bloodstream, the few preprogrammed white cells against yellow fever that Billy has had from birth will go into action. They'll make some antibodies and begin to proliferate and gamely carry on the struggle. But yellow fever viruses are terribly virulent: they easily overwhelm these few circulating antibodies; the big eaters are not summoned; Billy dies. His immune system never had the chance to get going.

When the microbe hunters of the U.S. Army, led by Dr. Walter Reed, fought yellow fever in Cuba in 1900, they noticed the natives never

Richard Colonno, research fellow for Merck and Company, Inc., displays the inhibitory effect of antiviral materials on rhinoviruses, which cause the common cold. (Photo courtesy Merck and Company, Inc.)

A chemical agent has been added to a cellular solution so that DNA begins to precipitate out. Here, a scientist, after swirling the glass rod in the liquid, is extracting pure DNA. (Photo courtesy Hoffmann-La Roche, Inc.)

A Roche scientist looks at DNA fragments separated on an electrophoresis gel. The bands are made visible by a dye that lights up under ultraviolet light when bound to DNA. (Photo courtesy Hoffmann-La Roche, Inc.)

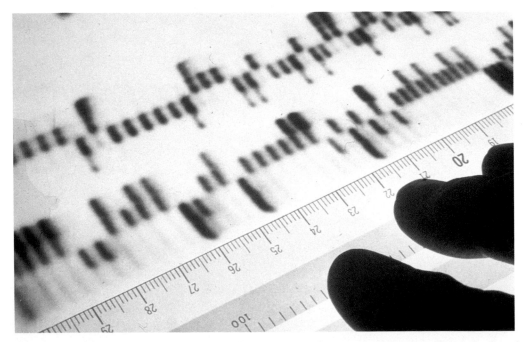

A Roche scientist "reads" the nucleotide sequence of a particular gene from the band pattern displayed on an electrophoresis gel. Each vertical band represents a nucleotide in the DNA. (Photo courtesy Hoffmann-La Roche, Inc.)

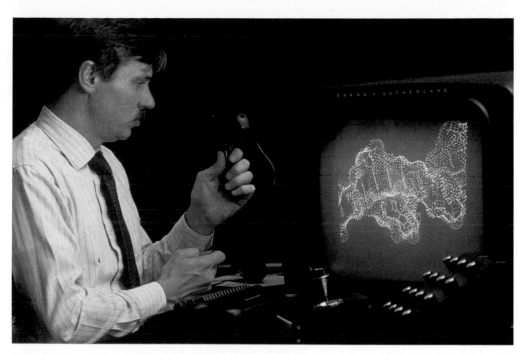

A Roche chemist, using computer graphics, studies a three-dimensional picture of double-helical DNA. (Photo courtesy Hoffmann-La Roche, Inc.)

Daniel Nathans used restriction enzymes to cut DNA at specific sites, enabling us to determine which genes coded for which proteins and paving the way for genetic engineering. (Photo courtesy the Johns Hopkins Medical Institutions)

Messenger RNA from a human donor cell is microinjected into a frog egg, which then produces a specific donor protein. (Photo courtesy Hoffmann-La Roche, Inc.)

seemed to get the disease. It was only the American doctors who came down with yellow fever, occasionally dying from it. The natives had all been infected with the virus as children, and those children who survived were immune as adults.

So how do we make people immune to grave infections without forcing them to risk death as children in order to acquire natural immunity? We vaccinate them! Just as Billy's initial flu infection provoked the white cells to make antibody and otherwise prepare, so does the "tamed" flu virus in the vaccine give his immune system a first jolt. White cells form against the specific germ; antibody circulates. Then if the vaccinated individual is hit with a real flu infection: *Blam!* The now prepared white cells go into action and Billy never even knows he's had the flu. Unfortunately, this flu scenario is imperfect because so many different varieties of flu virus exist that people are often attacked by kinds for which they have no preexisting immunity.

There are two approaches to developing a vaccine. In one, you find a not-so-virulent strain of the virus that infects animals, and inject that strain into humans, thus protecting them against the virus's more powerful cousins that are dangerous to humans. Edward Jenner's smallpox vaccine is an example of this. Jenner picked up on the folkloric observation that milk maids never got smallpox. The reason was because the cows they were milking were infected with a variety of smallpox called vaccinia (from *vacca* in Latin, meaning cow). Vaccinia, in other words, is smallpox of the cow. When the milk maids got their cows' vaccinia, the virus provoked in their human immune system the appropriate antibody formation to fight off the real smallpox. No matter how many times the smallpox virus entered the milk maids' bloodstream, the women never noticed symptoms, so primed were their white cells already from previous encounters with vaccinia. Thus, Jenner could prepare a smallpox vaccine from the blood of infected animals, inject it into humans, and safeguard them from the disease.

A second way to make a vaccine is by taming the virus over a long period. One does this by infecting successive generations of mice with the germ, or successive generations of eggs, so that in each new generation the virus is weaker than previously. Finally the live virus becomes so attenuated (tamed) that, when injected into humans, it will not give them symptoms of the disease. Instead the attenuated virus primes their white cells, making them immune in the future. Yellow fever vaccine, the most outstanding accomplishment of virus research before the polio vaccines, was developed along these lines.

Although yellow fever had disappeared from the United States in 1905, it remained endemic in Africa and South America. The advent of intercontinental air travel in the 1930s posed the risk of reimporting the disease into the United States, as the virus's incubation period was much longer than the duration of the flight. Thus, until a vaccine could be developed to nip yellow fever, the victories of the microbe hunters were only temporary.

Let's touch briefly on the making of a yellow fever vaccine, so that the process will seem familiar by the time we reach polio. Step one, growing attenuated strains of the virus in laboratory animals, was largely the work of the Rockefeller Institute in the 1930s. Staff member Max Theiler began by giving yellow fever to mice, attenuating the virus by passing it through a number of generations of laboratory tissue cultures, and then producing samples of the vaccine by growing it in eggs.[2] Step two, producing enough vaccine in the United States to immunize travelers, was the work of the National Institute of Health at its field station in Hamilton, Montana. Montana had been chosen because no mosquitoes live there capable of spreading yellow fever outside the lab. In February 1941, ten months before the entry of the United States into World War II, the lab began producing the vaccine.[3]

At this point yellow fever, an otherwise unimportant disease in twentieth-century America, offers us a model of what can go wrong in developing a vaccine. One must remember that viruses are extremely tiny particles. A comma on this page is about 1.5 millimeters long. Things much smaller than this are usually measured in microns, which is one one-thousandth of a millimeter. Thus, a comma is 1500 microns long. A single cell in the liver, by contrast, is only about 15 microns long, and a hundred of them, set end to end, would take up the space of a comma. In the world of microbes, however, sizes are much smaller still. The bacterium (bacillus) that causes typhoid fever is only two microns long. Internal details are scarcely visible with the best ordinary microscope, the maximum resolving power of which is one fifth of a micron. With a regular microscope most viruses are invisible: a typical one being about one tenth of a micron. Therefore one cannot simply look at a vaccine under the microscope and see if it is contaminated with any outside viruses that shouldn't be there.

To stabilize the tricky yellow fever vaccine, it was initially packaged in human serum, obtained from students at the University of Montana. But here's what can go wrong in preparing a vaccine: one of the serum donors must have had hepatitis, because hepatitis virus was in the emergency lots of yellow fever vaccine rushed early in 1942 to American troops in the Pacific. There had been no time for field testing. The war had started; the Japanese were advancing; the Marines in the Pacific had to be immunized against yellow fever, or, like the British army in the Crimea in the nine-teenth century, all would be lost to disease. Thus, one might argue that it was proper to omit crucial field-testing stages before disseminating the vaccines to the troops. But the contaminated vaccine was nonetheless given out, and 28,000 soldiers came down with hepatitis, 100 of them dying. Although the problem was repaired—the yellow fever vaccines going on to save thousands of lives among soldiers fighting in the Pacific and West Africa—the entire episode was a rehearsal for the encounter with the polio vaccine in the mid-1950s.[4]

The list of vaccines available to the average American in 1950 is a list of diseases that had been abolished in this country. An average American infant in 1950 would get a combination vaccine for whooping cough, tetanus, and diphtheria: all classic killers of children. There'd be a small-pox shot. If you had not already been exposed to tuberculosis (meaning that your tuberculin test was negative), you might get a BCG shot, stand-ing for *Bacillus Calmette-Guérin*, the two French researchers who had developed a vaccine usable in humans from cow tuberculosis. The BCG vaccine was tried for the first time in 1921, to keep a newborn baby whose mother had just died of TB from getting the disease. The infant did not get TB either from its mother or the vaccine, a relief to the vaccine's inventors, who hadn't known if the virus had been sufficiently tamed.[5]

Otherwise an average American in 1950 would be vaccinated only in special circumstances: for influenza if you were elderly; for yellow fever and typhoid if you were planning a trip to the Third World. Finally, if you'd been bitten by an animal feared to be rabid, you'd be given the painful, prolonged course of shots that rabies vaccine entailed. Some of the bacterial vaccines of the past (such as the difficult pneumonia vaccines) had been eliminated by 1950, a result of the advent of antibiotics. The revolutionary vaccines of our own day for mumps, measles, hepatitis, and so forth were still waiting in the wings. The immediate challenge, as scientists thought about vaccines in 1950, was polio.

The Young James Shannon, the Young Institutes

In a technological age such as our own, great science does not just happen. We no longer inhabit the world of Galileo, Koch, or Pasteur, where a gifted individual, brooding over a few simple instruments and calculations, could overturn whole conceptions of nature. Someone has to make it happen.

It was James Shannon, director of the National Institutes of Health in its explosive years of growth, who determined that the money Congress poured into health was translated into scientific discoveries. These were not modest discoveries. They have transformed in thirty years' time the way we think about events in the body. Of course, these discoveries were not made solely because Shannon brought good scientists to Bethesda or because of the NIH's funding of important university research. Nor is this work by any means the exclusive bailiwick of American scientists. But the fulcrum of the lever that created the new molecular biology—the chief new kind of knowledge—was in Bethesda, Maryland, in the years 1955 to 1968, the period of Shannon's directorship.

Words such as "vision" are used mainly at awards dinners. Yet no other word describes exactly Shannon's absolute confidence in the rightness of his belief that by bringing good men and women together and giving them the money they needed, they could study basic events in the body with results that would benefit health. For Shannon, health—rather than scientific knowledge in itself—was the ultimate objective. He often reminded his colleagues, "This is not the National Institutes of Science. It's the National Institutes of Health." But he also believed that only by understanding basic biological mechanisms could one determine how to intervene in disease. In retrospect the Shannon years served more than any other single event to make possible the American portion of the Health Century.

This story begins, as do so many others we tell here, in New York City. But Shannon came from an Irish, not a Jewish, family. In 1921 at the age of seventeen, he enrolled in New York's Holy Cross College. His major interest was basketball. He couldn't have cared less about science and medicine. Considered a possible candidate for the 1924 Olympics, he was captain of the basketball team in his senior year. Marks: mediocre. "I applied for medical school as a sort of afterthought at Harvard, Yale, P and S [Columbia], Cornell, and New York University. I was turned down flat at the first four." In his interview at Yale the dean told him, "You know, Shannon, we don't admit our medical students simply because they're good athletes." He got into NYU only because the dean of admissions had himself been a track star, and maybe because he glimpsed in Shannon something special.

Shannon got off to a slow start. "I didn't know what studying was. I remember we began the course of osteology [bones] and the first night I studied two hours and thought that was a very trying experience." When he discovered other students knew more than he did, he commenced to apply himself, and by his junior year was second in his class. And these were bright students. By his senior year in 1929 he was top of the class, having been president of the class for three of his four years at NYU.

James Shannon in 1924.

After finishing a two-year internship at New York's Bellevue Hospital, Shannon returned to NYU as a clinician in diseases of the kidney, while simultaneously working on a Ph.D. in physiology under Homer Smith. This was fast-lane science: Smith's group and Alfred Newton Richards's people at Penn were making big contributions with micromanipulators and micropipettes to knowledge of the kidney's regulation of sodium and potassium.

An elemental force in the man's personality starts to shine through. The class yearbook for 1929 showed facsimiles of a button for each graduate. The one for Shannon says: INFORMATION TO PROFS FREE![6] DeWitt Stetten, who interned at Bellevue at the time Shannon was becoming a specialist in kidney physiology, remembers a commanding presence. "He arrived on my ward one morning followed by a group of third- or fourth-year medical students and demanded to be shown a patient with renal disease." Stetten took him to a patient who was in profound uremic coma. There was nothing medicine could do for such patients in those days. "Shannon therefore turned to me and said, 'Dr. Stetten, do you have any thoughts as to what we might do for this man?' " The flustered Stetten gave a nonsensical answer that entailed cleaning the man's kidneys by draining off his cerebrospinal fluid. Shannon looked at him in bewilderment and finally said, "That is the craziest idea I have ever heard."[7] This was a man who did not suffer fools gladly.

Just before the United States entered the war in 1941, Shannon began his own experience with directing large-scale research: he was appointed head of NYU's research labs at the Goldwater Memorial Hospital on Welfare Island. We've seen the demands of fighting a war change other scientific work already—cortisone, penicillin, and yellow fever. Touching Shannon's life now was the problem of malaria. In collaboration with the pharmacologist Eli Kennerly Marshall of Johns Hopkins, the Goldwater research group was supposed to figure out how to replace the quinine supply from the Dutch East Indies (today Indonesia), which had become inaccessible as a result of the Japanese advance in the Pacific. Shannon later recalled: "With the beginning of the war, our first experience with knowing how little we knew about malaria was replacing men on Guadal-

The Shannon family, Mount Desert Island, 1937.

canal [a Pacific island that saw fierce fighting]. To start with, the First Marine Division was replaced by the Second Marine Division. Then that was replaced by the American Division, all in the course of one year. We had three divisions. They all were placed on the inoperative list because of the malaria casualties. They were evacuated to Australia, where they couldn't retrain because of malaria relapses."[8]

What to do? How about giving the men Atabrine, an alternative drug to quinine? The problem was that Atabrine had major side effects. Shannon said, "If you didn't get malaria, you were made inactive because of nausea, vomiting, and diarrhea because of drug dosage. You couldn't get the troops to take regularly Atabrine because the GI [gastrointestinal] symptoms incapacitated them."[9] So Shannon and Marshall did some experiments and determined that the immediate problem lay in excessive dosages: the troops could take considerably less, avoid the side effects, and still not experience the symptoms of malaria. The Goldwater group wanted to work more on new malaria drugs, but a government committee turned down their initial application. Alfred Newton Richards, by now head of wartime medical mobilization, was confident that Shannon and his team could do the job. According to Shannon, Richards told the committee, "If they say they can do it in New York, give them the money." This large international project went on to discover such new antimalarials as chloroquine. After the war Richards helped bring Shannon to the NIH.

Shannon learned a lot from directing this wartime program to find drugs for malaria. He learned how to apply the weight of the federal government to big issues in science: "I saw how fast one could move in a very complicated problem, provided very broad resources were available to one." So in 1949 Shannon came from New York down to Bethesda, and the government said they'd give him $5 million. But let's not get ahead of our story.

The National Institutes of Health came out of the Second World War scarcely changed. Indeed there were three hundred fewer people on the payroll in 1945 than in 1941.[10] In 1945 the NIH funded less than 5 percent of American medical research, two thirds of the total financed by the drug industry.[11] The NIH itself was still run by the commissioned officers of the Public Health Service who saw their first responsibility as microbe hunting rather than basic medical research. And the NIH directors from this period, although generally beloved by the staff, tended to fit more the mold of the good steward than the aggressive grant-getter. Part of their gentlemanly ethic was precisely that one was not pushy.

Rolla Dyer, director of the NIH from 1942 to 1948, had been a lifelong PHS officer. Although born in Ohio, he had received his medical training in the South and had spent his professional career in the South. William Sebrell, director from 1948 until 1955, was a Virginian. Though Sebrell made something of a scientific name for himself in the field of nutrition, he too had been a career PHS officer. Bernice Eddy, one of the NIH's female microbiologists, remembered Sebrell: "He was a nice man. I think he meant well."[12] Shannon by contrast she recalled as rather a nasty bit of goods.

The NIH's postwar expansion was organized along two lines, the first of which was growth of in-house research on the Bethesda campus. This in-house operation is referred to in NIH jargon as the intramural program. The second thrust would be outside the walls, extramural research, in which the NIH gave grants to academics all over the United States and even outside the country. Both have been extremely important in the postwar history of basic medical science. Four Nobel prizes have come from the in-house program, and a much larger number have been financed by extramural funds.[13]

In collaborating with Vannevar Bush's wartime Office of Scientific Research and Development, the NIH had already implicitly accepted the principle of funding private research. But a 1944 act of Congress explicitly empowered the Surgeon General (the head of the Public Health Service, of which the NIH is a part) to "make grants-in-aid to universities, hospitals, laboratories," and so forth. When the war came to an end, Bush's OSRD was abolished and Director Rolla Dyer contrived that the forty-four OSRD research contracts still running be transferred to Bethesda. This provided the NIH's initial bump-up in funding, a first ripple from which great waves of federal money would soon flow.[14]

In 1945 the NIH's support for research projects totaled $180,000. In 1984 NIH's grants and contracts to outside institutions amounted to $3.5 billion. Of the twenty-one thousand separate research grants the NIH made in 1984, almost two hundred went to foreign countries. Over the years French scientists, for example, have received over $6 million in NIH money, Israeli $25 million, Canadian over $1 billion.[15] So from these little wavelets of 1945 great breakers indeed have rolled.

To understand the corresponding rise of the NIH's in-house research, we have to introduce some new dramatis personae: a remarkable woman named Mary Lasker, her sister Alice Fordyce, and her good friend Florence Mahoney. What are these three women—none a trained scientist or researcher—doing in a story dominated thus far by men?

In 1940 Mary Woodard Reinhardt married the wealthy advertising executive Albert Lasker. Lasker, who had made his fortune through such inspirations as "Reach for a Lucky Instead of a Sweet" and "Lucky Strike

Green Goes to War," sold his ad business two years after marrying in order to devote himself full-time to public causes, especially health-related ones.[16] His bride Mary, a cum laude graduate of Radcliffe College and a successful businesswoman in her own right, already had a history of activism in public causes. In 1942 they created the Albert and Mary Lasker Foundation to lobby for federal support for mental health, birth control, and, after their cook was stricken with cancer, cancer research. The Laskers were thus lobbyists, but public-spirited ones in that they had nothing to gain from their activities over the next forty years. (Albert died of cancer in 1952, but at this writing Mary is still alive and participates actively in such Lasker Foundation programs as their highly publicized annual awards.)[17]

In the early 1940s Albert introduced Mary to his good friends Florence and Daniel Mahoney, owners of a newspaper chain, at Miami Beach. Florence Mahoney, who at one point had wanted to go to medical school, was herself attentive to medical matters, and the two women decided to begin lobbying a reluctant Congress to spend more on health. By supporting the reelection campaign in 1944 of Florida's Senator Claude Pepper financially and editorially, they had succeeded in interesting him in health. A sympathetic Pepper held hearings, which, however, seemed to run aground on the conservative attitudes of the Public Health Service. The Lasker people found the modesty of the federal service maddening. Dr. Dyer had noted, for example, "that NIH had never had its budget request denied by . . . Congress." Of course not; the sums requested had always been so tiny.

The scene now shifts to 1947. As a result of the Republican victory in the congressional elections of the previous year, the loyal Senator Pepper has just lost his chairmanship of the Appropriations Subcommittee. Mary Lasker has become terribly interested in heart disease, so Pepper encourages her to try out her ideas on the new chairman, Senator Styles Bridges of New Hampshire. Bridges is all the more receptive because he has just suffered a heart attack. Also he might, in historian Stephen Strickland's words, "be interested to know that no funds had ever been earmarked for research into heart disease . . . by the National Institute of Health."[18] In 1948 Congress passed the National Heart Act. The National Institutes became plural as the heart institute now comes alongside the preexisting National Cancer Institute (which had been created in 1937 and joined the NIH in 1944). Prominent cardiologist Paul Dudley White became head of the "advisory council" of the heart institute, and in 1949 James Shannon was invited to Bethesda as the institute's director of research.

The Tough Get Going

It was apparently on the advice of Alfred Newton Richards—Shannon's wartime boss—and the NIH's associate director Norman Topping that Shannon got the job. At the time Shannon was research director of Squibb, and took a two-thirds cut in salary, from $30,000 to $10,000 a year, to work for the government. "You'll be ruined," his high-powered medical friends warned him (in Shannon's later reconstruction of the dialogue). His scientific career would become entangled in bureaucratic red tape. "You can't afford to do it. They don't know how to manage, son." But the heart institute had given Shannon carte blanche in hiring and $5 million to play with. Actually, Shannon quickly corrected people who told him he had some nice blue chips to play with. He said, "I have them to *work* with."

Shannon wanted to apply the same management techniques at the heart institute that had worked so well on malaria at Goldwater Memorial Laboratories. That meant approaching the heart in the same way he previously had studied the kidney, as a very complex biological mechanism, but one that could be understood through quantitative laboratory investigation. This basic understanding could then be transmitted on the semiapplied level to physiology and pharmacology, for ultimate application to bedside medicine. His kidney physiology lab at Goldwater had ended up helping to keep the Marines fighting in the Pacific. So now it was a question of taking a categorical institute operating within a government bureaucracy and using it for basic study of disease. "That's something I'd like to try my hand at," he said.

The first problem was recruiting good people. Until this point scientists who wanted to stay on at NIH were expected to become PHS officers, a perfectly noble calling but not everyone's cup of tea, certainly not everyone like Burroughs Mider, whose major interest was leukemia and who had come to the cancer institute in 1939. Two years after his arrival they told Mider he should apply for a PHS commission, which entailed passing the physical (remember that the microbe hunters had to be tough) and "going to the Marine Hospital in Baltimore for two years to prove that he was a physician and not just a 'mouse doctor.' " Mider failed the physical because of his eyesight and was thereupon advised, "There is no future here for anybody who can't get a commission."[19]

Thus, Shannon was up against the tradition of microbe hunting. The PHS rules were designed to select men who could fight yellow fever in Panama. But Shannon wanted up-to-date scientists. "They sent me every scientist in the government who had twenty years of experience and a long list of publications and generally was over fifty or fifty-five years old. I used to send them back in piles, saying there is no suitable candidate for this." He wanted to find his own people in the academic environment, and tried a couple of them out on the Civil Service Commission: No dice. The commission said, "They are not acceptable. They don't satisfy our standards."

Shannon replied, "Your standards don't satisfy my needs."

So Shannon went to Director Dyer and said, "You asked me down here, saying that you wanted to exploit my capabilities in the development of this field of medicine. But now you ask me to operate within rules that defeat me before I even start."

Dyer set up a meeting between Shannon and the five members of the Civil Service Commission. He told them about his plans to get young people who had "the quantitative biological approach to serious biological problems with application in medicine." He also said that if he didn't get what he wanted he'd leave the government. They told him he could hire anybody he wanted, and this victory—however petty and bureaucratic it may seem in the retrospect of forty years—changed completely the recruitment of government scientists.

What Shannon wanted were young M.D.s interested in research. He was able to promise them patients in an institute hospital, the clinical center that would open in 1953. So in 1951 he went to see his best friends in the field of medicine, men such as Bob Loeb, the noted chief of medicine at P and S, or George Thorn at the Brigham in Boston. "I asked, would they separate for me the four or five people in their setup they think I would want." It helped in this enterprise, of course, that the Korean War had just begun and with it the doctor draft, so that young physicians who didn't want to spend two years looking at sore throats in Pearl Harbor could join this extremely high-powered team that Shannon was assembling.

"So the people came to me, people who had won extraordinarily high academic records or they wouldn't have had those assistant residencies; they had been highly productive within the experience of these professors of medicine who were very good personal friends of mine. There wasn't a single person I offered a job to of that group that didn't accept it."

The men whom Shannon recruited in those early years at heart read like a Who's Who of American science. Julius Axelrod, who in 1970 would win a Nobel prize, had been with Shannon at the Goldwater labs; ditto Robert Berliner, who later became a deputy director of NIH and is now Dean Emeritus of the Yale Medical School; Thomas Kennedy, a noted kidney specialist, had been a resident at Columbia; Christian Anfinsen from Har-

vard would win a Nobel prize in chemistry in 1972. Some of these early
heart recruits such as Bernard (Steve) Brodie stayed to become NIH's top
scientists; others, such as Sidney Udenfriend—today at the Roche Institute—drifted off to industry. In three years Shannon hired at heart a
hundred and fifty scientists.[20] They were a generation of brilliant recruits,
the first such exceptional American generation since the arrival of the
Germans in New York twenty years before.

"We Ran into a Buzz Saw on the Polio Vaccine"

In 1950 the average American never came into contact with malaria or
yellow fever. But "polio" was a word that struck fear into every parent's
heart, for in the late 1940s an epidemic of the disease had begun which
threatened to reach into every American home. In 1950 over thirty-three
thousand people, mostly children, came down with paralytic polio. Earl
Warren, later to become Chief Justice of the Supreme Court, was at the
time governor of California. There was a big election on, in which he was
swept once again to victory. Just after voting in Oakland, their legal resi-
dence, the Warrens got a call from the governor's mansion in Sacramento:
"Honeybear is awfully sick. The doctors say it's polio." Honeybear was
Nina, youngest of the three Warren daughters. When the Warrens arrived
home two hours later they found Honeybear, a high school cheerleader,
paralyzed from the waist down and scarcely conscious. She was rushed to
the hospital, but of course there was no therapy the doctors could begin,
polio being a viral disease inaccessible to antibiotics. Happily, Honeybear's paralysis did not extend to the muscles that control breathing, so
she was not put in an iron lung. But her legs were paralyzed.

When the Warrens were permitted to see their daughter briefly, she
reached for her mother's hand and whispered, "Polio's not so bad, once
you've got it and you're not afraid of what might happen." Then she
added, "Take Daddy home and make him rest. He'll be a wreck." Instead
of celebrating his electoral victory, Governor Warren found himself crying
in a corner.[21]

Polio had always been an endemic disease, for the virus, which resides in
the intestines, is spread by filth and poor sanitation. Children who lived in
the days before every family had a bathroom were exposed early in life to
polio; a few would be paralyzed or die. But most who contracted the
disease would remain without symptoms, and accordingly have natural
immunity to later infections. Paradoxically, as America became cleaner,
polio changed from endemic to *epidemic:* so many children had never had
an initial exposure that they never developed natural immunity; thus

"An early model of the Drinker respirator known as the 'iron lung.'"

when, at age nine, they contracted the virus from a schoolmate carrier, they might develop full-blown symptoms. The more children without natural immunity, the more quickly the epidemic would spread. The virus heads for the central nervous system, and when it lodges in the brain stem and spinal cord it kills those nerve cells that control the muscles, hence paralysis.

Nobody who is over forty today can forget childhood playmates with a paralyzed leg or a withered arm, the classmate who vanished suddenly to be placed in an iron lung, this can-shaped respirator in which the victim would lie, day after endless day, the great iron can creating a negative interior air pressure so that the lungs could be opened up by the pressure of the outside air (the muscles that ordinarily create the negative interior pressure are crippled).

It is 1950. Gene Roehling, a Southern California resident, has just been admitted to the San Bernadino County Hospital. "The nurse came quickly into the room, hesitated just a moment, then said matter-of-factly, 'Mr.

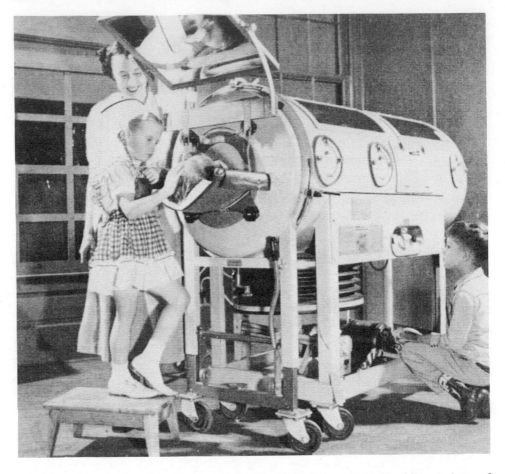

Gene Roehling in an iron lung. His family visits him on the Roehlings' sixteenth wedding anniversary.

Roehling, we're going to put you in a respirator, and I don't want you to be frightened.' "

He just lay there staring at the ceiling. His entire body was paralyzed. "I could not move an arm, a leg, a finger, a toe, or any single muscle. They told my wife Rosalie that I was dying."

The respirator itself was a "massive steel cylinder, about six feet long and a little less than three feet in diameter, raised to a convenient working height by thick, square legs, and it seemed to be literally covered with portholes, doors, hoses, bellows, and other appointments." Rosalie would come and visit him. Although he would keep a stiff upper lip during her visits, he would cry whenever she had gone.

"This used to annoy the nurses, who apparently expected me to be much braver, and they used to make a point of asking me what was

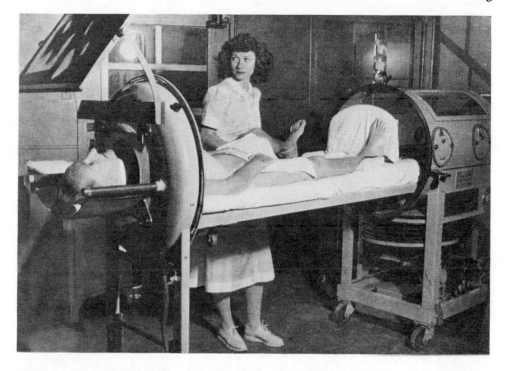

A physical therapist exercised Gene Roehling's arms and legs daily while he lived in the iron lung.

wrong." Roehling's nose would fill up from his tears, and he would have to summon one of these reproving nurses to blow his nose for him.[22]

A terrifying feature of the disease was that no one knew exactly how it was contracted, and so one didn't know how to avoid it. Was the cow's milk infected? Should we stay out of swimming pools? As the last great epidemic crested in the mid-1950s, there was a hysteria in the population comparable to the AIDS panic today. Dr. William Jordan, now a senior vaccine specialist at the NIH, was at the time head of the polio team at Case Western University in Cleveland. He remembers the terrible epidemic of 1952: "We ran out of respirators. The March of Dimes had to find some. I took care of one of our surgical residents, Jack Cole, who was critically ill. The people you see in wheelchairs with withered legs . . . it was a horrible business.

"My own daughter got polio. We were a young impoverished family. One of the first epidemics that summer hit a group of Boy Scouts, and she had been at camp on the same island. So you can imagine that when the daughter of the fellow running the program got polio, that was big news."[23]

Americans are very good at organizing huge voluntary efforts to combat national menaces such as polio, rather than relying on the state as the French do. So in 1938 the National Foundation for Infantile Paralysis (as poliomyelitis was then called) was formed. A dynamic lawyer named Basil O'Connor, who had once practiced law in New York City together with a famous polio victim, the paraplegic Franklin Roosevelt, would soon take command. The foundation's March of Dimes campaign captured the imagination of the nation. At halftime at basketball games in little Midwestern towns a big canvas would be spread on the court to receive showers of change from the spectators. The polio foundation commissioned from the Disney Studios a film strip featuring Mickey Mouse, Donald Duck, and friends marching off to fight polio:

> Heigh-ho, heigh-ho
> We'll lick old polio,
> With dimes and quarters
> And our doll-aaars—
> Ho, heigh-ho.

The March of Dimes' millions would, in fact, "lick old polio." But two preliminary scientific achievements made that possible. First, there had to be some practical way of growing the virus in a tissue culture and of knowing how much virus you had. Before, one could study polio in the lab only by giving the disease to monkeys: was a given strain sufficiently attenuated for a vaccine? Give it to a monkey and see if the monkey became paralyzed. The cumbersomeness of this kind of research is obvious, to say nothing of the risk of being bitten by the infected monkeys. In 1936 Albert Sabin, then at the Rockefeller Institute, had succeeded in growing some poliovirus in central nervous tissue of human embryos. But researchers were reluctant to use a vaccine prepared from human nervous cells because they feared it might damage the nervous systems of patients who received the vaccine. Also, you still needed monkeys to know if you had grown the virus successfully.

Then in 1947 John F. Enders, exasperated with the time spent teaching and administering, took leave from his post in the microbiology department at Harvard Medical School and opened a lab at the Children's Hospital of Boston. He was shortly joined by his former student Thomas Weller and another young man, also fresh from the military, Frederick Robbins. They applied themselves to growing poliovirus in tissue cultures made from human cells, and between 1948 and 1950 discovered how to keep the virus alive in cells from the human skin and intestine. They also developed a dye marker that changed color as the virus grew, thus permitting them merely to look into the microscope and see if they had any virus.

These accomplishments sound rather technical. Indeed they appeared sufficiently obscure to another polio researcher, John Paul of Yale, that when Enders casually mentioned he "had succeeded in growing Lansing poliovirus in human embryonic nonnervous tissue," Paul merely nodded politely. "For the moment, I was stupidly unaware of the implications that this finding held. At least it did not appear to me as an electrifying piece of news. . . . [It] hardly seemed to me a trick which could be put to any special or practical diagnostic use. How utterly mistaken was my preliminary judgment of this discovery to prove!"[24] It meant the beginning of the end of the monkey era and the rise of modern virus research in test tubes.

Second, nobody knew how many different kinds of polio virus existed. A

Nobel laureates Thomas H. Weller, John F. Enders, and Frederick C. Robbins, who discovered how to keep poliovirus alive in human tissue cells. They also developed a dye marker that changed color as the virus grew, permitting them to identify the virus through a microscope. This was the beginning of the end of the monkey era and the birth of modern virus research in test tubes.

vaccine was required against each strain, since the vaccines didn't cross-immunize. One reason earlier polio vaccinations failed was that a vaccine against one type would be made, only to have the children come down with another. In fact, three distinct strains exist, and to be fully protected

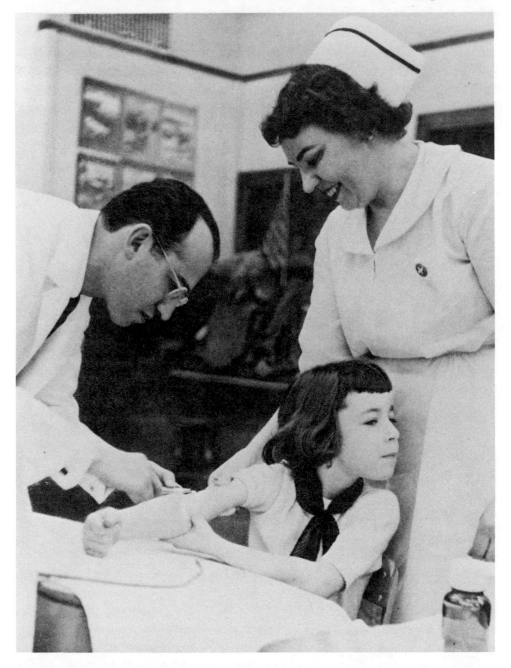

Jonas Salk injects a young patient with his inactivated polio vaccine.

one must be immunized against all three. Various researchers, using Enders's new tissue culture techniques and supported by the polio foundation, figured all this out by 1951. After that, to prepare a workable vaccine one needed only establish how to neutralize the virus so that it wouldn't give its recipients polio, and the problem would be solved.

Among the various scientists who plunged now headlong into this mission, Jonas Salk of the University of Pittsburgh gained the lead: by 1953 he had shown that his vaccine of killed virus immunized safely against all three types. In a meeting in January 1953 of the March of Dimes Foundation's scientific advisers at Hershey, Pennsylvania, a distinguished virologist named Joseph Smadel urged Salk, "What are you waiting for? Why don't you get busy and put on a proper field trial?" Salk then started large-scale testing of his vaccine, as O'Connor beamed. Nobody outside foundation offices knew exactly what was happening.[25]

Rather than staging a long series of careful field trials with appropriate scientific evaluation, Salk darted ahead on his own in the remainder of 1953 and 1954. The trials were successful. The foundation released the results to the press, and such were the nation's expectations that from that point there was no turning back. In August 1954 the foundation ordered five drug companies to begin producing mass lots of vaccine, on the basis of a formula for inactivating the virus with formaldehyde, according to a procedure Salk himself had devised. It must be stressed that the NIH's own vaccine laboratory would certify the Salk inactivated vaccine as safe for distribution to the public. On April 12, 1955, the first lots of vaccine were shipped.[26]

James Shannon remembered very well what happened next. At this point he had become the associate director of the NIH. "I was working over the weekend and I got a telephone call from Los Angeles, and this is eight or nine o'clock on Friday night. It was the Health Officer of the City of Los Angeles and he said they just had two reports of polio in some children who had been vaccinated nine days earlier. He wanted to know what should be done about it?"

One of the companies that contracted to make the vaccine, the Cutter Laboratories in Berkeley, California, had released several lots of vaccine that had been improperly inactivated. Live polio virus was being injected into children. The gratitude of the public turned to horror as the Cutter vaccine gave polio to almost 80 recipients; these children in turn went on to spread the disease to another 120 playmates and relatives; three quarters of the victims were paralyzed and 11 died.[27]

We dwell upon this grim incident because of its impact upon the history of the National Institutes of Health: it shows why good scientific leadership, able to resist both the pressures of Congress and the media, is so important. It is little known that NIH's Laboratory of Biologics Control, which had certified the Salk vaccine, had received advance warning of problems. And that warning came from its staff microbiologist, Dr. Bernice Eddy.

Dr. Bernice E. Eddy, whose lab tests found that the Cutter vaccine had been improperly inactivated.

In 1954 Eddy was fifty-one years old. Born in a mining town in West Virginia, she got a Ph.D. in 1927 from the University of Cincinnati and came to Washington during the Great Depression to work at the Hygienic Laboratory, as she continued to call it. Her job from then until she retired in 1973 was the safety testing of vaccines.

In 1954 the rush was on. Her lab had gotten samples of the inactivated polio vaccine to certify on a "due-yesterday" basis. "This was a product that had never been made before and they were going to use it right away," she recalled. She and her staff worked around the clock. "We had eighteen monkeys. We inoculated these eighteen monkeys with each vaccine that came in. And we started getting paralyzed monkeys." She reported to her superiors that the lots were Cutter's, and sent pictures of the paralyzed monkeys along as well. "They were going to be injecting this thing into children."

William Sebrell, the director of the NIH, stopped by the animal house where they were working, not to thank her for blowing the whistle but to ask if she and her co-workers wanted their children immunized with the vaccine, as it was in short supply. "I thanked him but said that my children had escaped polio so far and that I preferred to wait until the testing program was over before having them immunized," said Eddy. "Everyone there turned down the offer."

She heard nothing more about her report and never got the photographs back. "They went ahead and released the vaccine anyway, a lot of it. The monkeys they just disregarded."[28]

To understand what happens later, the reader must have some notion of how traumatic the Cutter incident was for the entire Public Health Service, not to say the NIH. We left James Shannon in his office on a Friday night. That was just the beginning. Shannon called the Surgeon General Saturday morning. Additional cases of paralysis continued to occur. "It seemed obvious that we had a crisis on our hands, the magnitude of which was unknown." Late Saturday afternoon a working group of senior virus specialists, whose advice the polio foundation had started to ignore a year earlier, began meeting in Shannon's office. Note that Shannon had completely taken charge of the crisis. "Sebrell was not the man to manage this," DeWitt Stetten recalled. "James Shannon was a man of quite different character."[29]

Shannon had brought in the Surgeon General, who called polio chief Basil O'Connor in New York. On Monday evening O'Connor and his advisers came down to Bethesda. Shannon wanted to withdraw the vaccine, "It was a very stormy meeting," he said. "O'Connor and the polio group in general disallowed any possibility of induced infections [as a result of the vaccine]. . . . So Basil O'Connor stormed out with dire warning of what he was going to do to the NIH and the Public Health Service. Further vaccination was stopped. I had many sleepless nights."[30]

The basic problem had really not been the carelessness of the Cutter company, which rightly or wrongly was exonerated in a later report. It was the difficulty in jumping from Salk's lab experiments with killing (formalinizing) the virus to large-scale industrial production. And the polio foundation had been so secretive that NIH didn't realize until too late how inadequate the formalinizing was. "There was no need for this ever to have happened," said Shannon later. "So NIH was painted into a box and made very bad decisions. Industry was painted into a box, and it was the forceful personality of O'Connor with the political support he had that was able to override some of the essential details of federal management of an important biological product."

But the government had to carry the can. "The fact was, everybody's head had to roll," said NIH's Alan Rabson in retrospect. "This was such a ghastly mistake." His wife Ruth Kirschstein, the director today of an important NIH institute, added, "The Cutter incident resulted in everybody up the line who had anything to do with it—very few people know this story—being dismissed because of it." All went out: the director of the microbiology institute lost his post, as did the equivalent of the assistant secretary for health. Oveta Culp Hobby, the secretary of Health, Education and Welfare (or Oveta "Culpable" Hobby, as she was known), stepped down. Dr. Sebrell, the director of the NIH, resigned. "And Shannon became the director," Kirschstein continued. "He said he would save the situation and he did."[31] The historic significance of the Cutter incident is that, among other things it made James Shannon the head of the NIH.

A Leader, Not a Coordinator

How typical of the federal government that the forty-odd buildings on the NIH campus of Bethesda are numbered in the order they were built. "Building One," the administration building, was thus the first, completed in 1938. Although everyone still refers to the administration as "Building One," the building itself no longer has a big red one on it, as all the other structures have numbers, but the words THE JAMES A. SHANNON BUILDING. In the lobby, directly in front of the main door, hangs a huge oil painting of Shannon. To the right of it is an impressive bronze of Shannon's torso and head, "presented by his friends," then various collections of photographs commemorating the unveiling of the bust or the renaming of the building in 1983. Aside from that there is nothing in the lobby except a big scale model of the campus.

The directors who have come after Shannon's retirement in 1968 have not had insignificant egos. One cannot grasp why they would allow such a shrine to remain in place without knowing that it was James Shannon who made the NIH what it is today.

"What does that mean?" Alan Rabson was asked, one of many to express the opinion that Shannon had "made" the NIH.

"Money," Rabson said.

One of Shannon's historic accomplishments is that he wrung from the Congress, against the wishes of the executive, far, far more money for health research than one would ever have thought possible. When Shannon became associate director in 1952, his boss William Sebrell told him, "Jim, one thing I can assure you is that [you need not] worry about budget. I will handle all the budget."[32] This turned out to be completely wrong. Sebrell, with the reticence of his generation, had no idea of the sums Shannon wanted. "Although William had committed that he would take care of all budgetary matters," Shannon remembered, "it just wasn't at that time feasible for him to do it." When it came time to testify before Congress about the budget, "William would make the presentation, but we had to set him up."

In the thirteen years that Shannon was director, he increased the budget of the NIH about fifteenfold. It took a special kind of personality to coax these enormous sums from the Congress. "He was a sort of Bobby Lane kind of figure, a real leader of men," one old hand recalled. A "leader of men": even the concept seems antique today. We prefer to talk about "coordinators." But leadership requires distinctive character qualities, not all of them agreeable ones. Shannon had a singlemindedness about mission that shaded easily into insensitivity and ruthlessness. As research director at the Squibb Institute just after the war he offered a taste of this: "Within the first two months I had to fire my deputy," he said. "I went away on a weekend trip and he was having some visitors. I told him how to behave in relation to them. It had to do with changing the program, and he didn't follow my directions. I fired him on the spot. I said, 'You're finished. We'll continue your pay for a month, but I don't want to see you around here anymore.' "

Ruth Kirschstein, a tough administrator herself, spoke admiringly of Shannon's autocratic qualities. "He was very serious and singleminded about it. He would get what he wanted and brook no disagreeing with him. He ran this place with an iron hand." Autocrats like it when the court shows up, and Joseph Murtaugh, a research planner who came to NIH in 1956, remembered Shannon's annoyance when courtiers were absent: "Elaborate devices were often resorted to by the various staff members to gain approval of leave plans. Often, even after having given prior approval to someone's absence, Jim would become annoyed upon seeing the vacant chair at the table, and demand to know [why] the individual was absent."[33] Jerome Green, who arrived in Bethesda the same year that Shannon became director, remembered him as a great mumbler. "He was like the surgeons who speak in a low voice because they expect complete silence."[34]

A lack of anything resembling ironical detachment in Shannon's character does not, therefore, surprise us. The man was completely humorless about his "blue chips," as he referred to the NIH. In medicine it is customary at something like the office Christmas party for the interns and residents to put on a bit of a skit that "roasts" the senior staff, mocking their behavioral peculiarities or whatever. These send-ups are thoroughly in the spirit of good fun. Thus at one NIH alumni reunion weekend, it was not out of the ordinary for the Ad Hoc Players, a quartet of campus bureaucrats, to rib the place a bit. For example, they sang:

> First you get the forms from DRG [Division of Research Grants]
> Everything you need is furnished free.
> Dream up a project that's nice and fat
> Then you add a bit of this and quite a lot of that.

Innocent enough humor, but halfway through Shannon stood up and stopped the show. "I was furious," he told an interviewer. "At a reunion of NIH scientists they were saying basically that the whole damn grant program was a rip-off. I thought they should stop. I wouldn't sit down until they stopped."[35]

But exactly this kind of driving magisterial personality was required to get money from the Congress, men who cannot be impressed but can be awed. So Shannon had a network of crucial allies on the Hill. John Fogarty, another Irishman who was chairman of the House Appropriations Subcommittee, saw absolutely eye-to-eye with Shannon. Fogarty was a Democrat from Rhode Island, and Shannon had been his personal physician for ten years. When Shannon could no longer look after Fogarty, he turned him over to Surgeon General Luther Terry. Melvin Laird, Fogarty's conservative Republican counterpart, was highly sympathetic. Thus, all was clear in the House. In the Senate, "health's" great ally was Democrat Lister Hill of Alabama.[36] Completing the foursome, Senator Norris Cotton, Hill's Republican opposite number on the Appropriations Subcommittee, also regarded NIH favorably.

The key figures were always Hill, Fogarty, and Shannon. Alan Rabson said twenty years later: "If Shannon is going to have sainthood, [it's because] he found these two, this senator and this congressman, and convinced them that their way to immortalize themselves was to support biomedical research. . . . So what do we have? We have a Fogarty center; we have a Lister Hill building, and we have a Shannon building."

In Shannon's own view the congressional leadership had joined forces, all of them saying: Let's push this as fast as it will go. How fast could it go?[37] When Shannon became director in 1955, Marion Folsom had just become Secretary of Health, Education and Welfare, replacing the ousted Oveta Culp Hobby. The NIH budget was then about $100 million.

Folsom to Shannon: "You asked for a $100 million increase? Well, I think I can get you at least a third of that. Remember that's a thirty percent increase, that's an unheard-of increase," said Folsom. Eisenhower approved the $130 million budget.

Now Shannon went to Fogarty and Hill. "Fogarty took the $130 million budget and increased it to $160 million. Hill took the $160 million and increased it to $200 million. So the budget we got for the next year [fiscal year 1957] was $200 million."

By 1960 the NIH budget had increased to $430 million, by 1968, the year Shannon retired, to well over $1 billion, and all this in a period of low inflation. With these new funds the campus institutes waxed mightily. The biologics division, which had blundered on the polio vaccine, was shunted off to a separate unit, where it was closely watched from "Building One." The microbiological institute, which had formerly housed biologics, was now renamed the Institute for Allergy and Infectious Diseases, a sexier name. As one wag put it, "Whoever died of microbiology?" Their major concern is currently AIDS. A series of new institutes was created.[38]

All this money did not appear by some kind of annual magic. It had to be, if not coaxed, at least justified in the presence of these sympathetic Appropriations Subcommittee chairmen. Although Shannon himself was, in Burroughs Mider's experience, "one of the finest witnesses I have ever seen," other medical figures, accustomed to scientific understatement of claims, were less sterling. Roscoe ("Spenny") Spencer at cancer, for example, testified before a Congressional Appropriations Subcommittee that "he did not think that an expanded budget for the National Cancer Institute was justified."[39]

The scientists were privately appalled at the politicians' scanty knowledge of health matters. DeWitt Stetten remembers testifying before the House subcommittee after Fogarty died and Daniel Flood, a Pennsylvania Democrat, had replaced him:

FLOOD: "Hey, Doc, what's new in deviated nasal septums?"
STETTEN: "We're working hard on it."

When Stetten appeared before Warren Magnuson in the Senate, Magnuson asked him about chiropractic. Magnuson's wife was evidently under treatment by a chiropractor.

STETTEN: "We'll try to look into that, Senator."

But we are selling the memory of James Shannon short if we talk too much about money. Because what the NIH prides itself on today is not its wealth. In fact, many of the buildings are shabby, the labs crowded, the sofas of the senior administrators covered with cracking plastic rather than leather. Shannon's inheritors pride themselves on the quality of the science, not their furniture. It takes a while to get used to this manner of expression. Historians do not talk about the "quality of history" done at

Surgeon General William Stewart, President Johnson, Secretary John Gardner (HID-
DEN), *James Shannon, and Philip Lee at the National Institutes of Health in 1967.
By 1968 Shannon had increased the NIH budget from about $100 million in 1955 to
well over $1 billion.*

R. W. Berliner, J. Orloff, and J. A. Shannon at the dedication of the James A. Shannon Building, NIH, 1983.

Yale or wherever. But for a scientist to say that someone does "good science" is to bestow high praise. And the NIH belief is that this tradition of good science, which makes the NIH "the most exciting place to be in the world," is part of James Shannon's legacy.

In retrospect Shannon was able to see the whole, wide horizon, from the molecular advances on one side to their practical application in the clinic far removed on the other. And as a leader with this vision he was able to inspire good people to accept work in the government service. Given ample resources by Congress, the NIH would inevitably turn into a power-house.

It is characteristic that he knew exactly what he wanted to do when he took office in 1955: "I felt that NIH then, which was still a very small operation . . . was ready to blossom. But to blossom it had to be radically changed, and I thought I was capable of changing it." Proceeding from the model he had established at the heart institute, his notion was to take the specific diseases that each institute represented and apply to them "quantitative concepts of biology . . . to understand the nature of disease and ultimately its management." This meant "erasing the basic difference between the fundamentally oriented scientist and the application of this new knowledge in the clinic." Thus, Shannon installed at NIH the basic plan of organization that will guide us through the remainder of this book: making advances in understanding basic mechanisms of disease, which lead to payoffs at the bedside, and in the health of the nation and the world.

FOUR

The Molecular Mainline

Picture yourself in an armchair on a quiet winter evening in 1887. "Where is medicine going?" you ask yourself. "What can my children expect?" You'd be lost in 1887 without some understanding of the germ theory of disease that Pasteur and Koch had been batting around, the notion that diseases are caused by microbes.

A hundred years later we ask ourselves the same question. But this time the theory we need to grasp has the word "molecular" in it. Wherever medicine is going today, molecular research will get there first. That is what this chapter is about.

Understanding molecular activity means simply understanding enough about basic chemical events in the body to "see" the molecules clicking together as the nucleic acids, or DNA, in the cell drive the machinery forward. With the electron microscope one can, for example, see the little trains of genetic material come chugging out of the cell's nucleus. One can see the antibody molecules forming "claws" in which they will entrap antigen, and know how each set of claws is shaped to fit a specific antigen.

We have now penetrated far beyond the level of the microscope to glimpse chemical events taking place within individual cells. When we can explain those events in terms of what the DNA—the basic genetic material—is doing at any given moment, we have reached the molecular level.

This molecular approach provides the basis of all new medical knowledge and drug research today. But it is so new that even many older scientists feel themselves left behind. In 1979 Herbert Carter, a biochemist from the University of Arizona, said in exasperation after hearing a paper by Felix Haurowitz, a chemist at Indiana University, on how DNA (the genes) governs the cell, "I am glad to see that somebody in my generation understands a little of the complexity of gene expression, to which I have been exposed for the last six months in seminars."[1]

These molecular fields move so fast that terms can go out of date in months, as happens now in immunology, rather than in decades. So in this fast-moving world let us make sure that we have one foot planted securely. In the normal logic of historical exposition, one starts at the beginning and finishes at the end. But in this chapter, to make sure no one gets lost, we shall act like a visitor to the forest: we shall plant a stake in the ground so that we can always follow the string back to where we entered. Thus, we begin with present knowledge of how things work, proceeding from that sure point back to the past.

A Stake in the Forest

There are a hundred trillion cells in the human body. Each one is like a little factory, having a nucleus with a full complement of DNA, RNA, genes, chromosomes, and so forth. Any one of these hundred trillion cells contains perhaps one hundred thousand enzyme molecules. The purpose of any enzyme is to accelerate a chemical reaction, and these different enzymes are responsible for perhaps a thousand to two thousand different kinds of reactions in each cell.[2] How may we sort out this bewildering complexity of molecules bumping and grinding together?

The heart of the human cell is the nucleus, with its long interlocking strands of DNA, or deoxyribonucleic acid, divided up into chromosomes. Each strand in this very long rope has a backbone of sugar and phosphate and a series of inwardly pointing chemical structures, parallel to the backbone, called bases. The bases of one strand make chemical bonds to the bases of the other, holding the two long strands together. The two bases constitute a base pair. And a number of base pairs, taken together, form a gene. As many as one hundred thousand genes are found in the chromosomes.

The purpose of a gene is to direct the chemical machinery of the cell to make a specific protein; this protein will then leave the cell and perform chemical work all over the body. For example, a typical protein is an antibody, made by certain kinds of white blood cells. So one gene, one protein.

When a gene orders a protein to be made, the two strands of DNA unzip. Then one of the DNA strands forms a strand of a closely related nucleic acid called RNA, or ribonucleic acid. The DNA does this by instructing a number of enzymes to produce these pieces of RNA. The RNA starts out bellied up alongside the master DNA strand, each of its pieces composed of bases that correspond exactly to the bases of the gene that has been switched on in the DNA. This strand of RNA then chugs its way outside the nucleus to begin, in collaboration with other kinds of RNA, making proteins.

The system is thus overpowering in its simplicity: DNA makes RNA; RNA makes proteins; these proteins in various forms then direct everything else that happens in the body. (The RNA actually makes amino acids, but a protein is simply a long string of amino acids.) When we fall ill, disease may be explained as a result of a derangement at this molecular level. For example, are the red cells of the body, normally doughnut-shaped, turning into pathological sickle-shaped cells? It's a result of a disorder in those particular DNA bases that form the gene for hemoglobin. Hemoglobin is the oxygen-carrying protein in the wall of the red blood cell. In sickle-cell anemia, a potentially fatal blood disorder affecting mainly black people, the hemoglobin is sticky; its molecules cling together unnaturally, pulling the red cell out of shape so that it is easily destroyed; hence the anemia. Hemoglobin is, like all proteins, composed of amino acids, and the particular defect in these sickling cells is the substitution of an amino acid called valine for the normal amino acid glutamate at a certain position on one of the hemoglobin chains. *Violà!* The molecular explanation of an important inheritable disease, a classic explanation in this case because it was in 1954 that Cambridge University's Vernon Ingram devised a technique for detecting amino acid substitutions in proteins. He came to MIT in 1959 and shortly thereafter explained the mechanism underlying sickle-cell anemia, the first of the molecular diseases.

Thus, we have our stake in the forest, a secure reference point to which we may always follow the string back. And the string goes: DNA makes RNA; RNA makes amino acids; amino acids in turn are the building blocks of proteins, the regulators of health and disease. Understandable? Yes. Perfection? No. Later in this chapter we shall discover a fiendish variation nature has devised upon this simple theme: in diseases such as AIDS, it is the viruses' RNA that directs the DNA of the host's cells (instead of DNA making RNA). It tells the host DNA to make more viruses.

Getting on the Molecular Mainline

Let's not exaggerate the ignorance of previous generations. Stanford's Sidney Raffel often has the experience of describing to young physicians or scientists "what biomedical science was like in my formative days about half a century ago. It is fairly apparent from the facial and verbal expressions of my dialogists—though they are usually discreet—that they regard the state of science of that period as belonging to a geologically distinct epoch." Every generation tends to think, as Raffel put it, that "developments in their own area evolved simultaneously with the kindling of their own interest."[3]

Scientists before the 1930s understood, for example, the general importance of proteins. Yet no one had any notion of their structure nor how they functioned. For example, the British physiologist William Bayliss pooh-poohed the whole idea that enzymes were proteins.[4] Nor did total ignorance envelop the body's two other major constitutents—fats and carbohydrates—although how the cell dealt with them was still obscure.

As for the nucleic acids such as DNA, they had been identified chemically before 1930 but were considered unimportant. To understand how DNA and RNA come to occupy center stage we have to keep track of two separate narratives: deciphering their chemical *function* and their physical *structure*.

Working out the chemistry of DNA is a New York story. It begins in the Rockefeller Institute in the early 1930s as a little man named Oswald Avery—he weighed less than a hundred pounds—pondered the findings of a British bacteriologist about the pneumococcus, the organism that causes pneumonia. This bacterium existed in several strains, and something about the virulent strains seemed to have the ability to make other nonvirulent strains equally dangerous. These strains transmitted this new virulence, moreover, to subsequent generations. So whatever it was that transformed them acted on heredity. Avery and his people were already extremely interested in the pneumococcus, given the great mortality from pneumonia in those days, and toyed with this curious observation. But after determining that the transforming ability seemed chemical in nature, they permitted matters to drift until September 1941, when young Maclyn McCarty arrived at the Rockefeller Institute.

A recent Johns Hopkins M.D., McCarty had become interested in microbes during a fellowship at NYU, and now wanted to work with Avery. Avery summoned McCarty to his office and "played a Red Seal Record," as associates referred to the carefully crafted but apparently extemporaneous speeches Avery would perform for neophytes. He waxed grandiloquently on the transforming principle of the pneumococcus, its ability, even when killed, to convey virulence on an inheritable basis to otherwise innocuous strains. "This is all it took," said McCarty later. "From then on . . . I was engulfed in the problem." Nine months later it was clear that the "transforming extract" must be DNA. Because Avery was a careful polisher of research—and because at that time scientific findings were not instantly announced to a worshipful press—two more years went by before Avery published the news that his lab had identified the molecule of heredity.

In the words of René Dubos, Avery had established "that bacteria can be made to undergo hereditary changes by treating them with . . . DNA extracted from other bacteria. This discovery turned out to be one of the landmarks of modern biology, because other investigators soon established that DNA molecules are the specific carriers of hereditary characteristics in *all* living things."[5]

Avery's finding created surprisingly little sensation. He did not win a Nobel prize. But one attentive reader was Columbia's Erwin Chargaff, whom we have met before. "Was it in the at-that-time still pleasant dining room [of the Rockefeller Institute]? Was it in one of the cheerless corridors of the College of Physicians and Surgeons? Anyway, somebody came and told me to read a paper by Avery in the *Journal of Experimental Medicine.* . . . It was obvious to me that I must work on the chemistry of the nucleic acids. The road to take was, in fact, clearly delineated before my eyes."[6]

When Chargaff and his team set out to analyze DNA in 1946, they profited from "an unusual combination of lucky circumstances," meaning that the technical devices they needed to make their discoveries had just become available. What were these devices?

First, paper chromatography had been introduced in 1944 for the segregation of tiny amounts of organic substances. You put a piece of something like coffee filter paper in the bottom of a glass jar; in the bottom of the jar is a mixture of liquids such as acetone and water. Then you pour in the substance you want to analyze: the more it resembles the acetone (nonpolar), it rises to the top of the paper; the more it resembles the watery filter paper (polar), it remains at the bottom. Elementary, but it beats the pants off previous techniques for discovering if X or Y was present in a particular solution.

Second, Chargaff's team had acquired a spectrophotometer made by the Beckman company, just as these high-quality devices became available commercially. This device shoots an infrared beam through a substance; whatever chemical bonds are present in the substance will vibrate at different wavelengths, and these vibrations will register on graph paper. Thus, the graph of a substance containing alcohol will look quite different from the graph of something with nitrogen. All proteins contain nitrogen, and spectroscopy offers a powerful tool for studying them.

There was one more happy circumstance. The bases of DNA belong to chemical families called purines and pyrimidines. Both contain nitrogen and may be studied with the spectrophotometer. Now, to understand how the two long strands of DNA coil together, remember that the purine bases are always attracted to the pyrimidine, and vice versa. How strange, thought Chargaff after playing around with wooden models of the molecules. The adenine base (a purine) seems always to go with the thymine base (a pyrimidine). He was within an ace of discovering the principle of complementary base pairing, the key to the architecture of DNA, yet no light bulb went on. Chargaff: "Later, I was often asked by more or less well-meaning people why I had not discovered the celebrated model. My answer has always been that I was too dumb."[7]

At this point the chemistry of DNA was fairly clear. But what was the molecule's structure? The question is not academic, because "molecular" anything means being able physically to visualize these big molecules as they twist and bond.

Now the scene shifts to Cambridge, England, in May 1952. Chargaff, who has just been to Switzerland in his third unsuccessful attempt to escape New York by getting a Swiss professorship, bumps into two scientists from the Cambridge physics laboratory, a twenty-three-year-old American postdoc named James Watson, "a gawky young figure" with a grin "more sly than sheepish," and Francis Crick, a thirty-five-year-old Englishman with "an incessant falsetto, occasional nuggets glittering in the turbid stream of prattle." They too were interested in DNA, and by collaborating with several crystallographers (scientists who study the microscopic image of substances through diffraction of X rays), the two had been groping toward its structure.

But perhaps on that day it was from Chargaff that the incessant stream of prattle came, for the two offered little as they picked his mind. Untrained in chemistry, they had not gotten far with the question: Which base goes with which? Crick, indeed, had forgotten the chemical differences among the various bases. So when they asked for information, Chargaff gave them everything he knew: "Adenine with thymine, guanine with cytosine [the names of the other two bases], purines with pyrimidines."[8] The rest is history. The two Cambridge scientists went on to postulate a two-stranded model of DNA, winding through the cell's nucleus in a double helix, as though a ladder had been twisted lengthwise. In 1953 they published their findings. The actual physical structure of DNA had now been revealed. One could visualize it, imagine where on the long chain to intervene. In 1962 Watson and Crick received a Nobel prize. Science was now firmly placed on the molecular mainline.[9]

From DNA to "Arthritis"

With DNA we've physically identified the very molecule of heredity. But how does it work? When someone comes down with a genetic disease such as sickle-cell anemia, what is the problem with their DNA? Does something in the DNA cause cancer? Answers to all these questions were unknown in 1953. Figuring out how DNA caused disease will be the basic agenda of molecular biology for the next quarter century, harvesting Nobel prizes one after the other.

Once again, the NIH is central to this story. In fact, a presidential commission in 1965 pronounced the NIH as "largely responsible for the biochemical explosion of the past two decades."[10] Two small groups of men had gathered in Bethesda long before Shannon's arrival, before anyone had heard of Watson and Crick. Both groups were composed of biochemists, people who study life systems by pouring chemicals together in test tubes rather than by making observations on animals, as Goldberger had done. One group, led by Jesse Greenstein, worked on cancer research. The other concentrated on DNA work; here we find Arthur Kornberg, Bernard Horecker, Leon Heppel, and Herbert Tabor.

In order to understand this story, the reader must recall a fact that today is often passed over in silence: America was once a substantially anti-Semitic society, not as bad perhaps as Europe but still a land where Jews in 1940 often felt distinctly unwelcome. Ruth Kirschstein, for example, who today is a high NIH administrator, was asked why, coming from Brooklyn, she went to medical school at Tulane in the late 1940s. Tulane is in New Orleans.

"It's not something I particularly like recorded," she said. "In 1947 a woman from New York City didn't get into medical school that easily and that was the medical school that accepted me."

Similarly, Jesse Greenstein, a workaholic biochemist, underwent a traumatic period in the 1930s, trying to be kept on at Harvard and Berkeley. "This period left a mark on Greenstein," his colleague Michael Shimkin later wrote. "He found how difficult it was at that time for a Jew to get a

Dr. Jesse P. Greenstein, the "workaholic biochemist" who made fundamental contributions to understanding the biochemistry of cancer.

permanent position, despite his arduous work and undoubted contributions to protein chemistry."[11] Then in the late 1930s the National Cancer Institute took him on. "Greenstein was a prodigious worker," fellow biochemist Alton Meister recalled. "He spent long hours in the laboratory and could be found there on most evenings and weekends." Once there was a lab fire. "I rushed in to see him vainly spraying CO_2 from an extinguisher on a violently burning tank of hydrogen. . . . The tank seemed hot enough to explode at any moment," Meister said. "I nervously suggested that we leave, if necessary by the second-story window. Greenstein, however, managed somehow to close the red-hot valve with his bare hand." Although the hand was, in fact, badly burned, Greenstein continued to work regularly in the lab "with a messy loose bandage on his right hand."[12]

In 1960 Greenstein wrote a major three-volume work on amino acids that Shimkin and many others regarded as "the best synthesis of the subject since the contributions of Otto Warburg in the 1920s," and he also made fundamental contributions to understanding the biochemistry of cancer. Later in our story we will return to the biochemists at the Cancer Institute.

The second group of individuals were to occupy themselves directly with DNA. The story begins in 1942 with Arthur Kornberg, a Brooklyn boy who had just received his M.D. from Rochester and knew nothing of biochemistry. "On the strength of research I had done as a student investigating my own jaundice, I was assigned to work on rat nutrition at the National Institute of Health." At this point Kornberg became fascinated, not by problems of vitamins in rats, but by enzymes. "I have never known a dull enzyme," Kornberg later wrote.

"One day in 1944, I was enthralled by a seminar on the 'one gene, one enzyme' concept by Edward Tatum based on his work with George Beadle." Tatum and Beadle are important figures in the DNA story because, even before the big discoveries of the 1950s, they had figured out from mold research that a single gene codes for a single enzyme. This reaped a Nobel prize for them in 1958, the year before Kornberg got his own.

When Kornberg arrived in Bethesda, he knew very little biochemistry. So he became friendly with a young biochemist with a Ph.D. from the University of Chicago named Bernard Horecker, who had come the year before. Leon Heppel showed up in 1942 as well, a "careful, meticulous, childish, and screwy" man who had a Ph.D. in biochemistry from Berkeley and an M.D.[13] Heppel had been friends with Kornberg when they were med students at Rochester, and had a number of bizarre mannerisms revolving around fear of germs and obsessive-compulsive rituals in the lab. And when Herbert Tabor, whom we met injecting penicillin into Mrs. Miller while a junior intern at Yale, arrived in 1943, the foursome was complete.

Led by Kornberg, this small band now began an intense period of intellectual activity, focused upon a daily lunchtime seminar. The purpose of the seminar was to teach Kornberg and Tabor, who were wild to plunge into research, some biochemistry. So there would be assigned readings, usually from the German, to be discussed the next day over sandwiches. It didn't matter if it was Christmas Day: the seminar met. Did they want to get tickets for the Budapest Quartet concert at the Library of Congress? No problem. They would hold the seminar while standing in line. One must imagine how unusual intellectual activity of this intensity was for staid Bethesda: some of the older scientists predicted that the four would develop ulcers. They did not.

In 1946 Kornberg was sent on a trip "to learn something about these things called enzymes," DeWitt Stetten recalled. "There was very little interest in enzymes around here. Kornberg went to St. Louis to study with Carl Cori, and with Severo Ochoa in New York. He came back with the spirit that: If we know the enzyme, we know the reaction. All biochemical events in the body are enzyme-catalyzed." When Kornberg returned, he interested the other seminar members in enzymes too. "That was the sparkplug event," said Stetten.

The four were, in Alan Rabson's words, "a close, elite kind of group. They were intellectually in a class by themselves. It was really a wonderful era, a very important period for biochemistry." The group broke up in 1953 when Kornberg went off to St. Louis and Horecker to NYU, but the ground had been laid for a series of important discoveries.[14]

As the DNA story broke, Kornberg selected for study an enzyme called DNA polymerase. A polymer is a big molecule, formed by a line of simpler repeating molecules. DNA is a perfect example of one. So a DNA polymerase is an enzyme that helps assemble the long DNA chain from scratch. (All enzymes end with "ase.") Although Watson and Crick had said nothing about enzymes, it seemed unlikely to Kornberg and other biologists that these complex substances just put themselves together spontaneously in the cell. While still at Bethesda, Kornberg and colleagues had started experiments putting into a test tube the following: (1) radioactively labeled pieces of DNA called nucleotides, meaning the base plus a portion of backbone; (2) longer strips of other DNA; and (3) a kind of bacteria commonly used in research, and common as well in the intestine, called *E. coli (Escherichia coli,* after its discoverer, German physician Theodor Escherich). The idea was that if an enzyme did indeed cause DNA to form, that enzyme—undoubtedly present in the *E. coli*—would cause the radio-labeled nucleotide to be incorporated onto the larger piece of DNA in the test tube. If they succeeded, they would be making DNA in the test tube.

Success! An enzyme was adding on nucleotides to the DNA. "Through this tiny crack we tried to drive a wedge," Kornberg said. The hammer he grabbed for this task was making purer and purer ingredients, and by late 1955 DNA polymerase was slowly emerging from the swamp of the bacterium's other enzymes.[15]

Where have we come in the story now? We know how to make DNA, but we don't yet know how DNA is subdivided into genes, nor how these genes code instructions to the rest of the body, miscoding them in the case of some diseases. It is the summer of 1957. A young biochemist named Marshall Nirenberg has just come from the University of Michigan to work in DeWitt Stetten's arthritis lab at the NIH. Nirenberg is described as "lanky, shy, and quiet." At this point the New World of American science goes on a collision course with the Old World of European science.

The Old World was represented by the Spaniard Severo Ochoa, whom we last met as a junior researcher in Meyerhof's lab in Berlin-Dahlem. Ochoa had come to New York after the Nazi takeover and by the 1950s was chairman of the biochemistry department of NYU. He and his team had already clawed down one Nobel prize in 1959 for determining how to synthesize RNA. But even though people knew how to make RNA in a test tube, they didn't know what those long repeating sequences of bases (nucleotides) meant: in some order the bases obviously coded for proteins. But which order? What was the genetic code? This is important in determining which pieces of DNA correspond to which genes: if one is going to undertake genetic engineering, one has to know exactly where a gene is on the DNA and precisely where to cut it.

Nirenberg had the good fortune at NIH to have his lab right around the corner from Leon Heppel's. Heppel kept a freezer full of RNA, which he compulsively inspected every morning, and which proved to be of great help to Nirenberg and his team. When asked to reconstruct his historic point of departure, Nirenberg recalled that he and Heinrich Matthei, a visiting German scientist, had determined that some molecules of RNA function as templates for the synthesis of protein in broken cells. They also found that RNA consisting of long chains of one of the four kinds of nucleotide bases was highly active as a template for the synthesis of a protein containing one of the twenty kinds of amino acids normally found in protein. These dramatic results gave them an RNA code word, he recalled, and thus they knew that other genetic code words could then be deciphered by varying the kinds and proportions of RNA bases used to direct protein synthesis. This knowledge gave them a sort of Rosetta stone to the mysterious genetic code. At this point a race began to decipher the entire genetic code.

The competitors were Nirenberg and his friends at the "arthritis" institute in Bethesda, and Severo Ochoa's large group of nearly twenty scientists at NYU. The Ochoa group had found out informally of Nirenberg's discovery, even before his announcement in the summer of 1961, and were now pressing ahead full blast. These races, although highly serious in terms of who wins Nobels, are conducted in something of the spirit of good fun, and Heppel was supplying both competitors with nucleotides. Ochoa himself remembers the race as "one of the most exciting moments of my life."

But it was frenzy more than excitement that prevailed in Bethesda. Stetten recalls, "The NIH mobilized. They were offended by the fact that Ochoa with his great pressure and his powerful lab team was muscling in on this problem. All sorts of people like Maxine Singer and Robert Martin contributed their peculiar talents to Marshall's work, often without recognition. They just pitched in and made compounds for him so that we could beat out these scoundrels from New York way who had a lot of money and a lot of experience. It was our finest hour because there was an element of selflessness in this participation that I had not seen on university campuses."[16]

Robert Martin, perhaps best known as the husband of Judith Martin, the columnist and writer Miss Manners, remembered the round-the-clock collaboration. "Maxine provided me with the enzymes and expertise and I synthesized the polynucleotides [for Marshall]. My wife was covering embassy parties for the Washington *Post* at the time—she called it the garbage run—so I worked her hours, from 2 or 3 P.M. till 1 A.M. [Another scientist] took the lobster shift from midnight to noon," to see if the ingredients had made any protein in the test tube. "We were in print with a large number of tentative code words by December of 1961."[17] That all this was done at the "arthritis" institute and had nothing to do with arthritis shows how basic science can flourish in the shadow of targeted disease.

Thus did Marshall Nirenberg take the lead in breaking the genetic code: in discovering that the sixty-four possible combinations of nucleotide bases along the strand of DNA are transferred onto a template of RNA with similar bases, and that these bases code in various ways for the twenty different amino acids. He received a Nobel prize for this in 1968.[18]

Was there a party after the discovery? DeWitt Stetten: "Marshall is not a particularly party person. He is shy and unassuming, intensely dedicated. He is a man who has no hobbies except his work. His reading is just the journals that come in that day."

Immunology

It is an October evening in the early 1960s. Birthday party guests have gathered in the Manhattan apartment of Baruj Benacerraf, a brilliant immunologist at NYU.

The guests are playing the J. S. Bach *Concerto for Two Violins.* Gerald Edelman of the Rockefeller Institute plays one violin, Lloyd Old of the Memorial Sloan-Kettering Cancer Center the other, and Benacerraf's wife Annette is playing harpsichord. The small circle of guests includes two musically inclined visitors from France, François Jacob and Jacques Monod. Monod is Annette's uncle, who is herself French.

Of those enjoying the Bach concerto that evening, all save Lloyd Old and Annette would later win Nobel prizes: Jacob and Monod in 1965, Gerry Edelman in 1972, and "Baruch" Benacerraf himself in 1980. What brought the guests together intellectually was the science of immunology and molecular genetics, but what brought them together that night was a love of music.

As this first generation of molecular scientists passes from the scene, one loses sight, in the glare of their scientific accomplishments, of what cultivated individuals they were. It was not merely because they had their roots in Europe. Michael Heidelberger, for example, the founder of the chemistry of the immune system, was born in New York, the elder son of a mother who herself had attended a finishing school in Virginia, who insisted that the children speak German at the table, and who hired for them a French governess; the governess took them to Central Park two afternoons a week and would "tolerate nothing but French." Heidelberger played the clarinet.[19]

Hans Clarke, the chairman of biochemistry at P and S, had recruited some of the best European scientists to come to these shores. He also played the clarinet. It was said in jest that Heidelberger—his lab two floors above—had never really been part of that department because he played the clarinet better than Clarke.[20] A Hungarian immunologist with the improbable name of Zoltan Ovary, brought to NYU by Benacerraf, circulated widely in the world of performing musicians in New York. Ovary's musical friends threw a surprise concert for Heidelberger on his eightieth birthday, and again chamber music on his ninetieth![21] As we see, these were highly cultivated individuals.

By contrast, the second generation of American immunologists were, if not exactly uncultivated, somehow much more . . . American. William Paul, a distinguished figure in immunology today, was a junior faculty member at NYU in Benacerraf's heyday. "When I came up for my first interview," he recalled, "Zoltan [Ovary] asked me if I was interested in music. Not wanting to overstate things, I said, 'Not particularly.' So thereafter Zoltan regarded it as a challenge to get me to those home concerts at Benacerraf's house."[22]

As Benacerraf's friends serenaded him on that birthday evening in the 1960s, the science of immunology was exploding about them. The invisible hand guiding the sciences works in strange ways. Before the 1960s the immune system was a narrow specialty within infectious disease, studied with the aid of rather vague serum this's and that's. In fact, all we had was the immunology of Pasteur and Koch: an antigen in the blood evokes somehow an antibody response. The mechanism was a mystery, all those little white cells swimming around inscrutably. Today immunology is a broad and deep discipline that flows across most areas of medical science. The new molecular immunology plays a big role in much disease research. In understanding AIDS, for example, it is essential to know how the immune system functions before AIDS breaks it down.

There are basically two kinds of white cells that destroy invaders, the big eaters (macrophages) that devour bacteria and a special kind of white cell called a killer T cell, which punctures the cells that it identifies as foreign—those cells invaded by viruses and cells from transplanted tissues. Where did these killer T cells come from? In the days of the microbe hunters, nobody had ever heard of one. Among the small white cells called lympho-cytes (which the microbe hunters did know about) two categories are now known to exist: the B cells that make antibody, and the T cells that coordi-nate the activities of the whole immune system. Some of these T cells are deadly killers, in on the endgame with the viruses. Others, known as helper/inducer T cells (also called T4 cells), function as a kind of radio command post, putting out chemical messengers far and wide to activate other white cells. Still other T cells, called suppressor T cells, turn the whole immune system off after the danger has passed. To show how recent all this knowledge is, the distinction between B and T cells was not nailed down until 1969.

Thus, when an invading bacterium comes, it's first identified by a big eater, which captures the invader and presents it, as a dog presenting a bone, to the helper T cell programmed for that specific antigen by its DNA. The T cell first checks a separate molecule on the surface of the macrophage to make sure the macrophage is playing on the home team. Then the T cell tells other T cells in that line to multiply, and it tells the appropriate B cells to release antibody. The floating antibody finds the bacterium and binds at one end to the invader; the other end of the antibody drifts toward a nearby big eater (macrophage). Like a moon rocket landing, the antibody lowers the bacterium onto the surface of the macrophage, and the macrophage gobbles it up.

When an invading virus comes, the scenario is a little different. The T cells have been participating actively in the above battle with the bacteria. But a certain class of T cells, the killer, or cytotoxic T cells, have the responsibility of destroying those cells of the body already infected by the virus. (Remember that antibody cannot penetrate into the interior of cells, where the virus particles have cached themselves.) The killer T cells do this by chemically puncturing the wall of the infected body cells and letting the contents spill out.

Meanwhile in this viral infection the helper T cells are coordinating the B cells' activities: the B cells are spilling out antibody particles, which have the shape of Y's. These Y's bind to the viral particles and deliver them over to the macrophages to be eaten up.

All of this activity is just the beginning. Once the few T cells and B cells that, from birth on, are preprogrammed for a given antigen go into action, they themselves multiply and produce a huge series of additional T and B cells in the same line that are equally specific. This continues until the invader is overwhelmed. Then the suppressor T cells switch everything off.[23]

Thus, millions and millions of possible antigens exist. The millions of different white cells against them are genetically coordinated, meaning that programs in their DNA fabricate receptors on their surfaces (and specific forms of antibody in the case of B cells) unique for each antigen. The different cells involved are constantly checking each others' receptors. This vast panorama of activity is orchestrated by the DNA, and determining how it works has been the assignment of molecular immunology.

The people attending Benacerraf's birthday party figured significantly in discovering all this. In 1959, for example, Gerald Edelman had established that antibody molecules have distinct light and heavy chains: certain variable regions of these chains would later be discovered as important in clasping to the antigen. Lloyd Old did work in the whole immunology of cancer. But the major figure in immunological discovery was the birthday boy himself, Baruj Benacerraf. Like James Shannon, Benacerraf illustrates what is necessary to move science ahead fast: imagination plus being a leader of men and women. Actually, Benacerraf had started out not as a scientist but as a banker with a medical degree who did immunology as a sort of hobby. A *banker?*

The story begins when Benacerraf's father, a poor North African Jew, immigrates to Venezuela at the turn of the century to find work. By dint of hard work, he and his brothers build a textile busines and ultimately establish a Venezuelan bank. Benacerraf is born in Venezuela in 1920, and five years later the family moves to Paris, where Benacerraf acquires a *lycée* education. The Second World War approaches; the family moves back to Venezuela, sending Baruj to the United States to be educated, and in fact he gets an M.D. degree from the University of Virginia in 1945. But in a Sephardic Jewish family, the sons are not considered free to find their own way, and Benacerraf felt himself under enormous pressure to take over the family business, especially since his father had just had a stroke. "My father's business interests were very intricate and involved complex partnerships with several difficult associates," he recalled. "The situation demanded a lot of attention and did not improve until sometime in the early 1960s, when I finally managed to successfully dispose of our South American interests. . . ."

Benacerraf ended up owning a New York City bank, the Colonial Trust Company, with offices in Rockefeller Center. But in 1956 he also received a faculty appointment in the pathology department of New York University.

We think back to previous chapters. NYU has already provided one of the great stem cell lines of American science: the German heavyweights coming there in the 1930s, plus James Shannon and Homer Smith in the physiology department, plus Severo Ochoa in biochemistry. But the man who appointed Benacerraf in 1956 was one of the new men of American science, trained not in Europe but at Harvard and the wartime Rockefeller Institute: Lewis Thomas. Today he is probably the senior statesman of the basic medical sciences in the United States. He had come to NYU as chairman of the pathology department in 1954, and proceeded to assemble a scientific team that rivalled that of Berlin-Dahlem in the 1920s. In Lew Thomas's department, the lightning was striking in immunology.

Benacerraf, as we know, came two years later, selling the bank around the same time. By force of personality and the ability to provide scientific leadership, he made his lab an urgent kind of place. It was to this lab, for example, that Michael Heidelberger came, at the time the most distinguished immunochemist in the country. There was an immunology club. Benacerraf later wrote, "We met regularly, discussed our results openly and passionately, and entered into frequently productive collaborations. I have a warm feeling, as I look back to this happy period, which fortunately coincided with the dramatic expansion of funding of immunology by the NIH. . . ."[24]

It is easy to forget that these scientists were not separated in a special research institute in Cloud Cuckoo Land: they had a line responsibility for teaching medical students. William Paul, then a junior member of the department, remembers lecturing to the meds: "It was a great honor to be asked to give a lecture to the medical students. The problem was, however, that all the other immunologists were there, so you didn't care about the med students. They were the last people you worried about." One can imagine what the bewildered students made of the latest findings. For latest findings there were aplenty. In these years much of the genetic control of the immune system was worked out.

Then disaster struck, at least for NYU. Benacerraf got a slap in the face: he was passed over for the chair of microbiology (which had by then become heavy-duty science, not just looking at germs under the microscope). Lewis Thomas, as dean of medicine, then asked Benacerraf if he would consider the chair in anatomy. "Yes," said Benacerraf, "if you'll rename the chair 'cell biology.'" NYU refused to do this, "so Baruch felt he had been insulted," said one insider. "He's a man who doesn't like to be insulted." So in 1968 Benacerraf decided to leave NYU. "I'll never set foot in the place again," he declared, although he later relented. Benacerraf, together with his young associates William Paul and Ira Green, went to the NIH.

Why the NIH, up to that time a kind of Sleepy Hollow in immunology? Here we encounter one of those technical circumstances on which history sometimes turns: the NIH happened to have a collection of inbred guinea pigs. Benacerraf's team was studying the genetic control of the immune system, and that means you need a set of experimental animals, all of whom have the same genes, meaning all of whom are inbred. At that time, the only place in the United States offering such guinea pigs was the NIH, which had a collection inherited from the Department of Agriculture.

Benacerraf's arrival crowned the NIH's own golden age in immunology. As the "New York mafia" swept onto campus, fear and trembling agitated the locals. "They were really nervous," Paul recalls. "The three of us arrived and it was them versus us, so to speak." But the other young people Benacerraf recruited and the research that he sparked filled the labs with energy. "He gave us a new stature in immunology," said William Rabson.

But it was not just Benacerraf. The very compactness of the Bethesda campus and the willingness of its immunologists to work together, to have seminars constantly, and wander in and out of each others' labs gave them a leg up. At centers where in-house competition was fiercer, such as Harvard, people were more secretive. At the state universities the sheer number of researchers, however excellent they were individually, did not achieve that critical mass. But the NIH, like Baby Bear's porridge, was just right.

Gene Shearer, today an AIDS researcher at the NIH, explained the importance of being a tight little band. "We have two seminars a week in which we have reports of what labs are doing. People can give feedback like 'I think you should try something else.' We exchange samples. I can get pig blood from Dave [Sachs] if we want to study something about suppressor cells in pigs. My door is always open; people can walk right in. You don't have to go through a secretary. It's not like some places where you've got to go through five big doors to get in."[25] Thus, if you take an institutional climate of informality and unlimited support, and bring the right people on board, something is going to happen.

Two other key people turned up to do immunology at the National Cancer Institute around the time Benacerraf arrived at the infectious disease institute: William Terry had become senior investigator at one lab in 1964, and Thomas Waldmann, whom we later encounter, took charge of another immunology lab at the cancer institute in 1965. By 1970

Benacerraf had already decided to leave for Harvard, but the juniors he brought with him from NYU—William Paul and Ira Green—went on to become international figures.[26] Like the names of most scientists conducting basic research, the names of these NIH immunologists are largely unknown to the general public (unlike the AIDS specialists who daily are in the papers). But the men are probably the most influential single group of immunologists in the world today.

What really broke immunology open was the ability to clone the genes that control immune response in the white cells. In the 1970s these rather dingy, crowded immunology labs in Bethesda shook with the excitement: figuring out how these white cells send each other messages chemically, and what kind of receptors they have on their cell membranes to receive those messages. In 1973 Alan Rosenthal and Ethan Shevach published their finding that the whole business begins when a big eater (macrophage) alerts a helper T cell that it has begun to gobble up something interesting. Robert Gallo's lab at cancer made a major breakthrough—the more remarkable for its completely accidental nature—in 1976 when they discovered the chemical that turns on T cells: a substance the first T cells to be activated secrete called interleukin two, or IL-2. The interleukins, or between-the-white-cells, are the protein substances that regulate communication within the immune system. Discovering them implies the ability to turn them on or off. Why would you want to turn them on? To get the immune system working again, as in AIDS. Why turn them off? To stop inflammation, as in arthritis, or to stop cancer, as in leukemia.

In 1981 Thomas Waldmann's lab discovered a protein that prevents activation of T cells, of potential importance in controlling those cancers in which T cells proliferate out of control. They called it anti-Tac. The following year William Paul's lab discovered another protein that activates B cells. The NIH immunologists have been on a roll ever since.[27]

The magnitude of these research accomplishments is seen in how greatly American immunology has now outdistanced the foreign competition. Although the Swiss, the Australians, the British, and the French continue to contribute, the big headlights shining down the track are those of the lead American locomotive. European postdocs now come to Bethesda and Harvard, rather than American postdocs going to Vienna and Heidelberg. In the 1960s, for example, the British were still able to keep their heads up with such Nobel winners as Peter Medawar (1960) and Rodney Porter (1972). "But now British immunology has been swamped by American immunology," said Michael Frank, director of the NIH's hospital immunology program. He had studied at Porter's Mill Hill Institute in London in the early sixties. Why this swamping? "We have large numbers of people who are well supported. British medical science has not been well supported. And overall progress in science is determined by resources and numbers of people."[28]

When Lister Hill and John Fogarty gave money to NIH to "fight arthritis," they didn't realize they were helping to found molecular immunology, which is part and parcel of this whole new way of looking at nature that is called molecular biology. As Lennart Philipson said in 1986, "During one scientific generation, molecular biology has developed from an embryonic philosophy to a basic science that concerns politicians, civil servants, the public, and scientists alike. For the first time we are on the threshold of being able to manipulate nature's own pathways to our design and advantage."[29]

As the word "molecular" has reverberated through this chapter, the reader may have heard the distant crashes of the established disciplines, their walls breaking down. "What is happening," said Lewis Thomas in 1985, "is the opening up of a new kind of basic biomedical science in which the old disciplines are being transformed into combinations of themselves. The barriers between departments and fields, once insurmountable in our universities and research institutes, are simply fading away. . . . Biomedical science is becoming, inexorably, all of a piece."[30]

This onmarch of things molecular, this ability to reach to nature's very heart, adds up to nothing less than a scientific revolution. It is not overdrawn to compare it, as Zacharias Dische did, to the revolution of humanism in the fifteenth century. Here is Dische, a refugee from Hitler who found shelter in Columbia's biochemistry department, commenting forty years later on the enormity of intervening events. "Those of us who, like this writer, were participants in this magnificent effort, which in a single generation resulted in the founding of the new biochemistry, can only be elated at the thought that they were witnesses and contributors to a major event in the history of human culture. One thinks of the enthusiastic exclamation of a German humanist of the fifteenth century. 'What a century, what arts and sciences! It is a joy to be alive.' "[31]

And yet as we raise our glasses in celebration of these achievements, the wine turns to gall in our mouths. At the writing of these lines an epidemic rages about us that the molecular revolution is powerless to control: AIDS.

AIDS

We are in the NIH's hospital, the clinical center. There are blue signs in front of the AIDS patients' rooms that say TAKE SPECIAL PRECAUTIONS.

Young men are lying on their beds, two to a room, watching TV. They form part of a drug trial, getting the drug intravenously, and only for that reason are they in this hospital. Generally, the clinical center doesn't take on advanced AIDS patients because the diarrhea and dementia pose too much of a problem for the nursing staff.

The first AIDS patients started to be reported in 1979, although nobody knew as yet the disease was AIDS, which stands for *A*cquired *I*mmune *D*eficiency *S*yndrome. Seven cases of peculiar pneumonias and cancers (the latter called Kaposi's sarcoma, a cancer of the lining of blood vessels, named after the nineteenth-century Viennese dermatologist Moriz Kaposi), were seen in young men that year, all of whom died. In 1980 there were forty-one cases, almost all of whom died within the year.[32] Only in the summer of 1981 did the Public Health Service clue in to the fact that something unusual was happening: a breakdown of the immune system, primarily in young men. Most patients were homosexuals; others had been shooting heroin intravenously. Their bodies, immune defenses lost, would be taken over by infections like PCP (Pneumocystis carinii pneumonia), raging attacks of herpes, Kaposi's sarcoma, tuberculosis, and the like, diseases that otherwise are never seen in young American men. Anthony Fauci, currently director of the infectious disease institute in Bethesda, which has primary responsibility for combatting the AIDS epidemic, recalls that by the end of 1981 he was going to "multiple meetings of PHS officials such as myself and Jim Curran from the CDC [Centers for Disease Control in Atlanta]. We got together and decided on the name AIDS. We used to call it the Opportunistic Infectious Kaposi Sarcoma Syndrome, but that was too long. Then there were slang words that none of us approved of, like the Gay Plague. . . ."

It was in March 1982, when Fauci was sitting one day with Curran in the cafeteria of the Humphrey building in downtown Washington, "that we were saying to each other, 'Damn it, this is an infectious disease. And if it is an infectious disease and is sexually transmitted it's going to explode.' That's when I thought enough of this really being a problem that I actually diverted my own personal laboratory toward AIDS." At this point Fauci was just a lab chief. "We didn't expect that people were going to say, 'Wow, here we have fifty or a hundred cases of this disease, let's just attack it like gangbusters.' But we had an ominous feeling that this was really going to get out of hand—and it did get out of hand."

Only in 1984 did Robert Gallo at the cancer institute discover that AIDS was caused by a virus. French researchers discovered it as well around the same time. But even before Gallo made the announcement, Fauci, whose group had been shooting specimens from AIDS patients into animals in an effort to identify the cause, knew Gallo was on to something. "Bob at that time was not particularly sharing. He knew he had something really hot and was hinting that he had something hot. He kind of told me there was going to be big news soon."

They were riding in a cab to the airport. Fauci had thought it might be a certain kind of virus, called a retrovirus, because this kind of virus is composed of RNA, not DNA; the virus reads in reverse (retro) the DNA of its host, in order to reproduce itself by forcing the host to make more RNA viral particles. Fauci's own group had found that in AIDS a certain kind of T4 cell (helper T cell) is depleted, those T4 cells responsible for recognizing antigen. Fauci knew that retroviruses had a selective attraction to these T4 cells.

Fauci also knew that Gallo had earlier stumbled across another retrovirus that was news. In 1979 Gallo had found a retrovirus that caused a cancer of the immune system. In the ponderous viral terminology of the day, Gallo had called that virus HTLV-I, which stands for *h*uman *T*-cell *l*ymphotrophic *v*irus, type *I*, a virus that makes straight for the T cells. But the cancers caused by HTLV-I are very obscure and nobody made much of the discovery.

Thus Fauci was braced. "I had been talking to Bob about this for months, that it was probably going to be a retrovirus that caused AIDS, and if anybody was going to find the answer you're going to find it because you're the honcho in retroviruses."

So there Gallo and Fauci were in the cab. "I said what the hell is going on? Is it HTLV-I?

"He says, no it's not HTLV-I but it's related to HTLV-I.

"I say, what is it?

"He says, well I really can't say anything about it now because it's the kind of thing that I want to . . .

"Come on, I said, stop the crap.

"He says, alright, it's a new virus." It was HTLV-III.

Three years after this cab ride, at the end of the Health Century, we know a little bit more about AIDS. The virus is now called simply HIV, or *h*uman *i*mmunodeficiency *v*irus. AIDS is a severe infection with HIV. In 1986, the most recent year for which statistics are available, one to one and a half million people carried this virus in their bloodstream, which we know because tests have been devised that pick up antibodies to the virus. We know that at least a quarter to a half of these infected persons will progress to full-blown AIDS within five to ten years, and that of these full-blown AIDS patients 75 percent will probably be dead within two more

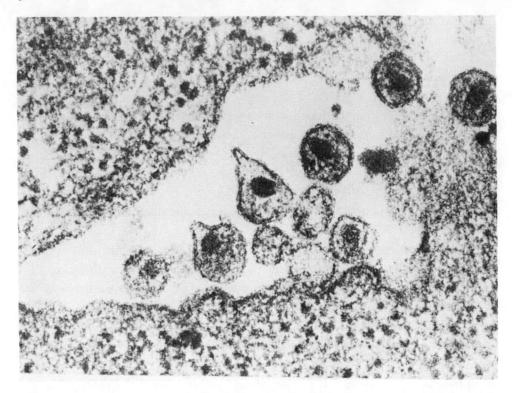

"AIDS virus particles, distinguished by their dark core of RNA, bud from the surface of infected T cells. The electron micrograph, made at the Pasteur Institute in Paris in 1983, is the first image of the earliest viral isolate, LA V; the following year the same virus was identified at the National Cancer Institute under another name, HTLV-III. . . ."

years. Because of the under-reporting of deaths to the CDC, these figures are on the low side.[33]

In 1986 the National Academy of Sciences projected a tenfold increase in AIDS cases over the coming five years.[34] "Here we've got a real humdinger," said DeWitt Stetten, "a disease that appears to be uniformly fatal. This makes it quite unusual, quite out of the range of plague or cholera, where there were immune people who could build a new stock. In this disease there are no survivors."[35]

But in addition to the hedge cutter mortality of AIDS, there is the nightmare of becoming a social outcast after one has acquired the symptoms related to the virus, such as persistently swollen lymph nodes or the whole AIDS-related complex of symptoms that includes fatigue and persistent fever.

Is AIDS today similar to yellow fever and the other plagues that the microbe hunters fought?

Howard Streicher, the administrator of Gallo's large lab and himself an M.D., said, "Yellow fever didn't disrupt social patterns as much. Today the social climate is to consider these people much the way syphilis was considered then. Someone with bad blood. Someone to be shunned." Streicher described getting telephone calls from surgeons who have AIDS, wondering if they should continue to operate. Homosexual health workers who contract the disease face a particularly agonizing dilemma.[36]

Yet as a result of the molecular revolution of the last twenty years, we know today enough about AIDS to feel sure that some kind of therapy or vaccine is not far away. Respected scientists at the NIH and in the pharmaceutical industry reflect this kind of restrained confidence. The mechanism of the disease is now clear, which is half the battle: the virus enters the T4 cell via a molecule on the cell's surface called the CD4 receptor. Once inside it makes new viruses that go on to inhabit other white cells, especially those responsible for calling the immune system into action. Thus, the body is overwhelmed. So a successful drug therapy might prevent the virus from replicating, or somehow coat the receptor so that the bug couldn't enter. A successful vaccine would target this particular virus without risking giving the recipient the disease.

Gallo's own work shows nicely how this new molecular science has placed us in the serendipitous position of understanding this disease at almost the exact moment it came along. The story goes back to 1970, when Howard Temin at the University of Wisconsin and David Baltimore of MIT discovered the enzyme that RNA viruses use to seize control of a cell. Called reverse transcriptase, it lets the viral RNA make in reverse a transcript of the host's DNA. Gallo was intrigued by this because a simple chemical test would let you know whether you had any reverse transcriptase in a tumor or not, i.e., whether the tumor was caused by a retrovirus.

Gallo had wanted to study T cell tumors, but encountered the technical problem of not knowing how to make the T cells multiply so they could be studied. Thus, in 1976 he stumbled across interleukin 2, which T cells send out to activate other populations of their own kind. Gallo thus had no intrinsic interest in HTLV viruses, certainly not in AIDS, which was just about to appear. He was simply a researcher trying to see whether viruses caused cancer. But he chanced across the technique for discovering the cause of AIDS just before the epidemic itself broke.

"If you'd had the AIDS epidemic twenty years ago, you'd be in a really tough position," Thomas Waldmann said. But chance favors the prepared mind, the classic phrase of Louis Pasteur.[37]

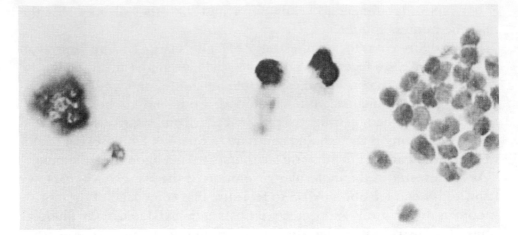

Infected T cells (LEFT) *contrast with normal T cells* (RIGHT) *because the AIDS virus causes the membranes of infected cells to fuse, yielding multinucleated complexes known as syncytia. The virus primarily infects T4 cells, which look like other T cells but differ from them in function and biochemical markers.*

Was the NIH's apparent preparedness for the epidemic an accident? William Jordan, a senior administrator at the infectious disease institute who for a period had the AIDS program thrown in his lap, said, "I don't like to call it an accident," he said. "It's a result of the federal government's willingness to support basic research. That we've learned how to grow T cells, that the tissue culture systems were already in place, that a prepared mind like Gallo's was at work is not an accident. Fortuitous is a better word."[38]

In the battle against this latest terrible epidemic, these men and women in the Public Health Service are keeping alive the traditions of the microbe hunters.

FIVE

Inaccessible Brain, Intractable Mind

In 1888 Emmy N., about forty years old, came to see Sigmund Freud in his office in Vienna. Although she was a youthful, attractive woman, "her face bore a strained and painful expression, her eyelids were drawn together and her eyes cast down; there was a heavy frown on her forehead." She kept her fingers tightly clasped because, whenever freed they exhibited a "ceaseless agitation." The muscles in her face and neck twitched convulsively. And from time to time she would interrupt herself by making a curious clacking sound with her mouth.

Even more strangely, every two or three minutes she would break off her story, turn to Freud with an expression of horror and disgust, and cry out, "Keep still! Don't say anything! Don't touch me." As she yelled this bizarre slogan she would stretch out her hands to Freud, fingers crooked, as though to ward him off.

Her symptoms had begun after her husband, a wealthy industrialist much older than she, died of a stroke. She found herself faced with raising two daughters alone, one a newborn, the other two. Since her husband's death, fourteen years ago, she had been constantly ill with varying degrees of severity. And even as Freud treated her she would complain one day of pains in her leg and chills, another day of stomach pain, and so forth.

What options were open to Freud, a young neuropathologist, or neurologist, who had just set up private practice in Vienna? There were the physical therapies of the day, little shocks of electricity on the affected part, or sending patients to a spa or nervous clinic to undergo some kind of shower-bath treatment. In fact Freud did apply a faradic brush to Emmy's benumbed leg. He ordered her to a private clinic where she was given warm baths and massage, with the usual lack of results. And he tried hypnotizing her, a fashionable new treatment at the time, made popular by the great French neurologist Jean Martin Charcot, from whose clinic in Paris Freud had recently returned.[1]

Drugs? Well, there were a couple. You could try to calm agitated patients such as Emmy N. with bromides, meaning salts of bromine, which had the great disadvantage of being toxic, thus not only calming patients but poisoning them too. Or you could quiet them with morphine or cocaine, a drug which Freud himself had recently discovered, addicting them at the same time as you calmed them. A whole generation of men and women turned into morphine and cocaine addicts at the hands of their neurologists.

That was it. The neuropathologist at the beginning of the Health Century had nothing else to offer his patients, no drugs that would give rest to their minds without sedating them, no particular psychotherapies aside from the reassurance that goes with the relationship between doctor and patient. Frustrated at his therapeutic helplessness, Freud went on to develop a kind of talk-it-out therapy he first used on Emmy. But it didn't make her any better. For the next twenty years she continued to hop from doctor to doctor, seeking relief through hypnosis and the like for her nervous symptoms. Her daughters, seeing their mother as a cruel and ruthless tyrant, sued her for their inheritance. Thus this nervous patient endured a life time of unhappiness and helped poison several other lives as well.

Although Freud was quite interested in Emmy's neuropathic heredity, by which he meant an inherited predisposition to nervous illness, he did not think that she suffered from organic disease of the nervous system. She didn't appear to have a lesion, such as a tumor or a hemorrhage into the brain. Yet as a neurologist, Freud saw a lot of patients who were without question organically ill. The big organic nervous disease of the day was neurosyphilis, a syphilitic infection of the brain and spinal cord, resulting first in paralysis, then in dementia and death. Because the disease was not yet recognized as a late form of syphilis, it was called descriptively dementia paralytica, or general paralysis of the insane. You became paralyzed, then you went insane, then you died. The victims were usually middle-aged men.

Moriz H., age forty-nine, had it. He was another of Freud's patients. Born a Jew in the Hungarian town of Pressburg, Moriz H. had come to Vienna to make his living as a merchant in the city's main shopping street. Somehow he contracted syphilis, perhaps in the pattern of the day from a prostitute. He would have had early symptoms, a chancre on his penis or groin with the regional lymph nodes swollen, then nothing more for years and years until one day he might notice a tremor in his hands or trouble in speaking. On May 27, 1902, Freud admitted Moriz H. to an expensive private nervous clinic near Vienna. Moriz's wife accompanied him. His principal symptom on admission: dementia. The case did not go well. Four months later Moriz's family withdrew him from the private clinic and placed him in the provincial insane asylum, what we would call a state hospital. We lose sight of him at that point, but if he indeed had dementia paralytica, which is what the clinic staff believed at discharge, he probably died in the public asylum.[2]

There is a spectrum of nervous disease that reaches from the physical lesions caused by the action of syphilis to disturbances of mood and perception in which one wonders if there is a physical lesion at all. Emmy N. is at one end, Moriz H. at the other. Freud indeed concluded several years after treating Emmy N. that a whole separate category of mental illnesses existed that had nothing to do with brain disease, illnesses that were instead the product of anomalies in early childhood socialization. These anomalies would later in life cause conflicts within the psyche itself, and these conflicts would produce psychiatric symptoms, such as Emmy N.'s bizarre clacking and crying out. In Freud's view, such symptoms could be abolished by treating the mind rather than the organic substance of the nervous system. Freud was not the first physician to treat psychiatric symptoms with psychotherapy, but he was the most influential. His distinctive brand of psychotherapy, which he called psychoanalysis, dominated American psychiatry in the 1940s and 1950s.

Before Freud, psychiatrists tended to see mind disease and brain disease as the same thing. Today the doctrine of psychoanalysis is being left behind. Although some kind of psychotherapy is still regarded as indispensable, the dominant trend is once again to see psychiatric symptoms as a result of the deranged molecular action of the brain. Thus both mind and brain disease start out as synonymous, in time become distinct entities, then meld together again, giving us the dynamic tension of this chapter. We shall begin by making the brain more scrutable through surgery and new techniques of imaging. Then we shall make the mind more tractable with new drug therapies as opposed to psychoanalysis. Finally we shall see how the molecular revolution in psychiatry is turning the wheel full circle to pre-Freudian times.

Penetrating the Brain

You are a neurologist, a specialist in organic diseases of the nervous system, at the beginning of the Health Century. A patient comes through the door with weakness in his left leg and a loss of feeling in the sole of his left foot, also with a recent history of terrible headaches. What's your diagnosis?

If only it had been a pain in the stomach! How much simpler it would be to diagnose, for only a limited number of things can go wrong with the stomach. But the brain and spine pose greater challenges, primarily because the brain has about ten billion nerve cells, with each of these cells making countless interconnections to others of the ten billion. Because the brain has no moving parts, there's nothing to watch in action. What you as a neurologist must first do is localize anatomically the reason for the leg's weakness, then consider the possible cause of the difficulty. The investigative techniques necessary for this localizing are quite straightforward and involve checking for differences in reflexes and such on each side of the body. Various European doctors developed these techniques only toward the end of the nineteenth century. That's one reason why brain surgery developed so late in time: you have to know approximately where in the brain the problem lies before you can operate (given that you can't move about freely inside the brain; it's packed tightly into the cranium).

Let's say your neurological investigation has now determined that the patient has a brain tumor in thus-and-such location. There's nothing more you can do in 1887. No drug therapy or radiation therapy exists for tumors, and only three years previously has the first successful operation for a brain tumor been carried out—by Francesco Durante in Rome. The Health Century would see, first, a series of practical operations for tumors and bleeding in the brain, and second, drug therapy for several important brain diseases.

Victor Horsley, a London surgeon, is generally regarded as the founder of modern brain surgery. Horsley had started doing brain operations in 1886 at the famous National Hospital for Nervous Diseases in Queen's Square, London. The torch crossed the Atlantic three years later as

Harvard's "Jack" Elliot watched Horsley operate in London, became interested himself in the whole question of localization of tumors, and returned to the Massachusetts General Hospital in Boston, one of Harvard's teaching hospitals, asking that his colleagues send him cases of brain tumor.

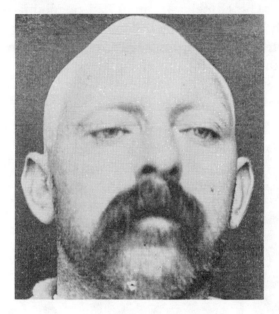

John Maloney, Harvey Cushing's first brain tumor patient.

It is now the summer of 1895. Young Harvey Cushing has just graduated from Harvard medical school and is assisting Elliot, who has yet to conduct a brain operation successfully. On June 27 John Maloney, age thirty-one, is admitted to the hospital with a huge, spongy tumor protruding from the back of his skull. Three years before Maloney had been struck on the head by a bucket of refuse falling about twenty feet. Within the past twelve months he'd become unsteady in his gait and had developed double vision, along with a constant severe headache. A large tumor had now formed on the lining of the brain. Called a meningioma, this kind of tumor—like a majority of brain tumors—had not spread within the brain. But it could become lethal by compressing the brain as it grew.

A week after Maloney's admission to hospital, Elliot and young Cushing operated on him. The tumor had already invaded the bone. As they bored in they encountered massive bleeding, which they tried to plug with wax, deciding to go no farther. Two weeks later they went in again, chiseling off the bony covering and shelling out the tumor with their fingers as best they could. A few hours later Maloney was dead from the bleeding. This was the infancy of brain surgery. Surgeons couldn't control the bleeding; they would know how big the tumor was only by observing it through the port they cut in the skull. The case made an impression upon Cushing, who salted away Maloney's photograph between the pages of a textbook on tumors.[3]

The following year Cushing went down to Baltimore to take up a post at Johns Hopkins as junior resident to William Stewart Halsted, perhaps the most famous surgeon of his day. The Hopkins hospital had opened its doors only seven years previously and had already become the epicenter of scientific medicine in the United States. Cushing later recalled of his arrival that "the surroundings at the Johns Hopkins Hospital were strange enough after what I had been through at the Massachusetts General. The talk was of pathology and bacteriology of which I knew so little that much of my time the first few months was passed alone at night in the room devoted to surgical pathology . . . looking at specimens with a German textbook at hand."[4]

Harvey Cushing at his laboratory desk, 1907.

Although Cushing interested himself in all kinds of operations at Hopkins, he showed a special flair for the nervous system. And if he did well in brain operations it was partly because he incorporated the new scientific methods of surgery he learned under Halsted. For example, he wore rubber gloves while operating, a procedure disdained by the more "artistic" Boston surgeons. Cushing's success was also due to his great meticulousness in sealing off bleeding vessels, until then the nemesis of brain surgery. But he was so slow in operating that later a distinguished general surgeon, watching him operate one day, would ask, "Harvey, do these tumors ever recur on you during the operation?"

Yet this carefulness brought benefits: by 1908, in his first 350 operations that opened the skull, he caused not a single case of infection, and in a series of 100 operations for brain tumors done by 1910 he had only eleven deaths, this at a time when the customary operative mortality for brain tumors was about 33 percent. In 1908 Cushing published a textbook of neurosurgery that marks the establishment of that field as a separate discipline.[5]

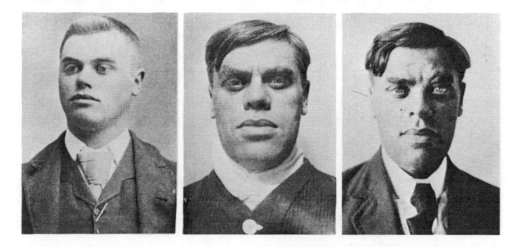

Development of acromegaly—from his first case of acromegaly, which Cushing dealt with surgically in 1909.

On April 15, 1931, Cushing did his two thousandth brain tumor operation. He is by now back at Harvard and has become the most famous brain surgeon in the world. He has a patient, a woman with a history of intense headaches who has lost part of her visual fields in both eyes. The bones of her toes, fingers, and jaw have also begun to grow again. Imagine how baffled you, a neurologist, would have been by this at the beginning of the Health Century. But by 1931 Cushing, and doctors generally, realized she was suffering from a disease called acromegaly. It is characterized by a huge lower jaw and a distinctive coarsening of the facial features. Its cause: a tumor in the pituitary gland which sits at the base of the brain. This woman's growing tumor was giving her headaches and threatening her vision by compressing her optic nerves. Reaching this tiny gland surgically poses many difficulties, such as cutting free a flap of bone on the forehead and carefully penetrating to the point where the two optic nerves cross. At that point, bulging from its little bony pit, Cushing found the swollen pituitary gland. He removed the tumor with suction, stitched the patient up, and at last report fifteen years later she was fine![6] Thus by the 1930s the main techniques of surgery on the brain had become well established.

When Cushing had gone to Hopkins from Harvard in 1896, he had brought one other thing with him aside from curiosity about the brain: a fluoroscopy tube. He simply took the one from Mass General, to the consternation of its staff. Fluoroscopy is a form of doing X rays so that one may observe through a fluoroscope, for example, the intestine bumping and contracting as it struggles with a barium meal. X rays had been discovered for medical use only the previous year in Germany, by Wilhelm Röntgen, but already in 1896 considerable excitement was rising in the United States because of the possibilities roentgenology offered for seeing the interior of the body.

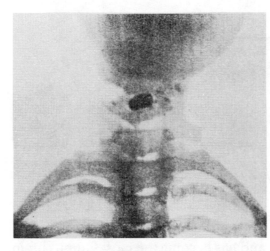

Cushing's early X ray of a bullet in a patient's spine, in 1896.

In 1896 Cushing used X rays for the first time to diagnose a disease of the nervous system. On November 6 a woman named Lizzie W. was admitted to the Hopkins hospital as a surgical emergency. Her bartender husband had shot her during a family argument, and the bullet had lodged somewhere in her spine. One side of her body showed signs of paralysis, and she had no feeling on the other side. You are the neurologist. Where is the bullet? You have only the entry site to go by, but the bullet could be nudging against the spinal cord somewhere far away, as bullets tend to migrate about once they enter the body. A doctor of the day would have little idea where to dig, but fortunately Cushing took several X rays. Lizzie W. had to lie under the machine for thirty-five minutes to make each one, but in the end they showed a bullet at C6, her sixth neck vertebra.[7] Neuroradiology, the imaging of the nervous system, had commenced as a specialty.

In the early days brain X rays served to diagnose mainly fractures and gunshot wounds, because X rays are unsophisticated about densities. They discern only four separate kinds of matter as they pass through a patient's body on their way to the photographic plate: air, fat, water (of which the body's other tissues are mainly composed), and mineral (as in bone). The X rays pass easily through air and fat, and so reach the photographic plate on the opposite side of the patient, darkening it. On the other hand, water and mineral offer much more resistance to the rays, and the plate behind remains white where the bones are, or where the bullet lodged in Lizzie W.'s spine. The problem for the neuroradiologist is that, due to the bony skull, one can't make out details in the tissue of the brain. Bullets and broken bone are visible, but not tumors and bleeding vessels unless they calcify or cause a change in the skull around them. Thus neuroradiology was late aborning. Only in 1907 does a German textbook begin to utilize X rays systematically in diseases of the nervous system.[8]

So how does one make the structures of the brain more visible in order to see if the pressure of a tumor or hemorrhage is shifting them about? In 1918 a student of Cushing's, Walter Dandy at Hopkins, hit upon an idea: inject air deep inside the brain into the big fluid reservoirs called ventricles. Normally these ventricles are filled with cerebrospinal fluid, or CSF. But if one removed some fluid and injected an equal amount of air, one could see if the ventricles had been displaced, collapsed, expanded, whatever: all these changes indicating that something pathological was going on in the surrounding tissues. Dandy called this technique "ventriculography." The following year he tried injecting air into the CSF that surrounds the spine, in order to diagnose tumors or malformed blood vessels. This technique was baptized myelography (anything that concerns the spinal cord begins with "myelo-"). Once injected in the spine, the air rises to the ventricles in the brain, making it unnecessary to bore a hole in the skull (pneumoencephalography). This represented a major step forward in the ability to localize brain lesions.

But these air injections were no fun for the patient. One radiologist remembered what it was like when the technique became popular. "We used to take patients and tie them backward on a chair." He indicated the back of the chair, where the patient's chin would be resting. "We needed three residents. As soon as the air was injected, they'd take the chair and turn it upside down." So that the injected air would fill all the portions of the ventricles. "It was horrible. The patient would be screaming and vomiting."

Wasn't there a better way? Ideally, the radiologist wants to see finer changes in the blood vessels in order to identify exactly where a tumor is. But the arteries are normally invisible. In 1927 the Portuguese neurologist

Egaz Moniz hit upon injecting sodium iodide into the major arteries that supply the brain (the carotid arteries) as a way of making the blood in the brain radiographically visible. This was the beginning of angiography, the study of arteries, not just in the brain but throughout the body, with a contrast medium.[9]

By the mid-twentieth century, neuroradiologists were able to diagnose those brain diseases involving considerable defects without difficulty. Neurosurgeons could then operate. The problem was that X rays, air studies, and angiography often couldn't find smaller but nonetheless serious lesions. Also, all the techniques then available carried some risk or discomfort for the patient.

Diseases from the Dark Cupboard

Not necessarily inventing, but *developing* drugs for disorders of the brain and mind has been very much an American project. Perhaps it goes hand in glove with the rise of neurosurgery and neuroradiology, also quintessentially American enterprises.

Take epilepsy. When abnormal waves of electrical activity run across the brain, they produce muscle fits, pauses of inattentiveness (absence seizures), and other psychological and muscular disorders over which the patient has no voluntary control. Epilepsy may result from tumors, blows on the head, or typically from no obvious cause.

Historically, epilepsy is one of those diseases that once made illness synonymous with martyrdom. Epileptics were thought to be possessed by demons, made social outcasts, and suffered the same kind of persecution as lepers did. Tales abound of epileptics thrashing into the fireplace and burning themselves horribly. Thus if any group of patients was deserving of help or a cure, it was the epileptics.[10]

Starting in 1857 bromine began to be used in the treatment of epilepsy. It did calm the fits, but only at almost toxic doses. Epileptics on bromine suffered as well a kind of ostracism, with their faces often covered with bromide pustules. Phenobarbital (Luminal), a nontoxic sedative introduced in 1911, started the following year to be used for epilepsy. Thus the problems associated with bromine were overcome, but "phenobarb" nonetheless caused sedation, an undesirable side effect for those who wished to have busy daytime lives.[11]

In 1923 young Tracy Putnam became a resident in neurology under Harvey Cushing in Boston. Cushing hated working with epileptics because they didn't have brain tumors: there was nothing he could cut out. He would put them on phenobarbital and discharge them from his service as quickly as possible. Putnam, who viewed things in a medical rather than a surgical manner, became intrigued with the possibility that epilepsy might be caused by a chemical abnormality in the brain. He noted, for example, that patients who "rebreathed" their own carbon dioxide by putting a paper bag over their heads got some relief. He asked himself, "Might an institution for the treatment of epilepsy be established adjacent to a brewery, and the content of carbon dioxide in the atmosphere metered so as to be tolerable and yet sufficient to prevent attacks?" But the more he thought about this project, the worse it seemed. What he did instead was to team up in the mid-1930s with Dr. Frederic Gibbs, who had just established at the Boston City Hospital the first laboratory in the world for the routine clinical testing of brain waves (known as electroencephalography or EEG). Putnam had just become the head of neurology in that hospital and so was in a position to get things done. They started administering electricity to cats in sufficient doses to cause convulsions and then seeing what chemicals raised the threshold for convulsions in these animals, that is, what chemicals could abolish epilepsy.

"I combed the Eastman Chemical Company's catalog," Putnam later wrote, "for suitable compounds that were not obviously poisonous. I also wrote to the major pharmaceutical firms, asking if they had available or could make suitable chemicals." He was looking for drugs in particular containing a benzene ring, because among the barbitals only phenobarbital, which also had a benzene ring, possessed the ability to suppress epilepsy. "The only one of them that showed any interest was Parke-Davis. It wrote back to me that it had on hand samples of nineteen different compounds analogous to phenobarbital and that I was welcome to them." But Parke-Davis also mentioned that it thought the exercise a waste of time since its testing had showed all nineteen to be inactive. Yet the pharmaceutical house had not used the tests that Gibbs and Putman devised. Of the nineteen, all save one were indeed inactive. And that one —later called phenytoin (Dilantin)—prevented the cats from getting fits without poisoning them.

In 1936 Putnam asked his chief resident, H. Houston Merritt, to try phenytoin on epileptic patients. "He accordingly did so. Our first patient was a man who had been completely incapacitated for years because he suffered one or more seizures daily, unrelieved by phenobarbital. He has remained seizure-free since."[12] In addition to marking a milestone in the liberation of humankind from disease, this whole story provides a nice instance of early collaboration between the drug industry and research scientists. Today Dilantin remains one of the drugs of choice in treating epilepsy.

Neurology is like a dark cupboard. At the back lie a number of little-known but perfectly dreadful afflictions whose course is irreversibly downhill. For some of them, such as Lou Gehrig's disease, or amyotrophic lateral sclerosis (ALS), there is still no cure even today. But among these gloomy disorders modern medicine has had one triumph, a palliation to be sure and not a cure, but nonetheless the conferral of incomparable relief compared to previous times. And that is over Parkinsonism, first described as paralysis agitans in 1817 by the English physician James Parkinson.

In Parkinsonism the patient loses the ability to bring about voluntary movements, although he can still move his muscles in his sleep. The joints seem to him as immobile as though fixed in concrete. A tremor develops in the hands and feet. Some patients feel a constant need to shift about. Napoleon III's chamberlain who had paralysis agitans had to get up from his seat and walk around every five minutes or so, contravening all the rules of court etiquette. In later stages victims start to develop a kind of locked-in syndrome: their minds are still clear but they are unable to talk or move. "The fate of the unhappy invalid is a wretched one," wrote the German neurologist Robert Bing. "With intelligence fully retained, he is condemned to absolute helplessness and must depend upon outside aid for the fulfillment of his most elementary needs, for example, in turning over in bed, wiping off the saliva which flows from his mouth, and so on. Death follows in about ten years after the onset."[13] Today about half a million Americans still suffer from Parkinsonism. They may experience some rigidity, and oscillate from good days to bad, as "on" and "off" are known, but they are vastly better off as a result of the work of George Cotzias and of the Merck company.

Cotzias looked and sometimes acted like a Greek peasant. But he was, in fact, the son of the mayor of Athens. As a medical student in Athens in 1941, at twenty-three Cotzias fled to America with his family in the face of the advancing Germans. When he arrived, he knew no English and was turned down by all the medical schools he applied to except Harvard, which somehow perceived through the language barrier a gifted individual. He graduated second in his class, did a residency at Mass General, and wound up at the Rockefeller Institute in the lab of Donald Van Slyke. In 1953 Cotzias followed Van Slyke to the Brookhaven National Laboratory in Upton, New York, becoming in time its medical director, just as he became simultaneously a professor of neurology at Cornell's New York City medical campus.

It was not any lack of distinction that gave Cotzias a sort of primeval quality. It was the way he acted. Bernard Patten, today a neurologist at

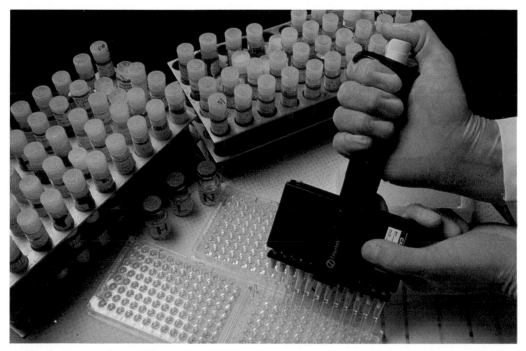

A Roche researcher adds reagent to a substance used to detect antibodies to HIV, the retrovirus that causes AIDS. (Photo courtesy Hoffmann-La Roche, Inc.)

An important retrovirus researcher at the National Cancer Institute, Robert Gallo codiscovered that AIDS is caused by a virus, HIV (Human Immunodeficiency Virus). (Photo courtesy Smokey Forester)

Anthony Fauci (seated), director of the National Institute of Allergies and Infectious Diseases, is a leading scientist in the federal government's war against AIDS. (Photo Smokey Forester)

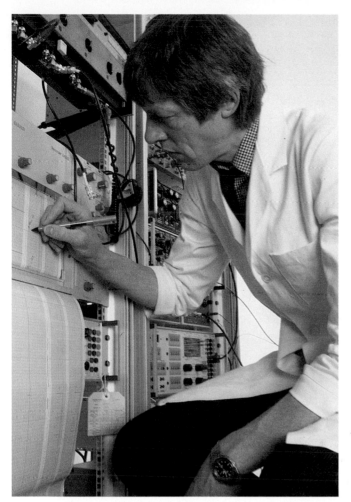

George Marshall, senior technician in neurophysiology at the Neuroscience Research Center in Hoddesdon, England, records and plays back electrical signals from brain tissue to measure the effect of a new drug on the brain's electrical activity. (Photo courtesy Merck and Company, Inc.)

One of the most distinguished figures in the history of understanding the brain's chemistry, Julius Axelrod won a Nobel prize in 1970 for his work on neurotransmitters. (Photo Smokey Forester)

Recipients of a 1985 Nobel prize for their study of the genetic regulation of cholesterol and its relationship to heart disease, Joseph Brown (right) and Michael Goldstein (left) represent a kind of teamwork almost unique in medicine: collaboration based on genuine friendship. (Photo Smokey Forester)

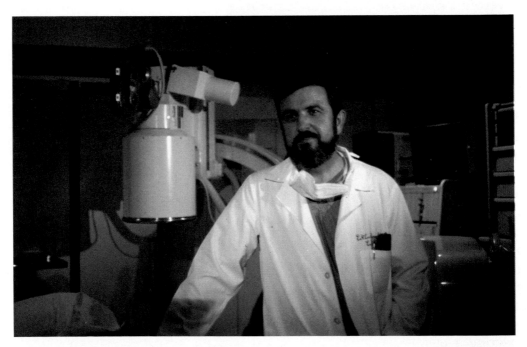

An M.D.-physiologist at St. Louis's Washington University, Dr. Burton Sobel pioneered in using the enzyme t-PA (Tissue-Type Plasminogen Activator) to dissolve blood clots. (Photo Smokey Forester)

Baylor College of Medicine in Houston, recalls being in the men's room at scientific meetings with Cotzias. He would cry out, "Oh God, it's great to urinate! I feel such relief!"

"Everybody would be looking at him," Patten said.

Patten, a clever young chemistry undergrad from Columbia, had arrived at Brookhaven in 1962 to help Cotzias in the lab. "Oh my God, Patten, you really are an ass," Cotzias would say. "Don't you realize we're in the research game primarily to earn a living—to make money so we can eat. Never forget that research is a business. But it's a special kind of business. You just can't decide to go into it. You have to be qualified by birth or training. Science is mostly instinctual, like fucking or killing."

Cotzias became interested in Parkinsonism in 1962, when the World Health Organization asked him to investigate manganese poisoning among Chilean miners, who developed symptoms similar to those of Parkinsonism. By that time it had become clear that Parkinsonism was associated with low levels of the chemical neurotransmitter dopamine. (A neurotransmitter relays nerve messages from cell to cell in the nervous system.) The dopamine failed to reach other centers deep in the brain called the basal ganglia, causing an inability to initiate movement. How about giving dopamine? The problem was that dopamine didn't cross the blood-brain barrier into the cells of the brain.

However, a chemical precursor of dopamine exists, which the body makes as well, known simply as dopa. It works best in a chemical conformation called L-dopa, and other researchers had tried it already in 1961, but not in sufficiently large doses. Cotzias did some basic research into which cells secrete dopamine and was led back to L-dopa. He started giving it in 1965 to Parkinsonians at Brookhaven.

Things did not go well at first because they couldn't get the doses adjusted. Discovering the right dosage rather than the right molecule is often the key to a drug's success. Thus what Cotzias discovered, in addition to the basic science of how the brain makes dopamine, was that you worked in increments from small doses up to large.

So at the beginning the patients suffered. But Cotzias said, "We can't turn back. Sure, the patients are suffering, but hell, what they're going through ain't nothing compared to what I went through when I was a sergeant in the Royal Greek Army. I was cold, wet, and hungry. I crawled through mud and slop. When the patients reach that degree of suffering, then we'll stop the study. But right now there's too much at stake." At stake in particular was the Nobel prize he thought he would deserve for discovering a major relief for Parkinsonism, an incurable neurological disease, by using a chemical the body makes itself.

But he didn't get a Nobel prize. And it added to his bitterness as he lay dying of lung cancer at fifty-nine that he realized he wasn't going to get one. Nobel prizes aren't awarded posthumously. "Of course he'd been a smoker," Patten said. "He smoked Camels. Inhaled them deeply. He hated the idea of dying."

In 1969 he did receive a Lasker Award. But he was bitter about the lack of esteem from neurologists. "Shit, if I'd listened to the neurologists I'd never have done anything," he told Patten. "They thought the disease was degenerative, irreversible." But the neurologists did think of Cotzias as something of a maverick "because he made some real neurological bloopers," Patten remembered. He presented a shaking patient with an obscure degeneration of the cerebellum and spine as a "nonresponding Parkinson patient." A visiting neurologist, Melvin Yahr, informed him that the patient didn't have Parkinsonism at all. Whereupon a huge quarrel ensued and Cotzias threw Yahr out of the lab.

Cotzias's achievement was showing that what had been considered a hopeless condition could be reversed. *Goodman and Gilman,* the Bible of drug treatment, calls L-dopa, or levodopa, "the first outstanding extension of [biochemistry] to a chronic degenerative neurological disorder."[14] But between Cotzias's beakers of L-dopa at the bench and the effective relief of patients lay a great gulf.

That gulch was filled by the Merck company. The large doses that brought relief also brought large side effects, such as vomiting, uncontrollable grimacing, and random, unwanted movements of the limbs. If the breakdown of L-dopa in the body could be slowed, one could give smaller doses with the same effect. Since the early 1960s Merck scientists had been working on this possibility, and in 1973 they created a combination of levodopa and a breakdown inhibitor called carbidopa. It was marketed two years later under the trade name Sinemet, and there is not a neurology department in the country where one does not hear daily references to Sinemet. Many patients become immune to it, alas, after about three years of treatment. But it purchases three golden years—in addition to extending their life expectancy about three years. These years are the work of George Cotzias.[15]

Psychoanalysis Rushes Onstage

Most of the material thus far in this chapter touches on brain diseases of clearly organic origin: if certain cells in the midbrain aren't producing enough dopamine, you get Parkinsonism. If you were deprived of oxygen at birth, you might develop epilepsy. The physical equation is that damage to the brain cells produces brain disease.

But in a vast range of disorders of thought and mood, it's unclear whether the cells of the brain have a lesion at all, either of an anatomical or biochemical nature. One group of researchers believes that psychiatric symptoms result mainly from disturbances of the mind, having little to do with underlying brain chemistry. Another group feels they are caused not by early childhood anxieties and traumas but by disorders in the underlying brain cells. These disorders may not be visible with the microscope in the way that neurosyphilis or Alzheimer's disease is. But they exist nonetheless, expressed in biochemical changes we only now are beginning to understand. Thus we have the controversy of brain disease versus mind disease, of biological psychiatry versus Freudian psychoanalysis.

For many years American psychiatry was dominated by the psychotherapeutic ideology, the view that mental illness arises from harmful social experiences and can be abolished by psychotherapy. What is psychotherapy? Any attempt to remove a patient's symptoms by acting on his mind rather than on the tissue of his brain. Such therapies as suggestion, group therapy, behavioral therapy, deep probing into childhood experiences—all are psychotherapy. Psychoanalysis, in other words, is only one kind of psychotherapy. But it became from the 1940s to the 1960s the most influential of the psychotherapies. Of these therapies, psychoanalysis offered the most opposition to the introduction of drugs for mental illness. Hence it deserves a place in our story.

It was Freud who devised, in Vienna in the 1890s and after, the system for investigating psychiatric symptoms and for understanding culture that he labeled psychoanalysis. The couch played a major role in Freud's analyses. His was a rich velvet one covered with an Oriental rug. He would seat himself behind the patients so they wouldn't be distracted by his expressions of approval, disapproval, or boredom. The mechanism of analysis was encouraging the patients to free associate, meaning to say whatever came into their heads, and not try to edit it for fear of the impression it would make on him.

As the patient talked, the analyst was to detect areas of resistance—things the patient seemed reluctant to get into. Then finally patient and doctor would discuss these resistances as evidence of the patient's efforts to ban from his conscious, adult mind memories of childhood sexual experiences and fantasies. These suppressed memories in a man might stem from his sexual desire as a little boy for his mother or in a woman from her memory of desiring her father's penis when she was a little girl. It was the repression of these childhood memories that was making the patient ill in the first place, and once the patient brought the memories out into the light of day, their pathological influence would diminish and the symptoms vanish. Later Freud extended this basic doctrine with an analysis of transference between patient and doctor, with theories of patients who remained fixated at certain stages of childhood development, and with much else. The doctrines of psychoanalysis fill libraries.

Freud died in 1939. The expulsion of psychoanalysis from the continent of Europe under Nazi rule brought about a great migration of European analysts to the United States. Not all were M.D.s. Such world-famous figures as Theodor Adorno and Herbert Marcuse, committed to applying Freud's insights to the understanding of society, added greatly to the prestige of psychoanalysis in nonmedical fields. But such M.D. analysts as Helene Deutsch, Kurt Eissler, and Bruno Bettelheim made a tremendous impact upon American psychiatry, just as did the arrival of the refugee biochemists upon their American counterparts.[16]

Yet even before the Europeans' arrival, some American psychiatrists had been trying their hand at psychoanalysis. William Alanson White, an early convert, had been elected head of the American Psychiatric Association in 1924. A group of American Freudians had begun research on psychosomatic diseases in the 1930s. So the coming of the Europeans merely provided icing, though of a terribly ornate and cosmopolitan variety, on a preexisting American cake.

How curious that, just as America became the world center for immunology after the Second World War, it also became headquarters of psychoanalytically oriented psychiatry as well, though for entirely different reasons. Progress in immunology stemmed from dollars and numbers and was quite unrelated to what was being written about lymphocytes in the *Saturday Review*. The advance of psychoanalysis in the United States, in contrast, had little to do with the onmarch of science, as the discipline's lore is entirely anecdotal and not verifiable by conventional tests or controlled studies. Rather it occurred because Freud's doctrines acquired currency among university intellectuals. Analysis is such a reflective exercise—pondering deeply what you imagine to be happening in your own unconscious, or in somebody else's, or in the collective unconscious of an entire culture—that its appeal to intellectuals is obvious. Because psychiatrists considered themselves to be intellectuals more than other physicians do, these exciting new theories, quite unaccompanied by the normal scientific tests of evidence, gained supremacy in university psychiatry.

If you think that psychiatry is just another medical specialty, like gastroenterology, you are wrong. Psychiatrists today are much closer to the general stream of medicine than they were in the 1950s. But still they consider themselves something of a breed apart. Other physicians agree.

They often don't trust psychiatrists to take blood pressures reliably, for example. In one large metropolitan hospital, the nurses usually put a red line alongside the notes made by clinicians in the patient's chart, meaning pay special attention to what the doctor says. The psychiatrists' chart notes receive no red lines. Thus the status of psychiatrists as intellectuals differs from the status of gastroenterologists as scientists.

As intellectuals, psychiatrists seem much more vulnerable to passing fads than are gastroenterologists, and this helps explain why the passion for Freudianism swept psychiatry so rapidly. By the end of the 1930s psychoanalysis had become the most important single influence among American university-based psychiatrists. As Gregory Zilboorg, himself a psychoanalyst, put it modestly, "Nowhere in the world did Freud's influence on medical psychology express itself so dynamically and so fruitfully as in America."[17] Walter Bromberg, a New York analyst, later wrote, "As the 1930s came to an end, it is safe to say that the new generation of psychiatrists had incorporated psychoanalytic thinking. Psychiatrists trained in the larger centers, such as New York, Washington-Baltimore, and Chicago, regarded those defense mechanisms arising from the unconscious as indisputable elements in psychopathology."[18] This is straight Freud.

Most psychiatrists are *not* certified psychoanalysts. In the 1950s and after, perhaps 10 percent of American psychiatrists had completed the additional lengthy training required to become a psychoanalyst (in addition to their four-year psychiatric residencies after getting the M.D.). But the analysts' influence disseminated much more widely than their numbers would have entitled. One distinguished academic psychiatrist, who requested anonymity, said, "In the 1950s and 1960s you pretty well had to be a Freudian in order to get anywhere in the big East Coast psychiatry departments."

By occupying the commanding heights in the main teaching hospitals, psychoanalytically oriented psychiatrists exercised much influence on residents, most of whom would not become certified analysts but simply go into practice. The residents would, however, carry with them the teaching of their staff men. Psychoanalyst and historian of the movement Reuben Fine says, "Most psychiatric residents who are taught psychodynamic formulations do not realize that they are learning psychoanalytic theory."[19] This wide diffusion of psychoanalytic ideas is germane to the Health Century because it gave both doctors and patients preconceptions of which therapies worked, and which did not. Drugs did not work, it was thought. Only long, long analysis.

Among middle-class people of the time, psychoanalysis had acquired an almost cult following, and it was a massive cult. Sniffed Mildred Edie Brady, a true believer, in 1947 in *The New Republic,* "A flood of uncritical popularizations of psychoanalytic concepts has been sweeping over the public via books, magazines, movies and radio." One writer gushed in *Science Digest* several years later that "modern psychiatry began with Freud," adding, "Nearly all psychiatrists today go along with the views of the Viennese pathfinder." New York *Times* reporter Lucy Freeman told in the bestselling book *Fight Against Fears* of how analysis helped her triumph over personal problems ("Inwardly, she was in a mess," *Time* confided). *Time* itself, although largely hostile to psychoanalysis, gave considerable play to such stories as "The Couch Cult" or "Is Freud Sinful?"

"Sure, Ralph Thompson eats, but his case is different—he's afraid of his father."

The middlebrow wit of the 1950s drew often on analysis. A *Saturday Evening Post* cartoon showed a little boy saying to his father at the table (a full plate of food still in front of him), "Sure, Ralph Thompson eats, but his case is different—he's afraid of his father." The reference is to Freud's concept of castration anxiety. In another cartoon we see a basset hound looking mournfully into the mirror: "I wish I could recall the youthful tragedy that marked me so!" Echoes of this are still heard today in the media attention given to a debunker of Freud's doctrines named Jeffrey Masson, who claimed to disprove the validity of all analyses that Freudian psychiatrists had ever conducted.[20]

Joseph Wortis, himself a true-believing Freudian, poked a bit of fun at the middle-class vogue for psychoanalysis: "There was a story that circulated years ago that described a simple method for screening people to

"I wish I could recall the youthful tragedy that marked me so!"

find out who might be suitable for psychoanalytic treatment. The story said all you had to do was design a house in which the prospective patient enters and finds himself in a room which has only two exits. One says 'You Loved Your Mother' and the other says 'You Hated Your Mother.' The person moves through the proper exit and finds himself in a second room where again, two doors are labeled, one 'You loved your father,' the other 'You didn't love your father,' et cetera, through a series of rooms, until you finally come into a room which again has two exits: one says 'Income above $30,000' and the other says 'Income below $30,000.' If you go through the door that says 'Below $30,000' you find yourself in the street."[21] In fact, analyses can be quite costly propositions, stretching on for years at three sessions per week at a hundred dollars per session.

If "depth psychiatry"—meaning psychoanalysis—worked, that would be one thing. But today there is growing doubt among psychiatrists about whether it actually does. Two scholars, Seymour Fisher and Roger Greenberg, who conducted a lengthy review of the evidence, concluded, "There is virtually no evidence that therapies labelled 'psychoanalysis' result in longer-lasting or more profound positive changes than [other approaches] that are much less time-consuming and costly."[22]

The problem is that the outcome of all the psychotherapies, psychoanalysis included, seems about the same. One study found that roughly four fifths of the patients get better, regardless of whether they receive family therapy, behavioral therapy, Adlerian therapy, Freudian therapy, or any other variety. What all the systems of psychotherapy offer in common to patients, in the words of the authors, is "a helping relationship with a therapist . . . [plus] suggestion and abreaction." Abreaction means simply retelling an experience in such a way that previously forgotten, or repressed, emotions associated with it are discharged. "Everyone has won and all must have prizes," the authors concluded, seizing one of the lines of the dodo bird in *Alice in Wonderland.*

There is one more thing. The authors found that what made a true difference in success rates was administering psychotherapy together with drugs.[23]

Schizophrenia and Chlorpromazine

A major mental illness is bad enough for the inability to think clearly and to function that it causes. But among the additional symptoms may be delusions—imagining the streets outside are swarming with people trying to break into your home—or hallucinations—believing that you can smell the odors of the crowds as they swarm about your dwelling. These fantasies, which are very real to their victims, tend also to make their victims uncontrollable. The numbers of schizophrenics are not inconsiderable: the disease affects at one time or another perhaps 1 percent of the population. In a country of 250 million people, we are talking about a lot of schizophrenics. In past times people who suffered from schizophrenia and the manic phase of manic-depressive illness would be institutionalized, and unless they could be subdued by endless wrapping in cold sheets or sedatives, they would end up in the disturbed ward.

Psychiatrist Frank Ayd remembers the disturbed ward as filled with "many screaming, combative individuals whose animalistic behavior required restraint and seclusion. Catatonic patients stood day after day, rigid as statues, their legs swollen and bursting with dependent edema [swelling]. Their comrades idled week after week, lying on hard benches or the floor, deteriorating, aware only of their delusions and hallucinations. Others were incessantly restive, pacing back and forth like caged animals in a zoo. Periodically the air was pierced by the shouts of a raving patient. Suddenly, without notice, like an erupting volcano, an anergic [abnormally inactive] schizophrenic bursts into frenetic behavior, lashing out at others or striking himself with his fists, or running wildly and aimlessly about."[24]

Psychiatrist Mary Holt of Pilgrim State Hospital in New York recalled, "Some years before the drugs came along, I was in charge of two buildings of regressed women here at Pilgrim; they were so wild that I just couldn't keep them decent. They'd soil themselves, tear their clothes off, smash the windows, and gouge the plaster out of the walls. One of them would even rip radiators right off the walls. We'd sometimes have to surround them with mattresses in order to give them sedative injections, and these would help for a while, but then they'd get addicted to the sedative and we'd have to take them off it."[25]

Did these people have mind disease or brain disease? Even today the question is hotly debated. Psychoanalytically oriented psychiatrists argue that schizophrenia is caused by faulty child rearing (the schizophrenogenic mother), biological psychiatrists that the disease may stem from a possibly genetic chemical imbalance in the brain or from a viral infection. The question was once academic, given the failure of either camp to provide successful treatment. But after 1900 schizophrenia itself became something of a national crisis, as the numbers of these patients increased steadily. Nobody really knows why this extraordinary apparent increase in schizophrenia occurred in the nineteenth and twentieth centuries, but there is substantial agreement that it did occur. The number of patients generally in state and county mental hospitals rose from 150,000 in 1904 to 559,000 in 1955; in 1904 only 2 Americans per 1,000 population found themselves in mental hospitals, in 1955 4 per 1,000. The incidence of hospitalizing people for mental illness had thus *doubled*. A majority of the acute, or urgent, admissions were for schizophrenia.[26]

In this context of helplessness in the face of a rapidly increasing mental illness, two new drugs named chlorpromazine and reserpine burst on the scene in 1954. They were the first antipsychotics, or neuroleptics, meaning drugs that act on the nervous system. Unlike sedatives, they calm without unduly sedating, so that people subject to schizophrenia and the mania of manic-depression are able to lead fairly normal lives. It's a stunning accomplishment.

The story begins in 1949 when Francis Boyer, having just become president of the pharmaceutical house Smith Kline & French in Philadelphia, went to France. He loved the French. "He spoke French with a terrible American accent but it worked," said his colleague John P. Young. "People could understand him."[27] At that point Smith Kline, basically a maker of patent medicines, was not one of the big players in the American drug scene. In 1936 the firm had a line of some fifteen thousand different products, including Eskay's Neuro Phosphates, Essence of Pepsin, and Norwood Compound Syrup of White Pine with Tar.[28] Boyer wanted to move the company into "ethicals," drugs that doctors prescribe, and out of patent medicines bought over the counter. But ethicals meant doing research: at the time, Smith Kline had a research staff of eight people, with an annual budget of $70,000. (In 1985, by contrast, the firm had a research staff of fifteen hundred and an annual research budget of over \$300 million.)[29]

Smith Kline was able to finance research under Boyer's leadership because in 1932 it had brought out a popular decongestant for colds called Benzedrine, sold in an inhaler. This is the way things work in the drug industry: you get a winner and the profits finance research on future winners. With Benzedrine the company had stumbled into a series of stimulants called amphetamines (street name: bennies). In 1944 they launched Dexedrine, an amphetamine pick-me-up used by truck drivers to keep awake and by dieters to curb their appetites. An epidemic of amphetamine abuse in the 1950s and 1960s forced doctors to cut back drastically on prescribing them.

Now Boyer had some chips to work with, and he turned to Europe as a possible source of new compounds that the company might develop. Thus he traveled in 1949 to France. But we know what the French are like. Boyer made overtures to the French drug house Rhône-Poulenc; they were a little bit snooty. There things rested.

The following year, while searching for a new antihistamine, Rhône-Poulenc came across something really interesting, a drug that seemed to enhance the effectiveness of anesthetics, to be also an antihistamine, and to have other properties. The story goes that Rhône-Poulenc first offered it to Merck and Company, and to the American Home Products Corporation (Ayerst Laboratories). Neither was interested.

Therefore at the end of 1951 a Rhône-Poulenc man traveled to Philadelphia. "I couldn't really figure out why he came," said Francis Grant, the Smith Kline executive responsible for European operations. "But early in 1952 we sensed that something was in the offing."[30] Like today's story of interferon, which we shall tell in a later chapter, industry people were following their noses rather than making finely calculated business decisions. Knowing the drug might be good for something but not exactly what, Boyer signed a licensing agreement with Rhône-Poulenc in April of 1952. Smith Kline paid around five thousand dollars for the drug, now named chlorpromazine, plus a royalty later negotiated at 10 percent of the profits. The company was not at all interested in testing chlorpromazine for its psychiatric properties. "Let's get this thing on the market as an antiemetic [antivomiting drug]," said Boyer, "and we'll worry about the rest of that stuff later."

Smith Kline began testing the drug. The French meanwhile had reported good results with psychiatric patients, so late in 1952 Dr. William Long, the medical director of the company, tried giving chlorpromazine to a psychotic nun. John Young remembers the case. "Long had a patient who was a severely disturbed nun, at the edge of violence and using extremely coarse language. Dr. Long, who was an extremely conscientious physician, was very concerned about the patient. He gave her some of this stuff.''

The results?

"Long couldn't believe it! She had been extraordinarily abusive, with most un-nunlike behavior. In the afternoon she was calm. He described it at the table in the lunchroom. What he described was a typical chlorpromazine result.''

But to test drugs more widely, drug firms are dependent upon university physicians to conduct clinical trials. Here Smith Kline started running into trouble with the psychiatrists, who viewed chlorpromazine as a glorified sedative. Committed to a psychotherapeutic ideology, academic psychiatrists had little interest in drugs. Heinz Lehmann, a German emigré psychiatrist teaching in Canada who did participate in the early trials, said, "At the time, no one in his right mind in psychiatry was working with drugs. You used shock or various psychotherapies.''[31]

Smith Kline brought Pierre Deniker, a French psychiatrist who had already used chlorpromazine as an antipsychotic, to the United States to help persuade American psychiatrists to cooperate. Because Deniker spoke poor English, Young accompanied him to see various greats of the day, such as the head of the American Psychiatric Association, or the doctors at the Michael Reese Clinic in Chicago, or a distinguished therapist named Jules Masserman. "These people were very skeptical,'' said Young. "They weren't willing to do anything.''[32]

Although Smith Kline did finally persuade some university psychiatrists to cooperate, acceptance was slow. Said Young, "You have to remember the context. There were no drugs. Those cases were in the back wards and that was it. The notion that you could ever do anything about it hadn't occurred to anyone. These doctors and nurses who went into McLean [a psychiatric hospital near Boston] at that time, their altruism was busted after six months. What this drug did was not to cure these patients, but to tip the balance enough so that the doctor and the nurse in the hospital said, 'Hey, maybe we can *do* something for these people.' ''

The real breakthrough came as chlorpromazine entered the state mental hospitals, where hundreds of thousands of patients were simply being warehoused as too dangerous to release but too numerous to treat. The company had formed a special chlorpromazine task force, and if the task force encountered foot-dragging at the state hospital, it would simply go to the state legislature and say, "We've found a drug that is going to save you lots of money.'' One state legislature was called into special

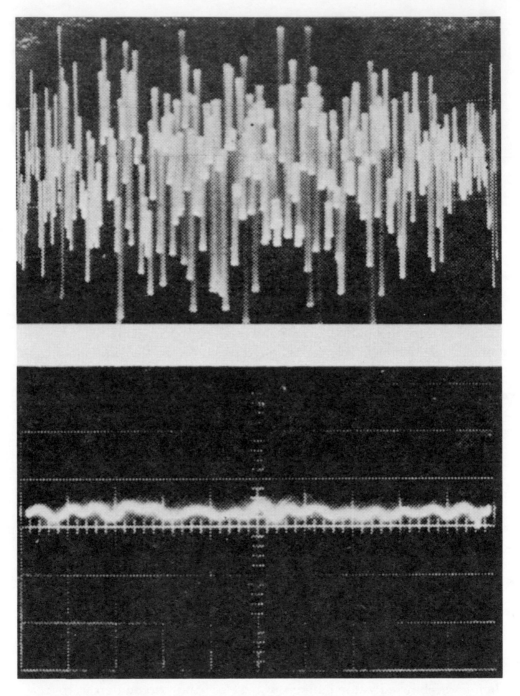

Recordings showing noise levels in disturbed ward of mental hospital before drugs (TOP) *and after* (BOTTOM). *Before drugs, the ward was 220 times noisier.*

session to hear about chlorpromazine. The proceedings were aired on the "Today" show.

Soon, like Saul on the road to Damascus, doubting psychiatrists were falling on their knees, having seen the light. Henry Brill of New York's Pilgrim State Hospital had been a skeptic. He said, "I remember walking into the dayroom and seeing this small group of patients dressed, quiet, cooperative and in surprisingly good contact—with their psychiatric symptoms wiped away. That was perhaps the most spectacular demonstration anyone can ask."[33]

It was thus thanks to the custodians of these great redbrick state hospitals, and not to academic psychiatrists, that the success of chlorpromazine was established. *Time* magazine later mocked the academic Freudians for their pretensions. "The ivory-tower critics argue that the red-brick pragmatists are not getting to the patient's 'underlying psychopathology' and so there can be no cure. These doctors want to know whether he withdrew from the world because of unconscious conflict over incestuous urges or stealing from his brother's piggy bank at the age of five. In the world of red bricks, this is like arguing about the number of angels on the point of a pin."[34]

In March 1954 the Food and Drug Administration (FDA) approved chlorpromazine for market. In its first decade, chlorpromazine was given to perhaps fifty million people around the world. Smith Kline's net sales jumped from $53 million in 1953 to $347 million in 1970, due "in no small measure" to chlorpromazine.[35] As a result not just of chlorpromazine but of the generations of antipsychotic drugs which came after it, the population of institutionalized psychiatry patients fell from nearly six hundred thousand in 1955 to about a hundred and fifty thousand in the mid-1980s —a decline of 75 percent.

Chlorpromazine and other drugs had thus initiated a major new era in the treatment of mental illness. *Life* magazine cheered in 1956 that these drugs "are proving to be one of the most spectacular triumphs in the history of medicine." In the possibility of giving chlorpromazine to the young, *Science Digest* saw a solution to juvenile delinquency![36]

Of course the hype has now gone sour. Among the drug's unknown side effects, the gravest side effect of all turned out to be the deinstitutionalizing of tens of thousands of mental patients whose psychoses were chemically planed out but who were, nonetheless, perfectly incapable of coping on their own. Once out on the streets, many failed to take their medication, sometimes because they were too disorganized to do so, sometimes because they feared the medical side effects, the involuntary twitching and the like, that even today accompany many antipsychotic drugs. Many of these unfortunate people, who had once found a relatively sheltered home in the asylums, were then cast adrift. It is the deinstitutionalized mental patients who currently constitute the bulk of the homeless. You have probably seen them in the big cities, sleeping over heating grates in their ragbag clothes, or raging incoherently on the street corners. Ironically, the antipsychiatry zealots who urged liberating them in the first place have now passed on to other causes.[37] The very real progress in treating psychotic illness has not been without its costs.

Valium: King of the Serendipity Drugs

We are in Krakow, Poland. It is 1938. Leo Sternbach returns at Christmas from Zurich, where he's working as a chemist, to help his father, a pharmacist with a shop in the heart of Krakow's Jewish ghetto. "War was in the air," Dr. Sternbach recalled many years later. "There were melées at the University of Krakow, people attacking Jewish students in the streets. My cousin, who was very much of a Pole, got hit, and I enjoyed it, because my cousin had always said, 'Oh, we are Poles, we aren't Jews.' Then he got hit over the head with something."

Fortunately the professor in Zurich with whom Sternbach had been

Dr. Leo Sternbach in his lab, 1941.

working got a new grant from the Rockefeller Foundation. Sternbach was able to return to Switzerland, and Valium was saved for the world.

But not so fast. Valium is an American story. It fits into this Central-Europe-to-New York tramline that occurs throughout the Health Century. In 1940, a year after returning to Zurich from Krakow, Sternbach went to work for the Hoffmann-La Roche drug firm in Basel. Twelve months later it sent him to its daughter firm in Nutley, New Jersey, the rapidly growing labs that vitamins, sedatives, and Elmer Bobst had built late in the 1920s. Why pluck Sternbach from Basel? Partly it was because Nutley needed good chemists—and Sternbach lived for chemistry—and partly because Hoffmann-La Roche wanted to get its Jewish scientists to safety, as the Swiss feared a German invasion at any moment.

Time passes. The war ends. Chlorpromazine, reserpine, and a minor tranquilizing drug named Miltown are discovered. It is 1955, and the Roche people in Nutley are eager to get into this exploding market for psychoactive drugs, drugs that affect the mind. Sternbach proposes working with a kind of chemical compound he had investigated much earlier in Europe while looking for dyes. He had thought it might make a good dye, but the compound and its analogues turned out to be useless for that purpose. There was nothing about it that suggested it might have any effect on the mind, merely that it could be synthesized easily and Sternbach was familiar with it. So for the next year and a half he and his assistant, Earl Reeder, added on this side chain and that side chain, and then sent the new compounds over to Roche's pharmacologist, Lowell Randall, for testing to see if they tranquilized lab animals and . . . nothing. No results. Finally, in May 1957, they were cleaning up the lab at the end of this series of failed efforts.

"The whole bench was full of various experiments, crystalline samples, bottles, containers with fluids." Sternbach told Reeder to tidy up and put everything in bottles with appropriate labels. Then Reeder said, "Oh look. Here's a sample we forgot to submit for animal testing." Sternbach remembers, "We were under great pressure by this time because my boss had told us to stop these foolish things and go back to more useful work. So I submitted it for animal testing. My boss said, 'Oh, this is just to finish up your work.' I thought myself that it was just to finish up."

Several days later the pharmacologist Randall told them, "This compound has very interesting properties. We would like to have more of it." This was the beginning of the Valium story.

But at the time, in 1957, they didn't know what they had. They analyzed the new compound and found it wasn't at all similar to other members of what supposedly was the same series, the series with which Sternbach had begun eighteen months previously. Instead, it was chemically a benzodiazepine, and Roche marketed it in 1960 under the trade name Librium. The generic name of this family of drugs is important, because today over a thousand different brands of benzodiazepines are on the market worldwide, taken by hundreds of millions of people. They seem to work by helping a neurotransmitter with the initials GABA (gamma-aminobutyric acid) reduce electrical activity in the brain.[38]

Sternbach and Reeder tested everything they made on themselves. Sternbach remembers taking one compound he'd made (a precursor of clidinium bromide, which is not a benzodiazepine) and hallucinating for two days. Mrs. Sternbach was frantic. On another occasion, while Librium was still being tested, a neighbor appeared at the Sternbach home and asked for some of the drug because he couldn't sleep. Leo was away at the lab. So Mrs. Sternbach found some green-and-black capsules and gave them to him. They weren't Librium at all but a much stronger sedative called Mogadon.

The neighbor said, "I should take two or three of these?"

"Yeah," said Mrs. Sternbach, "that's fine."

Jan 24. 1958   Ro 5-0690/1   See 144

One 50mg tablet at 8:30
Slightly soft in the knees 10-11.
Appetite not influenced. Cheerful.
1:35. Slightly sleepy
2:50 Sleepy.
4:00 Pretty sleepy.
5:30 Slight dizziness
6- No effect
8:30 " "

Leo Sternbach's handwritten account of his own experience experimenting with high doses of Librium in 1958.

The neighbor took them and fell instantly asleep. Consternation. Dr. Sternbach came home. Mrs. Sternbach asked, "What shall we do?"

"Let him sleep," said Leo. "He'll have a good night's sleep." Sternbach had great confidence in his drugs, and he tested Librium on himself as well, noting on the form that it merely made him drowsy.

Librium, introduced in February 1960, enjoyed a huge success as a tranquilizer that was stronger than Miltown but not a full-blast antipsychotic like chlorpromazine. It was the kind of drug that people could take who felt anxious before sales meetings.

Meanwhile Sternbach kept working. The problem with Librium was its bitter taste. "Even in capsules, always a trace of the dust stayed around, which was terribly bitter. So I acetylated it," he explained, mentioning a chemical procedure for altering the molecule. He made various other changes to the Librium molecule and ended up in 1959 with a drug that had almost no bitter taste and was five to ten times more powerful than Librium. Hoffmann-La Roche marketed it in 1963 as Valium.

For Sternbach, Valium represented the summit of his career. "For the medicinal chemist it's really very exciting, the pinnacle, to discover a new class of biologically active compounds." And Valium went on to become a milestone in a certain kind of pharmacological achievement as well: drugs that help people with worry and unhappiness.

But do people need medical help with unhappiness, as opposed to anxiety neurosis? Valium became, in the supposedly permissive sixties and early seventies, a symbol of breakdown, as people dosed themselves chemically for problems that earlier generations of pioneers were thought to have met with steely resolve. Sternbach has a copy of a German magazine in which his picture had been stuck on the body of a nude man, surrounded by two nude party girls. The message: Valium equals Party City.

Doctors think twice today about whether these anxiolytics (as they're now called) are appropriate, because the benzodiazepines have the risk of addiction. Addiction in this context means the symptoms the patient gets after stopping the drug are worse than the symptoms before starting it. But doctors' offices are filled with patients who have, not a formal diagnosis of anxiety neurosis, but a stress headache or abdominal pain. People come in who are genuinely under stress and their heads and tummies ache. What's a doctor to do? A forty-five-year-old businessman comes in who gets migraines twice yearly when he has a big conference. "He finds five milligrams of Valium helps him," says the doctor, "and I don't see anything wrong with prescribing it."

Nor does Dr. Sternbach, who is impatient with the kind of media scare

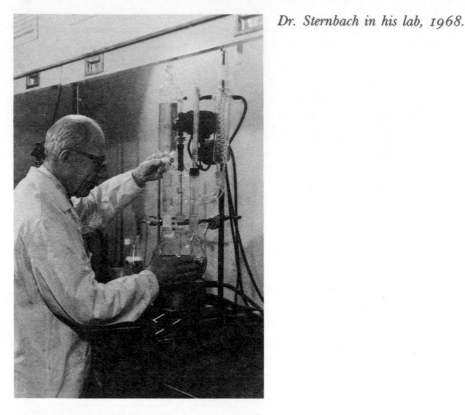

Dr. Sternbach in his lab, 1968.

stories about Valium that appeared following Barbara Gordon's bestsell-ing account of her own Valium addiction, *I'm Dancing as Fast as I Can.*[39] Sternbach says, "I feel the good Valium created was so much above its bad effects that it's definitely a classical [beneficial] drug. I considered these criticisms irrelevant because you don't talk about the thousands and mil-lions that it helped. You talk about the few that might have had some damage."

The millions indeed. By the end of the Health Century, psychoactive drugs such as Valium are being used by about 10 percent of the American population, or twenty-five million people. In the United States alone, the benzodiazepines are, in the words of pharmacologist Ross Baldessarini, "among the most prescribed drugs of *all* kinds, at rates approaching 100 million prescriptions per year and a cost of about $500 million."[40] In 1980 the company was making 30 million Valium tablets a day. In 1978 alone, Americans consumed about 2.3 billion Valiums. Roche's Valium patent expired in 1985.[41]

But Valium was the last of the important serendipity drugs, compounds discovered by blindly throwing things together. The next generation of drugs that affect the mind is being designed according to some rational

In the 1950s and '60s the pharmaceutical industry came of age. Merck entered the mental health field with an antidepressant drug, Elavil. Many doctors questioned whether all these drugs were necessary, or even appropriate.

understanding of brain chemistry. The kindly old man Leo Sternbach would have been wounded to the quick had he heard the words of Roche's current vice president for research, Ronald Kuntzman: "We've stopped doing research on the benzodiazepines. The era of these kinds of drugs is essentially past. We need now to know more about brain peptides in order to get new generations of drugs."[42]

The Rise of Biological Psychiatry

It was not biological psychiatry that created Valium and its generation of drugs. It was drugs like Valium that created biological psychiatry. Although studying the chemistry of the brain goes back considerably, the success of psychoactive drugs dramatized how much could be done for the mind by intervening in the brain, which is the essence of biological psychiatry. The first generation of antipsychotic drugs had been discovered more or less by accident: chlorpromazine was unearthed in a search for antihistamines; Valium was found in tidying up the lab bench. But later generations of psychoactive drugs would be prepared in the hope of fitting drug molecules into receptors in the brain. After all, this is what the molecular mainline is all about, designing molecules that will influence specific chemical events going on inside the cell, events that one knows about in advance rather than stumbling across them in the search for a new decongestant.

We find ourselves again in 1938. One of our characters, Otto Loewi, then a professor of pharmacology at the University of Graz, has been hauled off to jail along with the other Jewish males in this Austrian town. He has just finished the very last of a series of experiments that he began almost twenty years previously on how nerve signals pass from cell to cell. "When I was awakened that night and saw the pistols directed at me, I expected, of course, that I would be murdered. From then on during days and sleepless nights I was obsessed by the idea that this might happen to me before I could publish my last experiments." Finally a guard gave him a postcard and a lead pencil and Loewi scratched out the details. "Later in the day the guard came to tell me that he himself had mailed my card. I felt as relieved as if our whole future depended on that communication."

But in fact Loewi's future depended on his willingness to hand over to the Nazis the money he had received for winning the Nobel prize in 1936.[43] He duly signed over the funds; his wife gave them a family home in Italy, and he was permitted to flee to England.

The work that Loewi terminated in the Graz jail had begun in 1920, when he conceived a simple experiment to determine if a chemical was involved in the transmission of the nerve impulse. He called what he found vagus-material after the particular nerve he had worked with. The chemical was later identified as acetylcholine, the first known neurotransmitter. Such was the importance of Loewi's finding that Arnold Welch, a distinguished American pharmacologist, later wrote, "It was the work of Otto Loewi in Graz in 1920 that began the biochemical revolution."[44] In 1940 Loewi became a research professor at New York University.

In 1938 another of our heroes, Julius Axelrod, is twenty-six years old and working in New York City as a chemist for a laboratory that tests foods. He graduated from New York City's College in 1933, wanting to study medicine. "But at that time it was virtually impossible for a City College graduate [that is, a Jew] to be accepted by a medical school, and I was no exception." So for Axelrod it was the food lab, where he would stay until 1946, when he managed to get taken on as a research chemist by Bernard Brodie at New York University's Goldwater Memorial Hospital. How interesting it is to see the threads in this story come together, for it was this very lab that James Shannon had built up during the war doing malaria research. And even though Shannon was now at Squibb, Shannon's good friend, the great pharmacologist Brodie had become a lab chief there. Thus in 1946 Loewi and Axelrod, perhaps the two most distinguished figures in the history of understanding the brain's chemistry, found themselves at NYU. At the time Loewi was world-famous, Axelrod completely obscure.

When in 1949 Shannon was summoned to the NIH's heart institute, he brought his former Goldwater colleagues Bernard Brodie, Robert Berliner, Thomas Kennedy, and Sidney Udenfriend down to Bethesda as well. Axelrod, who had been trying to escape Brodie's lab at Goldwater, wrote James Shannon asking for a job. Shannon proceeded to put him back into Brodie's NIH lab.[45] At this point Axelrod was still a lowly chemist with no advanced degrees. Then in Brodie's lab he became interested in the question of how the body processes (metabolizes) drugs, and he started working on the amphetamines, then all the rage as "uppers." You give a rabbit amphetamines; the drug disappears in the rabbit's body. What happens to it? Ah, there's a special enzyme system in the liver that dismantles it? Very important, thought Axelrod, making major contributions to the discovery of this system.

In 1954 the National Institute of Mental Health, still part of NIH, asked Axelrod to head up the pharmacology section of one of its labs. Axelrod thought he had better get an advanced degree. He took a year off to fetch a Ph.D. in pharmacology, and upon returning to NIMH, began to study the possible role of adrenaline in schizophrenia. Adrenaline too is a neurotransmitter, and for his work on this and other neurotransmitters Axelrod won a Nobel prize in 1970.[46] Maybe we'd better pause here. Why is this subject so important?

The ultimate point is to find drugs that relieve the diseases of the mind and brain. But as Solomon Snyder of Hopkins, one of the current leaders in this research and earlier one of Axelrod's prize students, says, "Virtually every drug that alters mental function does so by interacting with a neurotransmitter system in the brain."[47] These neurotransmitters have such names as serotonin, noradrenaline, and dopamine. And it was Snyder of Johns Hopkins University who, in 1973 with Candace Pert, found the first site in the brain that a specific neurotransmitter plugs in to. These sites are called receptors. Snyder and Pert had discovered that cocaine and heroin bind preferentially to receptors usually occupied by natural brain neurotransmitters (these particular natural transmitters being the enkephalins and endorphins).

Hence we encounter once again a molecular concept. We saw it in the immune system, as protein molecules called leukokines cruise in the bloodstream looking for receptors on big-eaters and lymphocytes to plug in to. Similarly in the brain the nerve cells (neurons) have a number of different binding sites, or receptors. Various protein molecules coast about in the fluid outside the cell, looking for their specific receptor. When the molecule snuggles into its receptor, it initiates a series of chemical changes inside the cell that encourage anger, or thought, or dismay about a failed examination. These brain neuroreceptors and transmitters thus form the basis of mind.

Much of the molecular revolution of the last twenty years has concerned one specific portion of the vast wilderness of fluid surrounding the individual neuron: the small open space between the tail end of one neuron and the head end of the next. (The downstream neuron actually has a number of head ends, which are called dendrites, just as the tail end of the preceding nerve cell is called the axon.) For the nerve impulse to cross this open space, the tail end of the upstream neuron releases into the space a neurotransmitter; this transmitter crosses the space and is picked up by a receptor on the head end of the downstream neuron; that neuron then fires, and the nerve impulse is relayed further. The upstream neuron then reabsorbs again the neurotransmitter that it has just released. This whole process of release into the open space (synapse) and reuptake is mediated by a system of enzymes, and these enzymes may be modified by the action of drugs.

Thus the antidepressant drug imipramine blocks reabsorption of the neurotransmitter noradrenaline, prolonging the amount of time noradrenaline spends in the synapse. The longer the noradrenaline acts on the downstream neuron's receptors, the less the depression: so goes the theory. The opposite of depression is mania, and lithium today is the drug of choice against the manic phase of manic-depression. Lithium speeds up the reabsorption of the noradrenaline by the upstream neuron, thus diminishing the amount of time the noradrenaline may act on the downstream neuron's receptors. The less the noradrenaline, the less the mania: so, again, goes the theory.

Ditto for schizophrenia, thought to be caused by an excess of dopamine. Chlorpromazine is still often used against schizophrenia, and chlorpromazine evidently works by blocking the dopamine receptor sites in the downstream neuron. One can see in the mind's eye the dangerous dopamine molecules bouncing off the receptors as chlorpromazine molecules sit fast in the binding site blocking them.[48]

The solid line of discoveries about the chemistry of the nervous system that began with Otto Loewi has thus made organic psychiatry possible: treating disturbances of mind by addressing the chemistry of the brain. Although a Society of Biological Psychiatry was founded in 1945, it has been only since the 1970s that the biological group has started to get the upper hand over the psychoanalytically oriented psychiatrists. (Remember that few psychiatrists are simultaneously registered analysts; many, however, operate with Freud's insights about deep psychotherapy.)

The conflict between the two camps resulted in an open shoot-out late in the 1970s as the American Psychiatric Association struggled to bring its diagnostic manual up to date. The new edition, published in 1980, is referred to as the *Diagnostic and Statistical Manual,* third edition, or *DSM-III.* The forces of renewal wanted to remove all those labels that suggested the cause of the disorder was known to be in the unconscious, because so many psychiatrists simply no longer believe in Freud's unconscious.

Thus such diseases as Freudian conversion hysteria were marked for the high jump. Freudians think that conversion disorders, such as a leg that is mysteriously paralyzed for two weeks, are caused by repressed psychic energy that is converted into a physical channel, namely, the paralysis of the leg.[49] For the new school of psychiatry, however, the cause of such problems is simply unknown. And while it would be wonderful if psychiatric research someday discovers the true cause, in the meantime the anti-Freudians want to help the victim of the paralysis, not with depth psychotherapy dragging on expensively for years, but with drugs plus counseling.[50]

Freudians may object that the biochemical changes detected in schizophrenia or depression are consequences and not causes of the disease.

The biological psychiatrists respond that schizophrenia causes anatomical changes in brain structure as well as in brain chemistry; Schizophrenics may have enlarged fluid reservoirs, or ventricles, deep in the brain. Yet this enlargement also happens in a number of serious mental illness. What appears distinctive to schizophrenia is that the front part of the brain's temporal lobe is swollen. Changes of this nature seem unlikely to be the result of changed thought patterns. Thus schizophrenia, like some forms of epilepsy, is starting to be seen as an organic disease of the temporal lobe, caused possibly by a virus.[51]

Biological psychiatry is at the leading edge of what Francis Schmitt, the "dean" of the neurosciences, calls a molecular biology of the mind. He says, "If the fields of molecular genetics [what the DNA is doing] and neuroscience could be coupled, the impact may well be substantially greater than that of the Industrial Revolution in England over two hundred years ago, because one of its central targets would be the human brain and its product the mind."[52]

But to make the brain scrutable, one last step is required: imaging techniques that peer into its interior. Recently two of these have been developed.

A Walk Through the Body

New ways of visualizing the body are giving techniques used until only a few years ago the same kind of antique quality as descriptions of the early telephone. The problem with X rays, the reader will recall, is that they're unable to distinguish one organ from another: all the soft tissues look the same, and what the radiologist sees are only shadows left by the air in the diaphragm or by the feces in the colon. Beyond that it's a job for Sherlock Holmes. Is this displaced, is that displaced? And the more refined techniques such as arteriograms with contrast medium are invasive, uncomfortable, and a bit dangerous.

But how about taking a bunch of X-ray tubes and using them simultaneously to take pictures of the same cross section of the patient's body, but from different angles? Each X ray will see its own little pattern of densities, and a computer can put the patterns together in a picture of that cross section. The idea was that of Godfrey Hounsfield, an English electronics engineer, who built in 1971 an early prototype incorporating this principle. "In 1972 the first patient was scanned by this machine. She was a woman who had a suspected brain lesion, and the picture showed clearly in detail a dark circular cyst in the brain." It was clear that his machine was going to be able to do something regular X rays couldn't do: tell the difference between normal and diseased tissue. Hounsfield won a Nobel prize in 1979 for this discovery, which is called a CT scan, standing for computerized tomography. Tomography means doing X rays in sections.[53]

Spotting lesions directly with X rays was a major advance. "Suddenly you could see inside the brain," said Roger Smith, a neuroradiologist at Canada's Toronto General Hospital. "A hydrocephalic child is very, very obvious on CT scan. We simply don't see them nowadays." Hydrocephalus in newborn infants causes them to have large heads. Their cerebrospinal fluid, or CSF, is somehow blocked from circulating. Once these infants were diagnosed after air injections under a general anesthetic. Now the moment the condition is suspected, the child is scanned, the exact site of the blockage discovered, and an operation performed to relieve it.

CT scanning has within the last few years become the procedure of choice in diagnosing head symptoms. Resident physicians will do a history and a physical, perform a neurological exam, and order a CAT scan. One patient might have a movement disorder, his hands moving uncontrollably. "Yes, by God, there it is," the neurologists and radiologists might exclaim excitedly. "The head of the caudate's rotted away," mentioning a deep structure in the brain the destruction of which has produced the symptoms. Thus the physician is able to confirm the diagnosis of Huntington's chorea.

The second new imaging technique arrived in the mid-1980s. Called nuclear magnetic resonance (NMR), or magnetic resonance imaging (MRI), it has nothing to do with X rays. Instead, a huge magnet, requiring so much energy that it must be encased in a giant refrigeration plant and protected by concrete from external radio waves, subjects the patient's body to a powerful magnetic field. The patient doesn't feel a thing, but the magnet is strong enough to stop watches, erase the information on credit cards, and cause bunches of keys to fly through the air. What the magnet does is align briefly all the protons, or nuclei of hydrogen atoms, in the patient's body on a north-south axis; then a computer assembles this realignment into a picture. Since hydrogen atoms are found in water (H_2O), and since the soft tissues are composed chiefly of water, the technique is perfect for seeing even small differences: tumor versus nontumor, for example, or the subtle changes in the white matter of the brain that the disease multiple sclerosis entails. Because MRI ignores bone, little tumors may now be spotted that grow at the base of the skull or in the shadow of the spinal cord. (CT often misses these because, using X rays, it gives bone such prominence.)

MRI represents a variety of spectroscopy that goes back to the Second

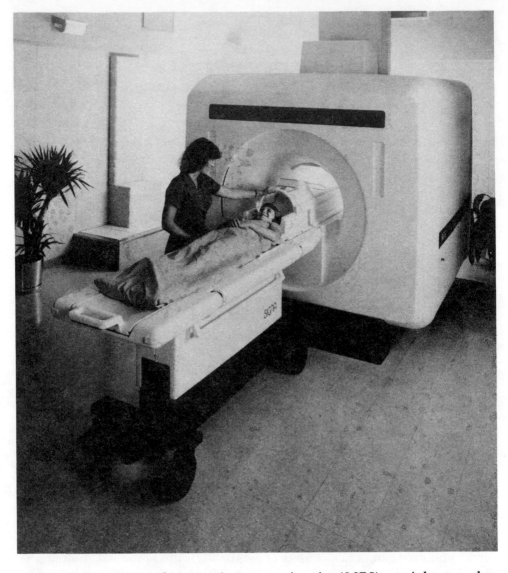

A young patient prepares for magnetic resonance imaging (MRI), a painless procedure that aligns the nuclei of all hydrogen atoms in the patient's body and produces an image so accurate that even tiny tumors can be seen.

World War, but only in 1967 was the first MRI coil built large enough to accommodate those body parts that are attached to live humans: the MRI at Oklahoma State University could image a human arm.[54] In the early 1980s coils big enough to image the whole human body were introduced. The clinical center at the National Institutes of Health acquired one in 1985.

The size of the structure might require a separate building and the

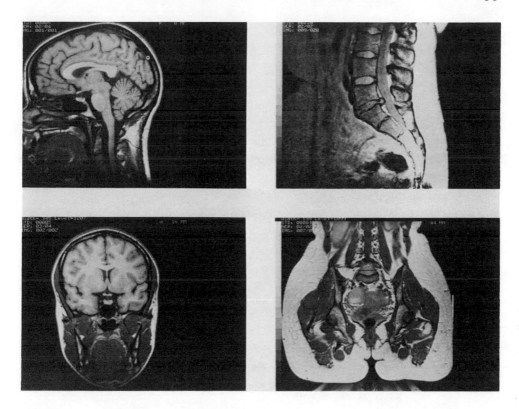

Four pictures obtained through magnetic resonance imaging (MRI). UPPER LEFT: *Image of a head demonstrating excellent soft tissue contrast and fine anatomic detail obtained at high magnetic field strengths.* UPPER RIGHT: *Image of this lumbar spine in the sagittal plane showing a herniated disk at the L5-S1 level.* LOWER LEFT: *A 3 mm image of the head in the coronal plane showing the pituitary fossa. The ability to achieve thin slices allows visualization of the pituitary stalk and small tumors of the pituitary gland.* LOWER RIGHT: *Image of the abdomen showing the psoas muscle, uterus, bladder, and pelvic bone marrow.*

machine itself costs about two and a half million dollars. That's a lot of dollars. But it's also a lot of information. According to Walter Kucharczyk, the neuroradiologist in charge at the Toronto General Hospital, MRI enables doctors to see the body in various planes, not just the cross sections that CT scan offers. That means being able to spot lesions like blood clots or tumors that you might miss in the particular plane at which you did the CT scan. Because MRI usually offers more detail, you can pick up tumors when they're smaller and operate on them. CT scan shows only quite substantial changes in the nervous system.

But where does it make a real difference? With AIDS, for example. Says Kucharczyk, "In AIDS you see nothing on CT scan, but the guy has real

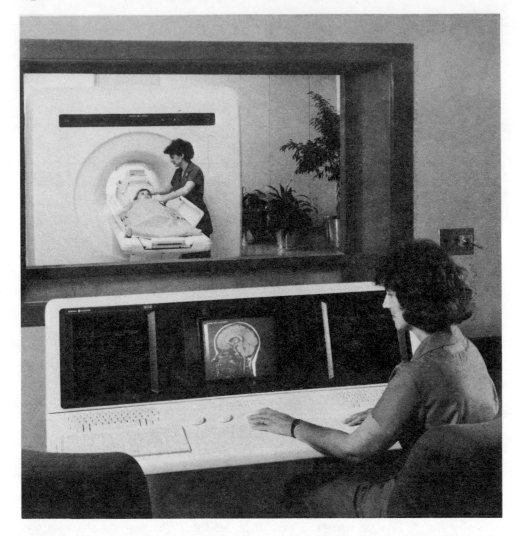

"Sit for a moment at the MRI operating console and find yourself as though in a Jules Verne submarine in the very center of the brain of a living person."

symptoms. With MRI we can see multiple lesions in the brain. We can tell the surgeon where to biopsy, and once the contents of the lesion are known, we begin treating the patient for toxoplasmosis or cytomegalovirus or whatever," he says, mentioning the opportunistic infections to which the central nervous systems of AIDS patients are prey.

Sit for a moment at the MRI operating console and look at the brain of a patient who's being scanned. You are looking at the brain stem, actually, the part at the back of the neck that controls the body's vital activities. The brain stem is quite vulnerable to tumors. So you start out looking at a section right at the middle of the body: the section is cut vertically, so that to the east and west are the walls of the neck. Above is the cerebral cortex, below is the spinal cord. You find yourself as though in a Jules Verne submarine in the very center of the brain stem of a living person and you can see clearly all the structures. As you begin your walk through the brain stem, a new section appears on-screen; you have moved a couple of millimeters toward the body wall and once again can see everything, the arteries and the different anatomical features; little tumors—fortunately in this case there are none—would show up clearly.

Mr. R., a young man in his thirties, has recently been admitted to the teaching hospital because of a violent headache after a period of inconclusive investigations elsewhere. Let's follow some of the diagnostic action for Mr. R. that uses this contemporary imaging technology, in this case, the CT scan. We begin at hospital rounds when a resident says, "There's big news. Mr. R. has a space-occupying lesion. It's been diagnosed with CT scan," which means the lesion is already pretty big. The pressure inside Mr. R.'s brain is very high as this space-occupying lesion expands. We also learn there's something in Mr. R's condition that is shedding protein into his cerebrospinal fluid. He's also gone blind.

We go down to Radiology. Sure enough, in the CT scan done with a contrast dye there's a big circle with a white rim and a black center in the left temporal lobe. The problem is, it doesn't explain his symptoms. Why would he be blind, since the various optic tracts and bundles don't run through that part of the brain?

The residents are all conversing about the lesion. They reviewed Mr. R. in rounds last week. Nobody noticed anything in his previous CT scans, not even the staff men. This is an exciting moment in neurology: discovering a lesion that is potentially treatable, since so many are not.

It is a week later. By now the neurosurgeons have biopsied Mr. R's left temporal lobe and reported the biopsy needle to be filled with gunk. It's probably a tumor. Surgery is possible but the tumor is growing rapidly and there is doubt about the success of an attempt to remove it. But at least the problem has been quickly diagnosed and the experts can make their decisions on the basis of hard information, not just informed guesses. Brain surgery—like all surgical techniques—has come a long, long way during the Health Century, and Mr. R. at least has a chance.

Our knowledge of the brain and how it works bounds ahead, but the era of real knowledge is just beginning. We understand the basics: For instance, how might Mr. R's tumor explain his blindness? "It might have started in the optic chiasma," theorizes one resident, "and worked along the optic nerve from there." The optic chiasma is deep at the base of the brain, where the optic nerves, coming in from the eyeballs, meet and cross. The theory is that a primary tumor here probably spread both to the temporal lobe and to the nerves of the eye. If so, the tumor has now spread so far as to be inoperable.

We go to Mr. R.'s ward. A neuroophthamology resident is there who knows everything about the case. "It's an optic glioma," he exults. "I've looked up the literature. It can't be anything but." He opens his briefcase and pulls out four or five Xeroxes of articles on optic glioma. A glioma is a kind of brain tumor. Sure enough, in the photographs in the articles we see the tumor in the optic chiasma, the cross-hatching indicating its spread to the orbital cavity, where the eyeball sits.

"We'll know for sure when we take a look at it," the resident says, casually reflecting the deadly nature of the problem. "Taking a look at it" means autopsy.

So it appears that Mr. R. won't survive. But years before he would not even have been diagnosed until the autopsy. A few years from now his diagnosis might take place at such an early stage in the tumor's growth that surgery or other treatment might be not only possible but successful. Medicine improves its knowledge and skill in increments, in the accumulation of thousands of clinical papers that fill the journals year after year. Patients too make marginal improvements, three months here for a Mr. R., six months there for someone else, to eventually extend life by years. But what we are learning about the brain and its functions may prove to be the most important incremental knowledge of all.

SIX

The Flagging Heart

It is in the area of heart disease that the last quarter of the Health Century has brought its greatest benefits, helping people still in their prime of life. For the fact is that heart disease strikes the middle-aged heavily and affects men in particular. A man's chances of having a heart attack increase 333 percent from his late thirties to his late forties.[1]

The waste is overwhelming. Over half a million Americans die annually of heart attacks, another two hundred thousand from strokes. As the number one cause of death, heart disease has become the "pneumonia" of modern times. But unlike pneumonia or yellow fever in the past, when death came within days, heart disease tends to be chronic. One may have it for years. Thus approximately forty million people today suffer from some kind of heart or circulatory disease that requires treatment.

While it is true that we all must die of something, most of these heart deaths are not inevitable. And twenty years from now people will be astonished that we once did accept them as inevitable. The drugs and surgical techniques that are the subject of this chapter are removing the inevitability of dying from strokes, heart attacks, and from kidney disease caused by high blood pressure. In no other field of medicine has this distinctive collaboration among university scientists, government health research, and the drug companies paid off so hugely as in reducing death rates from heart disease. It is a dramatic story.

First, an overview. In the twentieth century heart disease has seen a great rise and fall. Before 1900 deaths from heart disease were vastly overshadowed by deaths from such infectious diseases as tuberculosis. Then after 1900 heart disease underwent a great increase. From 1900 to 1963, the high point of this increase, cardiovascular and renal mortality in the United States rose 53 percent. Since the 1960s a major turnaround has occurred. From the early 1960s to 1984, heart disease deaths have declined by 36 percent.[2]

Thus we must be doing something right. But before we speculate what it might be, let us first look at problems that people get into when the arteries that supply the heart muscle begin to close down, then at problems and solutions surrounding high blood pressure.

"The Patients All Suddenly Fall Down"

The Earl of Clarendon lived in England early in the seventeenth century. As he reached sixty, he started to be plagued by what he thought was bladder stone, as he often had to rise in the night to urinate. Then he had shooting pains in his left arm such that "the torment made him as pale— he was otherwise of a very sanguine complexion—as if he were dead." And he used to say in having these attacks that "he had passed the pangs of death and he should die in one of those fits."

Finally the Earl of Clarendon left London for Salisbury and arranged a house to be made available near the great cathedral, "where he could perform his devotions every day." Early Sunday morning after his arrival he went on a tour of the local churches, "and when he returned, which was by eight of the clock, he told his wife and his son that he had been to look out a place to be buried in, but found none . . . the Cathedral only exempted." Indeed he had discussed with the sexton where he might lie, making "the choice of a place near a kinsman of his own name."

Next day the earl attended the morning sermon at the cathedral, "where he found himself a little pressed as he used to be," meaning he was having chest and arm pains again. He hurried home as best he could, went into a basement room to urinate, and "no sooner than having made water, and the pain in his arm seizing upon him, he fell down dead, without the least motion of any limb."

Some thought he might have had a stroke, but no, his face was not in the least contorted. "Nor could the physicians make any reasonable guess

The History of Cardiology, *two frescoes by Diego Rivera. Created in 1943–44 for the Instituto Nacional de Cardiologia "Ignacio Chavez," in Mexico City.*

Detail from History of Cardiology: *René Théophile Hyacinthe Laënnec (French, 1781–1826) invented the stethoscope and the method of mediate auscultation, and was the first to describe cardiac and friction murmurs. Established the anatomoclinical era.*

from whence that mortal blow proceeded." The earl's death was a mystery to all.[3]

Who could have resembled the Earl of Clarendon less than Peter Arthur, a poor Polish Jewish shoemaker who lived in Baltimore in the 1930s. In 1934 he had been admitted to the Johns Hopkins Hospital with a heart attack. By this time, medicine had advanced sufficiently to make the diagnosis: he had a kind of fatty plaque on the arteries of his heart (coronary arteries) called atherosclerosis. The plaque had considerably narrowed the arteries, limiting the amount of oxygen they were able to deliver to the pumping heart muscle. He apparently had a blood clot in one of the arteries as well (coronary occlusion). In addition he had high blood pressure (hypertension), emphysema (loss of lung tissue), and chronic bronchitis. None of these conditions was treatable with the medicine of 1934 and the hospital sent him home a month later.

Mr. Arthur was now too weak to make a living as a shoemaker and, borrowing money from a brother-in-law, he bought a small corner grocery store from a widow who was remarrying. His life henceforth consisted of lying on a sofa in the back room while his twenty-three-year-old son ran the store, helping the son with ordering, or waiting on customers at peak periods.

The one characteristic that Mr. Arthur shared with the Earl of Clarendon was chest pain. The underlying heart muscle, crying out for oxygen, gave both men the kind of pain that is called angina pectoris, or simply, angina. It's not that a thrombus (blood clot) sits in the coronary artery, merely that the artery has become so occluded that the heart tissue is not well oxygenated. Or that the coronary arteries are in spasm, squeezing shut even in the absence of much plaque, and cutting off the blood flow. Such chest pains are not identical to a heart attack, where the heart muscle actually dies (infarcts) from lack of oxygen, but they are on the same continuum of oxygen deprivation leading to cell damage, and these pains may easily end fatally.

Thus when Mr. Arthur returned to the hospital in 1936, they did not take his chest pains lightly. They quizzed him at length about stress, since internists in those days were considerably more interested in the psychological dimension of heart disease than now. And they noted that the blood vessels in his eyes were congested from the hypertension. But again, they could do nothing. Perhaps he fared well after that, for on his way home he was slowly able to walk up a slight hill.[4]

But perhaps he didn't. For as the English physician William Heberden wrote in 1772, these angina patients "all suddenly fall down, and perish almost immediately. Of which indeed their frequent faintness, and sensations as if all the powers of life were failing, afford no obscure intimation." It was Heberden who first described clearly the oppressive chest pain reaching into the arms, the sudden beginning and termination of the pain, the absence of shortness of breath (short, shallow breaths offer a sign that the heart is slowly, not suddenly, failing). "I have seen nearly a hundred people under this disorder," wrote Heberden of chest pain, which he called pectoris dolor. Three of his patients had been women, and one boy. "All the rest were men near, or past the fiftieth year of their age."[5]

Yet in an era of tuberculosis and typhoid fever, this kind of heart disease —involving narrowing of the coronary arteries and consequent lack of oxygen—did not dominate the attention of the physician. The heart problems that doctors saw before 1900 didn't stem so much from narrow coronary arteries as from the cardiac complications of the infections of the day, such as inflammation in the little leaves of the heart's valves (endocarditis), or inflammation of the heart muscle itself (myocarditis). Only in our own century does disease of the coronary arteries dominate the picture. It is this kind of heart disease that causes angina and heart tissue death:

myocardial infarction. Once known in medical jargon as coronary thrombosis, heart attacks now are simply referred to as "MI's." But in our own century they represent by far the number one cause of death and debility. In 1983, for example, 676,000 patients were hospitalized for acute myocardial infarctions.[6]

So sensitive are we to heart attacks, it seems amazing that before 1900 doctors had never even heard of blockages in the arteries of the heart, and that once they did hear of them, they didn't care.[7]

It was only in 1910 that James Herrick, a Chicago internist with a wealthy practice, described a heart attack for the first time in the American medical literature. A Chicago banker was having a midnight sandwich and bottle of beer after returning from the theater. Suddenly he felt severe pain behind his breastbone and, assuming it was the sandwich, induced himself to vomit. But the pain continued, the family doctor was called, and when morning dawned the family doctor called in Dr. Herrick. Herrick found the banker cold, nauseated, his pulse racing, and in great pain.

Today we may clearly interpret these symptoms: something was blocking a coronary artery; excruciating pain was radiating from the banker's oxygen-deprived heart; his skin was cold because the vital organs were saving for themselves the little blood the heart could put out, and the heart was racing wildly to compensate for the lessened amount of blood that each beat ejected. But Herrick, and the other high-powered specialists the family had summoned, were not even sure what organ was affected. John Murphy, a distinguished surgeon, arrived in case the problem lay in the abdomen: they had not yet even singled out the heart. Another distinguished consultant, Frank Billings, then dean of the medical faculty of the University of Chicago and past president of the AMA, thought it might be a sudden enlargement of the heart but knew no more.

But the doctors knew that, whatever the cause, the symptoms themselves were desperate. Murphy got on the phone to the banker's son in New York. "Come at once," he shouted over the long-distance wire. The son protested there was no immediate train.

"No! No! don't wait for the Century tomorrow. Go straight to Mr. ——— (a high New York Central official) and get a special. What's the matter with you? Get busy, come right away or you'll be too late!"

The banker's family asked the two high-priced consultants to spend the night, the better to look after the patient. So they slept in twin beds in the same bedroom. Herrick later remembered that "Murphy, hearing me turn in bed, but not wishing to waken me if I were asleep, would whisper, 'Herrick, are you awake? Say, are you sure about there being no pneumothorax [air escaping from the lungs into the chest]?'

"A little later from my bed, also in a stage whisper, 'Dr. Murphy, do you think this might be an acute pancreatitis . . . ?' Neither of us slept much. We got up once or twice during the night to look at the patient." Just imagine such a scene happening today!

In any event, the banker died shortly thereafter. Herrick told the pathologist, who apparently came to the family home to perform the autopsy, "Look for a clot in the coronary artery." The pathologist phoned him later that evening and said, "The clot was in the coronary artery, all right. But how in God's name did you guess it?" Guess, Herrick later confessed, was the right word. But he had made the diagnosis.

Full of pride, he wrote up the case in the *Journal of the American Medical Association* as an American first. The response? Silence, even though Herrick's article had run on the first page of the issue. Doctors at the time simply weren't interested in the possibility of blockages in the vessels of the heart. Their minds still organized diseases in terms of such familiar categories as infections, ulcers, and the like. Not until Herrick presented the subject again in 1918, showing slides taken at autopsy and the highly distinctive profile a heart attack makes on an electrocardiogram (ECG), did he elicit any curiosity.

Herrick had seen that particular patient a year previously. It was a fellow physician, whose severe angina had forced him to abandon his California medical practice and come to Chicago for a last-ditch consultation with Herrick. Herrick told him he thought the problem was an occlusion in the coronary arteries. The physician-patient told another doctor of Herrick's diagnosis, and this other doctor ridiculed the notion of such a diagnosis in a living patient.

Well, the physician with coronary artery disease died soon thereafter; Herrick's diagnosis was confirmed, and years later this other physician, the scoffer, phoned Herrick "in a feeble voice and in evident alarm," asking for advice because he had just diagnosed a heart attack in himself.[8] Thus a growing epidemic of heart disease obliged physicians to take interest. They were getting it themselves.

Even if earlier doctors weren't concerned with the arteries of the heart, they longed for ways to relieve angina in their patients. "Few things are more distressing to a physician," wrote the English physician T. Lauder Brunton, "than to stand beside a suffering patient [who is] looking for relief from pain which he feels himself utterly unable to endure." It was Brunton who in 1867 introduced the first helpful drug against angina: amyl nitrite. Up to then only brandy and ether had been able to overcome the sense of impending dissolution that Brunton's angina patients felt. Then Brunton saw a medical friend use amyl nitrite to decrease blood pressure in animals, and he thought that in patients with chest pain amyl nitrite might take the load off the heart as well.[9] He was quite right. All the nitrates dilate the blood vessels, thus decreasing the load against which the heart has to pump and opening up the coronary arteries to let more blood reach the heart.

Even before Brunton described amyl nitrite, doctors had been interested in all the compounds that link nitrogen and oxygen, particularly in one such "nitrate" that had been synthesized in 1846. It was called nitroglycerin. A physician in the English seacoast town of Brighton had been giving patients tiny doses of the substance, which made their heads ring and their hearts pound so that they forgot about their other pains. There matters rested with nitroglycerin—a drug that induced funny sensations but didn't seem to have any therapeutic use—until in 1879 William Murrell, a London doctor on the staff of a chest hospital, decided to try some on an angina patient. Familiar with Brunton's previous article on amyl nitrite, he thought nitroglycerin might have the same effect on the heart.

Murrell's first patient was a sixty-four-year-old bailiff, a "cool, clearheaded fellow little prone to talk of his sufferings," who had been accustomed to an active life, "seldom walking less than fifteen miles a day, often very fast." But recently pain had been seizing him as he walked, running down "as far as the elbow." "During the seizure the patient suffers most acutely, and feels convinced that some day he will die in an attack." The attacks had been increasing in frequency, and now the man could neither stoop down nor pull on his boots. Thus a formerly active man had been reduced to semi-invalidism by his heart's inability to get enough oxygen.

To make sure that his first test of nitroglycerin wouldn't be corrupted by the placebo effect (which Murrell referred to as "the effects of expectation"), he placed the man on some innocuous compound for a week. "It need hardly be said that he derived no benefit from the treatment." Thus, if the nitroglycerin worked, it wouldn't be just because the man believed that he felt better.

Murrell then gave his patient a mixture of nitroglycerin and water. "At the expiration of a week that patient reported that there had been a very great improvement." The attacks came less often and were less severe. "He found that a dose of medicine taken during an attack would cut it short."

Murrell administered nitroglycerin to several of his other angina patients, with similar results. A sixty-one-year-old laborer, who felt as though his chest would burst during angina attacks and whose pulse was irregular, was put on a 1 percent solution of nitroglycerin. "For four days he has not had a single attack, although he had a great deal of walking to do. When he felt any indication of the onset of the pain, he took a sip of his medicine, and it was all gone in a moment."[10]

We have dwelt on these early experiences with angina therapy because after 1879 doctors had virtually nothing else to offer patients with chest pain. Indeed nitroglycerin today is still the first drug they turn to. It works by dilating the blood vessels and thus decreasing the work the heart has to do: the heart pumps against less resistance and more blood stays in the dilated veins rather than returning to the heart. Nitroglycerin even seems to open up the big arteries of the heart themselves. But nitroglycerin is not a cure for disease of the coronary arteries, which sooner or later may become so clogged that even reducing the work load will not save a faltering heart.

This situation remained virtually unchanged from the 1880s until the 1960s, when a brilliant English medicinal chemist named James Black discovered the first of the drugs that give the heart a chance to rest by blocking the receptors in the muscle cells that drive it on. The sympathetic nervous system speeds the heart up, activating these particular receptors called beta adrenergic receptors. The beta receptors may be blocked by the drug propanolol. Thus propanolol (Inderal) and the generations of drugs it has spawned since it was first launched in 1964, are called beta blockers.[11]

More recently drugs that break up clots in the coronary arteries have been introduced. The first-generation parent of these drugs, streptoki-nase, reduces the risk of further heart attacks by restoring circulation to the area of affected heart muscle. We consider these in the last chapter. Still other drugs known as calcium-channel blockers open up coronary arteries that have gone into spasm and caused a heart attack by cutting off the blood supply. But until these adjuvants to nitroglycerin appeared in the 1960s, people who had the sequence of angina, heart attacks, and early heart failure skirted the risk of lifelong invalidism, at least for what re-mained of life.

High Blood Pressure: The Pump or the Pipes

A major accomplishment of the Health Century's last two decades has been calling attention to high blood pressure, a disease whose existence was scarcely known before 1900, and scarcely treatable before 1955. High blood pressure affects 40 percent of the adult population, including two thirds of the elderly.[12] Even moderate levels considerably increase one's chances of dying of a heart attack.

For reasons that are largely unknown, as we get older our arteries begin to constrict. The muscular layer within them begins to tighten. And as they narrow, the heart must beat more strongly to perfuse the body. High blood pressure, or hypertension, means simply that the heart muscle expels the blood with higher pressure. Thus moderate hypertension is said to begin at 140 millimeters of mercury when the heart is at the height of a contraction (systolic blood pressure), and 90 millimeters when the heart is between beats. Between beats the heart is resting, and this resting, or diastolic, blood pressure represents the constant minimum against which it must struggle day and night.

Any elevation of blood pressure can be a matter of concern. For one thing, the pressure may thicken the walls of the small arteries and arterioles (tiny arteries) of the kidney and brain, cutting off the blood supply to the tissues. And beating against this increased resistance at high pressure tires out the heart. As Karl Beyer, whose research has permitted millions of Americans to treat their blood pressure and still lead normal lives, explained, "These tremendous surges of pressure damage the walls of the arterioles that support the arterial pressure, reducing their elasticity. Eventually, something wears out. The pump or the pipes."[13]

Doctors historically have always been able to spot a "hard" pulse. And they certainly saw at the bedside symptoms that were associated with pounding hearts and hard pulses. But clinically apparent symptoms from high blood pressure develop only late in the disease. (A vexing problem in treating hypertension is that it generally is a disease without symptoms; patients feel fine, so why should they take something that makes them feel miserable?)

The first step in bringing down the nation's blood pressure was realizing that it was high. A practical device for measuring blood pressure was introduced only at the turn of the century. Before then, doctors had no reliable means of telling the pressure. Nor had they any inkling that heart attacks, kidney failure, and strokes occurred much oftener in patients with hypertension than in the population as a whole.[14] Indeed, about a quarter of the thirty-five million Americans with moderate hypertension today— meaning 160-over-95—do not know they have the disease. Thus until the Second World War neither doctors nor patients considered anything less than malignant hypertension, with diastolic pressures of 130 and up, a cause for concern.

It is astonishing how long it took awareness to dawn. From the earliest days of blood pressure measurement, it had been known that high pressures in the arteries led to their thickening, hence arteriosclerosis.[15] But doctors simply were not interested in high pressures of the blood and sooner considered low blood pressure, a nonexistent disease unless you're dying, cause for alarm. William Osler wrote in the 1918 edition of his textbook, "Frequently in keen business men, who work hard, drink hard, and smoke hard," the pressure of the blood "is permanently high—above 180—but as far as can be ascertained, there are no arterial, cardiac, or renal changes."[16] Henry Christian, the Harvard internist who inherited the editorship of Osler's textbook, considered the main problem in high blood pressure not the condition itself but the patient's attitude, as he wrote in 1938, "The patients suffer more from knowing that hypertension is present than from hypertension itself. They study their blood-pressure figures [like] the stock market. This should teach physicians to be chary of telling patients about their blood pressure." He advised his medical readers not to take their patients' blood pressures regularly nor stress them in the consultation.[17]

When in 1945 Irvine Page moved to Cleveland to become director of the famous Cleveland Clinic, many doctors still considered hypertension a necessary thing, for otherwise the heart wouldn't be able to get out the blood. At the time of Page's arrival, "hypertension had no place in the national arena, no committees and no journals. In 1939 the editor of the *American Heart Journal* rejected our paper on the discovery of angiotension [a body substance that drives up blood pressure] as being 'too chemical.' "[18]

Until the 1950s, the choice of therapies was limited when the patient's blood pressure went through the ceiling. David Riesman, a distinguished Philadelphia physician, said in 1931 that he treated high blood pressure by bleeding his patients, taking blood from the veins in a procedure with the dignity of centuries of injurious medical history behind it.[19] By 1938 bleeding was a bit much for Harvard's Professor Christian, but drugs offered no hope either. Clearly accustomed to the better sort of patient, Christian advocated "mental rest and quiet" and "long hours of physical rest." Best would be "a good vacation, often well spent at one of the springs. One day a week in bed or a low diet is useful." Everything in moderation: "it is well to reduce the amount of salt." Bathe in tepid water and keep the bowels open.[20] What would you do as a patient of Professor Christian's in 1938 with a systolic blood pressure of 200 and fearful about a stroke? Go to Warm Springs, Georgia? Stop working?

As they became aware of the dangerousness of hypertension, doctors started treating it in earnest. But these initial therapies entailed massive side effects and disruptions in the patient's life. In 1944 Walter Kempner of Duke University introduced his rice diet to bring down blood pressure. The patients would eat nothing but unsalted rice and fruit, and the diet worked. Exploding blood pressures did tumble down via the mechanism of semistarvation. Cardiologist Jerome Green, now a senior NIH official, remembered sending patients to Kempner's "stalag of twenty-nine cottages" in Durham, North Carolina. "Only the wealthy could afford it." And they hated it, as did most patients who went on this unpalatable, monotonous diet. Thus the rice diet failed because people couldn't stay on it long enough to benefit from it.[21]

In the fight against high blood pressure what were needed were effective drugs, but the great stumbling block in the drug therapy of hypertension has been side effects. Remember, early stages are asymptomatic. Why should people who feel fine take drugs that make them feel rotten? Of the drugs available before 1950, one had a choice between sedating oneself with phenobarb or injections of a toxic kidney stimulant (diuretic) containing mercury.

One approach, as we have seen, is to dilate the blood vessels, thus reducing peripheral resistance and decreasing the heart's work load. It is the autonomic, or involuntary, nervous system that constricts peripheral blood vessels. In 1950 British scientists devised various drugs called hexamethonium compounds that blocked the entire system, thus permitting peripheral blood vessels to open up. Although these drugs did, in fact, reduce hypertension, they also affected all the other functions of the autonomic nervous system, causing dry mouth, constipation, blurring of vision, heartburn, and sudden fainting. This was not the kind of drug the average fifty-year-old executive with moderate high blood pressure was going to take. But the hexamethonium drugs did provide relief for "malignant" cases, where kidney and heart failure were imminent. Edward Freis, a prominent figure in the field, remembered using these drugs just as he arrived at the Veterans Administration Hospital in Washington, D.C., in 1950. "The relief of signs and symptoms of congestive heart failure . . . was rapid and dramatic."[22]

But there's an alternative to turning off the whole involuntary nervous system. And that is to make the patients urinate with diuretics. Get rid of fluid, reduce the burden of blood the heart must pump, and the blood pressure will subside of its own. How do you make the kidneys pass water? Get them to pass salt, and the water will follow the salt. How do the kidneys handle sodium, chloride, bicarb, and the other atoms that pass in and out of their complicated system of tubules? The story goes back to James Shannon and the Goldwater Labs. The whole generation of scientists who did kidney physiology there and who later ended up at NIH helped determine where in the kidney each of these various atoms (ions, as atoms carrying a charge are called) goes in and out. The story also goes back to Cleveland's Western Reserve University in the 1930s, where a scientist named Harry Goldblatt learned how to induce hypertension experimentally in dogs by operating on their kidneys. This helped pin down the whole role of the kidneys in regulating blood pressure.

Karl Beyer, a young M.D. from Kentucky, learned these various techniques for kidney research as he taught physiology at the University of Wisconsin. In 1943 he took a job with the Sharp & Dohme drug company in Philadelphia, teaming up with the chemist James Sprague. They tried to develop drugs that would conserve the precious penicillin supply by keeping patients from excreting penicillin immediately in their urine. The drugs failed commercially because other companies like Pfizer had figured out how to make penicillin plentiful by the time they were marketed. But Beyer and Sprague thought these compounds might have other uses. Building on someone else's observation that one sulfa drug, sulfanilamide, caused patients to dump sodium, they tried sulfa compounds as diuretics. This approach didn't work because the drugs caused the kidneys to excrete bicarbonate as well as sodium, giving the patients an acidosis.

These stories typify drug development: you work for years and everything you make fails because it's toxic or events outrun it. But meanwhile Beyer and Sprague were acquiring lots of experience in altering the functions of the kidneys with drugs. In 1953 the Merck company bought Sharp & Dohme in order to expand into pharmaceuticals. Now this kidney expertise was teamed up with some first-class organic chemists; they energetically began synthesizing compounds.

The outcome of the story is ironical: in 1955 the team synthesized chlorothiazide, a new kind of diuretic which they thought had the same effect on the kidneys as the sulfa drugs did, except that it didn't get rid of the body's bicarbonate. In fact, the new drug didn't use that particular sulfa mechanism at all, but affected the kidney tubules at quite a different site. This is called serendipity, a happy accident. The history of drug discovery, which means stumbling across new drugs rather than designing them on the basis of known biological mechanisms, is full of happy accidents. Yet accidental or not, chlorothiazide did permit patients to secrete sodium and chloride, and therewith to pass off water, thus bringing down their high blood pressure with a minimum of side effects.

The first patient to receive chlorothiazide was a sixty-year-old man admitted to the hospital in Houston on November 9, 1956. He came in with heart failure, meaning that his tired heart, exhausted by the strain of pushing against a diastolic blood pressure of 144 millimeters of mercury was backing fluid up in his lungs and in his tissues. He was therefore short of breath, had swollen feet and ankles, and weighed 172 pounds. His doctor, Ralph Ford, gave him the medicines of the day and ordered a saltfrcc diet, but the man failed to respond. A week later his diastolic was still 140, his weight, 170 pounds.

On November 15, Ford started giving him half a gram of chlorothiazide twice daily. Immediately the man started urinating water and salt. A week later he had lost ten pounds of water, then ten more pounds over the next five weeks. "His shortness of breath and edema subsided," noted Ford. Two weeks after starting treatment his diastolic blood pressure had dropped to 120, and after the next five years on chlorothiazide it had reached 96. "The patient felt well and reported that he had been working every day."[23]

The FDA approved chlorothiazide (Diuril) in January 1958, and soon about a million patients in heart failure and half a million more with severe hypertension were using it in the United States alone. Tens of millions would end up taking it and its offspring. Merck's Diuril thus became the first of the antihypertensives that act on the kidneys without the use of mercury. It was a major achievement of American industry. Julius Comroe, the tracker of scientific achievements, wrote in 1977 that "oral diuretics . . . are one of the two most important new groups of drugs in the last seventy-five years," the other being antibiotics.[24]

Indeed, by comparison to what existed before, the thiazide diuretics were a marked improvement. But these early drugs had a side effect that was deemed at the time unimportant but that would later emerge as a major issue: they often increased, and certainly failed to lower, cholesterol levels.

Risk Factors

Late in September 1955, while visiting his mother-in-law in Denver, President Dwight D. Eisenhower found himself on the course of the Cherry Hills golf club. He'd had a bit of raw onion during lunch at the clubhouse, and as he resumed play later that afternoon he felt "a little touch of heartburn."

"Boy," President Eisenhower said, "those raw onions are sure backing up on me." But the heartburn went away.

Around 2 A.M. the next morning the President had a heart attack. Initially his physician, General Howard Snyder, told the press it was indigestion. But at five o'clock that afternoon the press was informed that the President had suffered a mild coronary thrombosis.

Ike recalled those early hours. He had felt his own pulse, *Time* magazine reported, "and found it laboring like a weary steam locomotive. 'Chug . . . Chug. Chug, Chug . . . Chuuuug.' " Fortunately the President was well again in a few months, although his heart attack almost prevented him from running for reelection the following year.

What were Ike's "risk factors"? A good deal of medical progress in the last decade of the Health Century has consisted of pinning down risks that the President and his doctors knew about only vaguely in 1955, if at all.

Just before the heart attack, Ike and his pals had been away at a fishing retreat outside of Denver. Ike loved hearty menus, and in the days before the heart attack he cooked for the stag party breakfasts of "fried cornmeal mush with chicken-giblet gravy and sausages," dinners of "spareribs and sauerkraut, corn bread and black-eyed peas." The morning of the heart attack Ike had stirred up a breakfast of "eggs fried sunny-side up, rashers of beef bacon, sausages, and steaming mugs of coffee." Who could resist it? *Time* beamed with pride upon the manly President for his all-American diet.[25]

Then came the unfortunate heart attack, but as the President recovered in the Denver military hospital, his appetite returned. The following Friday "he asked for, and got, a stump of his favorite beef bacon." Weeks of convalescence followed, and the President continued to eat, without gaining weight, his beloved servings of steak, prime ribs of beef, and so forth. As the President's plane, *Columbine,* finally droned eastward on November 11, Ike tore into an on board lunch of broiled steak.

No one can blame President Eisenhower for relishing the typical American diet of the 1950s. To his side in Denver rushed America's premier cardiologist of those days, Boston's Paul Dudley White. Dr. White was a distinguished physician who has added much to the treatment of heart patients. But it was the 1950s, and who had heard of risk factors? So Dr. White appeared at a press conference, annotating press secretary James Hagerty's account of the President's progress:

HAGERTY: "The President had a good bowel movement."

WHITE: "I put that in . . . I said the country will be very pleased—the country is so bowel-minded anyway—to know that the President had a good movement this morning."

HAGERTY: "The President enjoyed a breakfast of prunes, oatmeal, soft-boiled egg, toast and milk."

WHITE: "Some people might say, why did he have eggs, since eggs now are being deprecated against? *[sic]* We have to supply some fat to the body."[26]

Indeed in the 1950s the country was bowel-minded and not cholesterol-conscious. That the President's diet was swimming in cholesterol and that cholesterol deposits in the President's coronary arteries were the likely cause of his heart attack occurred neither to this distinguished heart specialist in 1955 nor to the watchful press.[27]

In the 1950s smoking was considered of such unimportance in heart disease that Ike's long smoking history—he had stopped cold turkey in 1949—was not even mentioned. Physiologist Ancel Keys at the University of Minnesota pooh-poohed the whole issue. "Despite their poverty, many peasant peoples smoke as many cigarettes as they can get, and often down to the last tarry fraction of an inch, without developing heart disease."[28] As for the risk of overweight, Ike was only five pounds heavier when he was stricken than he was as a cadet at West Point. Exercise? The President played golf and bounded often around the courses. No, his major risk factor was the cholesterol in his diet.

If we are now able to dissect Ike's risk factors, it is mainly because of a remarkable study, sponsored by the NIH's heart institute, of a little town in Massachusetts called Framingham, about eighteen miles west of Boston. Framingham had twenty-eight thousand people in 1948, when Assistant Surgeon General Joseph Mountin decided to push ahead with a study of heart disease. The study would follow a group of normal people for a period of years to see who among them got high blood pressure, heart attacks, and strokes. This kind of study is called epidemiological, not because it involves epidemics but because one wants to see how lifestyle and biographical factors affect your chances of getting a disease. Someone at Harvard had suggested Framingham because the town's doctors were known to be cooperative. The original plan entailed following a group of volunteers.

In July 1949, a year after the NIH's heart institute had been established, director Cassius Van Slyke asked for control of the Framingham program. He decided to shift the study group from volunteers (who might not be typical) to a random sample of Framingham's population. After much persuasion, the organizers got some five thousand local residents between thirty and fifty-nine to participate and then followed them with regular checkups between 1950 and 1974.[29] The organizers were overwhelmed at how many of Framingham's adults, free of disease in 1950, developed heart disease as time went on. Fully one third of the men who had been in their early forties when the study began had signs of heart disease by 1974. Of the fifty-five-to-fifty-nine-year-old men who had been healthy in 1950, two thirds had developed heart disease by the time the study ended.

None of this heart disease was inevitable: atherosclerosis is not a normal accompaniment of aging, and in many parts of the world people stay free of it all their lives. But the consequences can be fatal in the prime of life. Almost a tenth of the men who were early-fortyish and healthy in 1950 had *died* of heart disease before 1974. And the rate of heart disease in men was twice that in women. Thomas Dawber, the director of the portion of the Framingham study that ran until 1974, wrote in 1980, "Coronary heart disease is predominantly a male disease."[30]

Why were so many healthy Americans developing a potentially fatal disease in their prime of life, a disease incurable by the medicine of 1950? When the study began, it was unknown whether an increase in one's cholesterol level would increase later risk of heart disease; whether smoking played a role in coronary artery disease; whether exercise offered protection, and so forth.[31] It was the accomplishment of the Framingham study, one of the finest achievements of the NIH, to change heart disease from an issue in the doctor-patient relationship to an issue of lifestyle.

What were the risk factors?

First of all, smoking. Although cigarette smoking had previously been linked to lung cancer, the Framingham study showed smokers ran higher risks of getting heart disease than cancer. In 1950 Framingham males in their thirties who smoked had a subsequent heart disease rate of 222 per 1,000; the disease rate of nonsmokers was 109 per 1,000. Smoking thus doubled the later risk of heart disease.[32]

It is difficult at the end of the Health Century to imagine that doctors once considered smoking a harmless habit. Into the 1950s medical journals accepted ads from tobacco companies showing doctors smoking, and the cigarette once fitted into the tableau of gentlemanly dignity in which doctors like to see themselves. Until recently the Merck company displayed in the lobby of its research building a large portrait of its director of research in the 1950s, Arthur N. Richards. Richards is portrayed with a cigarette in his hand. James Shannon smoked. Several of the brilliant team that came with him in the early 1950s to the heart institute smoked.

The epidemic of smoking that broke out among American males around 1900 is doubtless partly responsible for the increase in coronary heart disease from 1900 until the early 1960s: in 1900 the average American fifteen years and older consumed 49 cigarettes a year; in 1962, 3,988 cigarettes a year.[33] It was the cancer scares of the early 1960s that began the great smoking decline, but simultaneously heart disease also began to fall. The parallel between both these rises and falls is significant.

Solid findings bring results: the respect of the American people for science is one of their finest characteristics. People have started to stop smoking. (In Europe, by contrast, the same findings have had little impact on smoking.) In 1965, three years after the first Framingham findings that smoking helped cause coronary heart disease, 52 percent of American males still smoked. Eighteen years later male smokers had declined to 35 percent.[34] Post-1980 findings from the study indicated that once you stopped smoking, your risk of coronary heart disease declines to the level of a nonsmoker's within a year.[35] In Framingham itself, as findings from the study got back to the local population, one third of the middle-aged male smokers had already abandoned the practice by the late 1970s.[36] Dr. Claude Lenfant, the director in 1987 of the heart institute, said that, of around one thousand institute staff, only four or five still smoke today.[37] Getting much of the American public to stop smoking thus represents a historic achievement.

Second, the Framingham study singled out high blood pressure. Although the dangerousness of malignant hypertension had been long known, doctors did not understand at the beginning of the Framingham study the risks of even mild and moderate elevations of blood pressure. The study hammered home the message that there was no such thing as benign hypertension. Previously, doctors had considered high blood pressure a result of the patient's other diseases, and if the patient had no other disease, doctors labeled the hypertension as benign. Farewell to benign. Of the men age thirty to thirty-nine who entered the study in 1950 with normal blood pressure, only 39 percent later developed coronary heart disease; of the young men who had any elevation of blood pressure beyond 120 mm/Hg., 73 percent later developed coronary heart disease. And the higher the blood pressure at the beginning, the greater the risk.[38]

But perhaps hypertension just accompanied heart disease without causing it? Another major investigation the NIH conducted simultaneously established that heart disease could be reduced by lowering people's blood pressure. In 1973 the heart institute started a big program to study people with hypertension over a period of time: What difference would treating their blood pressure actually make? Among the eleven thousand participants whom the heart institute followed for five years, those receiving "stepped care" high blood pressure medication had a 17 percent lower mortality than those receiving the standard treatments of the day.[39]

The heart institute in Bethesda has also run a big education program about blood pressure. It publishes annual statistics on heart disease. As Claude Lenfant recently recounted the spectacular success of this program, he pointed to a chart and excitedly drew an X at the spot where the graph of deaths from heart disease plunges downward. "That's it," he said, "the beginning of our national high blood pressure education program in 1972." The titles of these various programs sound so clunky and bureaucratic that one's ears close at their names (Multiple Risk Factor Intervention Trial). But they have brought great good to the American public.[40]

The Cholesterol Drama Begins

The most important factor in most of this country's heart disease appears to be deposits of cholesterol in the coronary arteries, rather than high blood pressure or smoking, which play a role by worsening the effects of the underlying cholesterol problem. We know this, for one thing, because previous efforts to bring down hypertension with drugs did not reduce heart disease as much as the organizers of the studies had expected. In Japan, heart disease had been rare despite the frequency of hypertension and smoking until the Japanese changed their diets and began eating cholesterol-rich American-style foods.[41] As William Castelli, current director of the Framingham study, observed in 1986, "Three quarters of the people on earth do not get atherosclerosis and therefore do not get coronary heart disease. Fat intake in these people averages only 20 to 30 grams per day." By contrast, Americans eat 60 to 150 grams of fat every day, and coronary heart disease is their most common cause of death.[42] Although hypertension is the principal risk factor in strokes (increasing their frequency around sevenfold), and although smoking greatly exacerbates underlying coronary artery disease, the principal culprit in atherosclerosis is cholesterol.

Atherosclerosis simply means the laying down of fatty plaques on the walls of the arteries, and cholesterol is the principal component of the plaques. As the plaques increase in size, they may cause clots to form, pieces from which break off, coast downstream, and plug the coronary arteries; or the plaques and clots may grow to such dimensions they occlude the artery; or, even while the plaque remains small, its presence may cause the coronary artery to go into spasm, cutting off the heart's blood supply. In all three scenarios cholesterol-heavy plaques emerge as the villain.

Cholesterol appears, therefore, a very sinister substance. But in fact it's a basic component of body chemistry, and if we didn't get enough in our diets, the liver would have to make it. It is cholesterol, in the membrane of each of the body's billions of cells, that makes possible the passage of fatty substances in and out of the cell. Cholesterol constitutes, therefore, one of the very chemicals of life. But when permitted to circulate in excess in the blood, it adheres in a complex process to preexisting lesions in the walls of the blood vessels, and it slowly jams them up. Why these original lesions occur is still a mystery.

Alerting the public to the dangers of cholesterol is mainly an NIH story. Providing the drugs that may finally permit us to do something about it other than going on diets of cracked grain is an industry story. Both have crowned the last two decades of the Health Century.

Scientists had know for a long time that populations with low cholesterol had little heart disease. What was not known was whether a threshold of blood cholesterol existed above which one would start to risk heart attacks. Many physicians assumed that, just as supposedly benign hypertension existed, benignly elevated cholesterol levels might exist as well. The patients had no symptoms. Why put them on one of the standard lipid-lowering drugs of an earlier epoch, or force them to abandon richly marbled steaks, if they were not really at risk?

The Framingham study began to sound the alarm about moderate serum cholesterol. Whereas only 4 percent of the men age thirty to thirty-nine who entered the study with low cholesterol (less than 200 milligrams per deciliter) later had heart attacks, 19 percent of those with high cholesterol (greater than 260 milligrams per deciliter) were later stricken. Fewer than a quarter of the low-cholesterol men in their fifties later had heart attacks; *more than 40 percent* of the high-cholesterol men in that age group later did so.[43]

In 1962 the first publications from Framingham on these risks commenced.[44] Cholesterol levels in the American public began to decline. In 1960–62, 27 percent of American adults had high-risk cholesterol levels; by 1976–80 only 22 percent did so. Sufficiently alarmed had the elderly become, for example, that the percentage of people aged sixty-five to seventy-four with high-risk levels dropped almost a third over that period.[45]

After 1980 one warning bell after another began clanging. The Framingham people published in 1983 a horrifying table showing a smooth increase in the risk of heart disease with every increase in cholesterol above 190 milligrams. Men above 300 milligrams had more than three times the risk than men with normal levels; the corresponding risk for women was almost as elevated.[46] It was obvious that there was no threshold. Any increase was dangerous. In 1984 the heart institute published a consensus development conference statement that summarized results of research. One important previous study had been an NIH lipid clinic started in 1971, which along with other work made clear that "reduction of blood cholesterol levels *will* reduce the rate of coronary heart disease." The conference recommended that adults at even moderate risk immediately begin eating less cholesterol-rich food, and less fat generally, and that people at high-risk levels start some kind of medication.[47]

You must remember that the NIH wasn't preaching to the public. It was preaching to the doctors. The problem in getting a nation to cut down on inch-thick sirloin steaks was persuading family doctors to counsel their patients. As for drugs, the medical profession, in Basil Rifkinds's words, had already "had their fingers burned" with earlier compounds that attempted to lower blood fats (cholesterol travels linked to a category of fats called lipoproteins).[48] In 1959 the William Merrell Company of Cincinnati had patented a drug (triparanol) that had to be withdrawn in 1962 shortly after it was marketed because it caused cataracts in several patients. Clofibrate, another touted cholesterol lowerer, turned out to be largely ineffective.[49] So there was a lot of medical skepticism.

Then in the early 1960s Merck and Company developed a drug, cholestyramine, to reduce the itching from jaundice in patients who had things like gallstones. The drug turned out to reduce cholesterol as well, and in 1971 Robert Levy at the heart institute began a large clinical trial, in its lipid clinics, to see if it was an effective agent. In 1984 the NIH decided that it was.[50]

But the problem with cholestyramine, as Merck's retired scientist Jesse Huff explained, was that the large dosage reduced patient compliance, or willingness to take the drug as prescribed; it tasted like rotten fish, and it was composed "of a granular material that sandpapered part of your anatomy on the way out." The drug tended to cause fecal impaction in the elderly. Also, it was ineffective in reducing moderate cholesterol levels, although it did bring down by 10 or 20 percent the very high ones.[51] Clearly cholestyramine wasn't something you were going to put the average thirty-one-year-old man on and keep him on it for years.

There's one more wrinkle. As cholesterol travels in the blood it is linked chemically to several kinds of lipoproteins. Lipoproteins are molecules consisting of fatty acids and protein, as opposed to the free-form fatty acids that travel in the circulation as well. One kind of lipoprotein, called low-density lipoproteins, or LDL, is the bad kind: LDL takes cholesterol about the body and deposits it on the walls of cells lining the blood vessels. Although these cells need some cholesterol, they don't need as much as they get with the red-meat American diet. Another main kind of lipoprotein is, however, the good kind. Called high-density lipoprotein, or HDL, it goes about the blood vessels sweeping up cholesterol and bringing it back to the liver for excretion. So you want as much HDL as you can get, and as little LDL. The problem in coronary artery disease is that patients have, in addition to overly high levels of cholesterol, too much of the cholesterol linked to LDL.

It was Donald Fredrickson and his people in the molecular diseases branch of the heart institute who worked all this out in 1967.[52] The papers were among the most frequently cited of that era. Not only did their work constitute an important scientific achievement, it also represented another case of James Shannon's picking stars, for Shannon had brought Fredrickson to the heart institute in 1953. Fredrickson in turn in 1975 became a director of the NIH and later president of the Howard Hughes Medical Institute.

The stage is now set. We have in place a population of thirty or forty million people with elevated serum cholesterol who are more at risk of a heart attack than they'd like to be; we have a line of therapeutics of some efficacy that lowers cholesterol but tastes like rotten fish; we have the world's premier biomedical organization in high gear for a cholesterol crusade; and we have the profit motive.

The Cholesterol Drama: Act II

Merck and Company, with its $4 billion yearly net sales, is one of the biggest players in the drug industry and known moreover as a highly competitive player. With perhaps seven hundred Ph.D.s and a hundred M.D.s, the thousand-odd scientists in the research labs of the company's pharmaceutical branch, Merck Sharp & Dohme, offer deep strength in every drug product line except perhaps gynecology, which few of the big players nowadays will go near. While Merck is determined to make a profit for its shareholders, the company—like all the other large and successful companies—prides itself on its science. Its president (now chairman), Roy Vagelos, had come from Don Fredrickson's institute at NIH; Edward Scolnick, former vice president and now president for research, had a distinguished career as a Bethesda NIH scientist as well. And Merck's now-retired Maurice Hilleman, developer of many vaccines, is considered one of the scientific heavyweights in this country since World War II. But the company employs many distinguished scientists, men and women who are able to link the search for knowledge to the company's mercantile interests. There is nothing distasteful about putting science to work in search of profits: those profits are generated by better drugs, drugs with greater therapeutic qualities, fewer side effects, a longer half-life, or drugs that offer some other improvement upon those of the competition. Much of the profit will be reinvested in further research.

All this being said, competition in the industry is fierce. So when in 1976 the Japanese drug house Sankyo announced it had found a drug that would block the formation of cholesterol in the liver, Merck became curious. The company had been attempting since 1953 to find a product that would inhibit cholesterol synthesis—an obvious strategem for lowering blood cholesterol. And indeed Carl Hoffman, a Merck scientist, had synthesized mevalonic acid in 1957, a key intermediate in the body's pathway of cholesterol synthesis.[53]

So Merck asked Sankyo to send over a supply of their new blocker, and as soon as it arrived, the company tried it out. Sure enough, it inhibited mevalonic acid, thus lowering cholesterol, just as the Japanese had claimed. So Merck worked out the chemical structure of the Japanese compound and started looking for its own analogue. This is the way you do things in a highly competitive industry.

The Japanese had made their blocker by fermenting it in systems of *Penicillium* fungus, so Merck tried different fungal systems—settling finally upon the species *Aspergillus terreus*—to see if it could produce something roughly similar. Merck drew upon its extensive screening program for fermentation compounds, and the product of fungus after fungus was put into test tubes to see if it would inhibit the liver enzyme that makes mevalonic acid, thus inhibiting cholesterol.

One day late in November 1978, the lab technician reported to Alfred Alberts, the project director, "Nope, once again no activity, except in one of the test tubes where we must have made a mistake because there's nothing left."

Alberts remembers, "My heart was in my mouth. 'Go back and check it again,' I said." Indeed the mass screening had stumbled across a highly active compound. But was it the same as the Japanese compound?

Merck's chemist Georg Albers-Schonberg recalls the excitement as in February 1979 the product arrived on his desk. A desperate rush was on: a Merck committee had to know by the following week if this fermentation product was different from the Japanese compound. The source of the rush was entirely internal. The committee had been about to cancel the fermentation screening program on the grounds of low productivity. But now success! The product was different from the Japanese. Merck wouldn't have to buy the license from Sankyo.

There's many a slip between producing something in milligram quantities and scaling it up for production in tons. Could Merck's fungus be scaled up? Carl Hoffman, who had synthesized the key intermediate to cholesterol, found himself on this particular team. It is a sign of the shortness of corporate memory that Hoffman's discovery of mevalonic acid had now been forgotten. Alberts, the team leader, dimly remembered the name "Hoffman" from college chemistry and was astonished now to find himself Hoffman's boss.

Merck applied for a patent in June of 1979, although one might point out that in the drug industry, getting the molecule is just the beginning of a development process that takes eight years on the average and costs between $50 and 100 million. One must be able to produce a drug that will cure humans and not poison them. For testing such blockers, Merck had already in place a cell-culture system that Roy Vagelos had brought with him from the NIH, via Washington University of St. Louis. He and other members of this Bethesda-St. Louis team set up the system in Rahway, New Jersey. This is important because, unless you have some kind of test tube system of liver cells, you have no way of knowing whether your blocker is actually inhibiting the formation of cholesterol. It was the first such system, set up by a young Harvard postdoc in 1953, that got research in this area going. Merck also possessed an appropriate animal system, meaning laboratory dogs that were found to react suitably, which Jesse Huff had organized. The company was thus all set to go with a compound now temporarily named mevinolin—from mevalonic acid.

Well, Merck was all set until reports arrived that the Japanese compound apparently produced cancer in test dogs ("the greatest known carcinogen in dogdom," someone cracked).[54] At this point, according to Basil Rifkind at the heart institute, someone upstairs at Merck seems to have become very nervous about mevinolin and stopped its development. So the heart institute got on the phone to the company saying, "You're sitting on a marvelous product and should be moving ahead with it." Thus, NIH scientists, now glowing white-hot about an epidemic of cholesterol-caused heart attacks, began to take a practical hand in health.

The process of animal tests and human clinical trials is very lengthy, its tediousness further extended by periodic FDA reviews. By the end of 1986 it had become apparent that mevinolin, now renamed generically lovastatin, offered major promise in reducing high cholesterol levels when taken in combination with cholestyramine, and in reducing moderate levels when taken alone.[55] "Lovastatin is going to have an enormous impact on practice," enthused Rifkind. "For the first time we've got potency plus ease of administration. Barring toxicity, five years from now the drug will be huge." Indeed, *The Wall Street Journal* at the end of 1986 was talking of $1 billion sales a year.

And the market! Rifkind continued, "If the 240's [people with serum cholesterol of more than 240 mm/Hg.] jump into lovastatin, that's 30 to 40 percent of the population." Although uneasy about treating a lifestyle disease this way, Rifkind nonetheless felt that lovastatin offered the possibility of changing enormously the public health: "We think you can actually eliminate coronary heart disease, and you can do that by lowering LDL." So Merck submitted its new drug application, or NDA, to the government in November 1986. Perhaps lovastatin will develop unexpectedly toxicity as it is "put into" millions of patients, or perhaps it will fulfill the expectations of *The Wall Street Journal.*

What transforms this drama from a standard scenario of drug wars to high science is the arrival of two independent players from academe: Michael Brown and Joseph Goldstein. They represent a kind of teamwork almost unique in medicine: collaboration based on genuine friendship. Jack Orloff, who as scientific director of the heart institute knew them well when they were in Bethesda, said, "Envy usually destroys these things. But Brown and Goldstein *alternate* prestigious lectureships." Indeed it is true. When they won the Nobel prize in 1985, both their names appeared on the single lecture.

The story begins in Boston, at the Massachusetts General Hospital, when Joe Goldstein, a South Carolina boy who is doing a residency in medical genetics, meets Michael Brown, a New Yorker from Brooklyn who's just come to Mass General as a resident in internal medicine, with an M.D. from Penn in his pocket. It is 1966. Two years later the two pals go to Bethesda to work in differing labs of the heart institute concerned with how genes regulate enzymes: Brown to Earl Stadtman's lab and Goldstein to Marshall Nirenberg's lab. Molecular genetics is exploding around them. Nirenberg has just won the Nobel prize in that year. Goldstein looks after some of Don Fredrickson's patients in the campus hospital who have a striking genetic disorder in which their cholesterol goes sky-high. The duo are intrigued by the yellow accumulations of cholesterol in the skin of these patients, and by their recurring heart attacks. "That was our mutual recognition that it was a really interesting disease," they said later.[56] At the NIH the partners also become addicted to duplicate bridge.

In 1970 the two pals move to the huge health science center of the University of Texas at Dallas. They work together on the genetic regulation of cholesterol, indeed sharing the same lab after 1974.

Now, the two briefly separate during a time in the early 1970s that Goldstein spends in Seattle. And in Seattle he discovers that about a fifth of all heart attack survivors have a significant hereditary component in their high blood lipids. Perhaps excessive LDL itself is somehow genetically controlled? That is exactly what Brown and Goldstein find out in their next seven years of research: a specific gene codes for a specific LDL receptor in the liver.

As Brown reconstructed it, the triumph goes back to the NIH days. "We had both been trained at the NIH in very basic, fundamental laboratories. . . . So in Dallas we set up tissue cultures, took skin biopsies from these patients, put the biopsied cells in tissue culture, and then we measured the ability of these cells to regulate their cholesterol production." If the cells have lost this ability, it suggests that the gene has gone haywire, reducing, or downregulating, the number of receptors for LDL-linked cholesterol in the liver; so the cholesterol will stay in the blood, ultimately finding its way onto the walls of the arteries and causing hypercholesterolemia and its accompaniment of atherosclerosis.[57]

Brown and Goldstein went on to explain lovastatin's mechanism of operation in patients whose high cholesterol is not genetically determined. Lovastatin interrupts the synthesis of cholesterol in the liver cells. We know that already; but this interruption causes the cells to increase the number of receptors for LDL on their walls: the more LDL receptors you have, the more they bind circulating LDL cholesterol, the less serum cholesterol you have. This Brown and Goldstein found out. Their work, and especially the discovery that lipid metabolism is under genetic control, won them a Nobel prize in 1985.[58]

They altogether deserve their prize, but giving all the credit to them for establishing the *practical* applications of their insight raised a few collegial hackles at Merck. Brown and Goldstein had been doing their test tube experiments at Dallas with the Japanese blocker that was mentioned earlier, and the reductase enzyme that the drug inhibits had been supplied by the Japanese as well. Fair enough.

But another version of the story—supplied by Jesse Huff and Alfred Alberts—is that Michael Brown attended a Merck meeting as a consultant. There he heard about lovastatin and how Merck had developed it, went back to Dallas "and immediately bought up every dog in Texas," said Alberts. What Brown heard that advanced his and Goldstein's animal research was that you have to do the studies on lab-bred dogs. They don't work on street mongrels. Second, you have to add cholestyramine to the lovastatin to bring down very high cholesterol levels. Both these concepts, claim Alberts and Huff, the two Dallas scientists got from the Merck scientists.

Huff and Alberts were in no way begrudging of praise toward the Dallas duo. "Brown and Goldstein showed us how this drug worked," said Huff, "that it fooled the body and induced these receptors. They were able to prove their own thesis and establish the mechanism of our drug."

But this rather poignant little story illustrates the larger point that drug company scientists can be touchy about the attenion received by academics.

When Robert Spiegel, an academic cancer researcher, was thinking about accepting a job at Schering-Plough, an important drug house, he discussed the matter with his friend Stephen Carter, whom we shall meet in the next chapter. Carter had been at NIH, knew the ropes, and was then working at Bristol-Myers.

Spiegel asked Carter what it was like to work for a drug company.

"You have to lose some of your ego," said Carter. "You are in charge of a scientific program at a company, and if you isolate a compound early in development and it looks very interesting to you and you put the resources behind it and hire some extra people and nurture this program and it works out, it goes into the clinic. When some investigator there finally does the study and writes the article in the *New England Journal,* the press is going to say, Dr. So and So found a new treatment for lung cancer. It's not going to be you."[59]

"He Died Last Thanksgiving on the Restaurant Floor"

We are looking down on Dr. Henry Spotnitz and a fifty-seven-year-old man who's just been painted orange. The scene is one of the heart surgery suites of Columbia-Presbyterian Medical Center in New York, now a bit dingy but still one of the great citadels of American medicine. Schoenheimer and Chargaff were at Columbia, but the new princes are the heart surgeons like Spotnitz, a short, intense man who asks the tough questions at rounds.

The patient, who worked in a car dealership, has a variety of heart disease that puts him at risk of sudden death: malignant arrhythmia. An arrhythmia is any disturbance in the normal beat of the heart, and while some arrhythmias are innocuous, this man's heart tends to start beating very rapidly (ventricular tachycardia, "tachy-" meaning "fast"). Then his heart might begin writhing in an incoordinated way, so that bundles of muscle fiber contract randomly rather than in a single coordinated squeeze (ventricular fibrillation). The heart is no longer pumping out blood at this point; then it stops altogether. Because the major complication of tachycardia and fibrillation in the ventricles is death, these are grave conditions. About four hundred thousand Americans die every year from such malignant arrhythmias.

This man had died the previous Thanksgiving, which is to say, his heart had stopping beating. It was in a restaurant; his psychiatrist wife stretched him on the floor and began to resuscitate him by pressing rhythmically on his chest (cardiopulmonary resuscitation, or CPR). But he'd been a cardiac cripple going back ten years before: a smoker, two previous heart attacks that had left scars. Because of atherosclerosis, one of the major arteries on the heart's right side (the right coronary) was completely plugged and the main artery on the left, the left anterior descending, or LAD, was somewhat blocked. Previous scarring and the inadequate blood supply meant the heart was only putting out a fifth as much blood as normal. Thus this wounded, inadequately oxygenated heart muscle, straining desperately to supply a bit of blood to the body, would periodically go into arrhythmia.

Spotnitz was going to do two procedures on the man's heart, bypass a portion of the right coronary artery with a piece of the man's leg vein (a coronary bypass operation), and implant an electrical device that would automatically shock the heart back into a normal rhythm whenever in the future it started beating abnormally.

The busy bees swarm about the orange man. They put a catheter in a neck vein to thread down to the right side of the heart and monitor the pressure; various tubes run in and out of his mouth. The patient is covered with green drapes. The surgeons begin their dramatic double-gloving, extending their arms in a high regal gesture as the nurses slide on the gloves. Spotnitz is now wearing a "miner's cap," a helmet with a pinpoint light attached.

What happens in open-heart surgery is very simple. A vertical incision is made in the middle of the chest; there is little bleeding. The surgeon takes a pneumatic saw and splits open the breastbone, or sternum. Big metal retractors, attached to a frame, winch open the chest. The membrane encasing the heart (pericardium) is sliced and peeled back. We're now looking at the beating heart.

Tubes (cannulas) are attached to the veins that return blood to the heart from the head and from the body. Another tube is attached to the root of the aorta. These tubes will be hooked up to the heart-lung machine that oxygenates the blood while the heart is stilled. Thus the tubes attached to the venous side will run into the machine, and the tube attached to the aorta will run out of it. Meanwhile the big disks of the machine will slowly revolve, introducing air into the blood in place of the bypassed lungs. Spotnitz makes a small incision in the aorta and punches the cannula right in.

Meanwhile, a physician's assistant is dissecting the saphenous vein from the leg. The leg has other veins that will take over once the saphenous is removed. Now another small cannula is punched into the aorta at its very root, where it leaves the heart. This cannula will pump a sodium-potassium solution into the coronary arteries, stopping the heart by chemically jamming the "pumps" of the muscle cells. The heart-lung machine is now going. The heart is beating very slowly. A net is slung under the heart like a cargo net at dockside to make it easier to manipulate the organ.

Spotnitz sews one end of the now-detached saphenous vein to the aorta, the other to the downstream end of the right coronary artery. An hour and three quarters have now passed since the operation has begun.

At this point, a resident comes up and dumps a bucket of cold water right on top of the heart; he just swooshes it out as though he were cleaning his kitchen floor. The heart has just stopped. The function of the cold water is to reduce the oxygen demands of the heart's cells, so that they won't die while the operation is on. Remember that the heart isn't receiving any oxygen while the bypass is in effect.

Of interest is what Spotnitz does next. He is implanting an AICD, or automatic implantable cardioverter and defibrillator. In a heart attack, if the heart begins tachycardia, it has to be cardioverted, or restored to normal rhythm. If the heart begins to fibrillate, it must be defibrillated. This machine will do both by supplying an electric shock whenever its minicomputer senses an abnormal rhythm. The minicomputer is programmed with an image of the normal rhythm and thus can recognize an abnormal one. The AICD has two sensing electrodes, which Spotnitz stitches to the wall of the right ventricle where the heart's electrical current originates in each beat; the AICD has two patches that emit the shocks. Spotnitz stitches these to the outside of the heart front and back.

Ten days later the generator will be installed in the wall of the man's abdomen. In preparation for this, Spotnitz makes a little tunnel through the fat of the thorax and abdomen, and he draws wires through it down to the pouch in which the generator will be placed. The generator will be good for two years, or a hundred shocks. Hopefully the man will not need any shocks, to say nothing of a hundred. Spotnitz has done twenty of these implantations so far with only one death, in a patient who already had extensive heart damage and ongoing disease in the coronary arteries.

From the heart surgeon's viewpoint, the touchy part of the operation now begins: Will the team be able to wean the patient off the bypass pump? Will they be able to start the heart again?

"Set the defibrillator," he says. He shocks the heart, and it starts beating again, very slowly. The heart needs to warm up. We look at the grafted vein now successfully implanted. It is filled with blood.

At this point the heart suddenly begins to fibrillate. It looks like a bag of worms as various muscle bundles writhe and twist. The ECG registers little blips on a screen showing the heart's electrical activity. They should march regularly across the screen. It goes flat. Spotnitz attaches another electrode to pace the heart with outside current. The ECG returns to normal but it's artificial. If the man's heart does not reacquire its own electrical rhythm, he cannot be weaned.

Minutes pass. Spotnitz removes the artificial pacing electrode. The man's heart begins its own regular beating. Little green blips once more file steadily across the screen.

Spotnitz calls out, "He's looking terrific."

These devices really do have the capacity to do great good. One woman, Lisa, who received an AICD was a retail salesperson. She had a heart disease in which her right ventricle was paper-thin and arrested on her wedding night. Her husband, a medical technician, resusciated her with CPR. Her physicians started her on the various drugs to control this kind of thing, but she arrested again. Once again, her husband was on hand and brought her back. She received an AICD. It has since fired twenty times. "That's twenty deaths," says one of Spotnitz's residents.

Another patient who received the AICD, Richard, was sixteen at the time he was seen. He had two sisters. One had been a sixteen-year-old with idiopathic hypertrophic cardiomyopathy, meaning that she had, for unknown reasons, a disease of the heart muscle that gave her an enlarged heart. Her parents had come home unexpectedly when her boyfriend was there; she gave a gasp of fright and dropped dead. A year later Richard's other sister dropped dead at nineteen. At that point Richard was evaluated at Columbia-Presbyterian and found to have a large heart too. He received an AICD, and as of two years later it has not yet fired.

At the end of the Health Century the United States strains at the very edge of change in heart surgery. But it was not long ago that surgery on the heart appeared infeasible. Sir Stephen Paget, one of the founders of chest surgery, said in 1896 that heart surgery had probably got about as far as it was going to go. "Surgery of the heart has probably reached the limits set by Nature to all surgery: no new method, and no new discovery, can overcome the natural difficulties that attend a wound of the heart."[60] From the viewpoint of these men the difficulties attendant upon heart surgery seemed insuperable. For starters, there was no way of knowing exactly where the problem lay: which artery was blocked, which portion of the muscle was scarred. No anticoagulants existed to keep the blood from forming clots that would cause heart attacks and strokes. For delicate operations on tiny coronary vessels and valves, surgeons need a highly visible (well-exposed) operating field and a motionless heart. But not until 1953 did it become possible to stop the heart and still keep the patient alive.[61]

The story of heart surgery before 1953 is the story of successful operations performed for unusual diseases, or unsuccessful operations performed for common diseases. A common "traditional" heart ailment, meaning before the epidemic of atherosclerosis began, was the cementing, or stenosing, in a half-open position of one of the heart's main valves, the mitral valve. It is the valve that opens the left ventricle so that blood may flow from the left atrium into the ventricle, and it is called the mitral valve because its two triangular flaps were thought by ancient anatomists to resemble a bishop's miter. Thus in mitral stenosis the stenosed valves don't open wide, keeping the ventricle from filling completely; instead, blood backs up in the atrium and, behind that, into the lungs. Nor is the half-filled ventricle able to supply the body's oxygen needs. The patient is tired, short of breath, and coughs up blood from the backup of pressure in the lungs.

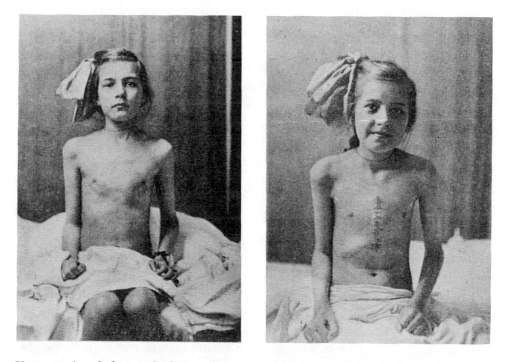

Young patient before and after cardiotomy and first successful valvulotomy for mitral stenosis, performed by Dr. Elliott Cutler in 1923.

That is what ailed the twelve-year-old girl whom Elliott Cutler saw at Boston's Peter Bent Brigham Hospital on May 15, 1923. She'd had episodes of sore throat until about age six, probably contracting the streptococcal infection called in those days rheumatic fever; the bacteria in her throat had caused an inflammatory reaction in the flaps of her mitral valve and plastered them rigidly together. Now she had a fast pulse, breathed in short little gasps, and was coughing up bright red blood. Her doctors could hear all kinds of rumblings and roarings in her heart as the atrium tried to squeeze blood into the ventricle, and as the ventricle tried to force it out into the body.

What was to be done? Previous doctors had attempted to operate on mitral stenosis in experimental animals, usually with the result of destroying the valve. She seemed about to perish anyway, so the Cutler team gave it a try. They plunged a hooked knife into the wall of the left ventricle. "The knife was pushed upward about two and one half inches, until it encountered what seemed to us must be the mitral orifice." They then fumbled around with the knife for a bit, withdrew it, and closed her up. Afterward they had no idea what structures they had reached nor what was going on in her heart. And although the operation hadn't killed her—history's first successful valvulotomy—she was no better than before.[62] By 1929 there had been six further operations for mitral stenosis, with only one patient surviving. Clearly, operating on the valves of the heart when one couldn't see what one was doing was not the wave of the future.

In the ensuing years everything changes. The most urgent heart problem becomes coronary artery disease and not sticky valves from strep infections. Surgeons become somewhat less wary about approaching the heart once catheterization lets them visualize radiologically its interior. And when in 1944 the Hopkins pediatrician Helen Taussig proposes to surgeon Alfred Blalock an operation on the heart's external tubes that involved reconnecting several of them—an operation that succeeded brilliantly in relieving a rare congenital heart condition—surgeons begin to think more aggressively about confronting heart disease.[63]

The two chief stumbling blocks become at this point stopping the heart so as to hold this squirming mass still for an operation, and visualizing the arteries of the heart so that one can see exactly where the blockage lies. They are solved only five years apart.

The story of the heart-lung machine began in 1931 at Massachusetts General Hospital, when John Gibbon, a young intern, was assigned by his chief, Edward Churchill, to monitor a woman with a pulmonary embolus, a blood clot in the artery leading from the heart to the lungs. "During that long night, helplessly watching the patient struggle for life, the idea naturally occurred to me that if it were possible to remove continuously some of the blue blood from the patient's distended veins, put oxygen into that blood . . . and then inject continuously the now red blood back into the patient's arteries, we might have been able to save her life." As it was, she became unconscious at 8 A.M. the following morning and stopped breathing. "Within six minutes and 30 seconds Dr. Churchill had removed the embolus and closed the opening he had made in the pulmonary artery, but the patient could not be revived."[64]

After getting a post at the University of Pennsylvania, Gibbon and his wife, Mary Hopkins Gibbon, a skilled technician, resolved to make such a

machine. Gibbon's colleagues thought the quest idiotic. His friend Eugene Landis gave him encouragement. But privately even Landis believed
the enterprise doomed.[65]

Yet the Gibbons pressed on, first inventing crude devices that kept
animals alive while their hearts were stopped. "I shall never forget the day
when we *did* succeed in performing all the work of the heart and lungs with
our machine, with no blood flowing through the animal's own heart and
lungs. My wife and I thought some sort of miracle had occurred." This was
in 1935.

Finally in 1953 they perfected a heart-lung machine that kept an eighteen-year-old girl alive while Gibbon repaired a hole in the wall between
her left and right atria. Did Gibbon go on to do a great series of operations? No. Having risen to the challenge, he lost interest in the heart and
turned his hand to liver disease.[66]

Five years later Frank Mason Sones and his colleagues at the Cleveland
Clinic accidentally solved the second obstacle to operating on the heart's
arteries. Sones was a cardiologist who also did angiography, injecting dye
into blood vessels with a catheter and then watching where it went on a
fluoroscope. Catheterizing the heart had been practiced since 1941. Indeed the discovery was of such magnitude that its inventors had won a
Nobel prize in 1956, three years after the Gibbonses invented their heart-
lung machine.[67] But, revolutionary though it was, "cardiac cath" involved
merely sending the tip of the catheter into one of the heart's big chambers
or great vessels. Coronary cath entailed inserting the catheter into the
entrance of one of the coronary arteries, which have their origin at the
base of the aorta just as it leaves the heart. It was deemed impossible in the
1950s on the grounds that the tip of the catheter might send the artery
into spasm, killing the patient. In 1958, as Sones attempted to cath the left
ventricle, he noted to his horror that the tip of the catheter had drifted into
one of the coronary arteries. It was clearly visible on the screen, but the
patient continued to be fine. "That fortuitous event taught Sones that,
contrary to views held at that time concerning electrical instability of the
heart, nonoxygen-carrying fluid could be injected into a major coronary
artery without untoward event."[68] In October 1958, Sones made the first
deliberate attempt to visualize the coronary arteries and began making
motion pictures of what he saw on the fluoroscope.[69]

A visitor to the Cleveland Clinic around this time, a small-town GP from
Argentina named René Favaloro, became intrigued by these films. He
would spend hours looking at Sones's home movies of coronary arteries.
The visitor soon turned into a permanent member of the clinic. Now
everything is in place: techniques for seeing where the blockage is and for

John and Mary Gibbon inspect their heart-lung machine, which was first success-fully in 1953, when it kept an eighteen-year-old girl alive while he repaired a hole in the wall between her left and right atria.

Human malignant melanoma cultivated in mice lungs allows immunologists to study the manner in which tumors spread from one part of the body to another, and to evaluate the ability of biologic response modifiers and chemotherapeutic drugs to halt their spread. (Photo courtesy SmithKline Beckman Corporation)

Human colon carcinoma cells are stored by cryopreservation in liquid nitrogen. (Photo courtesy SmithKline Beckman Corporation)

One of the major health lobbyists, Mary Lasker cofounded the Albert and Mary Lasker Foundation to secure federal support for research in mental health, birth control, and cancer. She is currently on the board of the American Cancer Society. (Photo courtesy Brown and Powers Associates, Inc.)

Gerald Laubach, president of Pfizer, Inc., exemplifies the new generation of pharmaceutical leaders highly attuned to the role of biotechnology. (Photo copyright Michele Singer, 1985)

Human cells—kept alive in the red nutrient solution—producing leukocyte interferon. The water surrounding the jars is kept at body temperature (98.6° F). The Styrofoam balls keep the water from evaporating. (Photo courtesy Hoffmann-La Roche, Inc.)

bypassing the heart so that it may be repaired. In 1967 Favaloro operated "under bypass" on a woman who'd been having angina for three years. Her coronary arteriograms showed a complete blockage of her right coronary artery. Favaloro took a piece of her saphenous vein and stitched one end to the aorta and the other to the downstream portion of the blocked artery. She recovered uneventfully and was thereafter free of angina. It was the first *published* instance of successful bypass surgery.[70] It is important to emphasize "published" because three years previously, in 1964, Michael DeBakey and his colleagues at Baylor in Houston had done a bypass operation but neglected to write it up.[71] By the time Favaloro returned in 1971 to Argentina from Cleveland, he and the Cleveland group had done more than twenty-two hundred coronary bypass grafts, losing fewer than 3 percent of their patients. By the mid-1980s more than a million Americans had undergone bypass operations, and around two hundred thousand are currently being done every year. The coronary artery bypass graft has placed in the shadow every other form of operation on the heart.[72]

We have almost reached Henry Spotnitz's operating room. In addition to a bypass operation, the reader will recall, Spotnitz also implanted in the fifty-seven-year-old car dealer an automatic defibrillator. Using a single large jolt of electricity on the skin of the chest to abolish the "bag of worms" and restore the heart's normal electrical activity goes back to Harvard's Paul Zoll. Zoll knew of some Russian research at the end of the Second World War giving an electrical current externally to a fibrillating heart. But how did one apply it to clinical use? Zoll first did a number of animal experiments, then in 1952 he applied a series of shocks to two patients whose hearts were at ventricular standstill. The first one died, the second recovered well.[73] This marked the beginning of much research on external electrical shocks for fibrillation and cardiac arrest.[74]

The outcome is well known to any follower of hospital life or the hospital soaps: the frantic race through the corridors once the arrest code has been called with such signals as 555 or code red, the nurses and residents tearing open the arrest kit and plunging in an intravenous line. Start the epinephrine. Apply the defibrillation paddles to the chest. Zap, zap. Nothing. Start the lidocaine. Zap, zap. Nothing. Start the . . . Thus implanting a defibrillator to replace this desperate and often unsuccessful chase was an idea whose time had come.

In the late 1960s Michel Mirowski and his co-workers at the Mount Sinai Hospital in Baltimore developed, in cooperation with Intec Systems of Pittsburgh, the first prototype of what we have already been introduced to as an AICD, or automatic implantable cardioverter and defibrillator. By the early 1970s they had overcome a number of technical problems, such as packing the large amounts of energy required into tiny lithium batteries. They established that not nearly as many joules are needed when the electrodes are planted directly against the heart as when they are applied externally to the chest; and they figured out how to program the AICD's minicomputer to recognize tachycardia and fibrillation.

After extensive animal trials, Mirowski's group implanted in February 1980 an AICD in the first human patient at the Johns Hopkins Hospital: a fifty-seven-year-old woman with intractable angina; she had a history of a heart attack eight years previously, followed by bypass surgery; the surgery had not overcome her persistent arrhythmia. She was a perfect candidate for sudden death, but with her new AICD the woman was discharged "well" and stayed well as long as they followed her.[75] These AICDs promise to end that thirty-year medical era in which the nurses and doctors would look at one another at the end of an arrest and say, "Well, I guess we can give up."

By the mid-1980s, nearly 345,000 deaths every year that would formerly have occurred from coronary heart disease are now being averted.[76] This number is staggering. More than a third of a million lives are spared every year thanks to our new understanding and treatment of the human heart.

SEVEN

Cancer

In 1953 *Today's Health,* the American Medical Association's magazine for the public, published a story about Mary, a three-year-old girl with chicken pox. She seemed to have a very hard case of it. Her body was covered with spots, and her normally sunny disposition had turned to crankiness. "What a joy she was before she became sick!" her mother said. "She could never stand still or walk. She had to dance and run. And sing? She sang all day long like a happy bird."

But then she didn't run or dance anymore. "She walked slowly, sometimes stiffly, as if it was hard to bend her knees. And she didn't sing anymore. Most of the time she sat quietly in her father's easy chair, looking at picture books or dozing."

The parents thought the chicken pox was dragging on for rather a long time. So they called the doctor, a real old-style family doctor who was important to residents of their small town. He examined Mary and said, "Children are like this. Mary'll be out of bed in a day or two." But as he spoke, he kept his eyes on Mary and didn't look at the mother, which was not typical of him.

One day Mary fell off her father's lap. "When we picked her up, we saw some ugly bruises on her, so her father went to call the doctor and I undressed the child. Before I slipped her nightie over her head, I noticed tiny marks like blood marks on her backside and legs. I didn't like the looks of those marks, and that was the first time I got the feeling that Mary was a very sick, a seriously sick child.''

But the family doctor reassured the mother and wrote out a prescription for a tonic. That Christmas, the Christmas of 1952, was a sad day. Mary fell asleep at the table after taking no interest in her presents. Her parents started thinking maybe they'd better see a specialist, but they didn't want to hurt their doctor's feelings.

"He might think we don't have faith in him," the mother said. "I didn't want to hurt our doctor. He didn't deserve to be hurt."

"Not Doc," said the father. One sees what the doctor-patient relationship once was. In any event, the family doctor was more than happy to arrange an appointment with a specialist.

"The city doctor examined Mary and took samples of her blood. Then he asked me if Mary had been getting orange juice." The doctor told the mother that Mary had one of two things, scurvy or . . . but he didn't mention what the second thing was. The mother's hands started trembling. She was unable to fasten the snaps on Mary's leggings.

The mother then watched Mary closely. "I saw the little-old-lady look in her face and bearing. And I couldn't believe she was the healthy, strong baby I had borne! My Mary had disappeared."

The next Saturday they returned to the specialist's office. The office was full of patients but the receptionist let them right through. The doctor's greeting was courteous, but short and gloomy. He read to them from a sheet of paper. "This is the report of your child's blood. Her blood shows an extremely large number of white cells." In an infection the blood will show many white cells, but these cells were peculiar. He told them Mary had leukemia. Mary had two or three months left to live, the doctor explained.

Although the parents did take Mary to cancer specialist Sidney Farber's ward in the Children's Hospital in Boston, where she remained alive until the article describing her experience was published in May 1953, it is unlikely that she lived much longer because in 1953 childhood leukemia was still a fatal disease.[1]

The story of young Mary is important because in cancers such as hers we have made great progress during the Health Century. But cancer is mainly a disease of the elderly, not of children like Mary. Although the fear of it begins with middle age, the disease affects mainly old people. Two thirds of those who die of cancer are over sixty-five.[2]

Nine hundred thousand Americans develop cancer annually. Let's talk about the third of them that are not elderly. For example, in 1984,

1,800,000 potential years of life were lost in people dying of cancer *before* the age of sixty-five. This contrasts with 1,600,000 potential years of life lost from heart disease, or 100,000 potential years lost from diabetes.[3] But even though the losses are terrible, we have made great strides in fighting the disease in the last two decades, and this chapter brings good news and hope.[4]

Early Struggles

Cancer is not a modern disease. The ancient Greeks told accounts of women who would develop hard lumps in their breasts, have pain throughout the neck and shoulder blades, become emaciated and die. Similar accounts of cancers that begin as local lesions then spread, or metastasize, fatally throughout the body, recur throughout Western medical literature. What is distinctive about the twentieth century is that now we can *do* something about cancer, where doctors were helpless before.

Consider how utterly helpless Ulysses S. Grant's physicians were when in 1885, at age sixty-three, the ex-President developed soreness around his right tonsil. His doctors saw an ulcer at the base of the tonsil, did a biopsy, and made a diagnosis of cancer. This was two years before the Health Century started. Beginning with the work of Berlin physician Johannes Müller in 1838, doctors had been establishing differences among types of cancers with the microscope and determining that cancer was not some foreign body but merely the body's own tissues growing out of control. So they were able to diagnose Grant's epithelioma.

But treat him? They gave him gargles of saltwater and iodine, dilute carbolic acid, potash, and yeast. Also cocaine to relieve his terrible sore throat. These remedies did not arrest the spread of the disease; soon much of his throat and small palate were destroyed. In this kind of cancer the major risks are bleeding to death, or suffocation if a piece of tumor clogs the windpipe, or starvation because one is unable to swallow. Grant's weight dropped from nearly 200 to 146 pounds. "After a severe spell of threatened suffocation during the night of March 29, 1885 . . . he passed his days and nights in a sitting position with his feet resting on a chair." Wanting to spend his last days in a pleasant setting, Grant had himself moved to Mount McGregor, New York, a small resort village near Saratoga, and instructed his personal physician to terminate the specialists' "desperate efforts to save me." Grant died five weeks after his arrival in Mount McGregor, the course of his illness differing little from other such deaths across the millennia.

Oh yes, there was one difference. Grant was a smoker, in a sense a victim of the Civil War in which he commanded the Union armies. He had apparently been quite a light smoker before he led the attack on Fort Donelson, a Confederate stronghold on the Cumberland River in Tennessee, in December 1862. This episode first brought Grant to national prominence.

After riding back to his troops from a visit to the commander of a federal gunboat, he was met by a staff officer who told him the enemy was attacking vigorously. While giving the order for counterattack, Grant rode forward carrying an unlighted cigar in his hand. Grant said, "In the accounts given in the papers, I was represented as smoking a cigar in the midst of conflict; and many persons, thinking no doubt that tobacco was my chief solace, sent me boxes of the choicest brands from everywhere in the North. As many as 10,000 were received. I gave away all I could get rid of but having such a quantity on hand, I naturally smoked more than I would have under ordinary circumstances, and I have continued the habit ever since."[5] Thus although the course of Grant's illness was thoroughly traditional, he became among the first cancer victims to die from a modern cause.

U. S. Grant's cancer was not typical in another respect as well: he was a man. Until late in the nineteenth century, cancer afflicted women much more heavily than men. One of the first cancer statistics comes to us from the Italian city of Verona, where between the years 1760 and 1839 doctors diagnosed cancer in 1,136 patients, 87 percent of whom were females. Whereas 17 percent of all deaths in women were attributed to cancer from 1700 to 1750 in the German town of Einbeck, only 7 percent of male deaths had that diagnosis. This imbalance is due partly to the ease of diagnosing breast and cervical cancer in women—the commonest cancers in women until recently. But the more deeply hidden cancers are equally distributed between the sexes, and there is no reason to think that until the nineteenth century, cancer was not chiefly a woman's disease.[6] Even within recent memory in urban America, cancer has struck women with more force than men. In Boston between 1903 and 1912, women had a 19 percent higher death rate from cancer than men. Men in Boston endured more cancer of the mouth from smoking clay pipes, but almost every other category of cancer was more common in women. The same was true in those years for Chicago, Pittsburgh, and Providence. In Philadelphia the female cancer death rate doubled that of the male, as in several other big cities.[7]

Then in the 1930s the staggering rise in male lung cancer began that overturned for the next forty years the historic preponderance of female cancers. In 1935 lung cancer deaths were still relatively infrequent, overshadowed statistically by malignancies of the stomach, intestines, and prostate, the important male cancers. In 1935 lung cancer was twice as frequent in males as in females, a reflection of men's earlier start in smoking.

As male smoking further increased, the frequency of lung cancer in men rose ninefold from 1935 to 1974, and lung cancer deaths in men became four times as common as in women. In 1974 lung cancer was far and away the commonest male cancer, representing a third of all male cancer deaths. By this point male cancer deaths had become *50 percent higher* than female cancer deaths.[8] Few graphs of medical statistics are more dramatic than the chart (see page 208) showing the dramatic rise of lung cancer at the same time as other kinds of cancer remain stable or decline. Because Ulysses S. Grant didn't inhale his cigars, he got cancer of the throat rather than of the lung. Lung cancer is a disease of cigarette smokers.

Lung cancer thus helps us understand something very interesting: the increasing tendency for women to live longer than men. In 1900 women's life expectancy at birth (forty-eight years) was only two years longer than men's (forty-six years). Today women's life expectancy at birth (seventy-eight years) is seven years longer than men's (seventy-one years).[9] An important reason is that from 1900 until about 1950 many more men than women smoked.

What progress have we made curing these terrible diseases? The three strategic routes to curing cancer are surgery, radiation therapy, and chemotherapy (drugs). Typically, the bulk of the tumor is reduced surgically, the stragglers of the tumor in the affected region killed with X rays, and the distant "mets," or metastases, treated with drugs. Of these three, surgery is the oldest form of treatment.

Surgery for cancer had to await such innovations of the nineteenth century as anesthesia and germ-free operating conditions (asepsis). Not until the 1880s did these operating room realities give surgeons enough experience that they felt able to tackle major procedures. In 1881 Vienna's Theodor Billroth first removed the malignant portion of a stomach; in 1898 Ernst Wertheim of Vienna performed the first radical hysterectomy for cancer of the cervix (the cervix is the bottom third of the uterus), removing the entire uterus and tissues surrounding it. Throughout the 1880s William Halsted at Johns Hopkins performed an operation for breast cancer that entailed excising the entire breast, underlying muscles and the lymph nodes in the arm pit; this was the now controversial radical mastectomy, which he reported in 1891. Although today this Halsted operation tends to be seen as surgical overkill for breast cancer, at the time it called the attention of American physicians to the feasibility of cancer surgery.[10]

With Wilhelm Röntgen's discovery of X rays in 1895, radiotherapy became a possibility for treating cancer as well. It was used for the first time by a Chicago medical student in 1896 named E. H. Grubbe who happened to own an electrical equipment shop on the side. Because he had the apparatus, his professors referred to him a woman with breast cancer.[11] For technical reasons, radiotherapy and treatment with radium advanced much more slowly than did surgery. Yet by the 1930s two of the three prongs—surgery and radiation—had increased overall survival rates in cancer from virtually zero to about 20 percent.[12]

What had not come into play up to this point was drugs, late off the blocks because one cannot give these potent substances to humans before first trying them on animals. And not until 1903 did someone devise a method of transplanting tumors into lab mice, without which there could be no practical drug research.

"We Were Practically Pseudo-Charlatans"

Chemotherapy for cancer ironically finds its origins in the mustard gas attacks of World War I. In autopsies done on mustard gas victims it was noted that their lymph glands were destroyed, their bone marrow wiped out, and that they had few white cells remaining, a logical consequence of the destruction of the bone marrow, which makes white and red cells for the blood. Around 1930 James Ewing, a cancer specialist at New York's Memorial Hospital (later part of the Memorial Sloan-Kettering Cancer Center), suggested to colleagues that they try mustard gas on various cancers. They found it too toxic for internal use, although it did work on skin cancer.[13] There matters rested until World War II made the American government once again interested in the uses of mustard gas.

In 1942 Yale University signed a contract with the wartime research office to study sophisticated new varieties of mustard gas, and Louis Goodman and Alfred Gilman—authors of the "Bible" of pharmacology— who were members of Yale's pharmacology department were assigned to the nitrogen mustards. To assess what happens to mustard gas in the body, Goodman and Gilman injected rabbits, then noted how quickly the rabbits' white cells disappeared from the blood. Their colleagues joked that the Germans weren't going to attack with hypodermic needles. No matter: Goodman and Gilman became extremely interested in what mustard gas did to white cells.

They asked their colleague Thomas Dougherty in the anatomy depart-

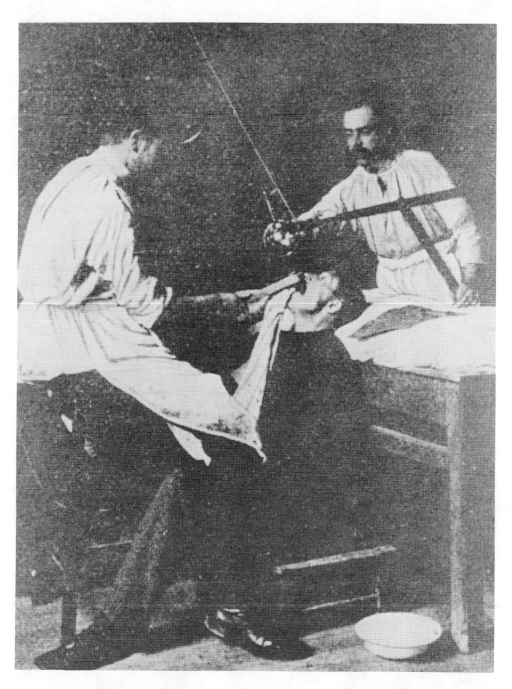

After Wilhelm Röntgen's discovery of X rays in 1895, radiotherapy became a treatment for cancer. Here we see an intra-cavitary treatment of carcinoma of the epiglottis, 1908.

ment to participate in a study. "Could one destroy a tumor with this group of cytotoxic [cell-killing] agents before destroying the host?" So they gave nitrogen mustard to a special mouse with an advanced lymphoma, a cancer of the lymph glands. The lymphoma softened and regressed. Recalls Dougherty: "I cannot remember exactly how many doses we gave, but the tumor completely regressed. This was a surprising event." They stopped treating the mouse for a while, the tumor returned; they started again, the tumor regressed; but after a while the tumor stopped responding to the nitrogen mustard, having become resistant. They had encountered what continues to be a big problem in cancer therapy: the tumors put up defenses to drugs.

Buoyed by their mouse success, in December 1942 the two pharmacologists persuaded a Yale surgeon, Gustav Lindskog, to give nitrogen mustard to a forty-eight-year-old silversmith in the hospital with advanced lymphatic cancer. As may be seen in the photograph on the previous page,

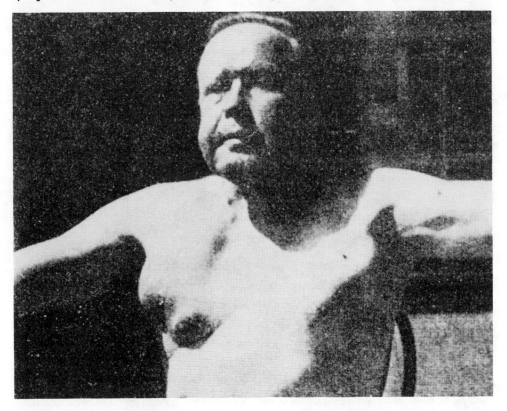

Patient in terminal stages of lymphosarcoma (lymphatic cancer) four days after initiation of tris (p-chloroethyl) amine hydrochloride *treatment by Yale surgeon Gustav Lindskog in 1942.*

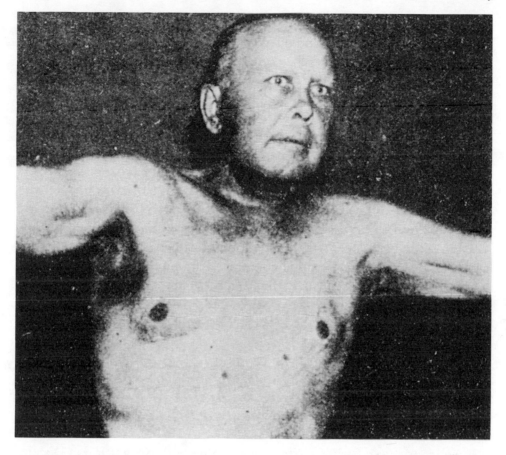

Patient in terminal stages of lymphosarcoma eight days later and two days after last dose. Note that the tumor masses receded.

the tumor masses had swollen his face and upper body. "Chewing and swallowing had become almost impossible, and a tracheotomy set [for cutting into his windpipe] was kept close at hand for immediate use." The patient's response was dramatic. The tumor masses receded. But then, as in the mice, the tumor grew back once the drug was stopped, and finally the tumor became resistant to the nitrogen mustard altogether. In June of 1943 the nitrogen mustard group at Yale moved on to other tasks, but in the meantime, researchers at Chicago and Memorial Hospital in New York had taken up the work. Because of the top secret nature of mustard gas, not a word of this had thus far been published.[14]

Nitrogen mustard is an example of a class of cancer drug called alkylating agents: they form permanent cross-links between the two strands of DNA in the cell's nucleus so that the cell can't divide, thus stopping the multiplication of cancer cells. Of course such agents also prevent every other cell in the body from multiplying, thus wiping out the hair follicles so that one's hair falls out, and the cells of the intestinal lining so that one has diarrhea. But historically they represent the first effective drug against cancer.

To keep our historical story straight, however, a second drug must be mentioned before we proceed with the first. In the late 1940s the scene shifts to Boston's Children's Hospital, where cancer specialist Sidney Farber, encouraged by such reports of success as Goodman and Gilman's, resolves to try drugs on the feared childhood cancer leukemia.

In leukemia, a single line of white cells in the bone marrow proliferates out of control, and as this line of cells grows wildly, it kills all the other white cells and the red cells, making the children liable to hemorrhage (because some white cells figure in blood clotting) and to infection (because, as in AIDS, the victim is completely immunosuppressed). Could another class of drug, less toxic than the nitrogen mustards, be found to stop cell division in the unchained white cells? Farber hit upon a member of the vitamin B complex called folic acid. Someone had found that folic acid caused the regression of breast tumors in mice. Did it do so in humans? No. Farber tried some out on his little leukemia patients and it made them worse. So how about something that blocked folic acid? Thus a folic acid antagonist? Farber asked the chief of the Lederle company's research labs, Yella Subbarow, to synthesize some folate antagonists, or antifoles, as they're known.

In February 1947 Farber started trying some of these, getting in December clear remissions with one called aminopterin. His staff would look at specimens of the child's bone marrow, and the leukemic cells would be gone. Nothing like this had ever been seen in cancer therapy before. Unfortunately, the patients all relapsed after an interval, most of them later dying.[15] So although aminopterin wasn't a cure, it set many researchers to thinking that leukemia could be beaten.

Now the scene shifts to Bethesda. Cancer research in the Public Health Service had begun in 1922, when pharmacologist Carl Voegtlin started studying the effects of metals on tumors that had been transplanted into mice, thus establishing the tradition of calling in-house cancer specialists at the NIH "mouse doctors."[16] The Public Health Service also set up a field station for cancer research in Boston, and it was the Boston group that Michael Shimkin, an irreverent young scientist like Erwin Chargaff, joined in 1938. Congress had established a special National Cancer Institute in 1937, and in January 1940, the Boston group joined the core Washington Hygienic Lab group in occupying the new building. Shimkin described the scientists and administrators of the Washington group as

Research staff of the National Cancer Institute at its regular weekly meeting. Projection on screen behind them is of a cancer specimen. This famous Life *cover was so stagey that it embarrassed the scientists who posed for it.*

"characteristically a silent lot, tending to sit on the back rows and to become involved in introspection. In the days before air conditioning, it was pleasant to drowse under the large, sunny windows."[17]

Nor did the original NCI types establish themselves as scientific fast-laners with the passage of time. When Shimkin came back to Washington in 1954 after a sojourn in the field, he realized that "the good-hearted Heller [John Heller, NCI director from 1948 to 1960] had a rest-and-rehab center for officers who had not met their mark in previous assignments or had various personal problems."[18]

The problem that afflicted not just NCI but all cancer research until the mid-1950s was the suspicion, indeed contempt, with which bedside doctors, or clinicians, viewed drug therapies for cancer. They believed cancer an incurable disease, and that putting these poisons into dying patients merely stripped whatever dignity they possessed in their agonal moments. "We were practically pseudo-charlatans *[sic]*," said Stephen Carter, who had come onto staff at NCI only in 1967. "People used to talk about the poison-of-the-month."[19] Vincent DeVita, now the director of the NCI, recalled of those early years, "As much energy was expended in the scientific community to stop cancer drug development as was exerted to get it off the ground."[20] At Columbia's medical school (P and S), clinicians refused to give biochemists access to their cancer patients.[21] Thus cancer research was, until the early 1950s, a "graveyard for scientific reputations," in scientist Michael Shimkin's words. "Many scientists of the time considered research on cancer a waste of time."

A series of events in the early 1950s turned cancer chemotherapy from a backwater to a rushing torrent of medical progress. One was the opening of the NIH's campus hospital in 1953, giving cancer researchers access to in-house patients.

Second, in 1953 Congress instructed the NIH to do something about childhood leukemia. "A stimulating factor . . . was that a neighborhood child of a staff member of an influential Congressman had died of leukemia," said Shimkin.[22] There were hearings. Sidney Farber came down from Boston with photographs of a leukemic child before and after therapy. Money became available.[23]

Third, the "doctor draft" coming on the heels of the Korean War suddenly threw up an elite cadre of young internists and surgeons who were happy to spend two years doing research in Bethesda rather than sewing shrapnel victims back together. In Gordon Zubrod's view, it was quite specifically their arrival on campus that brought "patients with disseminated cancer from the dark recesses of nursing homes into the bright light of medical care of university quality."[24]

Finally, in 1954 came Zubrod himself, a man with a considerable reputation in drug research, who'd been on Shannon's antimalaria team during the war and had recently done a stint at Hopkins. He had come to NCI as medical director of all these new hospital beds. In his charge fell the institute's new mandate to do something about childhood leukemia. Now the players are assembled.

Among the kinds of cancer that became curable in the years 1955 to 1965, we look at two: an unusual pregnancy cancer and childhood leukemia. Their importance lies in establishing the idea that cancer could be conquered. At the end of the Health Century this is the possibility, the hope, that now beckons to us.

The first cancer to be cured with drugs—not just put into remission but actually cured—is an unusual cancer that may occur in early pregnancy. As the conceptus begins to grow, some of its cells (those that would later form the placenta) begin multiplying out of control. This cancer, called a choriocarcinoma, once led to death in six months.

The pieces began taking shape when Roy Hertz became the chief of endocrine cancer research at NCI in 1947. Long interested in chorio, a kind of endocrine cancer, Hertz had started admitting patients with it to the clinical center as soon as it opened in 1953. Now other doctors joined this endocrine team, among them a young naturalized American named Min Chiu Li with an M.D. from Mukden Medical College in China, who'd done an advanced degree at the University of California, then spent several years in cancer research at Memorial Sloan-Kettering. As it came time for Li to do his doctor draft service, he opted to spend the two years at Bethesda, and thus was accepted in Hertz's service. Li had known of Hertz's work with endocrine cancers and had himself treated several such cancers at Sloan-Kettering, so it's not as though Li's mind was entirely unprepared.

One weekend in late August 1955, while Li was the physician on call at the clinical center, a woman was admitted through the emergency room who had had a huge stroke. She died shortly thereafter. Li became quite upset at hearing that her underlying problem was a metastatic chorio and that she previously had been left untreated. He wondered if methotrexate, a drug similar to Farber's aminopterin, might do something for the disease.

"Two months went by before I had my first opportunity to test the validity of my theory. One day we received a telephone call from Dr. William Lucas . . . a young medical officer of the Naval Medical Center across the highway from the clinical center. He stated that he had examined a twenty-four-year-old woman . . . who had a few metastatic nodules of chorioadenoma in the lungs." Lucas knew that Hertz's team was interested in the whole problem. Did the team have anything to offer?

"I met with the patient, her husband, and Dr. Lucas," Li continued. "After the patient's initial refusal and resistance, she was finally admitted to the clinical center in good physical condition." But while Li was organizing his plan of treatment in the next days, she suddenly had a huge lung hemorrhage and became moribund. Hertz's group had a conference and decided to leave up to Li whether he would proceed with his methotrexate plan or not. Li felt there was nothing to lose, as untreated she would die, and so he began to agonize about a key kind of decision in the story ahead: the size of the dose. Everything depended on this relatively technical matter: too little and people die from the cancer, too much and you run the risk of making their last days awful from the treatment. He and his associate pharmacologist, Paul Condit, settled on 50 milligrams of the drug to be given by IV. The patient started to improve. They gave her four more big doses over the next four days—more improvement. Good nursing care helped her over the terrible side effects during the next three weeks. She was able to leave the oxygen tent, to sit in a chair, and two months later she was virtually well again. Using the same dosages and plan of "intermittent" treatment, they cured a second chorio patient in March 1956, and a third in April. It was clear that the drug methotrexate, in Zubrod's words, "did indeed cure one type of metastatic cancer."[25]

A Nobel prize at once? Not exactly. The accomplishment was pooh-poohed, on the grounds that chorio had its origin in fetal tissue and thus differed from true cancer. The real test came with childhood leukemia, or acute lymphocytic leukemia (ALL), as it is known. Up to this point parents who brought children with leukemia to the hospital were simply told to take them home, and even Farber had extended the time of "remission" by only a few months. The NCI was taking on the most notorious disease of childhood.

Here a different team ran with the ball, not Hertz's endocrinologists but a group under Zubrod led by a young doctor named Emil ("Tom") Frei who had come from St. Louis to NCI in 1955. That year another powerful personality, as different from Frei as chalk from cheese but with a similar name, joined Frei's leukemia team: Emil ("Jay") Freireich, a Chicago boy with a Chicago M.D. "Jay is regarded by a lot of people as being strange, outlandish, highly outspoken, but brilliant," said Vince DeVita much later. "When I came to the leukemia wards, Freireich was my mentor. Frei's job in those days was to keep Freireich from getting in trouble. When he got in trouble it was smoothing the path over afterward. Freireich had a zillion ideas."

Stephen Carter, now the director of cancer research at Bristol-Myers, was at the cancer institute until 1976 and remembers Freireich as the real genius of the two, "in the sense that his mind was phenomenally fertile. Ideas would just pop out of the guy's head. But he was a terror, very, very difficult to deal with, very intolerant of anybody who he felt didn't understand what he was talking about." Freireich's arrogance used to make DeVita so mad that Freireich thought DeVita was going to hit him. For example, DeVita had learned as a resident at Yale that you didn't mix antibiotics. When DeVita came down to Bethesda in 1966, "it was Freireich wanting to give not only combinations of antibiotics, but intravenous antibiotics that said on the bottle never give intravenously. He'd worked all this out." Then Freireich would put DeVita up against the wall —DeVita is a big man but Freireich is huge—and argue at him until he'd convinced him. "You could see that he was right," said DeVita.

Frei, by contrast, was the smoothy of the team, "Mr. Inside," as opposed to "Mr. Outside," as someone said. Carter: "Tom took Jay's ideas and was able to implement them in a very effective manner. So that the two of them worked beautifully together." Thus Tom and Jay, Frei and Freireich, drove forward the conquest of childhood leukemia.

The first problem the team faces is controlling the infections and hemorrhages of the disease. They'll use massive antibiotics to handle the infections. Freireich solves the hemorrhage problem with the idea of giving transfusions of platelets, a blood substance involved in clotting. Getting enough platelets means huge raids upon the clinical center's blood bank. They win in a showdown with the blood bank director.

They decide to attack the disease itself in a quantitative manner, meaning not just collecting anecdotes of results but following on a daily basis what the bone marrow is doing and shifting drugs accordingly.

Their first trial in 1955 gives the patients methotrexate and one other drug, but *not* in combination. A fifth of the patients get complete remissions, meaning no more disease visible in the bone marrow, but relapse anyway, meaning they've still got leukemia somewhere.

Their second trial, undertaken in 1958, tries to increase the remission rate by giving combinations of drugs. That year a pediatrician named Myron Karon joins them who's had experience with combination therapy and with a new kind of cancer drug called the vinca alkaloids (vinblastine, later vincristine). They give various drugs, balancing the toxicity of these highly poisonous compounds against the results they're getting in the bone marrow. The remission rate climbs from 20 percent to 90 percent. This is clearly the right track: doing combination therapy. Hit the cancer simultaneously along a number of metabolic pathways so that it doesn't develop drug resistance. The problem is that the patients continue to relapse.

It is now 1961. The team realizes they're within reach of curing leukemia if they can just work out the drug schedule. The VAMP program begins, giving their little patients four powerful drugs at once: *v*incristine, *a*methopterin (methotrexate), 6-*m*ercaptopurine, and *p*rednisone. And not just quick doses of these toxic chemicals but long courses: each four-drug combination lasting ten days, with two weeks between, for a total of five courses.

But was that long enough? Will the patients die anyway after this exhausting therapy. Here the last hero of the leukemia drama arrives onstage: a Birmingham biochemist named Howard Skipper at the Kettering-Meyer Labs Southern Research Institute. DeVita is very sentimental about Skipper: "He's one of the greatest thinkers in cancer chemotherapy. . . . Even though he's not an M.D., he's one of the greatest mouse doctors in the world." What Skipper does is develop the cell kill hypothesis. How long do you have to give the drugs? Long enough to eradicate every last leukemia cell. How long is that? Here we do a few calculations, based on studies in mice of how long it takes a single leukemia cell to double, and for those two cells to double again, and so forth.

In one of our leukemia patients there are about one trillion leukemia cells, weighing about a kilogram. But it doesn't suffice to remove 99 percent of that kilogram. You must also remove the *last milligram* of tumor, even the last cell. Skipper says that it takes as much treatment to get that last milligram as the whole previous kilogram. He determines that treatment must be maintained for 164 days at least. Skipper's concepts are applied and we start getting not remissions but cures.

Elizabeth Good, one of many young patients whose acute lymphocytic leukemia is now in remission after treatment with asparaginase. The long-term survival rate for children with acute lymphoblastic leukemia has risen from 4 percent in the early 1960s to about 65 percent today.

Meanwhile another problem has lifted its head: after a period of remission, some of the children are getting headaches. The leukemia cells are hiding in the brain and multiplying there, because the VAMP drugs don't cross the blood-brain barrier. What to do? The solution is found at the St. Jude's Children's Hospital in Memphis, Tennessee: give radiotherapy to the central nervous system; participants in the project from other universities (group B) inject methotrexate into the spinal cord. This solves the hideaway problem. By 1963, scientists were reporting cure rates of 50 percent in this once-fatal disease of childhood.[26] Today, the long-term survival rate for children with acute lymphocytic leukemia is about 65 percent; for other childhood cancers cure rates are as high as 88 percent.[27]

What has been the secret of success? New drugs? Well, to some extent. The Eli Lilly company in Indianapolis donated supplies of vinblastine and, in 1961, vincristine as its scientists isolated them from a kind of periwinkle bush. The jawbreaker, "6-mercaptopurine," had been available since 1952 from the Burroughs-Wellcome Company, then at Tuckahoe, New York.

But unlike penicillin for pneumonia, curing leukemia involved more than grabbing a bottle off the shelf. The key turned out to be how you *applied* the medicines already available: massive doses, given over long periods of time, in combination with other drugs. And that was an organizational question. In fact, Gordon Zubrod had spent some time at IBM in 1961 learning how to organize a task force. It was the leukemia task force he set up after returning that swept the team on to victory. Stephen Carter on Zubrod's role: "These ideas would never have come to fruition without the organization, the ambiance, the intellectual stimulation he gave, and his ability to sell the concept to NIH."

The success of Zubrod's team with childhood leukemia led Congress to demand task forces for every kind of cancer.[28] In the years ahead the backs would be broken of Hodgkin's disease, kidney cancer in children, and other feared blood cancers. But important though these victories have been, the real success of the NCI's cancer drug program in the 1960s was to prove that it could be done, on the model of James Shannon's antimalarial drug campaign or the antibiotic campaign before it. When DeVita reflected back upon the campaigns against Hodgkin's and against another adult blood cancer in which he'd been active, he said, "These cancers are easily curable, easily. I think the important part of these experiments was just to show you could do it, that you could cure cancer with drugs."

Cancer Viruses and Two Brave Women

We go back to an earlier incident, the story of Bernice Eddy and her blowing the whistle in 1954 on the presence of live virus in Jonas Salk's supposedly inactivated vaccine. This discovery had not been well received at the NIH. Rather than promoting her and giving her charge of the polio vaccine program, the new administrators swept in by the Cutter incident took her off polio altogether and put her back on flu viruses. About this time Eddy started to become interested in cancer.

She'd always been interested in cancer. Back in the mid-1920s, doing a Ph.D. in bacteriology at the University of Cincinnati, she remembered palling around with the med students: "I had an apartment so we'd have dinner down there and harangue about all kinds of subjects and cancer was one of them. We didn't see why it couldn't be some kind of organism." She had done most of the first two years of courses with the meds. "I saw some of these cancer patients from time to time and, oh, they were horrible. It was one of the worst-looking diseases, you know. They'd still be alive and yet just in such terrible shape. I guess it just stuck with me that there ought to be something you could do for them."

So we have in 1956 a restless Bernice Eddy, age fifty-three, resentful about being punished as a whistle-blower and endowed with a long-standing interest in cancer. Enter Sarah Stewart. She too had been trained as a bacteriologist at the University of Chicago, and she came to the PHS in Washington in 1936, one year before Eddy. Both women had been part of that group of female scientists having bag lunches in the sun on the steps of the Hygienic Lab in downtown Washington. They were fast friends.

Unlike Eddy in biologics control, Stewart had an appointment from 1947 onward at the National Cancer Institute. And she was extremely interested in possible viral causes of cancer. Up to this point cancer virology virtually did not exist. Then in 1953 Ludwik Gross, working alone in the basement at a veterans hospital in the Bronx, had discovered a virus that produced tumors in mice. This officially had broken open the field. Using some techniques Gross had developed, Sarah Stewart published a paper in 1953 on an apparently viral agent that caused leukemia in mice. But in this kind of research she didn't have what scientists call an "assay system," a laboratory culture in which you could reliably grow your virus and do experiments with it. Precisely such cell cultures were Bernice Eddy's area of expertise, and around 1956 Eddy showed Stewart how to grow her suspect viruses in a mouse cell culture. The two women then in 1957 made a major discovery. They found that the virus Stewart had been working with caused cancer in every animal it was given to. They called it the SE polyoma virus.[29] "SE" means Stewart and Eddy. "My contribution was the poly, and hers was the oma," said Eddy. The polyoma was particularly important because, up to that time, scientists had thought of viruses

Sarah E. Stewart. Working with Bernice Eddy in 1957, she found the first virus—named the SE polyoma virus—that caused cancer in a wide range of animals. Until then, scientists thought viruses caused cancer mainly in birds.

as causing cancer mainly in birds (Peyton Rous having discovered the first such chicken cancer virus in 1908).

The name Ludwik Gross is now legendary in cancer virology. The name Sarah Stewart remains virtually unknown. Why is that? At least part of the answer lies in a certain disregard for the work of women that earlier dogged the culture of science. Alan Rabson, now a senior administrator at NCI, remembers the events: "When I got here in 1955, they told me that Sarah Stewart was an eccentric lady who thought that tumors were caused by viruses. No one believed her. . . . She was what people called an intuitive scientist. She really did not know how to do science the way rigorous scientists do."

Apparently the established bacteriologists at NCI didn't like her work. Her experiments were thought badly conceived and carelessly conducted. Rabson says, "The thing that bothered them all was that she said she was going to prove that cancer was caused by viruses."

The honchos explained to her that "you don't do science that way. You don't set out to prove something." Sarah said that she really didn't care. Rabson comments, "She thought that they were picking on her because she was a Ph.D. and not an M.D."

So Sarah Stewart went to med school. She enrolled in Georgetown Medical School at the age of thirty-nine and became the first woman M.D.

to graduate from there, interning at the same PHS hospital on Staten Island at which Joseph Kinyoun had been.

Rabson continues the story. "She came back and said now she was ready to prove that cancer is caused by viruses. The director said not around here you won't. So they wouldn't let her come back." Finally Burroughs Mider, the scientific director of the cancer institute, found her a lab in the PHS hospital in Baltimore.

"She did these classic experiments on the polyoma in Baltimore. She used to periodically come over to the campus and bring her slides and show them to the pathologists in our lab. They all thought she was very eccentric."

Why did these male scientists think Sarah Stewart eccentric? "First of all she was very secretive, because she thought Gross was trying to steal everything from her, and that everyone was trying to steal her work, which was true, because she was onto a very important discovery. She would show us slides but never tell the details of the experiments. So when she would show us a very unusual tumor which we'd never seen anything like before, we would ask how did you produce it?

"She would giggle and say it's a secret. She drove everyone crazy."

Stewart never did "controls," meaning study what happens to mice who didn't get the virus. She and Eddy would grind up tumors from cancerous mice and isolate the virus from those tumors. The scientists wanted to know if the noninjected mice got cancer.

"I remember," Rabson continues, "that one day Sarah looked at me and giggled and said, 'I never do controls. They only confuse you.' In fact, it turned out at that point that all the mouse colonies on the campus here were riddled with latent polyoma virus, and if she had done controls, she would have gotten tumors with the controls. So she was right. It would only have confused her."

Sarah Stewart and Bernice Eddy's discovery of the polyoma in 1957 marked the real takeoff of theories about virus and cancer. "It was a major, major discovery," says Rabson. "All of a sudden real virologists jumped in. It could be destructive like polio, but produce tumors at the same time. Suddenly the whole place just exploded after Sarah found polyoma."[30]

Although Stewart was later promoted within the cancer institute, she did not in her lifetime win the recognition she deserved. She died of cancer in 1976, Bernice Eddy remaining close to her until the end. "She was a forceful individual who did not let anything stand in the way if she could help it," said Eddy.

This is an interesting story, but in terms of drama it's nothing compared to what happens next. At the same time in the late 1950s that Eddy and

Stewart were producing cancers in animals with the polyoma virus, Eddy had sneaked back to the polio vaccine. Remember from chapter three what a chamber of horrors Salk's inactivated polio vaccine had been for the NIH in 1955. Surely all the problems with the polio vaccine had then been cleaned up?

Not exactly. "I did things on the side which I wasn't assigned to do," Eddy said. One of them was starting to conduct safety experiments on the polio vaccine in June 1959, from which she had officially been removed four years earlier. In observing cells from the kidneys of rhesus monkeys under the microscope—the kind of cell preparation from which the polio vaccine was being made by private drug companies—Eddy had noted spontaneous degeneration, meaning that the cells would start to die without any apparent cause. She did more experiments with these cells, and on July 6, 1960, reported to her chief, Joseph Smadel, that when she injected preparations from those monkey kidneys into hamsters, the hamsters got cancer. Tumors grew in newborn hamsters at the site of injection; probably a virus in the monkey cells was causing the cancer.

The story that follows is such a sad one, partly because Smadel himself was a distinguished scientist, not just a petty bureaucrat. Shannon had made him associate director of the NIH in 1956 to help clear up the polio vaccine mess following the Cutter incident. Smadel had remained in Building One until the end of June in 1960, when, finally tired of administering, he became the virus lab chief at the biologics division where Eddy worked. But even in 1956 Smadel had taken a lively interest in the biologics division and was presumably well informed about the escapades of its members. Thus he was not pleased, just after assuming his new post in viral research, when Eddy threw this time bomb onto his desk: the possibility of a cancer-causing virus in the polio vaccine.

In August he sat down with Eddy, went over her data, and dismissed the findings as "lumps." He thought her lumps unrelated to the degenerative changes (vacuolation) that other scientists had observed in the kidney cells of other monkey species, and he dismissed the possibility that the lumps might be cancer or cause the disease in humans. He must have been very nasty at the time, for he later wrote to Eddy, "It is my recollection that I was not even diplomatic in telling you that you had no basis for either statement." This was not out of character for Smadel, who was generally known as brusque and authoritarian, although his earlier relations with Eddy while he had been at Walter Reed had been cordial. DeWitt Stetten remembers Smadel as "a very difficult man to work under . . . a heavy-handed man, arbitrary and difficult."[31] Even Maurice Hilleman, a close friend and an admirer of Smadel's, said, "You only got along with Joe if

you could outcuss him. Anybody who was bright didn't do so good; anybody who was a little bit retarded did very well because Joe felt sorry for
them. Joe was very humanitarian."[32]

The Eddy problem landed again on Smadel's desk when, in October of
1960, she gave a talk at the New York meeting of the Cancer Society. At the
meeting she described finding a cancer-causing virus in the monkey cells
from which the polio vaccine was grown. Thomas Rivers of the March of
Dimes Foundation was in the audience and later told Smadel what Eddy
had said. Smadel hit the roof. "Smadel called me up," Eddy said, "and if
there was anything in the English language—any awful name—that he
could call me, he did. Oh, he was mad. I never saw anybody so mad."
Smadel wrote Eddy a letter later that day forbidding her to speak in public
again without clearing a written text of her remarks specifically with him.
That was just the beginning.

In the meantime, events were moving ahead in the outside world. Maurice Hilleman, developer of many famous vaccines, had gone at this point
to the Merck company, one of the companies making Salk's inactivated
polio vaccine as well as Sabin's activated variety. Sabin's vaccine was then
in massive field trials in Europe and the Soviet Union. Quite indepen-
dently of Bernice Eddy, Laurella McClelland, a viral specialist in Hilleman's vaccine division at Merck, had noted something funny in the
monkey kidney cells on which the vaccine was being safety tested. These
were cells not from the kidneys of rhesus monkeys, from which the polio
vaccine was being produced, but from a species of African green monkey.
Hilleman had asked the director of the Washington, D.C., zoo to bring
some monkeys in for him other than rhesus because the rhesus variety
were all infecting one another with these weird viruses en route from
Africa to their American laboratory homes. So the zoo director was supposed to bring in some green monkeys via Madrid, where there was no
other animal traffic. The greens were flown to Philadelphia, where Merck
drivers picked them up. Hilleman's team then put into the kidneys of the
green monkeys extracts from the rhesus monkeys' kidneys, and the green
monkeys' kidneys started to show pathological changes. For some reason
the viruses the rhesus monkeys were carrying didn't destroy their own
kidneys, but they destroyed those of the greens. (In Hilleman's view the
AIDS virus reached North America via these African monkeys.)

So Hilleman had to give a paper on some subject of interest for the
Sister Kenny Foundation, the counterpart for Sabin of the March of Dimes
Foundation that was backing Salk. He decided upon "How to Detect
Undetectable Viruses." It was clear to Hilleman that a number of different

viruses remained in the vaccine. He warned Albert Sabin, who was to be in the audience, that bad news was coming.

"I said, listen Albert, you and I are good friends. But I'm going to talk about a virus that's in your vaccine now. You're going to get rid of the virus. Don't worry about it, you're going to get rid of it. So of course Albert was very upset with me."

Hilleman told Sabin there was something special about this virus. "I don't know how to tell you this, but I've been around vaccines for a long time. I just think this virus may have some long-term effects."

Sabin said what?

"I said cancer. I said Albert, you probably think I'm nuts, but I just have that feeling."

In the meantime, Hilleman said, "we had taken this virus and put it into hamsters." Their hamsters got cancer, just as Bernice Eddy's had. "So the joke of the day was that we would win the Olympics because the Russians would be loaded down with tumors." (Sabin had field-tested his oral polio vaccine extensively in the Soviet Union.)

Hilleman presented his own findings formally at a conference in Copenhagen at around the same time Eddy was having her unpleasant conversations with Smadel. Hilleman, accepting the suggestion of a colleague at Eli Lilly, named the virus responsible for the microscopic changes in the kidney cells SV 40, or Simian Virus 40, meaning that thirty-nine other of these monkey viruses had already been identified. A Yale group with an electron microscope then determined that SV 40 and Sarah Stewart's polyoma were basically the same virus, but one infected mice, the other monkeys. Nothing about SV 40 causing cancer had yet come out in either the scientific literature or the press, although insiders were aware. Alan Rabson, who with his wife, Ruth Kirschstein, attended the Copenhagen meeting, said, "Everyone in the grapevine knew that."

Since both polio vaccines had at this point been given to millions of children, members of the grapevine were now frantic to find out what was going on. "Everyone was very excited," said Rabson of the reaction at NIH. Hilleman had thought that the inactivation procedure used on the Salk vaccine probably killed SV 40.[33] But it was only recipients of the Salk vaccine who became infected with the SV 40 virus because the inactivation procedure didn't kill it. Only they had antibody traces of the virus in their blood. Recipients of the Sabin vaccine had no SV 40 antibodies. The virus was killed in their intestinal tracts.[34] The Russians, supposed to show up at the Olympics dragging with tumors, were safe![35]

In the spring of 1961 all became clear. One of Eddy's co-workers published the news that indeed live SV 40 virus was present in the polio

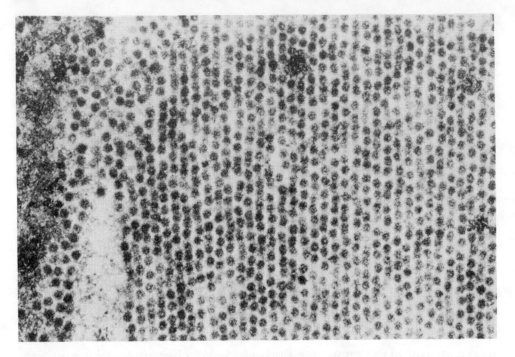

SV 40 virus particles. This cancer-causing virus was present in some of the monkey cells from which the polio vaccine was grown.

vaccine. The director of the biologics division, Roderick Murray, notified the Surgeon General that steps were being taken to ensure that future polio vaccines would be free of SV 40.[36] Finally, in July 1961, Eddy herself established that the cancer-causing agent in hamsters was SV 40, although she was not permitted to publish this finding until a year later.[37]

Only at this point does the drama, under way for eighteen months in the corridors of power, begin to come out in the press. On July 26, 1961, the New York *Times* reported that Merck and Parke-Davis, another vaccine manufacturer, were withdrawing their Salk vaccines "until they can eliminate a monkey virus." Nothing was said about cancer. The story ran next to an account about overdue library fines on page 33. Not until February 1962, did *Times'* readers, in a story on page 27, find out anything about cancer.[38]

Was this silence merely the incompetence of the press in the face of a complex scientific question, or was there a deliberate effort to keep a lid on the story? Albert Sabin was asked thirty years later why the silence? "I think to release certain information prematurely," he said, "is not a public service. There's too much scaring the public unnecessarily. Oh, your children were injected with a cancer virus and all that. That's not very good."[39] One recalls how badly the whole public health system had been burned by the Cutter incident five years previously. A second hue and cry in 1960 might have shattered public confidence in vaccines so badly that the toll in unnecessary disease would have been far greater than the risk of the contaminant. Still, a cancer-causing virus had been identified but not announced.

Do all those people who received the contaminated Salk vaccine in particular between 1955 and 1961 have cause for alarm? As Ruth Kirschstein, director of one of the Bethesda institutes, has pointed out, there are people walking around today with antibodies for SV 40, meaning that the virus has entered their bloodstream.[40] But while particles of SV 40 have been recovered from tumors in several humans, there is no evidence that the virus has caused cancer in the population. Those who received the vaccine, however, are still discretely being monitored by public health officials.[41]

Eventually, Bernice Eddy lost her labs. In successive measures she was denied permission to attend scholarly conferences, her papers were held up, and finally she was removed from vaccine research altogether. Her treatment became a scandal within the scientific community and was discussed in Senate hearings.[42]

What got Stewart and Eddy into trouble? Sexism within the PHS? Eddy didn't feel the men she worked with were "sexist;" the very term clangs unfamiliarly in the mouth of this woman now in her mid-eighties. Ruth Kirschstein was asked if Sarah Stewart would have had an easier time of it as a man. "Sarah would say so," Kirschstein responded. "I'm not so sure."

It may be that these women were treated as they were not because of overt discrimination but because they evidenced a somewhat different scientific style than did many of their male colleagues. Stewart's intuitive sense that cancer was caused by viruses is a case in point, and her attempts to prove something that she felt in her heart to be true met with great skepticism.

Why had Smadel gone after Bernice Eddy? Maurice Hilleman: "Well, because she never had definitive experiments. When you set up an experiment, you set up the controls to go with it. You can't have public health being upset by experiments that may not be meaningful and that are not definitively run. They tore the hell out of her for that." In Eddy's defense, she was aware at the time that all the campus lab animals she might have taken as controls were contaminated with the virus. But what Hilleman and other men were saying, in essence, was that these women lacked rigor, lacked system, that they were too intuitive. "And yet she was right," added Hilleman.

By contrast, when Hilleman told Smadel the same thing that Bernice Eddy had told him, Smadel listened. Eddy and Stewart had soft scientific styles; Smadel and Hilleman had hard styles, and hard personalities to go with them. Whether Eddy and Stewart had the right style or not, their polyoma virus and SV 40 went on to form the basis of the revolution in biotechnology, which is the story of the scientific present and future.

The War on Cancer

It helps to have connections. NIH directors James Shannon and Donald Fredrickson both attended important politicians as personal physicians. When New York lawyer Roy Cohn lay dying with AIDS, he was admitted to the NIH campus hospital, the premier center for AIDS research in the world. When Senator Orrin Hatch, then Republican chairman of the Senate committee that controls the NCI budget, felt a lump under his arm, whom should he call but Vince DeVita, the cancer institute's director.[43] So when retired Air Force Colonel Luke Quinn, then a lobbyist for the American Cancer Society, fell ill with cancer in the late 1960s, his physician in Boston, Dr. Rita Kelly, called DeVita. Quinn had wanted to be treated in Washington where he worked, and DeVita, although not yet director, already had the reputation as being a sort of prince among princes.

"What did the patient have?" DeVita asked Kelly. "She said that he had a cholangiocarcinoma [cancer of the bile duct]. I said that we don't see patients with that kind of illness. She said that we should do it as a favor. I said, 'Sure, describe the case.' She described something in the case over the phone that didn't make sense with the diagnosis—he had axillary lymph nodes [swollen armpit lymph nodes]. Cholangiocarcinomas just never develop axillary lymph nodes. So I said that it sounded interesting, and to send him down." DeVita at this time was very involved in lymphomas, cancers of the lymph nodes, and was developing a drug attack similar to VAMP for leukemia that would lead to cures for three quarters of the patients with the lymphoma called Hodgkin's disease.

"I thought maybe by chance he had lymphoma. We could treat that. He couldn't be treated for the other tumor for which we have no therapy."

They biopsied Colonel Quinn's lymph nodes and discovered that indeed he had a lymphoma. Quinn was treated with the experimental drugs then in use and lived for about three more years in remission. The story is important because, as a lobbyist for the American Cancer Society, Quinn knew Mary Lasker well. In fact, as a result of what happened to Luke Quinn, Mary Lasker got very interested in chemotherapy. Lasker had pulled strings for years behind the scenes on the Hill for more health dollars. Seeing the extended remission of Quinn, it began to dawn on her that something might be done about cancer.

Using the public relations skills of a lifetime in lobbying, Mary Lasker organized in 1969 a Citizens' Committee for the Conquest of Cancer. Large ads appeared in the New York *Times:*

"This year, Mr. President, you have it in your power to begin to end this curse. . . . We are so close to a cure for cancer. We lack only the will and the kind of money . . . that went into putting a man on the moon.

"Why don't we try to conquer cancer by America's 200th birthday [1976]?"[44]

Thus was born, in a high wind of hype, the War on Cancer, Congress's attempt to cure cancer in time to celebrate the nation's bicentennial. Of course the program never had a chance. The early victories over the leukemias and lymphomas we saw in the 1960s stemmed from good planning, not fundamental scientific breakthroughs. Those leukemias and similar cancers offered easy targets for chemotherapy: a high percentage of their cells are dividing at any one time and drugs blitz all those dividing cells at once. But in the major killers, such as lung, bowel, and breast cancer, only a small proportion of the tumor is dividing at any one time, and the cells have ample time to develop resistance to whatever drugs are thrown at them. The moon shot had worked because we knew the scientific principles of making rockets. The War on Cancer was doomed not to conquer cancer because nobody had solved such fundamental questions as how to prevent resistance to chemotherapy? But the war did *quadruple* the budget of the cancer institute in seven years, from $190 million in 1970 to $815 million in 1977.

History works in strange ways. Congress thought it was financing revolutionary cancer therapies. What it did was to help finance with cancer money the revolution in biotechnology. For one thing, about half of the cancer institute's budget would be spent on basic research rather than on applied studies.[45] Simultaneously the budgets of the other NIH institutes swelled as well.

The payoff? The War on Cancer paid, for example, for Daniel Nathans's research on such tumor viruses as SV 40. With SV 40 Nathans worked out the whole logic of restriction enzymes that permits DNA to be recombinated. Alan Rabson said, "You can set all types of targeted research. The scientists will figure out how to do important things in the face of people making plans for them. In the cancer program, that's what they did. The leaders set up all these plans with goals and targets, but out of it came most of the biochemistry of recombinant DNA technology."

In the molecular biology of cancer itself, the decade from 1977 to 1987 saw major discoveries. How do tumor cells spread? They somehow break into the basement membrane, or protective wall, of other tissues by binding to a certain receptor on the basement membrane, the laminin receptor. If that receptor could somehow be plugged, the spreading cancer cells wouldn't be able to bind to it. A huge amount of science goes into uncovering such possibilities for therapy.

Oncogenes, to take another example, have now come into view since the War on Cancer began. These are genes on the long strip of DNA that seem to go out of control and start making far more protein than they're supposed to. This waterfall of excess protein pushes the cancer cell forward. Elsewhere on the strip are the genes that control the resistance of the tumor to drugs. Learning about all these genes, and how their proteins make cancer cells differ from normal ones, results from the War on Cancer. DeVita contrasts the difference between 1971 and now as, "the difference between a black box and a blueprint. We will eventually unravel the blueprint and understand why a cancer cell becomes a cancer cell. In 1971, they would have put me in the booby hatch for saying that."

In terms of the nation's health, the major payoff of the War on Cancer has been quite unexpected: the war on smoking. Once upon a time the cancer researchers had an almost cozy relationship with the tobacco industry. The famous cancer geneticist and director of the American Cancer Society, Clarence C. Little, for example, became scientific director of the Tobacco Industry Research Committee. The NCI's Howard Andervont consulted for the tobacco industry. Cancer scientist Michael Shimkin, who was sufficiently persuaded by the accumulating evidence to stop his own smoking in 1957, remembers locking horns with Little in lecture tours. Shimkin tried stirring up audiences by showing cigarette ads, producing usually no effect other than amusement. "I recall one such lecture to a meeting of the Lost Chord, a society of laryngectomized individuals [voice box removed, usually for smoking-caused cancer], where the air was thick with tobacco smoke." Because the mouse doctors in Bethesda were unable experimentally to produce smoking-related cancer in mice, they assumed smoking didn't cause cancer in humans either. And many such as Andervont smoked themselves. W. Ray Bryan, a colleague of Shimkin's at the cancer institute, died in 1976 of emphysema caused by the cigarettes he continually smoked. Shimkin concluded, "All this demonstrates why few research scientists are in policy-making positions of public trust. Their training for detail produces tunnel vision."[46]

Nor did the PHS formerly play any leadership role in discouraging Americans from smoking, despite the mounds of scientific evidence that had been accumulating. John Heller, director of the cancer institute from

1948 to 1960, felt himself immobilized by the inability of his in-house staff to reach any consensus. And the surgeons general, nipped at by the tobacco industry, remained discretely mute on the subject.

The War on Cancer has made perhaps its greatest contribution to the nation's health by giving ammunition to a new generation of antismoking public health leaders. In 1972 the institute set up working groups on lung cancer and on tobacco, in the context of a larger program on the causes of cancer. In 1974 these groups transferred into a special NCI Smoking and Health program. In general, the 1971 Cancer Act returned to the cancer institute the whole concept of prevention (cancer control), previously fielded out to weaker government agencies for fear of offending the American Medical Association and the tobacco industry.[47]

Once the scientific leadership had declared smoking a legitimate subject, the facts began to flow. Study followed study on the dangers of smoking:

· Pancreatic cancer caused 22,000 deaths in 1981. Smoking was responsible for perhaps 40 percent of those deaths in men, 25 percent in women.

· Bladder cancer caused 10,000 deaths in 1981, half of them due to smoking.

· In 1981, 90,000 Americans died of lung cancer, 91 percent of those deaths in men caused by smoking, 77 percent in women.[48]

The cancer institute estimated that if smoking were reduced by two thirds, and if people followed suitable diets and had regular checkups for cancer, the nation's cancer death rate would be cut *in half* by the year 2000.[49] Given that 130,000 cancer deaths a year are now caused by smoking, that would represent 75,000 saved lives per year.

Armed with these statistics from the War on Cancer, a new generation of public health officials has begun to campaign against smoking with the fervor of Richard the Lionhearted. Due not inconsiderably to the militancy of C. Everett Koop, who became Surgeon General in November, 1981, smoking has now been banned from federal buildings and from public places in several states. The new cancer hunters, inheritors of the tradition of microbe hunting of the early days of the Public Health Service, have the prospect of saving hundreds of thousands of lives from cancer, just as those who fought against yellow fever and malaria in their day also saved hundreds of thousands.

Finally, the War on Cancer has paid off in increasing the survival chances of those who get cancer today. The overall survival of cancer patients has risen from 38 percent of those diagnosed in 1960–63 to 49

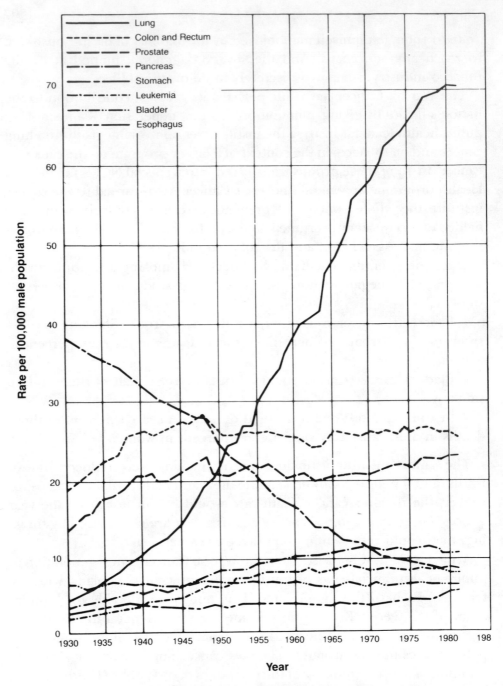

**Age-Adjusted Cancer Death Rates* for Selected Sites
Males, United States 1930–1981**

*Age adjusted to the 1970 standard.
Source: SEER Program. Biometry Branch. NCI

Age-adjusted cancer death rates for selected sites, males, United States, 1930–81.

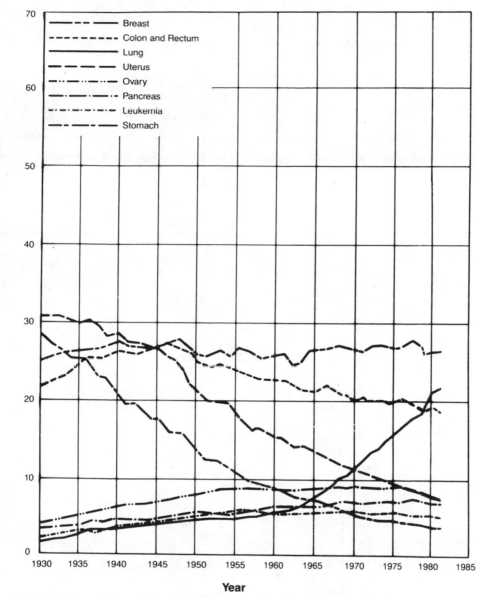

Age-Adjusted Cancer Death Rates* for Selected Sites
Females, United States, 1930–1981

*Age adjusted to the 1970 standard.
Source: SEER Program. Biometry Branch. NCI

Age-adjusted cancer death rates for selected sites, females, United States, 1930–81.

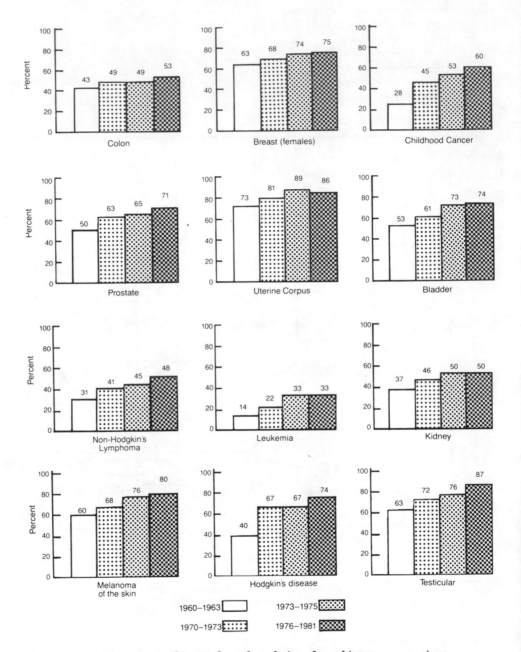

Five-year relative survival rates for selected sites for white cancer patients.

percent of those diagnosed in 1976–81. Over that period the survival of patients with cancer of the bladder increased from 53 to 74 percent; cures in testicular cancer improved from 63 to 87 percent, breast from 63 to 75 percent.[50] These improvements result partly from better therapies, partly from earlier diagnosis. The War on Cancer has contributed to both.

Indeed, if a cancer of the colon is caught early, 88 percent will survive it today; 94 percent of those diagnosed early will live if they get a skin cancer called a melanoma. Ovarian cancers caught early are now cured 82 percent of the time, as are 83 percent of breast malignancies that are caught early.[51]

Stephen Carter used to ask his medical students which patient has the greater probability of being alive in five years—one who was brought in with a diagnosed case of colon cancer or one with congestive heart failure. "Most students guessed the heart patient. They were wrong. Today the odds favor the cancer patient."

If Ulysses S. Grant had fallen sick today as opposed to 1884 with his throat cancer, his chances of responding well to therapy would now be 50 percent, up from 30 percent in 1973. His chances of surviving would now be 40 percent, as opposed to no chance at all at the beginning of the Health Century.[52]

And little Mary who died of leukemia in 1953? She would very probably be alive and well. While we haven't yet cured all cancers, the progress made in the past twenty years is phenomenal, and perhaps the greatest medical achievement of this century—the cancer cure—is now within sight.

EIGHT

Aging

One of the oddities of science is the nude mouse. This species of inbred mouse is *born* wrinkled, so it's not exactly like aging. But in the accompanying photo you see the mouse, wrinkled like an old Serbian peasant. And then the mouse is given some pharmaceutical preparation that is supposed to remove wrinkles in humans, and lo, these natural, inborn mouse wrinkles go away, leaving a smoothness any truly modern mouse would be proud to exhibit.

The problems of aging humans, of course, exceed wrinkles. But some of them respond as wrinkles do. The last two decades of the Health Century have seen great progress in easing the natural physiological changes—and treating the diseases—that accompany growing old. There is no inherent physiological reason why we should get sick as we get old. As one specialist in the health problems of the elderly put it, "The medical approach to aging is not to let people live forever, but to enhance as much as possible the portion of the life span which is conducted at a fully functional level." We needn't, in other words, decline before dying. "Even if the maximum life span is ninety, people should be able to spend eighty-five or ninety years of that in a fully functional state."[1]

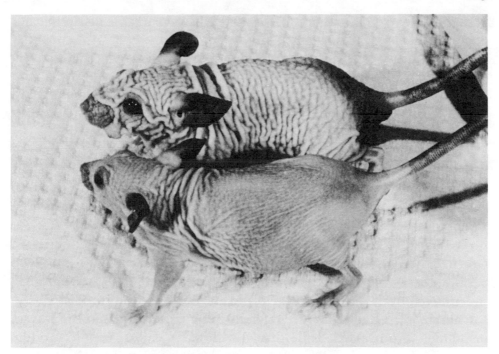

*Research with rhino mice, which are genetically wrinkled, shows that topical applica-
tion of Retin-A™ decreases wrinkling. Mouse pictured on top has not been treated;
mouse pictured on bottom has been treated for 10 days. In the treated mouse, wrinkles
are effaced and the skin appears smooth, with a decrease in sagging folds.*

Patterns of Aging

We grow old in various ways. Winston Churchill showed one of them.
When, in May 1940, he became Prime Minister, Churchill was already over
sixty-five. And as he navigated the British Empire through the desperate
early struggles of World War II, he suffered the medical problems of the
elderly.

In December 1941, while staying at the White House to confer with
President Roosevelt, Churchill felt hot in the night. He rose from bed to
open the window. "It was very stiff," he told his personal physician, Sir
Charles Wilson (later Lord Moran). "I had to use considerable force and I
noticed all at once that I was short of breath. I had a dull pain over my
heart. It went down my left arm. It didn't last very long, but it has never
happened before." Just as the Japanese had bombed Pearl Harbor, British
ships were blowing up like firecrackers on the North Atlantic, and the
Germans had invaded Russia, the lion of battle had a heart attack.

In the days to come, Churchill would use his remarkable discipline and personal buoyancy to separate himself from the kinds of problems that beset the elderly—such as heart attacks. He had outside help, though. The Prime Minister loved alcohol. When asked in August 1942, as he was about to inspect the British positions at El Alamein, if he would like a cup of tea, Churchill responded, "Young man, I have long made it a rule of my life never to drink nonalcoholic drinks between meals. I would like a large whiskey and soda."

Despite his age, Churchill showed remarkable stamina. Admiral Sir Henry Moore describes a typical Churchillian evening during the war. "We were late starting dinner, which did not end till about ten-thirty. Then we all had to attend a movie (a regular Hollywood type)—then about twelve-thirty we started the meeting about 'Torch' [the coming landings in North Africa]. About 3:00 A.M. the Prime Minister said, 'It's time you people went to bed; I am going to do my papers,' and went into his small sanctum to do so." He was up again at eight-thirty the following morning.

Churchill had this wildly irregular sleeping pattern because he was an insomniac, another malady he shared with many elderly people. And he downed red barbiturate pills when at last he felt he must sleep. Nor was he unmindful of the effect of heavy drinking and sleepless nights upon his own health. In fact, he was something of a hypochondriac, and after his first heart attack, for example, he frequently asked Wilson to take his pulse.

Yet through Churchill's weekly sieges of throat aches, earaches, eye aches, and itchings emerges a picture of an old man with spectacular *joie de vivre.* Here we are in North Africa: up at 6 A.M., then "motoring in clouds of sand, long walks between troops, addressing groups of troops, talks with officers, in fact, a nonstop tour of inspection." This done, he plunges into the sea, rolls on the waves, does a handstand on the bottom, and makes the V sign with his legs sticking out of the water.

Even though aging is not a disease, sooner or later the normal physiological changes of aging shade into disease. Thus in his late seventies Churchill began to go downhill. He suffered his first stroke in 1949, another in 1952. In July 1953 he had still another stroke that left him in bed paralyzed for a while. But did this indomitable seventy-eight-year-old turn his face to the wall? No. He had in the meantime become Prime Minister again, and in 1954 he was able to meet with Ike in Washington. Yet even when he was Prime Minister (1951–55) his mind had begun to wander. "I made an exhibition of myself today," he told Dr. Wilson. "I get maudlin. It seems a feature of this blow [stroke]. Why am I like this, Charles?" The deterioration became more severe. By 1959 people were speaking of "Winston's waning faculties." One friend who had passed some time with him said, "There were long pauses, and sometimes Winston began a sentence and then could not remember what he meant to say." In the course of a cruise on Aristotle Onassis's yacht in 1960 Onassis chattered to the Prime Minister, "You are in a meditative mood, not talkative."

CHURCHILL: "My mind is very empty all day." Churchill became demented in the last five years of his life, dying in 1965 at ninety.[2]

There are various patterns of aging, rather than a single, unitary process by which everyone becomes old and dies. Churchill exemplifies one pattern: continuing to function well, absence of disease, then a sudden, catastrophic decline.[3] Churchill's previous heart attack had not impaired him; he had recovered completely from his various pneumonias, operations for hernia, and so forth, and even in his early seventies was able to bound up stairs two at a time. Then a sudden series of strokes demented him. The source of his mental deterioration would be known medically today as "multi-infarct dementia," rather than Alzheimer's disease or some other form of mental deterioration. Despite drinking vast quantities of alcohol all his life, he seemingly did not suffer from alcoholic dementia.

But from research done at the National Institute on Aging, following groups of individuals year by year through old age, we know that alternative patterns of aging to Churchill's also exist:

• *Stability prevails until dying,* meaning that the individual undergoes not even the standard physiological changes of aging, such as loss of kidney function or reduction in problem-solving ability. A swift death then terminates what has been a healthy life.

• *An early decline from illness:* all of a sudden in the aging process disease begins, such as cardiac insufficiency, arthritis, or dementia—all medical conditions, none inevitable, none inevitably bound up with aging.

• *A slow decline in function occurs,* even in the absence of disease, such as loss of kidney function or a reduction in one's problem-solving ability. These are not really "medical" conditions but common physiological accompaniments of growing old. The person does not develop outright disease until the very end.

• *Changes occur, stemming not from the body's own cells but from the culture:* one's underlying organs may be perfectly fine, yet one's health is changed by cultural expectations, such as (on the positive side) lowering one's cholesterol or (on the negative side) entering a nursing home for no reason save the convenience of the relatives.[4]

Thus there are many patterns. We should differentiate between the physiological problems of aging and medical symptoms falsely associated with aging. Jumbling the two together previously has created a number of myths.

Mythbusting

The elderly (over sixty-five) have risen so rapidly in numbers—their percentage trebling over the last hundred years—that misinformation about what aging entails has mushroomed as well. One person out of eight is already over sixty-five. As Robert Butler, the first director of the aging institute, points out, "Already eighty percent of all death occurs after sixty, and you can imagine it will be even more striking in the next century as more and more people survive to their later years, unless we have an absolutely devastating AIDS epidemic."[5] What are common misunderstandings about this population?

"Old age once did not exist." This belief, often encountered in media stories about aging, is a myth. We often read that old age has only recently become a problem because in past times life expectancy was low and there were no elderly. Even if the average life expectancy at birth in the past was only twenty-eight, or thirty-five, or whatever low number you chose, it was so low only because infant mortality in those days was so high. Half of all children might never see a twenty-first birthday. This mass of deaths thus dragged down overall life expectancy.

It makes much more sense to ask what percentage of the people who had reached twenty might reasonably look forward to old age. That percentage was considerably higher. If in Massachusetts in 1850 you made it to age twenty, you'd have an even chance of reaching age sixty. Thus perhaps half of those who survived to twenty would reach the threshold of old age, and of course many of them would live to be seventy or eighty.[6]

The elderly were never a high percentage of the population mainly because birth rates were so high, making the average age quite low. In New York State in 1786, for example, only 4 percent of the population was over sixty—the same for New Hampshire in 1767. In the United States as a whole in 1870 only 3 percent of the population was over sixty-five.[7] Thus it is correct that few old people existed relative to the huge bulk of babies and adolescents. But in absolute numbers the United States had in 1870 a million and a half people over sixty-five. So the elderly existed.

"Old people have never been cared for in the family." Before 1900 the elderly did, in fact, tend to live with their families. According to one study, around 1900 only one old person in four lived alone or with a spouse. Almost 60 percent lived with one of their children, whether that child was married or

not. And another 13 percent lived with relatives or friends. By contrast, in 1975 over eight out of ten old people lived alone or with their spouse; only 12 percent lived with a child, and only 4 percent with kin.[8] Thus in our own times the elderly have very much drifted out of the care of families.

Another myth touches the benefits to the elderly of medicine. Some people argue that the health care system today has done little to improve the life expectancy of the elderly.[9] But in fact the life expectancy of the average sixty-five-year-old American has risen by 17 percent in the last quarter century. In 1960 at the age of sixty-five you could expect to see another 14.3 years of life; in 1984, the most recent date for which statistics are available, the average sixty-five-year-old will reach 81.8 years.[10] Of course, these extra years do not stem solely from improved treatments for hypertension and angina. Yet the beta blockers and calcium-channel blockers and diuretics of the Health Century have played an important role.

There is a stereotype that growing old means getting sick. The reality is different. According to one study, in 1982 three fourths of men in their late sixties were still able to do heavy work such as shoveling snow. Almost a third of those over eighty-five could still do such work. Organized by the aging institute, this study of two rural counties in Iowa showed that 86 percent of the women over eighty-five were able to bathe themselves without assistance; three quarters of them were able to walk across a room without assistance.[11] Accordingly, for the vast majority of elderly, growing old does *not* mean disablement.

To understand aging we must separate the specific diseases elderly people get from the underlying process of aging itself. Says Edward Schneider, a senior scientist at the Institute on Aging, "Much of what we've thought due to aging is due to specific diseases, many of which can be prevented. For example, women lose bone with aging. Is it aging? No, it's a disease called osteoporosis. You can give women exercise regimens and they can prevent loss of bone." Or take the added risk the elderly are thought to run in surgery. Schneider: "Most surgeons have now realized that the risk of surgery has nothing to do with age. It's all to do with the amount of disease in your heart and lungs. Someone who's ninety with good heart and lung function has a very low risk of death in surgery."[12]

Yet while aging is not synonymous with increased illness, let's not conceal from ourselves the reality that far more elderly people than younger people have disease. Of men and women aged twenty-five to forty-four who were polled in 1983, 72 percent felt in good or excellent health. Only 36 percent of those over sixty-five did so.[13] One study estimated that 80 percent of older Americans have at least one chronic ailment. And another

survey calculated that, of the elderly with chronic conditions, four out of
ten have some limitation on their activity.[14]

So what does go wrong? Here myth differs totally from reality. The
elderly have corns, constipation, and ingrown toenails, right?

Wrong. Only 4 percent of those over sixty-five have ingrown toenails, 5
percent corns and calluses, and 7 percent constipation, although this
latter figure is the highest incidence of constipation in any age group.
Furthermore, the percentage of elderly with hemorrhoids (7 percent) is no
higher than in the middle-aged.

Only one elderly person in seven has cataracts or diabetes. And as for
migraine headaches, the incidence is far higher in the middle-aged, especially females (6 percent), than in elderly persons of either sex (only 2
percent).

For old people, the diseases that are truly common are quite serious,
particularly heart disease and cancer. One elderly person in three has
heart disease, and almost four in ten have high blood pressure.[15] We don't
know what Churchill's blood pressure was because there is no evidence
that Lord Moran ever took it (although he frequently took the Prime
Minister's pulse). But almost certainly it was through the ceiling. Churchill
also experienced the chain of strokes that may follow hypertension.

Although Churchill never developed cancer, one out of five elderly
women surveyed in 1982 in East Boston had had a cancer at some point in
their lives (one out of ten men over sixty-five).[16] The elderly are more
often bedridden, spending seventeen days a year in bed sick, as opposed
to five days a year for those aged twenty-five to forty-four. Old people
experience another two weeks of "restricted activity" every year, on the
average.[17] But that means eleven months out of twelve they're maintaining normal lives.

A final myth, one cultivated perhaps, by the patent medicine ads on TV,
is that when the elderly bump into the "health care delivery system," they
are likely to receive compassionate, concerned care. And bump into it they
do. In 1983 elderly women visited the doctor 4.6 times a year, a third more
frequently than younger women. Elderly men went 4.2 times a year, almost three times as often as younger men.[18]

Doctors who equate aging with disease make unsatisfactory medical
attendants. Edward Schneider discovered that firsthand when, himself on
staff at New York Hospital in the 1960s, he decided to admit his grandfather.

"My grandfather was in excellent health. One day in his seventies he
developed heart failure. I took him to the emergency room, because I
thought it was one of the best hospitals in the United States at the time.

"I took care of my grandfather's heart failure, and then I had him admitted to a teaching ward of that hospital, and when I finished work in the emergency room I went up to visit him. I found him delirious, disoriented, confused, agitated, and distraught. He was tied up in bed with restraints. And he was lying perfectly flat—which he shouldn't have been, because if you have heart failure you should be sitting up in bed. So I went to the nurse's station to find out what had happened. What had happened was that when he came up to the ward they had asked him to go to the bathroom with a urinal and a commode and do it in the bed because they were worried about him walking to the bathroom. Well, this man had never been in a hospital before. And when he wanted to go to the bathroom, he wanted to go to a bathroom, not to have to go in bed. So he struggled with the nurses to go to the bathroom and they finally sedated him.

"Well, the drug they gave him for sedation turned out to have the opposite effect, because a certain kind of drug which when they give it to young people causes sedation, when they give it to old people, in fact, causes agitation. These are the barbiturates. He was given this drug and he became agitated. And now they had to restrain him in bed. So I found him delirious, confused, disoriented, and constrained in bed and very, very angry. So I spoke to the resident. We decided the best mode of action was to check him out of the hospital. We brought him home and he lived another seven years and was never again in a hospital."

For many doctors, reluctance to separate aging from disease begins with their training. As they encounter the elderly for the first time in "Emerg," they become resigned about the possibility of treating them. Myron Miller, head of the new geriatrics program at New York's Mount Sinai Medical Center, described the young doctor's experience when old people show up in the hospital's emergency room, "often with multiple medical problems and very little understanding of them. They might be taking fifteen different medications, no idea what they are and for what purpose. And there'd be a string of people like this and you're faced with seeing them in a very limited time period. There's a tremendous frustration on the part of the individuals who are supposed to provide the care. How can I do this? I can't get a reliable history. The individual doesn't know what his problems are. He can't tell me what they are. I'm not even sure if the information I get is reliable. And when I finish with this—it's going to take me three hours and I've got twenty minutes—there's another one just like him right behind." So the "house staff" in hospitals become exasperated with the elderly, especially with the elderly poor. They become drained emotionally. "I've seen this over and over again every day," said Miller.

A case in point: in the neurology service of one big-city hospital, the resident physicians often roll their eyes whenever the chief physician announces a "consult" must be done on a patient over seventy. Although they purse their lips in irritation, they say nothing because this particular chief is a militant believer in spotting in elderly patients any condition that might be reversible and reversing it. One recent consult was in the ward for elderly women, a kind of warehouse with the distinctively urinous odor of the nursing home. It was an eighty-year-old woman who couldn't walk and who had a recent history of "hip pain." As opposed to just glancing at her and supposing her to have some degenerative nervous or bone disease, the chief did a full neurological examination and insisted on X rays. There in the X rays the team saw two broken hips that the hospital's other medical staff had missed. The woman was operated on, successfully, for these conditions.

"When You Look into Fran's Face . . ."

Dementia, the organic loss of intellectual function, is not a normal result of aging. It is a disease. Yet for hundreds of years "senile dementia" was seen as normal in the elderly. Within the past ten years our views of the "inevitability" of senility have been revolutionized.

Among the heirlooms of a Nova Scotia family is a needlepoint sampler embroidered by a woman in 1790. The writing on the needlepoint is perfectly normal. But if one follows the later letters, the handwriting betrays a clear mental decline. Of particular interest in the dementia of the Nova Scotia woman who made the sampler is that it ran in the family. Seven generations have been born since the 1790s. The family immigrated from England to Canada in 1837, and a kind of dementia called Alzheimer's disease—named after German neurologist Alois Alzheimer, who first discussed it in 1906[19]—has appeared frequently in each generation. One early member of this family might be described as "getting lost in a field. He would go to someone else's house and he wouldn't know where he was." Linda Nee, a social worker of the National Institute of Mental Health, is studying this group of families.[20]

Nee had received in 1977 a present-day member of this family for a consultation. Realizing a "familial" problem might exist, she started to follow it up. Now she has spotted about eight families, all descendants of the needlepoint woman, in whom perhaps sixty family members have Alzheimer's disease. On average, the disease begins in these families at fifty-three. This early onset characterized Dr. Alzheimer's own German patients as well, which is why the phrase "presenile dementia" was for a

long time synonymous with "Alzheimer's." The condition was deemed a
rare form of senility beginning in middle age.

Our views of aging have been turned topsy-turvy by the discovery in the
late 1960s and early '70s that this supposedly rare disease is in fact com-

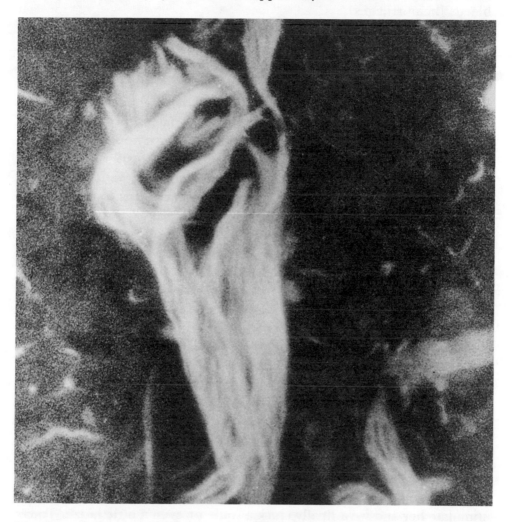

Tangles and plaques in brain tissue of Alzheimer's disease patient.

mon in the elderly. Exactly the same pathological changes in the brain that
occurred in these rare cases of "presenile dementia"—tangles of brain
tissue and a fatal reduction in the overall size of the brain—are often
found in the very elderly.[21] Alzheimer's disease has now been demonstrated to be a major issue in aging. But how recently this realization has
come!

Edward Rall, a senior physician at the arthritis institute and NIH administrator, remembers his own discovery of Alzheimer's. He was at a meeting in New York in the 1970s and saw Fred Plum, a neurologist at Cornell Medical School. "Something came up about Alzheimer's and I said, 'Yeah, yeah. Rare, but you know, you get senile with one of those strokes and bleeds [hemorrhages].'

"Fred says, 'Like hell you do.' He says, 'Alzheimer's is probably one of the major causes of dementia in the elderly.' Grumble grumble grumble.

"Well, three days later I get a whole sheaf of twenty reprints from Fred showing me how wrong I was, because the figures on senile people from a London hospital showed that about a third of the aged senile had serious brain damage from strokes either due to hemorrhages or infarcts [loss of blood supply]. About a third of them seemed to have nothing but Alzheimer's disease, which in the EM [electron microscope] shows neurofibrillary tangles [tangled plaques of brain tissue]. Whatever patients were left were a mixture of strokes and Alzheimer's. So Alzheimer's seems to be a dominant factor in senility in the aged."

Dr. Trey Sunderland of the National Institute of Mental Health estimates that at sixty-five about 3 to 5 percent of the population has dementia, about half of that caused by Alzheimer's; at eighty, one person in three shows some dementia, and again Alzheimer's causes about half of it. Thus Alzheimer's is responsible for perhaps 40 to 60 percent of all dementias. Affecting two to three million Americans, Alzheimer's is, according to Edward Schneider, the fourth commonest cause of death in the United States today.

Linda Nee introduces us to a member of the Nova Scotia family who's looking after "Fran," one of the disabled relatives. "Every time I get back from the nursing home everybody naturally asks, 'How is Fran?' It's kind of a normal question. 'Does she know you?' I go down for a week to ten days each time to see Fran, and maybe seven or eight of the days Fran would show absolutely no response to me being there. I would do my best to stimulate her and maybe one of the nurses would come around and stimulate her and we'd finally crack a smile or even a little laugh. Today, with all the attention that Fran got, there's no question she was very well stimulated and responded enormously.

"So Fran's brain isn't completely dead. We must remember Fran cannot walk. She has absolutely no use of her legs whatsoever. She cannot feed herself at all. She doesn't want to eat. The nurses have a real problem getting food into her right now. Fran has really no interest in doing anything other than sleeping. We know there's reaction in the brain, because when you look into Fran's face sometimes, it looks as though she's fighting a private war, simply because of the contortions to her face."

The recent discovery of the commonality of Alzheimer's has provoked great concern. Linda Nee: "The last five or ten years have seen the big focus on Alzheimer's. You know, medicine is like anything else, it has its voguey things and it reacts to pressure, as any other field does." In addition, the Alzheimer's patient groups have "really put it in the newspapers," in Nee's words. Thus funding for Alzheimer's research has boomed, and three different institutes at NIH have substantial programs.

One major result of all this research is that *the gene that causes Alzheimer's disease has been discovered.* Researchers at the Massachusetts General Hospital have found the defective gene to be sitting in chromosome number twenty-one.[22] The discovery that Alzheimer's is indeed a genetic disease—previously suspected because of its "familial" pattern—does not mean a therapy is yet in sight. But it does give Alzheimer's, formerly a "disease of theories," now about the same scientific status as AIDS: we know what causes them both, although the causes are very different. And molecular biology has determined a sufficient portion of the "mechanism" for each that scientists may at least begin thinking about intervention. In the case of Alzheimer's, the process might entail searching out the protein this particular gene makes and seeing whether that protein causes the problem. It is difficult to speak of a cure, because untangling these plaques of brain fibers would be like unfrying an egg. But once the excess protein is discovered, some kind of prevention might be possible.

How about preventing the disease by not marrying, and thus not transmitting it to the next generation? Dr. Sunderland downplays such extreme sacrifice. Even though Alzheimer's does run heavily in a few families, such as those being studied now in Italy, Michigan, and Nova Scotia, "the vast majority of cases are what we call sporadic Alzheimer's, where there might be one or two members in the family but not that many. Certainly it is not a family disease [i.e., you would have a fifty-fifty chance of getting it if you've got a parent with it]." Sunderland added, however, that if the brothers and sisters of Alzheimer's patients are followed long enough, maybe half of them do get it, "if they're lucky enough to live until eighty-five or ninety." So it may be that Alzheimer's is a genetically transmitted illness with "such a late onset in life that most people die of other causes before it's even expressed." (The abnormal gene begins producing its upsetting proteins when a genetic disease is "expressed.") Thus Sunderland feels that that counseling people whose parents had Alzheimer's not to have children is unnecessary, "because there's such a late onset of illness."

This sober assessment of the facts lets us counter some of the media hysteria on Alzheimer's. So pervasive is this kind of hysteria that it has reached into the lives of children. A TV producer says, "I suppose we all know somebody who has it. I mean, my ex-wife's mother, who had always led a very vibrant, electric life, apparently got Alzheimer's disease. She's had it for the last couple of years. It's tough stuff to deal with. The kids are upset about it, you know, whether they're going to inherit it or not." This kind of exploitation of people's fears, however unwarranted, is not uncommon.

A team from the CBS show "Sixty Minutes" wanted to do something on Alzheimer's. So they got onto one of these Alzheimer's families in Canada where the disease has passed from generation to generation. "What the producer found was that people were coping," reported Linda Nee with relish. "She [the female producer] was upset. She said, 'Oh, these people are coping and I didn't expect it.' " These families are proud that they're doing well under the terrible strain of seeing loved ones become demented.

Nee said, "I had to laugh, frankly, when that producer got back in touch with me. I could hardly wait to tell the family that they were coping and that wasn't the kind of story 'Sixty Minutes' was after."

Easing Arthritis

Nothing about arthritis is inevitable. Edward Schneider tells the story of a ninety-five-year-old man who comes to the physician's office complaining of pain in his right knee. "He looks at the physician and says, 'Doc, I've got some pain in my right knee, it's killing me.'

"The doctor turns to this man and says, 'But you're ninety-five years old; you have to expect some pain in your knee.'

"The man is smart enough to turn back to the doctor and say, 'But my left knee is ninety-five years old and it's doing just fine.' "

But there's a difference between inevitable and common. According to the arthritis institute at NIH, arthritis and related diseases afflict nearly thirty-seven million Americans; $25 billion a year are lost in wages, for example, owing to arthritis.[23] Only 5 percent of people aged eighteen to forty-four suffer from arthritis; 47 percent of those over sixty-five do so.[24] And even though arthritis doesn't kill anyone, it "cripples older people," in Edward Schneider's words, "and takes them from being independent, living at their home, enjoying life, to being dependent, living in a chronic care facility, and pain."

A variety of arthritis called osteoarthritis, or the arthritis of aging, most afflicts the elderly. Unlike rheumatoid arthritis, more a disease of youth in which the lining of the joints becomes inflamed and proliferates out of control, in osteoarthritis the cartilage that protects one bone from crunch-

ing against another deteriorates; inflammation ensues, and the joint becomes painful and immobilized.

With a disease that cripples and agonizes tens of millions of people,
powerful commercial inducements to research exist. Although no one has
yet found a cure for arthritis, discovering drugs that will relieve its symptoms has spurred the drug companies. Recently there has been big news.

Let's back up for a second. When we discussed earlier the use of cortisone and prednisone for arthritis in the mid-1950s, we passed over the
fact that these drugs are steroids, most of which the adrenal glands produce to drive metabolism. When the body gets them, the adrenal glands
think they've done their duty and stop making a number of other natural
steroids essential for life, so long-term steroid therapy can have major
complications, including death. Thus, although steroids brought miracu-
lous short-term relief to those bedridden cases of the 1950s, they did not
represent a lasting solution to this chronic disease.

Given the financial stakes, it is unsurprising that many companies tried
their hand at nonsteroidal anti-inflammatory drugs in the 1950s and '60s.
The Geigy company in Switzerland had put a candidate on the market in
1952. Merck introduced a rival, Indocin, in 1965. Many others were available too, all for patients no longer getting relief from aspirin, the front-
line therapy for arthritis, then as now. The problem was that all these
nonsteroidals had a degree of toxicity that could not be bred out of them.
Phenylbutazone, for example, was estimated in 1984 to have caused at
least 445 deaths in Britain during the preceding twenty years.[25] Indometh-
acin (Indocin and others) tended to give patients indigestion and ulcers.
Also, the drugs had to be taken several times daily, an added expense for
hospitals and a nuisance for patients.

It is at this point that Joe Lombardino and Edward ("Ted") Wiseman of
Pfizer come onstage. Readers without exposure to the pharmaceutical
industry may have trouble understanding the intensity of team spirit in
one of these big drug houses. When, for example, the drug that
Lombardino and Wiseman discovered was approved many years later, in
1982, at least eighty of the several hundred people who'd worked on it
gathered in front of the Pfizer research lab in Groton, Connecticut, to
cheer. These are professional scientists, Ph.D.s and M.D.s who are members of editorial boards of journals and who have long lists of scholarly
publications. All would acquire an urgency in their voices as they describe
how they set out to "discover drugs."

So when, in 1962, Lombardino and Wiseman set out to find a nonsteroidal anti-inflammatory drug for Pfizer, it was as though they had been
entrusted with a piece of the Shroud of Turin. They were both in their late

Central research team gathers in front of Pfizer lab in Groton, Connecticut, to cheer approval of anti-inflammatory drug Feldene.

twenties. Lombardino starts synthesizing away; Wiseman does the animal tests. About five years later they discover something that improves marginally upon the competition, "meaning multiple doses would be necessary and our drug will make your ears ring, too," as Wiseman put it. The two investigators suggested that their company not go ahead.

Here we come to the theme of advances in basic science producing health payoffs that is the keynote of the Health Century. The two had thought a lot about how to inhibit a kind of natural chemical involved in inflammation called the prostaglandins. They had in mind a molecule that would do just that, a molecule that would be baptized an oxicam. But the conventional wisdom held that the synthesis was impossible. Wiseman was in a car accident and could come into the lab only on crutches and perch on a stool in his body cast, listening to an increasingly fed-up Joe Lombardino report on the latest synthesis. "Joe brought some very weird-looking crystals down to me on December 14, 1966, and said, 'Ted, if this doesn't work, that's it. I just can't justify going on for another year of synthesis.' And we tested it that day and didn't believe the results. I came back in the next day and it was clear that Joe had broken the synthesis."

But the question that haunts all drug discoveries is not: Will we be able to get the molecule; but: Is it toxic? Are we going to spend a hundred million dollars developing this thing and then find out that it gives old ladies anemia? Toxicity is a problem that had bedeviled all the other nonsteroidals. So Lombardino and Wiseman would test one version and it would poison the lab animals, and another would make it through the lab animals only to be somehow inappropriate in the first human volunteers—volunteer medical students—they would put it into (in the drug industry you "put drugs into" animals and people).

There are many pitfalls in turning a molecule into a product, the road of drug development. "We lost one drug," said Wiseman, "because it interacted with every glass bottle we could find. Upjohn lost a very promising drug because it interacted with sunlight, and they couldn't handle it. I heard another fascinating story of an anti-inflammatory that died because it somehow crystallized rock-solid in every pharmaceutical formulation that anybody could think of. Capsules literally went to pieces of rock while sitting."

And these drugs have to survive the "hurly-burly of the commercial world," as Wiseman calls it. "Going to sit on the pharmacy shelf, patient takes them home in the glove box of the car, cooks them for a while, probably stores them in the cabinet in the bathroom, steams them every morning. It's not unknown in a large number of cultures to wash your drug down with a glass of beer, or certainly a glass of wine. There's smog on top of all of that. They take other drugs, too [that may interact]." This is what can go wrong when your beloved drug leaves the lab.

Six more years pass, and finally in 1976 Lombardino and Wiseman have discovered a good oxicam they could test in humans. Three years later it receives in England its first approval for marketing. Pfizer has by now invested seventeen years and $80 to $100 million in the drug, which it will call Feldene. The Lilly company had a similar drug, Oraflex, which developed toxicity and had to be withdrawn in 1982.[26] The losses ran into many millions of dollars. Now we begin to understand why all those employees were cheering. The emotional commitment is incredible. "I know of people within our corporation," said Wiseman, "individual scientists, who've lost what looked to be an extremely fine drug somewhere, and their careers never really surmounted that. You can look at them and say you know the steam went out of that man when so-and-so happened. They still function very well in the laboratory but that spark is somehow gone."

So Feldene emerged to help Auntie Edna. Mrs. Wiseman had an aunt back in England, Auntie Edna, who had suffered from arthritis as long as Wiseman could remember, from the time he went to high school with his wife in the early 1950s in Portsmouth. He took some Feldene to her local doctor in 1980. Did it help her?

"Oh. She could start to walk down to the shops to do her shopping again. And she had not been able to get from upstairs to downstairs before Feldene.''

The world is filled with Auntie Ednas, who will not get a cure for their disease but who would like fewer side effects or a drug that's simpler to take. The market for Feldene was vast, and by the mid-1980s it had become one of the world's ten bestselling drugs. Now, the purpose of this story has not been to show how much Pfizer has helped the elderly but to demonstrate how enormous that pool of suffering is, and by what slender threads hang the few drugs that can provide relief. Feldene could have run off the rails at a dozen switch points before it reached Auntie Edna. When one thinks that before 1900 there was nothing for arthritis, that before 1950 there was nothing save aspirin, one understands how recently progress in science has begun to drain that pool of misery.

Tagamet

Few who practiced medicine before the 1950s will forget the typical ulcer patient. "Pain is perhaps the most constant and distinctive feature of ulcer," wrote William Osler in 1892. "The attacks may occur at intervals with great intensity for weeks or months at a time, so that the patient constantly requires morphia. . . . One patient during the attack would lean over the back of a chair; another would lie flat on the floor, with a hard pillow under the abdomen."[27] These "peptic" ulcer patients had a lesion in the wall of their stomach or duodenum caused by the hydrochloric acid the stomach secretes.

Once peptic ulcer disease heavily affected young women. Only recently has it become most frequent in the elderly. Although the reasons for this upward drift in the age of ulcer patients are unclear, today in the United States it is the elderly who suffer most. In 1983, 41 elderly persons per thousand had ulcers; among the middle-aged, only 35 per thousand. Elderly women had the highest ulcer rates of all.[28]

Before recent progress in treatment of peptic ulcer, the major therapy was restricting one's diet. John Alexander-Williams, a distinguished British stomach surgeon, remembered putting his patients on "a glass of milk and water on rising; strained porridge for breakfast with a small cup of weak milky tea; an egg in a cup of warm water at eleven and at lunchtime two tablespoons of steamed plaice [a kind of flounder the British eat] or a little minced chicken, followed by two cups of semolina. A cup of milk and water was to be taken two hours later, and another at teatime. At six, some lightly scrambled eggs or soft roe, followed by junket [sweetened milk set with rennet] or egg custard. No gourmet's paradise, to be sure!" The alternative was surgery, in which one patient in thirty died.[29]

In the United States something known as the Sippy diet, introduced in 1915 by Chicago physician Bertram W. Sippy, was in vogue until after the Second World War. Aimed at protecting the stomach walls from acid, the patient would drink "three ounces of milk and cream mixture every hour from 7 A.M. until 7 P.M. In addition, three soft eggs, one at a time, and nine ounces of a cereal, three ounces at one feeding, may be given each day. . . . Cream soups of various kinds, vegetable purées and other soft foods may be substituted now and then, as desired."[30] To neutralize stomach acid, doctors recommended large doses of magnesia powder and sodium bicarbonate powder between "feedings," as meals would henceforth be known.[31] You'd be on some version of this for many years or the rest of your life.

If one hears relatively little about stomach ulcers today in any age group, it is because chronic ulcers, which ultimately could cause death by perforating an artery or letting the stomach contents spill out into the abdomen, have virtually disappeared. And they have disappeared because of a drug called Tagamet (cimetidine), introduced in the United States in August 1977. But the development of Tagamet was a cliff-hanger.

We encounter a familiar face, Francis Boyer, president of the Philadelphia drug company Smith Kline & French, who brought over the antipsychotic drug chlorpromazine. The profits of chlorpromazine had permitted Smith Kline, previously a marginal vendor of remedies, to turn itself into a big player. Boyer needed research to do this. To tap into British pharmacology (itself the product of intensive post-1933 tutoring by German émigrés), Boyer founded in the late 1950s a Smith Kline research lab at Welwyn Garden City in the English countryside. Philadelphia executives rubbed their hands. Now there would be new drugs. But despite the millions of dollars spent on research and the hundreds of scientists hired, there were no new drugs, no discoveries. By 1964 the company had invested over $100 million in research and had nothing to show for it.

Part of the problem was that traditional methods of drug discovery really did depend on luck. One scientist characterizes it as the "man and a boy" type of research in which one chemist plus his lab assistant would "create molecules by the pound and send them to pharmacologists, who would screen them for their activity in the hopes that luck would strike." It was called research "untouched by the human brain."[32] To end this streak of bad luck, in 1963 Smith Kline raided Imperial Chemical Industries (ICI) to bring to Welwyn a top-notch M.D.-pharmacologist named George E.

Paget. And Paget immediately brought two pals from ICI with him, pharmacologist James Black and a biochemist named William Duncan.

Black we have met briefly before in connection with a beta blocker heart medication called propanolol in the heart chapter. Black believed there were such things as "receptors" in the body, to which specific molecules could be tailored. Hence drug "design" rather than drug "discovery." After propanolol, Black had turned his attentions to a substance in the body called histamine. Just as too much histamine will give you a runny nose (hence antihistamines), Black thought, on the basis of other people's research going back some years, that there might be other kinds of histamine receptors in the body. Maybe the stomach's gastric-acid cells had such receptors, different in kind from those in the sinuses. If they could be blocked, the stomach's secretion of acid could be stopped. This seems so logical now. In 1963 it was all brilliant guesswork.

Now, Black had wanted to pursue this intriguing hypothesis when with his former employer, ICI, but it for some reason refused. He was therefore happy to accompany his friends to a job with the pushy Americans at Welwyn Garden City. Industry colleagues deemed going to work for the Americans "like leaving the *Times* and going with the *Daily Mirror* [a tabloid]." The three friends from ICI didn't care: they were going to apply science to drug making.

Black, a Scotsman with working-class roots (his father had been a coal miner who worked his way up to manager), possessed enormous personal dynamism, a kind of leadership ability sociologists call charismatic, the ability to get people to follow you even if reason tells them you're an idiot. So Black called the various departments together at Welwyn and said, "Look, I believe there is a possibility of drawing an analogy between the alpha- and beta-adrenergic receptors [of the heart and blood vessels] and histamine receptors." They discuss what will be needed and soon they're rolling. By mid-1966 the chemists have found some compounds that turn *on* one kind of receptor but not the other, but the problem is to turn the stomach receptors *off*.

Many months pass fruitlessly. One member of the team described the frustration. "When you get a compound and it turns out to be inactive, you do not know why it's inactive, you only know that it is." So, one inactive compound after another.

Meantime, the Smith Kline headquarters in Philadelphia was getting impatient. Said one executive, "Our earnings levels had been essentially flat. There were no new products to speak of, and none on the horizon. The situation was extremely difficult. And as it turned out, it got a lot worse before it got better." Despite misgivings in Philadelphia, Black insisted on pursuing the "antisecretory program."

In early 1968 Philadelphia's patience ran out and it decided to stop the program. Duncan, now deputy research director at Welwyn, returned to England and said, "I've been told to stop. We're not going to, but it means that the pressure is now on." To fool Philadelphia, they decide to rename the project the H_2 receptor program ("H_2" means the second histamine receptor, on the stomach cells).

They start to get their first breakthrough, discovering they hadn't been giving their rats enough histamine. So they had no way of knowing whether the hundreds of previous compounds they'd synthesized really blocked the rats' receptors or not. Things now heat up. "We saw each other every day. Every lunchtime became a conversation about chemistry."

Meanwhile, by 1969 the earnings crisis in Philadelphia was dictating huge cuts. Research at Welwyn was to be chopped 50 percent, and first to go would be the "new" H_2 receptor program. "Give it one more year," Duncan pleads. Philadelphia refuses. So Duncan cut every other program at Welwyn to give the money to the H_2 blocker team. Duncan later recalled, "It was a considerable gamble. Many of the people who knew—in Philadelphia, in the [Welwyn] Research Institute, and our consultants— thought it was a very unwise policy, risky in the extreme. Of course, they were right. But, they were also wrong."

Things begin coming together at Welwyn. They go back to an earlier compound improperly deemed inactive and begin lengthening its side chain, a chain of atoms striking off from the molecule's core. They tack a sulfur atom onto the side chain, then make the chain still longer, until they figure that the shape of the molecule is close to the shape of the receptor pocket in the cell wall, the conformation of which is unknown to them.

All this lengthening and adding takes two years. It's now 1970 and they've got something they're ready to test on humans. First two team members test it on themselves, then they give it to patients at University College Hospital in London, and finally they get some success.

More chemistry ensues; an even more powerful compound comes from the lab, named metiamide. Black, thinking the game over with the discovery of metiamide, resigns that autumn and goes to a prestigious chair in academe. Then at Christmastime 1973, just as the team is preparing massive field trials of its discovery, the first reports of metiamide's toxicity in patients start coming in. It has wiped out a certain kind of white cell in an ulcer patient in Edinburgh; in April 1974 a second such report comes in. Metiamide must be killed. One team member, Robin Ganellin, remembered of this moment, "Bill [Duncan] called me into his office. He told me, 'Work has got to stop.' I had an enormous reaction. It was as if the ground had opened up."

This particular story has a happy ending because, while metiamide was being tested, back in the lab the chemists had continued to meddle, removing the sulfur atom—traditionally associated with toxicity—from the molecule and replacing it with a pleasing little pair of nitrogens. This drug they called cimetidine. It was their only backup, and they had no idea if it was toxic.

On the other side of the Atlantic, management decides to undertake a gamble, a true do-or-die situation since the company has nothing else in the research pipeline. They had started to build an expensive plant in County Cork, Ireland, to produce metiamide, which has just died. Cimetidine is still in a jar on the shelf, the possibility of its having unacceptable side effects unknown. "We decided to use that plant for cimetidine," Henry Wendt, now Smith Kline's chief executive officer, remembers. "We put a lot of money into it before the clinical testing even began."

The last scene of the last act now transpires: the earlier ulcer patient who had developed the side effect of a decline in white cells is now terribly ill from the ulcer; the patient's physician asks for cimetidine, because cimetidine itself had been successfully given to a few human patients before the whistle had been blown on metiamide. The team now faces a choice: if cimetidine has the same toxicity as its parent, it will make the patient worse and that will be the end of the whole program. If, on the other hand, cimetidine cures the ulcer without poisoning the patient, it probably is not toxic. They give the drug, and the rest is history.

Introduced in England in 1976 as Tagamet, cimetidine immediately won banner headlines. *The Guardian* trumpeted, "New drug can beat ulcers." Elsewhere the press raved: "Breakthrough on ulcer-cure drug," or "If you've an ulcer, read on." But it wasn't just hype. Cimetidine, now brand-named Tagamet, healed most ulcers within four weeks. In August 1977 the American FDA approved Tagamet.[33] No more Sippy diet.

Cimetidine has dramatically changed the management of peptic ulcer disease. "Tagamet?" said one doctor. "It's put the gastric surgeons out of business. All they've got left is appendix and gallbag [gallbladder]. There aren't any more V-and-Ps." The *v*agotomy-and-*p*yloroplasty, cutting the vagus nerve that drives gastric secretion and reopening the scarred pylorus (the exit to the intestine from the stomach), had once been the bread and butter of adominal surgeons. Now surgery residents rarely have a chance even to learn it. Similarly, radiology residents no longer see the stark picture of a perforated peptic ulcer. When the chief of radiology brings in a film of a rare one, the residents do not even recognize it. The chief is astonished, because in his day it was as common as grass. Some doctors now speak of the "pre- and post-Tagamet era," in the way they once spoke of pre- and post-tuberculosis eras. Tagamet, of course, has joined the world's top-ten list of drugs.

Drugs. Drugs. The sense of well-being of the elderly depends heavily on drugs: antidepressants to overcome depression. Tagamet for ulcers, Feldene for arthritis, the scads of beta blockers and calcium-channel blockers and other drugs that now ease the heart's work load or dilate coronary vessels in spasm. The list could be still lengthened. Are we attempting the impossible? "After all, we see death unavoidable," wrote Puritan minister Cotton Mather in 1724. "My Angel of Bethesda, that has expressed so much concern to arm his readers against the approaches of death, yet confesses, I cannot by any means redeem thee; nor find a remedy for thee, that thou shouldest live forever, and not see corruption."[34] Nobody today is trying to escape death, yet who can reproach us for making gentler its slow approach?

NINE

Biotech

Biotechnology is about isolating particular genes on the long strip of DNA, removing them from the original DNA, and getting them to work productively for humankind. The story of biotechnology involves many people from diverse backgrounds. One important tale, that of Daniel Nathans, begins around 1900 when his father, Samuel, aged fifteen and full of rebellion against an Orthodox Jewish family, came from Russia to Philadelphia. Ten years later he married Sarah Levitan and, in 1928 in Wilmington, Delaware, Daniel was born. Like many people who were part of the great wave of Eastern European Jews who fled Tsarist persecution in the early 1900s, the Nathans were quite poor but loved and encouraged their son tremendously. Recalling details of his childhood in his 1978 Nobel acceptance speech, Nathans said, "My father lost his small business and was for some time unemployed. Our house was cold and leaky, and (I learned later) my parents sometimes went hungry." Nathans wanted to acknowledge the role his parents' love and support played in his rise from such humble beginnings to the pinnacle of medical science.

From Science to Health

Nathans is an interesting transitional figure, straddling the end of the Health Century. One leg is in the past. He had studied medicine at Washington University in St. Louis, at the time Arthur Kornberg and Carl Cori were there. He interned at Columbia's P and S, under the great clinician Robert Loeb. He studied protein synthesis at the National Institutes of Health with Michael Potter. Nathans encountered the German refugees from Hitler as in 1959 he started working in the laboratory of Nobel prizewinner Fritz Lipmann at the Rockefeller Institute. (Lipmann had left Germany in 1932 just before the Nazi seizure of power.) Then in 1962 Nathans arrived at Johns Hopkins just as the great waves of sixties science were breaking around him. Marshall Nirenberg was cracking the genetic code; other Nobelists were uncovering the mechanics of DNA and RNA with the aid of viruses that attack bacteria. Heady times.

Viruses that cause cancer interested Nathans in particular. To learn more about them, Nathans spent the first half of 1969 on leave at the Weizmann Institute in Israel. That spring he received a letter from his Johns Hopkins colleague Hamilton ("Ham") Smith.

Smith, three years Nathans's junior and the son of two genteel professors of education at the University of Illinois at Urbana-Champaign, came from a different world. "My entire boyhood was spent in this small midwestern academic community," Smith later wrote. "At home, an atmosphere of intense intellectualism was maintained. My father was perpetually working and writing." Nathans's father, by contrast, had been a bankrupt merchant. Smith remembered, "My brother and I received private French lessons during our preteen years. I began piano lessons at age eight." But despite their diverse backgrounds, the two scientists worked closely.

In a letter in the spring of 1969, Smith described his discovery in some bacteria of an enzyme that seemed to cut DNA. A DNA virus invades the bacteria, and bacterial enzymes cut the invader into ribbons. Nathans found Smith's discovery most intriguing, as it opened the possibility of cutting DNA into portions for study; indeed, of isolating particular genes. Upon returning to Baltimore that summer, he set to work chopping up DNA with enzymes. The particular DNA he selected came from a virus already familiar to readers of this book. It was SV 40.

Here was Nathans's reasoning at the time: "If the genomes [the genes] of DNA tumor viruses could be dissected in this way, and if individual fragments of viral DNA could be isolated, one might be able to determine . . . which segments of the genome were responsible for the various biological activities of the virus." Thus Nathans and co-workers took several cutting, or "restriction," enzymes from various bacteria, such as *E. coli,* and saw that the enzymes did, in fact, cut the SV 40 into fragments. These fragments could be separated on the basis of their weight in an

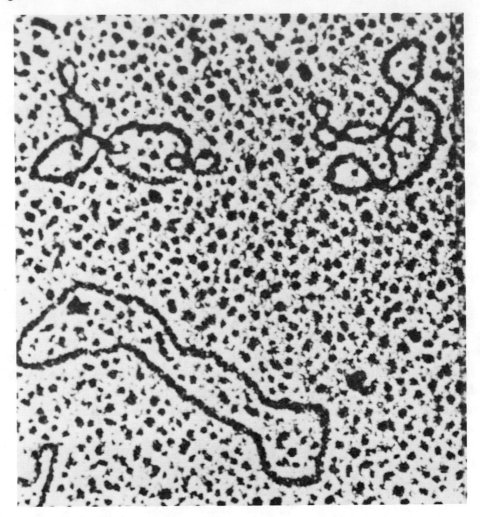

Electron micrograph of free SV 40 DNA.

analysis called electrophoresis. Moreover, each enzyme appeared to cut the DNA *at a specific site,* rather than as a lawn mower might.

By 1971 Nathans and his group were able to assemble these fragments into a map, knowing what position each fragment occupied on SV 40s little circle of DNA. They realized that "the circular SV 40 genome can be opened at any one of several different sites by single-cut enzymes, and small or large fragments can be prepared from virtually any part of the molecule." When in 1975 Frederick Sanger in England made available techniques for determining the exact sequence of base pairs in any strip of DNA, it became possible to know, chemically, which specific base pairs composed each gene. This was a momentous advance, because it meant

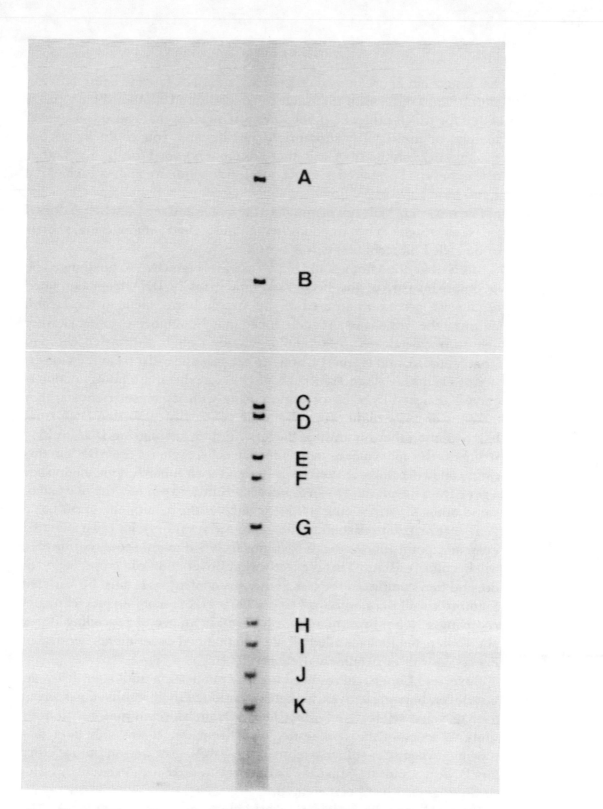

Autoradiogram of 32p-SV 40 DNA after digestion with Hamilton Smith's Hin d enzyme and electrophoresis from top to bottom in 4 percent polyacrylamide gel (25). The largest fragment is near the top (A), and the smallest is near the bottom of the gel (K).

that one could figure out which genes in the DNA (a gene being nothing more than a series of a thousand to two hundred thousand base pairs) coded for which proteins. If you knew the protein that caused sickle-cell anemia, or insanity, or superbright intelligence, you could figure out exactly where on the DNA strip that protein was coded for. By 1978 other researchers had prepared an exact nucleotide sequence map of each of the 5,226 base pairs in SV 40.[1]

The next step: Why not manipulate the genes and see what SV 40 does if we remove some genes or add others? Thus genetic engineering, shortly to be called biotechnology, was born.

But Nathans had not yet added pieces of foreign DNA to anything. The recombinant part of the story, marrying strips of DNA from unrelated organisms, occurs on an area of the map hitherto silent in the Health Century: the West Coast. Actually, it began in November 1972, in a kosher deli at Waikiki Beach in Honolulu. Stanley Cohen, a bearded clinician from Stanford, and Herbert Boyer, an enzyme specialist from the University of California's San Francisco campus, had been attending a conference. Exhausted by a day of conferencing with Japanese scientists, they talked over a late-night snack about the possibility of putting DNA from bacteria into other organisms. Bacteria, rather than having DNA in long strings in chromosomes as in mammalian cells, organize their DNA in tiny rings called plasmids, scattered throughout their innards. One might slice a gene from the plasmid of an *E. coli* bacterium and put it in the plasmid of some other organism entirely. For example, the salmonella germ has a gene that makes it resistant to the antibiotic streptomycin. If we take that gene and put it into *E. coli*, *E. coli*, normally vulnerable to streptomycin, will become resistant. That is exactly what Boyer and Cohen proceeded to do, and they completed the task in the spring of 1973. It must be said that Stanford's Paul Berg, who worked out the logic of recombinant technique, receiving a Nobel prize in 1980, came within an ace of preceding Boyer and Cohen, but he had called off his own planned experiments because of expressions of environmental concern.[2]

Boyer and Cohen had resolved to delay publication until later that year, but Boyer, bursting with excitement, mentioned their results in passing at a small, select science conference in New Hampshire on June 14. Nobody quite understood the significance of his remarks. It was only later that morning when some other scientist said, "Well, now we can put together any DNA we want to," that the hall began to buzz with excitement. Biotechnology had just been created.[3]

Lewis Thomas has called the technology of recombinant DNA "the single most profound, and at the same time most significant, advance in biological science in the twentieth century . . . a fundamental research tool for studying the inner working of cells. It now begins to seem as if there are almost no interesting questions [about cells] that cannot be answered by the use of these techniques."[4]

While these ennobling perspectives were evident to Thomas, more commercially lucrative vistas opened themselves to other observers. It is a sign of the marketplace naïveté of Boyer and Cohen that they entirely failed to appreciate the practical applications of their discovery. Neither thought of taking out a patent. And only when the Stanford University patent officer read an article about their work in the New York *Times* a year later, just before the expiry deadline for the application, did the commercializing of recombinant technology begin.[5] Actually, it was not until drug companies "developed" these test tube molecules that they acquired the potential of contributing to health. Otherwise recombinant DNA would have remained a scientific curiosity. Boyer (who would soon become a founder of Genentech) and Cohen ceded any royalties from the invention to their respective universities.

Why is recombinant technology so important? It matters because this altered DNA, when placed in systems of bacteria, yeast, or mammalian cells, is able to make proteins which the human body normally makes, proteins which, if given in therapeutic doses, might modify the response of the body to disease. These proteins are large molecules, so they cannot be artificially synthesized in the way the sulfa drugs were created from scratch. Our own cells make such tiny quantities of them that extraction by other procedures is impossibly expensive.

If the human genes that make these proteins are put into lower organisms such as bacteria, the bacterial DNA will happily give orders to produce them, via the usual route of messenger RNA, and so forth, along with all the other proteins the bacteria simultaneously produce for their own internal use. The bacteria can then be killed and split open and the desired human protein extracted from the soup of other proteins. The hope is that huge added doses of these natural proteins will help us better fight off viruses, as in AIDS, or resist cancer, for cancerous cells sometimes are identified as "foreign" and attacked by the body's own protein defenders. Gideon Goldstein, who has made several important contributions to the field, said, "We've definitely entered the molecular age of medicine." He mentioned one protein now being bioengineered, erythropoietin, which stimulates the formation of red blood cells. "Maybe fifty such proteins will be applied to medicine over the next ten to twenty years. As a result, we have a whole new therapy that we never had before. We were never able to give these proteins."[6]

There are even more gripping possibilities. Maybe these natural human proteins can be chemically modified, by artificially jiggling the gene. Such compounds would be even easier to patent than the body's own proteins. And they could be targeted to specific diseases in a way that natural proteins may not be. These simple hopes are most of what the multibillion-dollar biotechnology industry is all about.

Interferon

It is July 1956. Jean Lindenmann has just arrived from Zurich to spend a research year at the National Institute for Medical Research in London with virus specialist Alick Isaacs. He and Isaacs have tea together in August and discuss a curious phenomenon: once a person is infected by one kind of virus, he almost never comes down with a second viral disease simultaneously. The phenomenon is called viral interference. The body, once attacked by a virus, must secrete something that protects against viruses.

By November 1956 the two researchers had discovered the substance, which Lindenmann called interferon. Once a virus enters a cell, that dying cell liberates a kind of "Paul Revere" protein that races ahead to other cells and warns them that a virus is coming. These cells begin secreting their own defensive proteins, so that when the virus enters them it is blocked, unable to reproduce further or exit from them. The implications of such a substance are profound when used medically against viral infections.[7]

In 1963 the Finnish virus specialist Kari Cantell of Helsinki's Central Public Health Laboratory dedicated himself to making available a small supply of interferon, extracted from donated blood. Human white blood cells, among other kinds of tissue, produce interferon. But the amounts Cantell could derive were tiny. From 45,000 liters of blood he was able to extract only 400 milligrams of interferon—about one one-hundredth of an ounce. And even that tiny amount was only 1 percent pure, the other 99 percent of the solution he shipped out to various researchers being other white-cell proteins, so it was impossible to get an interferon pure enough even to analyze its chemical composition. The effort was so painstaking that, to be used therapeutically, a pound of interferon would have cost between $10 and $20 billion.[8]

Yet even those minute quantities seemed to produce spectacular therapeutic results. A Stockholm doctor found that interferon evidently prevented the spread of bone cancer in children. Dr. Jordan Gutterman of the M. D. Anderson cancer hospital in Houston flew to Stockholm, and when

Joshua S. Boger, research fellow for Merck and Company, Inc., studies a structural model of an enzyme closely related to one called renin, found in the human bloodstream, attempting to discover a compound to control high blood pressure. (Photo courtesy Merck and Company, Inc.)

Ruth Kirschstein, Director of the Institute of General Medical Sciences at the NIH. (Photo Smokey Forester)

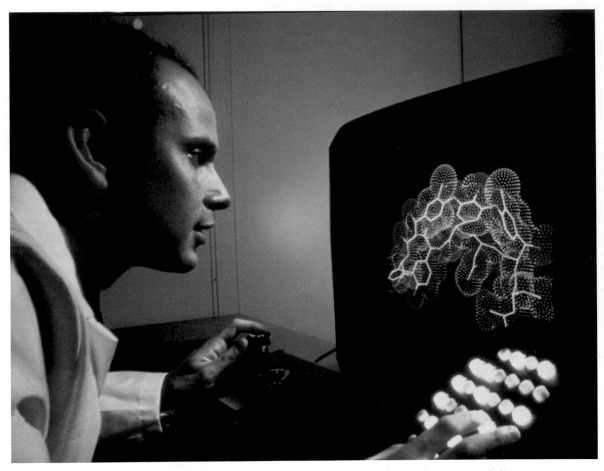

A SmithKline Beckman scientist uses a computer-generated molecular modeling system to help design new molecular structures and examine existing ones. (Photo courtesy SmithKline Beckman Corporation)

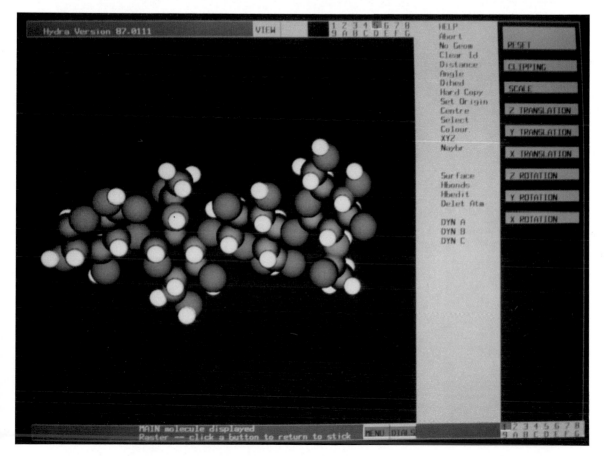

Polygen Corporation's HYDRA™ is a software system that allows researchers to construct, display, and manipulate chemically accurate three-dimensional images of molecular structures. (Photo courtesy Polygen Corporation)

DeWitt Stetten, a senior NIH official, directed an NIH laboratory from which many distinguished scientists emerged. (Photo Smokey Forester)

These four scientists were colleagues at NIH during the exciting 1960s when Marshall Nirenberg cracked the genetic code and won a Nobel Prize. From left: Philip Leder, Chairman, Department of Genetics, Harvard Medical School; Marshall Nirenberg, Chief, Laboratory of Biochemical Genetics, NIH; Maxine F. Singer, Chief, Laboratory of Biochemistry, NIH; C. Thomas Caskey, Director, Institute for Molecular Genetics, Baylor College of Medicine. (Photo Smokey Forester)

he saw the results and became so excited that he demanded a supply for his own patients. Even the tiny amounts available produced positive results: for example, in seven of Gutterman's seventeen patients with breast cancer, in his patients with multiple myeloma [a blood-cell tumor in the bone marrow], in his lymphoma patients. Gutterman applied to the American Cancer Society for money to purchase more of the incredibly expensive interferon, telling them of his first breast cancer patient, "She had a mass under her left arm, and couldn't raise her arm. Within forty-eight hours of her first injection she could lift it." The excitement was starting to build.

While Frank Rauscher was still director of the cancer institute in Bethesda, people had urged him repeatedly, as he said, "to do something about interferon." But he was cautious. "I didn't believe the results." After he became research director of the American Cancer Society in 1976, his attitude changed. Many reports of cures were coming in. And when Gutterman's request arrived for $1.5 million for further interferon purchases, Rauscher went upstairs to the ACS executive. "It's time to bite the bullet on interferon," he said.

But the person who ended up not just biting this particular bullet, but waving interferon before her as a sword in battle, was Mary Lasker. Lasker sat on the American Cancer Society board and, as we have seen, acted as a major health lobbyist in her own right. She and the ACS mounted a tremendous public relations campaign to force the cancer institute at NIH to buy interferon for larger trials. Stephen Carter, then at NCI, recalled the "oncopolitical hyperbole about interferon." "The pressure was unbelievable. Interferon was the worst example I ever saw of politicizing the scientific decision-making process." In retrospect he feels that if he had spoken out against interferon in the late 1970s, his career would have been through.[9] Vincent DeVita, at the time director of cancer treatment at NCI, said of the Lasker forces, "Mary was like a train roaring down the tracks on us. They pulled every stop out, and Mary had a few stops. She was able to get coverage on the front of magazines."[10] According to DeVita, it was the only time Mary Lasker had ever meddled inappropriately in medical matters. Finally the NCI gave in and announced in 1979 that it would buy $9 million worth of interferon.[11]

Yet the facts seemed to speak for themselves. The New York *Times* in 1979 cited "promising results." The NIH had already issued a big report on interferon. *Time* magazine featured interferon as the "IF" drug on its cover of March 31, 1980. When the Cancer Society's Rauscher was asked if the drug worked, he said, "The answer is yes. There is definitely action against cancer. Abundantly, clearly, yes." A nation was given hope.

Flash Gordon cartoon about interferon (1960). There was enormous public pressure on the NIH to move ahead with interferon research, even though many doctors were suspicious of its effectiveness.

This revolution of rising expectations is central to understanding why the drug companies were willing to commit such enormous sums to a drug about which so little was known. A source cited in *Science* said: "Worldwide sales . . . could reach $3 billion a year by 1987." Cancer researcher Robert Spiegel, on the staff of the Schering-Plough Corporation today, explained somewhat defensively after all the dust had settled, "You had twenty years of expectation building up. The only thing missing was enough material. The money was there. The interest was there. Everything was there."[12]

But how to get enough interferon? Here the drug companies, lured by the NCI's proposed purchase of the drug and twenty years of hype, rushed on board. The Searle company set up a $12 million plant in Britain; Abbott Laboratories, Warner-Lambert, and others plunged into interferon. The idea was to identify the gene that made the stuff, "clone" it by putting it into bacteria, harvest the interferon from the resulting soup, and offer the product to what was considered an enormous market. Hoffmann-La Roche in Nutley, New Jersey, crossed the finish line first, although no one knew it at the time.

One might in retrospect appreciate how bewildering this inrush of unfamiliar new biotech was for the drug companies. Traditionally, they had functioned on the Valium model: a team of organic chemists synthesizes compound after compound; another team of pharmacologists puts the compounds into mice. The mice either fall asleep or they don't. The compound goes to the "drug killers" in "animal tox," where it usually perishes. Finally, a more or less predictable number of antibiotics and decongestants reach the market.

But with these new bioengineered proteins, the traditional staff had to be augmented with squads of new protein chemists and immunologists. There were no animals in which something like interferon could be tested because the substance is species-specific, meaning that human interferon doesn't have any effect on mice, and vice versa. The companies, furthermore, had to undertake much basic scientific research on DNA.

To understand why Roche crossed the finish line first, we must back up a moment to 1967, the year in which the company set up its own research institute, the Roche Institute for Molecular Biology, in which scientists would do basic research not closely tied to drug development. This was Roche's solution to the problem of entering an unfamiliar new technology: establishing a sort of mini-NIH. Virginius Dante Mattia, a Newark lad who had gotten an M.D. and come on staff of nearby Roche as its general manager, had conceived the idea. In 1967 Mattia lured John Burns, another M.D. scientist then working for a rival firm, to come and get the institute off the ground. Burns then set up a kind of pipeline from Bethesda to Nutley: going to NIH, grabbing high-quality scientists by means of high salaries, and plunking them down in the hopes that, in addition to producing scholarly papers, they might develop compounds that were therapeutically useful. And therapeutically means commercially: there is no doubt at all that successful drugs are better medicines.

Burns recruited two aces from NIH. One of them, Sidney Udenfriend, had once been a graduate student of Severo Ochoa at NYU; he became in 1968 the Roche Institute's first director. The other was a biochemist named Herbert Weissbach, whom James Shannon had brought to the heart institute in 1953; Weissbach became in 1969 associate director of the

Roche Institute. These men have distinguished scientific pedigrees. And young scientists trained at the Roche Institute have spread throughout university life.

Yet here the story darkens a bit, as the needs of science for openness and the requirements of commerce for exclusivity conflict. In 1969 the Roche Institute also raided from Marshall Nirenberg's lab at NIH a young molecular biologist named Sidney Pestka. Pestka was brought in to develop interferon, and by 1978 he had succeeded in purifying it sufficiently to determine its structure.[13]

The scene now shifts to Los Angeles. It is 1977. A fifty-nine-year-old man lies dying of an obscure kind of leukemia. "For the sake of scientific research," as Nicholas Wade reconstructed the story, "he agreed to a painful procedure of no medical benefit to himself, the sampling by suction from his bone marrow of the cancerous blood-forming cells. Two months later he died."

Two blood specialists at the U. of C. medical school, Phillip Koeffler and David Golde, took the leukemic cells and succeeded in making them grow in a medium so that they would reproduce themselves generation after generation. A splendid tool for research. In the interests of science, Golde sent a sample of the cell line to Robert Gallo at the National Cancer Institute, who wanted to test them for viruses. Gallo noted incidentally that the cells produced interferon. He casually mentioned this to his former colleague Pestka, who asked for a sample of the cells, as indeed Gallo had given Pestka all his previously tested cell lines. Pestka took the cells back to the Roche Institute and, after several months of hard work, turned them into "superproducers of interferon." The cells had thus passed from being objects of disinterested scientific investigation to a potential $3 billion property.[14]

Still, what Pestka did with the cells was highly scientific: he used them to find the gene that makes interferon. Here is how he "fished out" the gene from the DNA of the leukemic cells, and we follow the process because, quite simply, it's how you do biotechnology. Pestka asked a researcher at the City of Hope Medical Center in Duarte, California, to determine for him the sequence of amino acids. (Amino acids are the building blocks of protein; their sequence in the protein is determined by the sequence of base pairs in the gene.)

Then he asked a small biotech firm, Genentech, Inc., in south San Francisco, to synthesize a piece of DNA called a DNA probe that corresponded to that amino acid sequence. Genentech, cofounded by Herbert Boyer, was an obvious candidate for such business; it had already "cloned" in 1978 the gene for insulin.

Now, Pestka's clever plan was to extract all the messenger RNA (mRNA) from the leukemia cells. Because the leukemia cells were already making large amounts of interferon, much of their mRNA would be for interferon. He instructed Genentech to cut the mRNA into tiny fragments with restriction enzymes.

Genetech then made DNA copies of each of these RNA fragments. But which DNA fragment was the interferon gene?

Now the researchers took Genentech's previous probe of artificially made interferon DNA and put it together with each fragment. The fragment it bound to was the interferon gene![15] (The artificial probe by itself didn't suffice for recombinant purposes because it lacked a lot of the base pairs representing instructions needed to get the gene to make interferon.) The above is a difficult step in bioengineering: identifying the complete gene. In June 1980 Genentech announced its success, and the ensuing media furor created enough investor interest to let the firm go public.

Now Roche and Genentech put the interferon gene derived from human leukemia cells into bacterial plasmids, using again the kinds of restriction enzymes and other techniques that Berg, Boyer, Cohen, and Nathans had developed. The bacteria multiplied wildly and, instructed by the new gene that had just been spliced into them, began making interferon.

All this is a far more complicated marriage of science and fermentation art than it appears. How exactly each of these steps is conducted represents guarded "proprietorial" information. In fact, those bacteria that do take up the recombinant plasmids are spread out on a big plate of nutrient gel, where they are cloned, the biologist's equivalent of large-scale lettuce farming. On this farm the recombinant DNA bacteria busily produce the interferon, in addition to all the other proteins the bacteria normally make. The point is that now interferon was becoming available in quantities sufficient to permit extensive clinical trials.

But making drugs that benefit the population is not just a matter of inventing a molecule. The drug must be developed, produced in large enough quantities to make it available at less than five thousand dollars a dose. If Roche had produced a triumph of genetic engineering, it was the Schering Corporation that produced a triumph of biotechnology. In 1978 Schering had acquired a one-sixth interest in a small Swiss biotech company named Biogen. At the time Schering wasn't thinking about interferon. It was desperate just to get something on the market because it had run out of new products. "When we did that Biogen deal," said Schering scientist Frank Bullock, a bulldog of a man who lives and

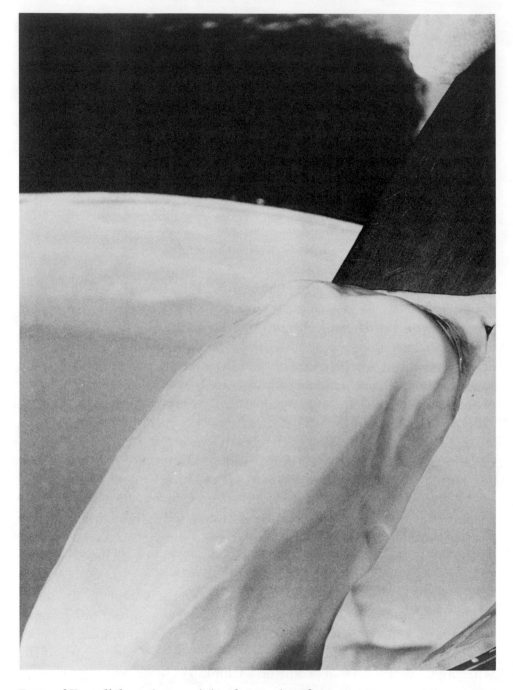

Paste of E. coli *bacteria containing human interferon.*

Biogen's Walter Gilbert.

breathes the making of drugs, "we had not the slightest idea that in fact we had a pregnant cow."[16]

It was Charles Weissmann, a Biogen founder and biochemist at the University of Zurich, who had impregnated the cow. He had been trying to clone the interferon gene for two years, succeeding late in 1979. He informed the board of directors in January 1980, and immediately Biogen staged a big press conference in Cambridge, Massachusetts, to announce the discovery. The story played prominently on the front page of the New York *Times,* along with a picture of another founding scientist of Biogen, Harvard's Walter Gilbert. For the public, this was really big news: an economical way had finally been found to make the fabled interferon. The year 1980 was to be a banner one for Gilbert, as he later that year won the Nobel prize, although for accomplishments not related to interferon. It would be his last banner year for a while.

Genentech is thought to have had the gene in hand for some time, but for commercial reasons did not make the announcement until June 1980. With that announcement, the race commenced between Schering and Roche, each haunted by a sense that it was running out of new products. One way to win is to knock out the other guy's patent. Here Schering had made a terrible blunder. Normally a company does not spend $100 million to develop a product unless it expects to control the patent. Schering had thought it controlled the American patent on interferon, but its lawyers had somehow goofed, failing to realize that Roche, producing the interferon it had developed in collaboration with Genentech, also had a

patent on interferon purification. Robert Luciano, Schering's chief executive officer, ground his teeth together as he recounted the story several
bitter years later. Lawyers for Roche and Schering finally agreed that the
companies would not sue each other under their respective patent rights.

Another way to win such a race is being the first to demonstrate that
your product is safe, that it cures, and prove it to the FDA. The Schering
scientists, already behind because of Roche's surprise announcement that
it would begin testing the drug on patients by January 1981, now entered
upon a desperate race. That one drug house tries to beat another is not of
particular interest to the general public. What is of interest in this story is
how Schering mobilized its staff for an intense team effort that recalled the
penicillin days.

In the tumult of changing science, this is an important public question:
How do you take these huge bureaucratic organizations, bobbing in the
backwash of biotech, and turn them around so that, in the case of the NIH,
they may continue to produce high-quality science, or in the case of
Schering and Roche, they will produce drugs that will be of great good?
The last chapter in the book attempts to answer that question. But here
let's see how Schering pulled interferon together.

Schering was so far behind Roche because Charles Weissmann's bacterial clones produced only minuscule amounts of interferon. Luciano:
"Somebody had to get the damn stuff out, purify it, extract it. There was a
great deal of hostility initially between the Biogen group, who viewed
themselves as university scientists who've invented this great advance and
want to know why the hell isn't it moving forward [and our people]. Well, it
isn't moving forward because you can't even find enough of it [using
Biogen's technique] to move it anyplace. Our people inside resented the
notoriety surrounding the discovery, while they worked in anonymity. The
collaboration wasn't working well."

Luciano brought the two groups together in his office, a beautiful
mohaired and mahoganied affair, and tried to get each to see the value of
the other's contribution. To an outsider, this might sound like settling a
quarrel among third graders, but it worked. "Biogen saw that, hey, there
was a hell of a contribution to be made in development here. Paul Leibowitz began production of the clone and Renato Fuchs began the scale-up.
[T.L.] Nagabhushan developed a unique extraction and purification process in rapid time. Something that had never been done before. That was
good, unique scientific work. The Biogen people formed after that a
healthy respect for our people. Finally, our people began to feel equal.
Otherwise, interferon would have died."

Paul Leibowitz brought Schering's scale-model plant—in which you do everything in miniature to make sure it works—on line by December 1980. In these drug-producing bacteria, as one scales up from very small containers to giant ones, every step is fraught with anxiety. Bugs that work well in small scale may quit or somehow change their product as the scale grows. "How do you think I lost all my hair?" joked the balding Elliot Stupak, who headed Schering's team.

In 1982 Schering's Renato Fuchs had completed the big production plant, using 34,000-liter fermenters similar to those once used to make certain antibiotics. Fuchs, from a Yugoslavian family that escaped the Holocaust by fleeing to Colombia, is a short, intense man with huge horn-rimmed glasses who takes a kind of imperial pride in his work. The giant fermenter is filled with nutrients, then 10 liters of bioengineered *E. coli* bacteria containing the interferon gene are poured into it. Each cell takes about an hour to divide, and redivide, and redivide, so that in about sixteen hours one to two tons of bacteria have grown. The bacteria are now killed and centrifuged. In a special process that Walter Gilbert developed (but that Schering had to buy from Harvard in 1983 because Gilbert had resigned his professorship), the proteins are centrifuged from the bacteria, and in a further series of purification steps the interferon at last is separated from the other proteins. At the end of the process, 34,000 liters of culture and two tons of bacteria have produced about 15 grams of interferon, enough to hold in the palm of your hand, but more than the entire world's supply in 1979. Whereas the interferon of 1979 was only 1 percent pure, this is 99 percent pure. One starts to get a sense of what biotechnology can accomplish.

Did Schering beat Roche? Frank Bullock: "I'll give you a truthful answer. I think we were a little more desperate than Roche. We're smaller. We don't have the business base. Roche on a worldwide basis is currently healthy and powerful and totally intimidates me. As do our friends down at Rahway [Merck]. They totally intimidate me."

In being able to complete its clinical trials of interferon at about the same time as Roche, Schering had going for it this totally *un*intimidated staff, for that is what Bullock was really saying: "The staff as a whole, coming out of a situation like this, gets a derivative psychic income, a mental state they take to every other project. It's a certain swagger almost. In any [drug] discovery enterprise, knowing the odds [are that] most things are going to fail, you've got to have a pretty extraordinary level of self-confidence about what you're doing and about yourself. . . ."

It is possible that this race turned out to be largely in vain, for some observers consider the first generation of interferons to be a drug that has failed. The years from 1982 to 1986 were filled with one crushing discovery after another as all the original diseases interferon was thought to cure remained stubbornly uncured. None of this could be determined in advance because you can't discover if human interferon works by testing it on animals. "We can't find what it's good for," said Schering-Plough's Allen Endlich. Stephen Carter at Bristol-Myers is even more direct: "Interferon is clearly a failure. It's damn expensive and it's damn toxic. So how long is a doctor going to give something to a patient that makes him feel absolutely terrible, costs a fortune, and doesn't work?"

But failure to meet exaggerated expectations and failure to help people at all are two different things. Interferon remains one of the most promising of the current bioengineered drugs because, according to Dr. Robert Spiegel, the director of Schering's clinical testing program, it does help 20 percent of the patients with such cancers as AIDS-related Kaposi's sarcoma, or 40 percent of AIDS patients with the bacterial infection pseudomonas. The disappointment was that interferon didn't help 90 percent of the patients and that the drug had unexpected toxicity.

In only one obscure kind of leukemia, called hairy-cell leukemia because the cells have little hairlike projections, did interferon cure almost all those afflicted. The FDA approved it for this "indication" in June 1986. But there are only about two thousand people in the United States with hairy-cell leukemia, and Schering had invested more than $100 million developing the drug, to say nothing of what Biogen and Roche had spent.

As interferon failed to do well in the marketplace, the risks of biotech started to become evident. Biogen fell upon hard times. Ex-professor and Nobelist Walter Gilbert was forced out as its president. A rueful Charles Weissmann said in 1983, "We have eight interferons in search of a disease. We really don't have the slightest idea where we are going with interferon."[17]

Yet interferon is currently being tested in AIDS, breast and skin cancer, and the common cold. There may be surprises to come.

Guided Missiles

Many diseases in the body stem from a single kind of cell that may be growing out of control, as in cancer, or invaded by a virus, as in AIDS. But in 1950s-style therapy nothing existed for going after such rogue cells. Antibiotics, for example, do well in zapping bacteria so that they burst in the bloodstream, but the drugs that built the big drug houses don't help us with the alarming diseases of the last quarter of the twentieth century. Here is where a kind of biotechnology called monoclonal antibodies comes in. They may be targeted for specific diseases in the manner of guided missiles.

This story begins in 1957 when an elderly Hungarian immunologist named Jules Freund became head of the new immunology section of the Infectious Diseases institute in Bethesda. Shortly thereafter he fell ill, dying in 1960 of a disease called multiple myeloma. In multiple myeloma a given line of B cells, or antibody-producing cells, goes malignant in the bone marrow. The symptoms of the disease are a lot of bone pain and frequent fractures as this clone of B cells proliferates out of control.

Freund may have died of this disease because of injecting himself—accidentally or for experimental purposes—with one of the substances that causes it.[18] It was a substance he himself had invented back in 1942 called Freund's adjuvant, a mixture of mineral oil and TB germs. He had devised it to induce immune responses in experimental animals. Neither he nor anyone else at this point was thinking of cancer. But if you inject the substance into some strains of mice it has the ability to give them a raging multiple myeloma. "It's a very evil thing," said immunologist William Paul many years later.

Three years before Freund died, his colleague at the cancer institute Michael Potter had become quite interested in how one kind of antibody differs from another. But how to get enough antibodies to study? Pathologist Thelma Dunn, also at the cancer institute, gave him a couple of mice who had the disease Freund was shortly to die of. Potter analyzed their blood and found the tumor was producing massive amounts of antibody.[19]

In 1960, for reasons independent of Freund's death (although Potter often saw his dying colleague), Potter wondered if the adjuvant might not induce multiple myeloma in mice. If so, before they died the mice would produce enough quantities of antibody from the same cell line to do research on. It seemed logical to induce the disease in a part of the mouse where the tumor cells would thrive easily, hence the belly. Soon Potter learned that simple injections of mineral oil alone would suffice. He started getting back a lot of antibody and went on to study the DNA, RNA, and so forth, of the cells that produced them. These were the first monoclonal antibodies, antibody-like substances from a single (mono-) B cell line.[20]

Why are monoclonals important? Potter's discovery was the first step that would lead to drugs that can be aimed at specific diseases because they are *antibodies already primed for that disease.* If you want to cure cancer, give a drug that is specifically targeted for that particular cancer, that sees, in other words, that cancer as an antigen. That is what all the excitement is about, but to understand why researchers today are so enthusiastic, we must pick up the thread in Argentina.

In the 1970s a colorful Argentinian named Cesar Milstein would find himself in Cambridge, England. Under his direction the first monoclonals with known targets are put together. How did he get there? The Milstein story could be a carbon copy of Nathans's: "My father was a Jewish immigrant who settled in Argentina and was left to his own devices at the age of fifteen. My mother was a teacher, herself the daughter of a poor immigrant family. For both my mother and my father, no sacrifice was too hard to make sure that their three sons (I was the middle one) would go to university."[21]

Milstein, however, must have disappointed his parents' expectations because in Buenos Aires he was an indifferent medical student and spent much of his time politicizing. After squeaking through his exams, he started out with a biochemistry lab and almost lost his position as he broke successively "3 five-liter round-bottom flasks out of a total of 5." Milstein must have had something on the ball, however, for in 1958 he won a fellowship in biochemistry in Cambridge, England. This is just about the time Michael Potter started to think about antibodies.

More years pass; Milstein goes back to Argentina, back to England again. Early in the 1970s Milstein's Cambridge biochem lab received from the Salk Institute in California a line of myeloma cells in culture. (This was a line that Potter had earlier sent to his colleagues at the Salk Institute, which now was reaching England.) Milstein needed antibodies for research and, as we know, myeloma furnishes plenty of them. In 1973 Milstein and a colleague had succeeded in fusing two myeloma cells, a neat trick but one of no obvious practical importance. Milstein traveled to Basel that year to present his findings, and captured the curiosity of a young German doctoral candidate doing research there named Georges Köhler. The following year Köhler came to Cambridge to work with Milstein.

Thus in 1974 Köhler was burrowing away on the problem of mutation in myeloma cells (a natural protective reaction), but he couldn't get the myeloma cell line Milstein had obtained from the United States to produce enough antibodies in tissue culture. So Köhler began experimenting with fusing different varieties of myelomas in order to break this roadblock and, six months after his arrival in England, had become quite proficient at the technique. "I was still thinking of trying to get a line [of myeloma cells] which was specific for a given antigen," said Köhler. All antibodies are specific for something, but with myeloma antibodies you have no idea what it is.

"I had the idea in bed, before going to sleep, and then I couldn't sleep at all. I told it to Claudia, my wife, the next morning. Then I went to the lab, and I talked to Cesar [Milstein], down in the basement where the tissue culture was.

"One of the things about Cesar is that he listens. If you come to him with a crazy idea, instead of dismissing it he will try to find out the good things about it. When I presented this to him, I was very uncertain, and I am grateful that he didn't turn it down immediately."

Köhler's idea was, rather than continuing to fuse myeloma cells together, to fuse a myeloma cell to a normal B cell that was producing known antibodies. The energetic myeloma would reproduce indefinitely; the lazy B cell would provide antibody to a known antigen, or invader. The hybrid of the two would provide buckets of material. The problem was that both B cells and myeloma cells were supposed to be poor fusers. So Köhler risked wasting the rest of his fellowship year in England pressing ahead with this plan.

But press ahead he did. To get a known antibody, he injected into the spleen of a mouse a particular antigen: some red blood cells. The B cells of the spleen would make antibodies to the invading red blood cells. Then in a test tube he fused the B cells and the myeloma cells. Would his fused "hybridoma" now make the desired antibody?

By Christmastime the crucial experiments were ready. He would know if they had been successful by the appearance of a "halo" in the medium of red blood cells in which he was trying to grow these hybrid cells, their antibodies specifically directed against those blood cells.

Having started the experiment, he went home for dinner, intending to return to the lab later in the evening. "I asked Claudia to come with me," Köhler remembers, "because it would be so boring to score a negative result. She was trying to calm me down. But she came with me. We went down into the basement of the institute, which has no windows. I looked at the first two plates. I saw these halos. That was fantastic. I shouted. I kissed my wife. . . ."

Thus Köhler had created a small factory that produced one particular, absolutely pure antibody of a known specificity. Remember that this specificity business is crucial: that gives the missile its "guided" dimension. Milstein and Köhler called the new cells hybridomas. The specific antibody had come from the white B cells in the mouse's spleen; the immortality had come from the tireless myeloma cells. And this neat exercise won them a Nobel Prize in 1984. The two scholars could foresee practical applications for their invention and asked the British Government if it wished to take out a patent. There was no response, and British science lost the opportunity to benefit from the hundreds of millions of sales dollars that monoclonals would produce.[22]

The American pharmaceutical industry was not slow in seeing biotech applications for these things. You could make a monoclonal specific for anything you wanted to investigate. A certain cancer? Inject the mouse spleen with tumor cells and create a monoclonal targeted for that cancer. A given disease you wanted to diagnose? Inject cells from that disease into the mouse's spleen and get a diagnostic test for that disease. Thus monoclonals arrived with a bang in medical *diagnostics* in the late 1970s.

But in one particular area of *therapy* they have arrived as well. This new technology is actually making people well again, rather than just improving doctors' ability to diagnose disease. Therapeutic monoclonals are helping patients with transplanted organs, such as transplanted kidneys, avoid the body's natural tendency to reject the transplant. They have blossomed under Ortho's Gideon Goldstein.

Goldstein, an M.D.-immunologist from Melbourne, Australia, was thirty when he landed at NIH in the Infectious Disease institute. He had come to these shores to do one thing: develop his "baby." Now, what his "baby" was, a hormone the thymus puts out called thymopoietin, is not part of this story. With the ability to switch T cells on and off, it is turning into an interesting drug that regulates the immune system. It is even being looked at as a possible AIDS drug. But thymopoietin is not a monoclonal antibody. To do research on it, Goldstein needed to develop a line of monoclonals. This rather technical research requirement resulted in an important new monoclonal drug.

Goldstein had discovered thymopoietin as a graduate student in Australia under the great immunologist Sir Frank Macfarlane Burnet. And when he came to NIH in 1967 it was to develop various tests of its effectiveness on T cells. T cells, which mature in the thymus, are the cells that thymopoietin controls. To purify thymopoietin and determine the order of amino acids, Goldstein went the following year to NYU. For the next decade in New York City, first at NYU and then at Memorial Sloan-Kettering, Goldstein was obsessed by the idea of turning his beloved thymopoietin into a drug and consulted with various companies about it. In 1977, therefore, Goldstein left New York City for Ortho Pharmaceutical's big, empty new labs in Raritan, New Jersey. Owned by Johnson & Johnson, Ortho was trying to reposition itself from a maker of birth control pills to high-tech science.

Goldstein became the head of Ortho's new department of "immunobiology." "My original concept," he later said, "was I would putter around in a couple of labs myself and do my research as I had always done. I was never an empire builder in academe. I just liked learning new things and so on. The company would develop the drug." Goldstein soon realized this was a mistake. Developing a drug costs $100 million. It can't be done two afternoons a week.

To help organize the research on T cells, the target of thymopoietin, Goldstein brought to Ortho in 1978 a young immunologist from Taiwan named Patrick Kung. Kung's story, which is disputed by Goldstein, is that he had worked on hybridomas (which make monoclonal antibodies) at David Baltimore's lab at MIT, and for Du Pont. Kung says that Goldstein knew nothing of hybridomas, but to test the effects of thymopoietin they needed some monoclonals that would go after specific surface markers on T cells. So Kung worked out a series of monoclonals targeting the various T cells, number one in the series, number two, and so on. The way experimental drugs are often labeled, it would be *Orth-Kung-T* cell, number *1*, number *2*, etc. Hence OKT-1, OKT-2.

Then it dawned on Kung that these monoclonal antibodies specific for T cells could be used to go after destructive T cells in the body and bind to their receptors, thus knocking them out. When may the body's own T cells be destructive? When, for example, they cause transplants to be rejected. It struck everyone like a thunderbolt that OKT-3 in particular, which had been designed to target only T cells, would be perfect in reversing transplant rejections. It coats the receptors of T cells and prevents them from attacking the transplanted tissue. The commercial possibilities were enormous, given the size of the transplant market. (Such previous drugs to combat transplant rejection as cyclophosphamide and the steroids had the disadvantage of knocking out the entire immune system, not just the T cells. OKT-3 is more specific than cyclosporine, another popular drug, for T cells.)

Goldstein became exasperated at this turn of events, because Ortho was now turning from his baby, thymopoietin, to develop a product that had originally occupied a quite ancillary position: OKT-3. Kung resented Goldstein's continued attempts to relegate the OKT series to second place, quarreled with Goldstein, and resigned from Ortho in 1981. The story is presented now as though Goldstein had discovered OKT-3 and the others. But in fact he initially was impatient with them.[29]

Yet Goldstein, too, became enthusiastic about the OKT series when the drug turned out to be significant in understanding AIDS and other diseases by delineating T-cell subgroups (remember that the AIDS virus attacks T cells). If you make an antibody specific for a given T cell, it will go after only those cells. The whole current T cell nomenclature, for example "CD4" in one version, or "T4" in another, was devised on the basis of the different T cells that the Ortho series targets. Goldstein said,

"It's enormously gratifying to me to see them as part of the English language now. I go and see a play on Broadway about AIDS and they talk about the T4-to-T8 ratio. It's all come out of this lab. Our monoclonals defined those cells."

Although monoclonals represent biotech, they do not stem from genetic engineering. Nobody manipulates the DNA, for the two cells join after being chemically treated. Nor do the monoclonals require anything more high-tech than the belly of a mouse for their production. The mouse's belly is "primed," then injected with a solution of hybridomas. The hybridoma cells multiply merrily until they have almost killed the mouse, at which point the mouse is sacrificed and the antibodies are extracted from the fluid that has accumulated in the belly. Straightforward purification techniques then separate the desired antibody from the mass of other proteins.

Among the many other uses to which the monoclonals are now being put, we mention merely one. Although still speculative, it offers considerable possibilities in cancer therapy. All monoclonals are guided missiles, but might it be possible to make an *armed* guided missile directed at cancer? Previous generations of anti-cancer drugs did halt the reproduction of cancer cells, but they also terminated all other cell division in the body, causing enormous side effects. Could one not devise monoclonals for particular cancers, hitch the antibody to some kind of cancer-destroying material, and then launch the whole thing at the cancer? When the monoclonal binds to the target, the deadly chemicals it carries destroy the tumor cells. That is the theory, at least.

Talk about drug wars. The race to get these guided missiles off the ground preoccupies many research directors. A kind of closed expression comes over their faces—they who normally are so glad to discuss their contributions to human welfare—when asked about their cancer chemotherapy programs. The Hybritech company of San Diego is supplying monoclonals armed with radioisotopes for patients with liver cancer. Eli Lilly and Company is linking the cancer drug vinblastine to Lilly monoclonals. Bristol-Myers, with a long list of cancer drugs still under patent, is reaching to its own shelves to put warheads on the missile. There are many strategies.

Perhaps these drugs will pan out, or not. The underlying idea, however, is quite breathtaking: using the peculiar quality antibody molecules have of being specific for targets in order to aim them at and destroy those disease targets. The potential benefit that the monoclonals offer humankind is incalculable.

Clotbusters

So the reader won't think "biotech" is all hype and obscure things grown up in mouse bellies, we mention one solid success: a bioengineered drug that breaks up clots in the arteries of heart attack victims. When a thrombus, or clot, forms in somebody's coronary artery, causing a heart attack, the affected portion of heart muscle doesn't die immediately from lack of oxygen. There's a crucial window of a few hours in which intervention can prevent the ischemia (lack of oxygen) from turning into necrosis (tissue death). In the 1970s several heart attack drugs were discovered, called streptokinase and urokinase, that would dissolve the clot and restore blood to the dying heart muscle. But to be most effective, these substances had to be injected directly into the affected coronary artery, and such injections require cardiac catheterization, a procedure not always available immediately after a heart attack (when it will do the most good). If you inject streptokinase into an arm vein, for example, it acts upon the entire body, creating the risk of bleeding, especially into the brain. Thus, although these drugs represented a big improvement on what was available previously to dissolve clots (nothing), they were not the penicillin of heart attacks.

Then in 1978 a Belgian scientist at the University of Louvain named Désiré Collen began to unravel exactly how the body deals with clots. It turned out there was a natural enzyme system, produced by the cells lining the blood vessels, that dissolved clots. Yet, faced with a massive clot in a big artery, the body didn't make enough of this enzyme to suffice. Could the body's own anti-clot system be reinforced? Collen identified the crucial enzyme. This enzyme, a natural substance that he called plasminogen activator, would get only those parts of the anti-clot system going *that were already bound to a clot.* The enzyme, "*t*issue-type" *p*lasminogen *a*ctivator, as opposed to other types of plasminogen activators, became called, for short, t-PA or TPA.

In the early 1980s Collen sent a paper describing his research to an American journal; this has become the norm for European scientists today. They publish in English and if possible in the flagship American journals of the various disciplines. An M.D.-physiologist at Washington University of St. Louis named Burton Sobel was on the editorial board of this journal, saw a copy of Collen's manuscript, and wrote Collen asking for samples of TPA. Sobel began doing research on dogs in St. Louis and realized immediately how effective TPA was in dissolving clots in dogs with induced heart attacks. Sobel's group would give it to a dog. Fifteen minutes later the clot, as followed by angiography, was gone. "And the animal looked healthy as a clam [sic]," Sobel said in an interview. A year following the animal studies, the St. Louis group began giving TPA to humans. But natural TPA exists in such minute doses that, as with interferon, it was difficult to collect enough to do research on it.

Then TPA research, like that on interferon four years before it, burst wide open when in 1983 Genentech, Inc., cloned the gene and expressed it in the same kind of bacterial system that interferon had been cloned in. Collen had been a consultant of Genentech's and brought with him, from Belgium to California, enough information to let them fish out the gene. He also brought knowledge of how to test it and determine its activity.

Genentech financed the clinical trials. Sobel said of those trials in St. Louis: "Once we began the pilot study in humans, the verdict was clear right away. The very first patient that we administered the drug to was very seriously ill and responded remarkably to the intervention. The clot dissolved."

In that same year, 1983, the heart institute in Bethesda organized a huge trial of TPA at thirteen different medical schools, comparing it to streptokinase. The double-blind aspect of this trial—in which neither doctors nor patients know if TPA or streptokinase is being given—was ended in February 1985 because TPA did so much better.[24] It would have been irresponsible to withhold this therapy from the patients.

According to Sobel, "TPA works acutely [immediately] in about 75 percent of the patients with documented clots." And it works by injection rather than by catheterization, thus theoretically permitting ambulance attendants to give it on the way to the hospital. The earlier the treatment, the less permanent the damage to the heart. TPA was clearly going to be a superb drug.

Given (1) that almost 700,000 patients are admitted to hospitals every year with a heart attack, (2) that TPA might be given routinely to all of them (since there's no quick way to tell if the heart attack was caused by a clot), and (3) that the cost will probably be two to three thousand dollars a dose, the mercantile possibilities for TPA are considerable. Many drug companies have therefore hopped on board with versions of TPA that are designed to bind to the clot more tightly or stay in the blood longer. And why not? This kind of profit-driven innovation produces better drugs. Genentech is not, after all, a charitable foundation.

Smith Kline, for example, will try to topple Genentech's patent, then press ahead with their own improved version of TPA. They have a licensing agreement to develop the particular TPA for which Biogen has cloned the gene. We remember Biogen from interferon. One sees how small this biotech drug world is, how few the number of big players. But the players may advance on the board only by contributing something. Smith Kline's scientists are working on drugs which, in combination with TPA, may heal the underlying lesion on the wall of the coronary artery, the lesion that has caused the clot to form in the first place.

Is this kind of "me-tooism" unproductive? Smith Kline, for example, is making its TPA in a culture of mammalian cells, something on the order of Chinese hamster ovary cells, because mammalian cells produce more exact copies of human TPA than bacteria are capable of turning out. It is in such technical but crucial details that marketplace competition has become a major motor of medical progress at the end of the Health Century. "We're a couple of years behind Genentech," says Smith Kline's Barry Berkowitz, "but we're very close to Burroughs Wellcome."[25]

At the beginning of the book we talked about the United States becoming, after the Second World War, the lead locomotive of medical research in the world as the result of a singular collaboration among universities, the National Institutes of Health, and the private sector. At the end, the reader might well imagine that the word "collaboration" is used ironically, for what we have seen in this chapter has been tooth-and-claw rivalry: the highly competitive drug companies struggling to lure away NIH's best scientists; academics in a race to clone genes and becoming in the process wealthy individuals; well-meaning lobbyists endeavoring to impose uninformed priorities on federal scientists.

And yet, and yet. From these behind-the-scenes rivalries have come unusual partnerships and great discoveries for the common good. As the drug companies battle one another for profits, we get better, cheaper penicillins. As the health lobbyists bend ears on the Hill, the NIH gets more money. As the academics rival one another in private biotech companies, gene after new gene is cloned. It is not an accident that the major triumphs at the end of the Health Century have occurred in the United States, where, more than in any other country, the public purse has encouraged science, and the private purse has encouraged competition.

Epilogue

Think of the progress we've made. "In my own early professional life when I was an intern on the wards of the Boston City Hospital," said Lewis Thomas in 1985, "the major threats to human life were tuberculosis, tetanus, syphilis, rheumatic fever, pneumonia, meningitis, polio, and septicemia [blood poisoning] of all sorts. These things worried us then the way cancer, heart disease and stroke worry us today. The big problems of the 1930s and 1940s have literally vanished."[1] In this book we have seen why they have vanished.

Lewis Thomas is a vigorous seventy-four years old. The dean of American medicine has lived through three quarters of the Health Century. And young interns today literally have no idea what he is talking about. Says Nobelist Joseph Brown, "You know, if you ever watch a movie about something in the nineteenth century, the minute the heroine coughs a little you know she's going to be dead of consumption in the next reel. We don't have that fear anymore."

But how will the next hundred years deal with the problems we do have today? How will *The Second Health Century,* to be published in the year 2087, represent life in 1987? Will historians write, "Back at the end of the twentieth century, the leaders of the day, spending more than $11 billion a year on medical research, had it in their power to do great good. And then they fell short"?

Huge government bureaucracies and giant drug companies do not automatically produce great good for the nation's health. Millions of dollars may sink silently into useless piles of "me-too" drugs and unimaginative mouse-doctoring. These large organizations require leadership. In this epilogue we look at the leadership styles that are emerging for tomorrow, leadership that must link the enormous resources of the public and private sectors to genuine improvements in health.

"I Fully Expect You to Fail"

Nobody at the drug companies talks in unwatched moments about "the future challenges of health." They talk about the coming crisis in profits. "By 1990 the patents of nearly all of the top 200 prescription pills in the U.S. will have expired," writes one observer. As the old reliables of the 1960s go off patent, growth rates in the pharmaceutical industry have already fallen from about 15 percent a year in the 1970s to 5 percent a year in the 1980s.[2]

Thus the challenge for the drug industry is to develop new products that doctors will want to prescribe and that will keep up profits. Here biotechnology enters as the most promising field for developing important new drugs.

You're a chief executive officer of a company with $4 billion annually in sales. You've come up through the business side. And some bright scientist comes through the door and encourages you to invest $100 million in a bunch of white cells in a test tube with no proven record of curing anything. "Biotechnology is immensely confusing," says Gerald Laubach, the president of Pfizer Inc. "There are a hundred and one little firms running around, underfunded, trying to develop, and inexperienced. It's very complex to deal with."[3] Laubach, an austere Pennsylvania Dutchman, is the head of a multibillion-dollar corporation. He has to figure out how to steer Pfizer through the narrows of biotech and onto the silver seas of continuing profitability.

So the obvious answer is to hire a lot of scientists, plunk them down in front of their benches, and let them go to work. But here things get tricky, because, unlike widgets, science can't be called forth at command. Says Robert Luciano, chief executive officer of Schering-Plough, "Drug discovery is a creative process, not a linear process. If it were a linear, production process, you'd just put so many units of labor and capital and resources in here and it goes along the production line, and widgets drop off at a predetermined rate. But this is a creative process."[4] You can't count on something being created, in other words. Or as George Cotzias, the maverick Greek scientist of the Brookhaven Labs, put it, "Science is guts, luck, and intuition, and you can't plan that. Only the fools in Washington think you can."[5]

Here is where leadership comes in. It makes the difference between bringing together scientists who mull aimlessly, and a group such as the members of Pfizer's Feldene team who, fired by enthusiasm, make useful contributions to the nation's health. But how to do it? How to lead such people, who are notoriously averse to being led?

Scientists do not respond well to battle hymns. The chief executive officer may no longer stand at the head of the column and cry, "Forward, boys!" in the way someone like John McKeen, the former managing director of Pfizer, once did. Laubach calls McKeen "one of the great leaders of this industry, an autocrat of the old school. He was a nineteenth-century manager-leader, complete with starched shirt collar. He was autocratic, domineering, abrasive, and impatient. It worked wonders for the company."

James Shannon shared something of this style at NIH, although his collars weren't starched. Indeed his grooming was often so poor that *Time* is said to have scrubbed a cover shot of Shannon because one of his shirt cuffs was frayed in the photograph. Laubach continued, "McKeen's style would not go down well with the several thousand scientists who have to create successful innovation or we as a corporation don't make it." The scientists of today do not respond well to autocrats, in other words.

What kind of leadership style does go down well with scientists? Where does one place oneself if not at the head of the column? The lunchroom perhaps? If one thinks back to scenes in this book that have set the stage for discovery, one of them has been lunch. Remember Arthur Kornberg's lunches with the pals at NIH, James Black's lunches at Welwyn Garden City when he was driving Tagamet forward. What memories did Michael Heidelberger have of the Rockefeller Institute in 1912? It was the lunchroom. Who might be having a sandwich there? Heidelberger recalled Jacques Loeb, the great German-American biologist, Peyton Rous, discoverer of the first cancer virus, Alexis Carrel, first to outline experimentally all the major heart operations.[6] Indeed, Rockefeller's great Oswald Avery himself, who in 1944 found DNA to be the mechanism of heredity, was said to thrive at the Rockefeller Institute not because of the laboratories but because of the conversation.[7]

Given that half of all science research in America today is done in the private sector, how does one re-create that intense excitement about discovery that surrounded Oswald Avery? One strategy is the "charismatic" style of leadership: beaming forth so much excitement yourself that those around you become swept up. A perfect example of this is Stanley Crooke.[8] Crooke, who although a midwesterner has retained some of the southern accent he acquired while studying for an M.D. at Baylor, came to Smith Kline in 1980 as director of research. He was brought there by chief executive officer Henry Wendt. Wendt, determined never again to let the cupboard go bare, wanted to reposition Smith Kline as a biotech company. The company built a huge new research lab near Philadelphia. Crooke was to run it.

Crooke does not feel that "pure research" is somehow nobler. "The notion of making drugs is inherently good," Crooke says. He repeats the phrase "inherently good," as he warms up. "The better the drug is, the better it is for patients. So no societal justification is required. It's a goddamn good thing to do. Everything about me is geared to making drugs because I think it's good."

When Crooke arrived, he faced the problem of lining up the hundreds of new scientists Smith Kline had just hired to work productively. And one does that by creating a distinctive, in-house scientific culture, a climate in which people work together, not because they are fear-driven by the threat of losing their job, or profit-driven by the promise of bonuses, but because they are science-driven, determined to apply the powerful light of molecular biology to developing new drugs. Thus, for Crooke, leadership means getting the hundreds of Ph.D.s and M.D.s now on staff enthusiastic about doing what they already do best. "The problem is how to align good people in the task of making drugs," he says. "The process of drug discovery is thrillingly complex, one of the few businesses really based on research."

And how do you know if you've succeeded in creating this culture of science? Crooke is very interested in lunch. Wendt is very interested in lunch. Weekly Crooke travels from the rustic research labs to see Wendt, and Wendt asks him about things like what are people saying over lunch, is there an air of excitement in the little conversation areas we've created, and so forth.[9]

The chief of a company with annual sales over $2 billion asks what the scientists are talking about over lunch?

Absolutely.

As these companies build new labs to accommodate molecular biology, a lot of thought is given to how to maximize conversations about science. In Merck's new lab wing in Rahway, the big rectangular lab bench is put in the middle of a room, so that everybody will constantly be walking past everybody else and there'll be constant interaction, no loners brooding away in cubbyholes. At Bristol-Myers's new research labs in Wallingford, Connecticut, scientists' offices are put together in common rooms across from the labs, so that they'll constantly cross paths as they go from lab to office, minimizing the kind of pouting and feuding that happens among powerful individuals who don't see each other very often. At ends of corridors little clusters of armchairs casually sprout, with a blackboard nearby, just in case people happen to be chatting and are seized by an idea. . . .

Thus one way to link together the thousands of new molecular biologists the drug companies are bringing on board is to inspire by example, and to hope the enthusiasm is infectious, in the style of Stanley Crooke.

Another tactic is to remove the penalties for failure, so that one's scientists are encouraged to be bold. It's hard, in a commercial world long attuned to searching the bottom line every three months, to convince one's people that failure doesn't matter as long as they have attempted the finest science of which they are capable. Thus Schering's Robert Luciano, the adopted son of a New York Italian family, offers an old-shoe image quite different from that of the tightly compressed Wendt.[10] He fingers in his pocket a gold tooth cap that has come off while shaving that morning. "I had to create an atmosphere that led our scientists to believe there was no penalty for failure. The only penalty for failure is for incompetence. I fully expect you to fail. It's in the nature of the process. In that case, you just go back and reconceive a new program."

For Luciano, leadership means letting one's scientists know the track is clear. "Even as a layman it seemed to me compelling that if you got the best people and gave them a certain amount of direction but largely allowed them to pursue their work in a relevant field, it would work. It's mainly a matter of getting the right people, creating the proper atmosphere, and then standing back and seeing if it works."

Luciano was told about Henry Wendt following those conversations in the lunchroom. Luciano looked stricken: that's not his style *at all.* "The biggest contribution management can make to research," he said, "is to show interest, provide the resources, and build a degree of confidence and security in the scientists." Given that Schering invests hundreds of millions of dollars every year in research, this kind of hands-off policy has risks. "It's a lot of money," Luciano says, somewhat regretfully. Yet if Schering's scientific culture does come together in the manner of the Rockefeller Institute lunchroom, the company will ride the wave of biotechnology handsomely.

Luciano's self-effacing quality causes him to downplay his own leader-

ship role. It is lab director Frank Bullock at Schering who projects that
Crookeian kind of enthusiasm. Yet Bullock credits Luciano as the driving
force pushing Schering from decongestants into biotechnology. This was
the logic of interferon. "Luciano came here [in 1978] with a view that he
really wanted Schering to be a research-driven company. With interferon
he achieved in one stroke a transformation of the image of the company
and put us on the road to being research-driven. I don't know if you were a
CEO what you would pay to do that, but I think you would pay a lot."[11]

Thus the leadership challenge for executives of these big drug companies is to survive the 1990s by becoming science-driven rather than market-driven. A big shake-out is coming in the industry, comparable to the
shake-out that has already occurred in Silicon Valley among the high-tech
microelectronics firms. At $100 million a try, bringing a drug to market
has become so expensive that the companies are dividing into the science-
driven discoverers, the takers of table scraps, and the "generics," the
companies that copy drugs that have gone off-patent.[12] Proud old names
like Parke-Davis have already disappeared from the scene, folded into the
Warner-Lambert empire.

The companies you read about here are among those that want to stay
among the ranks of the discoverers. But until the past decade or son, many
drug executives appeared unaware of what it takes. In the late 1960s, for
example, Pfizer's president Gerald Laubach conducted a poll among industry executives on whether they thought company management understood what was happening in research and development. Seventy percent
confessed they did not.[13] It is a sign of the changing times that creating an
in-house culture of science is now viewed by many industry leaders as
among their greatest challenges. Says Reginald Jones, the former chief
executive officer of General Electric, "Every company has its own culture,
and there are no two that are just alike. A CEO definitely has an impact on
that culture, just as an Iacocca has re-established the morale at Chrysler."[14]

Chrysler succeeds by being market-driven, and that is a matter of interest mainly to the shareholders. But the great majority of all new drugs
today, as opposed to forty years ago, are created by the drug industry. And
it is in the public interest, at the end of this Health Century, to hope that
the leaders of the pharmaceutical industry assimilate successfully what
being science-driven is all about.

"I'm Not Very Oriented Toward Money"

The National Institutes of Health confronts the Second Health Century as
well. And the leadership problems of this great biomedical organization,

which Lewis Thomas has called "the most brilliant social invention of modern times," entail attracting young people rather than maintaining profit rates.[15] The NIH once had, according to the immunologist William Paul, "the most fantastic recruiting device. It was fear of the draft. So it got absolutely the smartest M.D.s who wanted to do science to work here."[16] Many of the great names in modern American medical science are among that generation whom the alternative to military service pushed to Bethesda. These men then went out like Johnny Appleseeds and sowed molecular biology across the universities of the land.

The problems began when the doctor draft was abolished and working at NIH somehow lost its urgency for many bright young men. The NIH itself lost none of its scientific cutting edge. Jeffrey Schlom, a senior scientist who, to his wife's dismay, as he puts it, has rejected many fat offers to leave says, "It's still the place to be. There's a mystique at the NIH, the center of power in the medical community. It's the place where everybody has to come. That yellow list of lectures—there's no other list like it in the world."

The NIH list of lectures (which is yellow) showed for the week of December 15 to 21, 1986, a time when universities were shutting down for Christmas, over sixty lectures scheduled. If you wanted to figure out where to eat your lunch Tuesday noon, you'd have to chose among an immunology seminar on "Human MHC Class I Genes," a talk on the development of the lens of the eye in embryos, and a presentation by someone from Cornell on how some microorganism caused cancer in certain cell cultures.

So a scientist doesn't have to go to the scholarly conventions, the "meetings," Schlom continued. "Just go to a lecture or two a day and you'll know what's going on. The speakers give their *unpublished* data." He emphasized the unpublished part as the real edge, for in the hierarchy of scientific presentations, lesser audiences hear only the already published findings.[17] This excitement is everywhere at the Institutes. "It's just an electric place," said Tony Fauci, the AIDS specialist and director of the infectious diseases institute. "The NIH has to be the most exciting place in the world from the scientific standpoint."[18]

If it's so exciting, what's the problem? The problem is that excitement does not compensate for the low government salaries that scientists are forced to subsist on. They can easily double or triple their civil-service wages by going to private industry, and of course many have already done so. The crunch usually comes when the children reach school age, when their parents wish to put them in private schools. Government employees often cannot afford such schools.

Since paying more is impossible, how does one otherwise persuade bright young scientists to stay on? Here is where leadership comes in again. This time it does not consist in pointing out the importance of basic science, as Shannon did. Shannon's distinctive vision was to recognize that clinical progress would come only through fundamental research, or what Lewis Thomas calls "undifferentiated research." Thomas says, "No committee convened in the early 1950s to survey the future prospects . . . could possibly have guessed at the things that lay ahead."[19] But Shannon saw what lay ahead and mobilized government funds behind basic research rather than the purchase of additional iron lungs.

Everyone knows now that the future lies in molecular biology. The leadership of the 1990s must get the next generation to commit itself to *do* the basic research. And here new leadership figures are presenting themselves.

The future of NIH depends on keeping more people like Thomas Waldmann. Who is Thomas Waldmann? Nobody outside the scientific community has ever heard of him. He is in his office in stocking feet, a small teddy bear of a man.[20] His shirt is stained where his ball-point pens have leaked onto the fabric. One of his wool socks has a hole in it. Waldmann grew up in New York City, the son of an engineer and a mother who taught science. They'd immigrated from Czechoslovakia in the 1920s. As a boy, he'd run the nature program at his Connecticut camp; from fourth grade on, he'd done little projects with toad eggs. He wanted to be a scientist.

Waldmann finished an internship at the Massachusetts General Hospital in 1956. "The Korean War was over but the doctors' draft was still on." He came to NIH.

Waldmann, a very distinguished scientist with over four hundred papers to his credit, has a natural charisma. One can see it immediately. He talks about his research, out there on the forefront of how to turn T cells on and off, and is transported by the details of what he's working on. There are enormous depths of scientific curiosity resounding here, and the resonance of them attracts younger scientists.

He meets with his lab group of eight or nine young people, including a Japanese and an Austrian. A young female scientist starts talking about not being able to get the gene that codes for some protein, and Waldmann begins giggling. They look at him. He tells the story of the lions tearing the Christians limb from limb in the Roman Forum.

Suddenly a little boy in the stands starts crying.

"Johnny, why are you crying?" asks his father.

"That poor lion over there hasn't got a Christian," says Johnny.

This is apropos the poor protein that doesn't have a gene. These young scientists laugh. They love Waldmann, who has had many offers to leave the government service.

Why hasn't he accepted them?

"I'm not all that interested in money," he replies.

Thomas Waldmann is the latter-day equivalent of the dedicated microbe hunters who built the Public Health Service and who started the National Institutes of Health. But bravery in thc late 1980s frequently consists of renouncing the overwhelming material abundance of a consumer society in favor of dedication to what Waldmann calls "bringing molecular biology to the bedside."

One of his patients is a young man with an obscure but devastating leukemia. Waldmann has cloned a particular gene and extracted the protein that is making this young man better. He may not stay better. He is Waldmann's first patient with the disease. But Waldmann, and others like him, will keep looking for the solution. We are at the beginning of a new Health Century.

NOTES

The name of the publisher has been omitted from citations to books published before 1945.

Abbreviations used in notes:

JAMA = *Journal of the American Medical Association*
NEJM = *New England Journal of Medicine*
Goodman and Gilman = Alfred G. Gilman et al., eds., *Goodman and Gilman's The Pharmacological Basis of Therapeutics,* 7th ed. (New York: Macmillan, 1985).

CHAPTER ONE

1. F. I. Knight, "The Contagiousness of Tubercular Disease of the Lungs," *JAMA* 9 (October 15, 1877): 505.

2. The New York *Times,* November 19, 1986, p. 8. It is a sign of medical progress that this case was taken, not from a news story, but from an advertisement for the hospital.

3. As nationwide life-expectancy statistics do not exist for the United States before 1900, the figures offered here for 1887 are taken from the state of Massachusetts for 1890. U.S. Bureau of the Census, *Historical Statistics of the United States, Colonial Times to 1970. Bicentennial Edition, Part 2* (Washington, D.C.: Government Printing Office, 1975), table B, 126–35, p. 56. Life expectancy at twenty for males has risen 29 percent, from forty-one more years in 1890 in Massachusetts to fifty-three more years in 1983 for the United States as a whole; 1983 is the most recent year for which statistics are available. National Center for Health Statistics, "Advance Report of Final Mortality Statistics, 1983," *Monthly Vital Statistics Report,* vol. 34, no. 6, supp. 2, DHHS pub. no. (PHS) 85–1120 (Hyattsville, Md.: Public Health Service, September 26, 1985), p. 12.

4. National Center for Health Statistics, *Health: United States, 1985,* DHHS pub. no. (PHS) 86–1232, Public Health Service (Washington, D.C.: Government Printing Office, December 1985), tables 17 and 18, pp. 48, 50. The last year for which data are available is 1984. To calculate "annual rates of decline," I subtracted the 1984 death rate from that of 1950, and divided by thirty-four years.

5. This list omits many important medicines that were not specific for a given disease, such as ether and chloroform anesthesia, and a whole series of drugs that stimulate or depress the heart and central nervous system. An excellent review of this whole subject may be found in Walter Sneader, *Drug Discovery: The Evolution of Modern Medicines* (New York: Wiley, 1985).

6. Arthur Hertzler, *The Horse and Buggy Doctor* (New York, 1938), p. 78.

7. William Osler, *Principles and Practice of Medicine* (New York, 1892), pp. 76, 276.

8. Selwyn D. Collins, "Age Incidence of Specific Causes of Illness," [U.S.] *Public Health Reports* 50, no. 2, (1935): table 1, p. 1409.

9. The story of sulfanilamide is told in Sneader, *Drug Discovery*, pp. 282–88.

10. *Goodman and Gilman.*

11. Bess Furman, *A Profile of the United States Public Health Service, 1798–1948* (Washington, D.C.: Government Printing Office, 1973), p. 194.

12. Information about Kinyoun's early life comes from his Public Health Service personnel file in the St. Louis Federal Records Center. Dr. Victoria Harden kindly communicated to me a copy of this file. How the myth of his supposed "training" before 1887 in Europe established itself is unclear. If he had, in fact, studied in Europe before 1887 under Koch, Pasteur et al., as later biographers claimed, he would surely have mentioned it in his résumé for the examiners. He did make several later trips to Europe to observe research in the laboratories of these men.

13. Marine was retained in the title, to be dropped ten years later.

14. Details of Public Health Service history are taken from Ralph Chester Williams, *The United States Public Health Service, 1798–1950* (Washington, D.C.: Government Printing Office, 1951), pp. 490–551.

15. Furman, *Profile*, pp. 244–48.

16. See the Roll of Honor in Williams, *Public Health Service*, pp. 546–50; for old photographs of the microbe hunters in the field, pp. 132–33. The phrase "microbe hunters" was popularized by Paul De Kruif's book *Microbe Hunters* (New York, 1926).

17. Victoria A. Harden, *Inventing the NIH: Federal Biomedical Research Policy, 1887–1937* (Baltimore: Johns Hopkins University Press, 1986), p. 38.

18. Elizabeth W. Etheridge, *The Butterfly Caste: A Social History of Pellagra in the South* (Westport, Conn.: Greenwood, 1972), pp. 66–67; and Martin Kaufman et al., eds., *Dictionary of American Medical Biography*, 2 vols. (Westport, Conn.: Greenwood, 1984), vol. 1, p. 296.

19. Goldberger ms. diary, entry of August 9–11, 1915. In archives of the History of Medicine Division of the National Institutes of Health. The diary covers the period from November 28, 1914, to August 11, 1915.

20. Etheridge, *Butterfly Caste*, p. 72.

21. Joseph Goldberger, "The Etiology of Pellagra," [U.S.] *Public Health Reports* 29 (June 26, 1914): 1685; Goldberger wrote a fuller report, discussing eggs, meat, and other dietary factors, "The Cause and Prevention of Pellagra," *Public Health Reports* (September 11, 1914): 2354–57.

22. Interested readers will find a clear account in Lubert Stryer, *Biochemistry*, 2d ed. (San Francisco: Freeman, 1981), pp. 244–49.

23. Samuel D. Gross, *Then and Now* (Philadelphia, 1867), pp. 32–33; the R.A.C. pill was propagated by a quack doctor named John Esten Cooke of Transylvania University at Lexington, Kentucky.

24. Details in I. G. Farbenindustrie Aktiengesellschaft, *Fifty Years of Bayer Remedies, 1888–1938* (Leverkusen, Germany, 1938).

25. See Sneader, *Drug Discovery*, pp. 28–30, 83, on aspirin. The British Government broke the German patent on aspirin during the First World War, so that the drug is now generically called aspirin rather than by its proper chemical name, acetylsalicylic acid.

26. I.G. Farben, *Bayer Remedies*, p. 84.

27. On the conditions generally in pharmaceuticals, see Jonathan Liebenau, "Scientific Ambitions: The Pharmaceutical Industry, 1900–1920," *Pharmacy in History* 27 (1985): 3–11.

28. Elmer Holmes Bobst, *Bobst: The Autobiography of a Pharmaceutical Pioneer* (New York: McKay, 1973), p. 148.

29. Details in Thomas H. Maren, "An Historical Account of CO_2 Chemistry and the Development of Carbonic Anhydrase Inhibitors," *Pharmacologist* 21 (1979): 303–4. An offspring of this dynasty is Senator Lowell Palmer Weicker, Jr., of Connecticut.

30. Alfred D. Flinn, "Research Laboratories in Industrial Establishments of the United States," *National Research Council Bulletin* 3 (December 1921): 1–81.

31. Abbott Laboratories," *Fortune* 22 (August 1940): 67–68.

32. On this interwar expansion in research activity, see John Parascandola, "Industrial Research Comes of Age: The American Pharmaceutical Industry, 1920–1940," *Pharmacy in History* 27 (1985): 12–21.

33. Bobst, *Autobiography*, p. 153.

34. Sneader, *Drug Discovery*, p. 231.

35. *Fortune*, p. 104.

36. Bobst, *Autobiography*, p. 157.

37. Arnold D. Welch, "Reminiscences in Pharmacology: Auld Acquaintance Ne'er Forgot," *Annual Review of Pharmacology* 25 (1985): 8.

38. Francis Boyer, "The Pharmaceutical Manufacturer and Academic Research, *NEJM* 228 (April 29, 1943): 529.

39. A senior figure in science who requested anonymity told me this story.

40. National Institutes of Health, *NIH Almanac: 1985*, U.S. DHHS, Public Health Service, NIH Pub. No. 85–5 (Bethesda, Md.: NIH Division of Public Information, September 1985): 139; and interview with Dr. Bernice Eddy, December 4, 1986.

41. Harden, *Inventing the NIH*, p. 157.

42. In Harden, *Inventing the NIH*, chs. 7 and 8 chronicle these developments in detail.

43. National Institutes of Health, *NIH Almanac*, pp. 150–52.

CHAPTER TWO

1. Erwin Chargaff, "A Fever of Reason," *Annual Review of Biochemistry* 44 (1975): 13.

2. Richard H. Shryock, *American Medical Research Past and Present* (New York: Commonwealth Fund, 1947), p. 89.

3. George Rosen, "Patterns of Health Research in the United States, 1900–1960," *Bulletin of the History of Medicine* 39 (1965): 209.

4. Robert F. Kohler, *From Medical Chemistry to Biochemistry: The Making of a Biomedical Discipline* (Cambridge, Eng.: Cambridge University Press, 1982), p. 173.

5. Chargaff, "Fever of Reason," p. 10.

6. Thomas Kennedy's interview with James Shannon of January 11, 1984; and transcript in archives of the History of Medicine Division of the National Library of Medicine.

7. René Dubos, *The Professor, the Institute, and DNA* (New York: Rockefeller University Press, 1976), p. 22.

8. Ibid., p. 23.

9. L. Emmet Holt, the founder of American pediatrics, Christian A. Herter, a specialist in the chemistry of diseases, and Simon Flexner, the first director of laboratories of the

Rockefeller Institute, were also on the board. In addition to Dubos's book, a concise account may be found in Rosen, "Patterns of Health Research."

10. The statistic "a third" from Thomas Bonner, *American Doctors and German Universities: A Chapter in International Intellectual Relations, 1870–1914* (Lincoln, Neb.: University of Nebraska Press, 1963), p. 23. "At least a third and perhaps a half of the best-known men (and women) in American medicine of this era received some part of their training in a German university."

11. David Nachmansohn, "Biochemistry as Part of My Life," *Annual Review of Biochemistry* 41 (1972): 2–8.

12. Severo Ochoa, "The Pursuit of a Hobby," *Annual Review of Biochemistry* 49 (1980): 2–6.

13. David Nachmansohn, "Highlights of a Friendship," in *Reflections on Biochemistry in Honour of Severo Ochoa,* ed. Arthur Kornberg et al. (Oxford: Pergamon Press, 1976), p. 403. Also present were Francis O. Schmitt, Ken Iwasaki, and Paul Rothschild.

14. Hans A. Krebs, "Dahlem in the Late Nineteen Twenties," in *Lipmann Symposium: Energy, Regulation and Biosynthesis in Molecular Biology,* ed. Dietmar Richter (Berlin: Walter de Gruyter, 1974), pp. 9–10.

15. Erwin Chargaff, *Heraclitean Fire: Sketches from a Life Before Nature* (New York: Rockefeller University Press, 1978), p. 66.

16. This statement is not true of Meyerhof himself, who landed at Penn in 1940, after being permitted to stay on at the Kaiser Wilhelm Institute in Heidelberg until the astonishingly late date—considering that he was Jewish—of August 1937. But Meyerhof did not thrive in the New World. Nor is it true of the physicist Hans Delbrück, who ended up at the California Institute of Technology.

17. Erwin Chargaff, review of Dubos's *The Professor, Nature* 266 (April 28, 1977): 780.

18. Details in Kohler, *Medical Chemistry,* pp. 279–80.

19. Author's interview with DeWitt Stetten, December 6, 1986.

20. Chargaff, *Heraclitean Fire,* p. 64.

21. Sarah Ratner, "A Long View of Nitrogen Metabolism," *Annual Review of Biochemistry* 46 (1977): 6–7.

22. DeWitt Stetten, "Rudi," *Perspectives in Biology and Medicine* 25 (1982): 367.

23. Anker and Rabinowitch quotations from Laura Fermi, *Illustrious Immigrants: The Intellectual Migration from Europe, 1930–41* (Chicago: University of Chicago Press, 1968), p. 319.

24. James Phinney Baxter, ed., *A Memoir of Jacques Cartier . . . His Voyages to the St. Lawrence* (New York, 1906), pp. 190–91.

25. For a brief history of scurvy, see I. M. Sharman, "Vitamin C: Historical Aspects," in *Vitamin C: Recent Aspects of its Physiological and Technological Importance,* ed. Gordon G. Birch and K. J. Parker (New York: Wiley, 1974), pp. 1–15.

26. Elmer Holmes Bobst, *Bobst: The Autobiography of a Pharmaceutical Pioneer* (New York: McKay, 1973), pp. 173–74.

27. Details in ibid., pp. 174–78. It was the chemist Charles Glenn King, later to become a prominent nutrition expert, and W. A. Waugh, who crystallized vitamin C at Pittsburgh. "Isolation and Identification of Vitamin C," *Journal of Biological Chemistry* 97 (1932): 325–31. But delineating its chemical structure occurred the following year at the University of Birmingham in England. See R. G. Ault et al., "Synthesis of d- and of l-Ascorbic Acid," *Journal of the Chemical Society* 1933 (ii): 1419–23.

28. See Samuel Mines, *Pfizer: An Informal History* (New York: Pfizer, 1978), pp. 51–52. The major use of these barrelfuls of vitamin C was not scurvy therapy but as an additive in soft drinks.

29. Merck and Company, *The Merck Manual,* 14th ed. (Rahway, N.J.: Merck, 1982), p. 1177.

30. William Osler, *The Principles and Practice of Medicine* (New York, 1892), p. 285. It was then known as arthritis deformans.

31. This account of events at Merck and the Mayo Clinic has been assembled from the acceptance speeches given by Edward Kendall and Philip Hench when receiving the Nobel prize in medicine in 1950. Nobel Foundation, *Nobel Lectures: Physiology or Medicine, 1942–1962* (Amsterdam: Elsevier, 1964), pp. 270–90 and 311–43. They shared the prize with Tadeus Reichstein, who had determined the structure of compound A (which he called something else) in 1936, two years before Kendall. Reichstein, of course, had determined a commercially viable method for making vitamin C around the same time. On cortisone trials at the Mayo Clinic, see "Preliminary Report: The Effect of a Hormone of the Adrenal Cortex . . . . ," *Proceedings of the Staff Meetings of the Mayo Clinic* 24 (April 13, 1949): 181–97. This article broke the cortisone story to the world. Merck and Company, in an end note, expressed its regret, "that because of the exigencies of manufacture no supplies of compound E are expected for treatment or additional research until sometime in 1950 at the earliest at which time supplies still will be exceedingly small."

32. Kalamazoo *Gazette,* May 15, 1986, p. G 10.

33. On prednisone, see Walter Sneader, *Drug Discovery: The Evolution of Modern Medicines* (New York: Wiley, 1985), p. 224. Information on 1957 sales from the Schering-Plough Corporation.

34. Ernst Chain, "A Short History of the Penicillin Discovery," in *The History of Antibiotics: A Symposium,* ed. John Parascandola (Madison, Wisc.: American Institute of the History of Pharmacy, 1980), p. 15.

35. A good account of these events, based in part on Fleming's unpublished diaries, is found in Gladys L. Hobby, *Penicillin: Meeting the Challenge* (New Haven: Yale University Press, 1985), pp. 3–14. Previously a microbiologist at Columbia University, Dr. Hobby went to work for Pfizer Inc. in 1943.

36. These details are recounted in Chain, "Short History," pp. 20–21.

37. Quoted in Alfred Newton Richards, "Production of Penicillin in the United States (1941–1946)," *Nature* 201 (February 1, 1964): 441.

38. On these early efforts, see W. H. Helfand et al., "Wartime Industrial Development of Penicillin in the United States," in *History of Antibiotics,* ed. Parascandola, pp. 31–56. The authors point out that Roger Reid, a graduate student at Pennsylvania State College, developed the strain of penicillin from which Dawson of Columbia worked around 1933 (p. 31).

39. Details from Hobby, *Penicillin,* pp. 73–75.

40. Mines, *Pfizer,* p. 71.

41. Details in Richards, "Production of Penicillin," p. 441.

42. Stetten interview of December 17, 1986.

43. George J. Dohrmann, "Fulton and Penicillin," *Surgical Neurology* 3 (1975): 278–79.

44. Mines, *Pfizer,* pp. 73–74.

45. Ibid., pp. 84–86.

46. Richards, "Production of Penicillin," p. 443.

47. U.S. Bureau of the Census, *Historical Statistics of the United States, Colonial Times to 1970. Bicentennial Edition, Part 2* (Washington, D.C.: Government Printing Office, 1975), p. 58.

48. For most recent statistics on the relative mortality from lung cancer and rheumatic fever, a streptococcal infection, see National Center for Health Statistics, "Advance Report of Final Mortality Statistics, 1984," *Monthly Vital Statistics Report*, vol. 35, no. 6, supp. 2, DHHS pub. no. (PHS) 86–1120, (Hyattsville, Md.: Public Health Service, September 26, 1986), pp. 13–14, table 5. On the extreme infrequency of lung cancer in past times, see Edward Shorter, *Bedside Manners: The Troubled History of Doctors and Patients* (New York: Simon & Schuster, 1985), pp. 225–26.

CHAPTER THREE

1. A. J. Mercer, "Smallpox and Epidemiological-Demographic Change in Europe: The Role of Vaccination," *Population Studies* 39 (1985): 287–307; statistic from p. 307.

2. A brief account in H. J. Parish, *Victory with Vaccines: The Story of Immunization* (Edinburgh: Livingstone, 1968), pp. 171–72.

3. Ralph Chester Williams, *The United States Public Health Service, 1798–1950* (Washington, D.C.: Government Printing Office, 1951), pp. 223–24.

4. Details in ibid., pp. 223–28.

5. The taste of triumph soured in Albert Calmette's mouth in 1930 when his vaccine was blamed for causing a tuberculosis epidemic in the German city of Lübeck. Biochemist Erwin Chargaff escaped the Nazis so effortlessly three years later only because Calmette, pleased that Chargaff had helped exculpate the BCG vaccine in the Lübeck epidemic, wrote to him in March 1933, asking him to accept a post at the Pasteur Institute in Paris. Chargaff, "A Fever of Reason," *Annual Review of Biochemistry* 44 (1975): 15.

6. Saul J. Farber, "Presentation of the George M. Kober Medal to James A. Shannon," *Transactions of the Association of American Physicians* 95 (1982), p. 141.

7. DeWitt Stetten, "Bellevue Hospital New York, July 1934–December 1936," *Perspectives in Biology and Medicine* 28 (1985): 557–58.

8. This and other Shannon quotes in this chapter are taken from the transcript of Thomas Kennedy's interview of Shannon in 1984, in archives of the History of Medicine Division of the National Library of Medicine.

9. Atabrine is the trade name for quinacrine hydrochloride, first used (against tapeworm infestation) in 1939.

10. In 1945, 1,100 employees, down from 1,400 in 1941. National Institutes of Health, *NIH Almanac, 1985,* United States DHHS, Public Health Service, NIH pub. no. 85-5 (Bethesda, Md.: NIH Division of Public Information, September 1985), p. 139. Subsequent details about NIH staffing, organization, and budget, unless otherwise indicated, are taken from this publication.

11. Richard H. Shryock, *American Medical Research Past and Present* (New York: Commonwealth Fund, 1947), p. 136. Of the $40 million that the drug companies spent in 1945 on medical research, most went, of course, to applied studies of drugs.

12. Eddy interview of December 4, 1986.

13. For a listing of the Nobel prizes to which NIH funding has contributed, see National Institutes of Health, *NIH Almanac, 1985,* pp. 164–65.

14. George Rosen, "Patterns of Health Research in the United States, 1900–1960,"

Bulletin of the History of Medicine 39 (1965): 220; and Stephen Strickland, *Politics, Science, and Dread Disease* (Cambridge, Mass.: Harvard University Press, 1972), pp. 28–29.

15. Facts from National Institutes of Health, *NIH Data Book, 1985*, U.S. DHHS, Public Health Service, DHHS pub. no. PHS 85–1261 (Bethesda, Md.: NIH Division of Public Information, June 1985), p. 17; and National Institutes of Health, *NIH Almanac, 1985*, pp. 136–38.

16. On Lasker's life, see John Gunther, *Taken at the Flood: The Story of Albert D. Lasker* (New York: Harper and Brothers, 1960).

17. This section depends on Strickland's well-researched account in *Dread Disease*, pp. 32–54. Strickland is adulatory of the Lasker forces, whom many NIH-ers have seen over the years as power-seeking meddlers.

18. Ibid., p. 51.

19. Transcript of Wyndham Miles's interview with George Burroughs Mider, 1968, archives of History of Medicine Division of the National Library of Medicine. I thank Peter Hirtle for bringing this uncatalogued collection of interviews to my attention.

20. The statistic "150" from Saul Farber, "James A. Shannon," p. 1430.

21. Katherine Ames Taylor, from story "Honeybear's Miracle," *Reader's Digest* 63 (September 1953): 197–98.

22. Gene Roehling, as told to Jim Stangier, "I Live in an Iron Lung," *Saturday Evening Post* 223 (March 24, 1951): 26–27.

23. William Jordan interview of December 17, 1986.

24. John R. Paul, *History of Poliomyelitis* (New Haven, Conn.: Yale University Press, 1971), pp. 373–74.

25. Ibid., p. 419.

26. These events are chronicled in "Technical Report on Poliomyelitis Vaccine," *Public Health Reports* 70 (August 1955): 747–49.

27. Paul, *History*, p. 437, summarizing a WHO report of 1956. Other companies too had problems with inactivating their vaccines, but the greatest culprit was the Cutter product.

28. This account of Eddy's life and involvement in polio vaccines is taken from the following sources: (1) a summary transcript of Wyndham Miles's interview with her in 1964, currently in the archives of the History of Medicine Division of the National Library of Medicine; (2) the author's interview with her of December 4, 1986; (3) her letter to the author of December 11, 1986; (4) extensive documentation on the tortured history of the Laboratory of Biologics Control, which became in 1955 the Division of Biologics Standards, presented to the Congress in 1971. *Congressional Record—Senate, Proceedings of October 15, 1971*, pp. S 16291–99; December 8, 1971, pp. S20902–14; (5) *Consumer Safety Act of 1972: Hearings before the Subcommittee on Executive Reorganization and Government Research of the Committee on Government Operations, United States, Senate, Ninety-Second Congress, Second Session on Titles I and II of S. 3419* (Washington, D.C.: Government Printing Office, 1972). Items 3 and 4 delve into wider problems in the Division of Biologics Standards in addition to the division's treatment of Dr. Eddy. I have seen no evidence that the director's office of NIH received word of Eddy's 1954 discovery that the Cutter laboratory's vaccine lots contained live virus. A brief account of Eddy's life and tribulations is presented in Elizabeth Moot O'Hern, *Profiles of Pioneer Women Scientists* (Washington, D.C.: Acropolis Books, 1985), pp. 151–60.

29. Stetten interview of December 6, 1986.

30. Shannon transcript. On the rupture in October 1953 between NFIP and its scientific advisory committee, see Paul, *Polio*, pp. 423–24.

31. Interview with Alan Rabson of December 5, 1986; and interview with Ruth Kirschstein of November 21, 1986.

32. This and all subsequent Shannon quotes, unless otherwise indicated, from the transcript in the archives of the History of Medicine Division of the National Library of Medicine of his 1984 interview with Thomas Kennedy.

33. Joseph S. Murtaugh, "Some Reminiscences of Working with Jim Shannon," Murtaugh Papers, Ms. C 310, 1968, archives of the History of Medicine Division of the National Library of Medicine.

34. Jerome Green interview of November 21, 1986.

35 Natalie Davis Spingarn, *Heartbeat: The Politics of Health Research* (Washington, D.C.: Robert B. Luce, 1976), p. 20.

36. DeWitt Stetten, Jr., *NIH: An Account of Research in Its Laboratories and Clinics* (New York: Academic Press, 1984), p. 481. Lister Hill was the son of the surgeon Luther Hill, one of the pioneers of American heart surgery. Luther had named his son in honor of the great Glasgow surgeon Lord (Joseph) Lister. To make things even cozier for health in the Congress, the Surgeon General of the PHS, Luther Terry, had also been named after Luther Hill.

37. Shannon was, in his own recollections, conspicuously silent about the role of the Lasker forces in booming the NIH's budget. He had little time for Mary Lasker and spoke slightingly of the special interest groups; he praised Congress for its willingness to "leave the decision how best the funds could be distributed to the professionals at NIH."

38. Among the new institutes Congress authorized were: Child Health and Human Development in 1962; Environmental Health Sciences in 1964; and the National Eye Institute in 1968. Other preexisting institutes (diseases of the nervous system, arthritis, teeth, and so forth) were expanded with new funds. Of the NIH's eleven institutes devoted to categorical diseases, only two were founded after Shannon's departure: the National Institute on Aging in 1974 and an institute for arthritis and musculoskeletal disorders, hived off from the diabetes institute in 1986. A twelfth institute, the National Institute of General Medical Sciences, was founded in 1963 to administer the extramural grants of those other institutes that do not administer their own. Unlike the other institutes, it has only a small in-house research program. In addition to the institutes, the NIH operates a number of other ancillary divisions, including the distinguished National Library of Medicine.

39. Michael Shimkin, "As Memory Serves—An Informal History of the National Cancer Institute, 1937–57," *Journal of the National Cancer Institute* 59 (1977): 573.

CHAPTER FOUR

1. In P. R. Srinivasan et al., eds., *The Origins of Modern Biochemistry: A Retrospect on Proteins, Annals of the New York Academy of Science*, vol. 325 (New York: New York Academy of Sciences, 1979), p. 47.

2. These very general estimates are from James Bordley and A. McGehee Harvey, *Two Centuries of American Medicine, 1776–1976* (Philadelphia: Saunders, 1976), p. 526.

3. Sidney Raffel, "Fifty Years of Immunology," *Annual Review of Microbiology* 36 (1982): 1, 3.

4. Cited in N. W. Pirie, "Purification and Crystallization of Proteins," in Srinivasan et al., eds., *Origins of Modern Biochemistry*, p. 24. See also Joseph S. Fruton, "Early Theories of Protein Structure," *Origins of Modern Biochemistry*, pp. 4, 10.

5. René Dubos, *The Professor, the Institute, and DNA* (New York: Rockefeller University Press, 1976), p. 89. For the above account, see also Maclyn McCarty, "Reminiscences of the Early Days of Transformation," *Annual Review of Genetics* 14 (1980): 1–15. McCarty wrote a more extended account of these events in *The Transforming Principle: Discovering that Genes are Made of DNA* (New York: Norton, 1985). For an assessment of the reasons behind Avery's own scientific caution, see Arthur M. Diamond, "Avery's 'Neurotic Reluctance,' " *Perspectives in Biology and Medicine* 26 (1982): 132–36.

6. Erwin Chargaff, "How Genetics Got a Chemical Education," in Srinivasan et al., eds., *Origins of Modern Biochemistry*, p. 350.

7. The above account based on ibid., p. 351; and Erwin Chargaff, *Heraclitean Fire: Sketches from a Life Before Nature* (New York: Rockefeller University Press, 1978), pp. 98, 103.

8. This account from Chargaff, *Heraclitean Fire*, pp. 100–2; and Robert Olby, *The Path to the Double Helix* (Seattle, Wash.: University of Washington Press, 1974), p. 389. Olby argues that Watson was silent not out of duplicity but because he feared embarrassment and didn't want to "admit any knowledge which Chargaff could test out."

9. James Watson has retold his side of the story in *The Double Helix: A Personal Account of the Discovery of the Structure of DNA* (New York: Atheneum, 1968).

10. *Biomedical Science and its Administration: A Study of the National Institutes of Health* (Washington, D.C.: The White House, February 1965), p. 141. This document is often referred to as the Wooldridge Report, after the chairman of the NIH Study Committee, Dean E. Wooldridge.

11. Michael Shimkin, "As Memory Serves—An Informal History of the National Cancer Institute, 1937–57," *Journal of the National Cancer Institute* 59 (1977): 575.

12. Alton Meister, "Recollections About Enzymology and Amino Acid Biochemistry at NCI," in *NIH: An Account of Research in Its Laboratories and Clinics*, ed. DeWitt Stetten, Jr. (New York: Academic Press, 1984), pp. 239–40.

13. The description of Leon Heppel—". . . screwy, but always calculatingly so"—is Robert G. Martin's, "A Revisionist View of the Breaking of the Genetic Code," in Stetten, *NIH*, p. 287.

14. The above account from Arthur Kornberg, "For the Love of Enzymes," and Leon Heppel, "My Interrupted Association with Potassium," in *Reflections on Biochemistry in Honour of Severo Ochoa*, ed. Arthur Kornberg (Oxford: Pergamon Press, 1976), pp. 243–51 and 377–79. Also on Herbert Tabor, "Early Enzymological Research," in Stetten, *NIH*, pp. 222–29; and interviews with Stetten, Alan Rabson, and Tabor.

15. Arthur Kornberg recapitulated the story in "The Synthesis of DNA," *Scientific American* 219 (October 1968): pp. 67–68.

16. DeWitt Stetten interview of December 6, 1986.

17. Robert Martin, in Stetten, *NIH*, pp. 293–94.

18. Sources for the above are Robert Martin, in Stetten, *NIH*; Severo Ochoa, "The Pursuit of a Hobby," *Annual Review of Biochemistry* 49 (1980): 20; and interviews with Tabor and Stetten. Although Nirenberg was at the heart institute at the time of receiving the Nobel prize in 1968, he had remained until 1962 at the National Institute of Arthritis and Metabolic Diseases, later called the National Institute of Arthritis, Diabetes, and Digestive and Kidney Diseases.

19. Michael Heidelberger, "A 'Pure' Organic Chemist's Downward Path," *Annual Review of Microbiology* 31 (1977): 1–5.

20. Chargaff, *Heraclitean Fire*, p. 73.

21. Michael Heidelberger, "Reminiscences," *Immunological Reviews*, no. 83 (1985): 19.

22. Paul interview of December 4, 1986.

23. The general reader will find clear accounts of the immune system in Peter Jaret, "The Wars Within," *National Geographic* 169 (June 1986): 702–33; and Jeffrey Laurence, "The Immune System in AIDS," *Scientific American* 253 (December 1985): 84–93. Scientifically oriented readers will find helpful Ivan Roitt, *Essential Immunology*, 5th ed. (Oxford: Blackwell, 1984).

24. Baruj Benacerraf, "Reminiscences," *Immunological Reviews*, no. 84 (1985): 17.

25. Gene Shearer interview of December 5, 1986.

26. This account of Benacerraf's life and journey from NYU to NIH is based on his published "Reminiscences," and on interviews with William Paul, Alan Rabson, Thomas Waldmann, and another senior scientist who preferred to remain anonymous.

27. These discoveries are reviewed in William Paul, "Genetic Control of Cellular Interactions and Specific Immune Response Genes," in Stetten, *NIH*, pp. 167–75.

28. Michael Frank interview of December 17, 1986.

29. Lennart Philipson, "The European Molecular Biology Laboratory: An International Collaborative Effort," *Perspectives in Biology and Medicine* 29, no. 3, pt. 11 (1986): S98.

30. Lewis Thomas, *The Lasker Awards: Four Decades of Scientific Medical Progress* (New York: Albert and Mary Lasker Foundation, 1985), p. 5.

31. Zacharias Dische, "Reflections on the Relevance of Biochemistry for the Understanding of Living Systems," in Kornberg, ed., *Reflections on Biochemistry*, p. 224.

32. Statistics from "Update on Acquired Immune Deficiency Syndrome (AIDS)—United States," *Morbidity and Mortality Weekly Report* 31 (September 24, 1982): table 1, 507.

33. Institute of Medicine, National Academy of Sciences, *Confronting AIDS: Directions for Public Health, Health Care, and Research* (Washington, D.C.: National Academy Press, 1986), pp. 5, 7, 73.

34. Ibid., p. 5.

35. DeWitt Stetten interview of December 6, 1986.

36. Howard Streicher interview of December 16, 1986.

37. René Vallery-Radot, *The Life of Pasteur*, trans. R. L. Devonshire (Garden City, N.Y., 1923), p. 76. "Chance only favors the mind which is prepared."

38. William Jordan interview of December 17, 1986.

CHAPTER FIVE

1. Details in Josef Breuer and Sigmund Freud, *Studies on Hysteria* (1895), trans. James and Alix Strachey (1955) (Harmondsworth: Penguin, 1974), pp. 130–43, 167–68. The Stracheys situate the case in 1888 rather than 1889, the date Freud gives in the text.

2. Case taken from the discharge register (Protokoll) of the Sanatorium Fries, now deposited in Vienna's Stadt- und Landesarchiv in the city's Rathaus. The register is listed under M. Abt. 209.

3. Details from John F. Fulton, *Harvey Cushing: A Biography* (Springfield: Charles C Thomas, 1946), pp. 256–60; and from Edward W. Taylor, "Two Cases of Tumor of the Brain, with Autopsy," *Boston Medical and Surgical Journal* 134 (January 16, 1896):57.

4. Fulton, *Cushing*, p. 121.

5. Ibid., pp. 111–25; and William H. Sweet, "Harvey Cushing," *Journal of Neurosurgery* 50 (1979):7.

6. This account from Harvey Cushing, *Intracranial Tumours* (Springfield, 1932), p. 3; and Fulton, *Cushing*, pp. 288, 604.

7. This account from C. Gutiérrez, "The Birth and Growth of Neuroradiology in the U.S.A.," *Neuroradiology* 21 (1981):227; and Fulton, *Cushing*, p. 122.

8. J. W. D. Bull, "The History of Neuroradiology," in *Historical Aspects of the Neurosciences* ed. F. Clifford Rose and William F. Bynum (New York: Raven, 1982), p. 256. Fedor Krause's three-volume textbook *Surgery of the Brain and Spinal Cord* was translated into English in 1910. Bull considers Arthur Schüller, however, the true father of neuroradiology.

9. The name Egaz Moniz was later associated with a particularly ghastly set of operations perpetrated upon psychiatric patients, but this early accomplishment may be thought to counterbalance some of the later harm the man did. See Elliot Valenstein, *Great and Desperate Cures: The Rise and Decline of Psychosurgery and Other Radical Treatments for Mental Illness* (New York: Basic Books, 1986).

10. See Owsei Temkin, *The Falling Sickness: A History of Epilepsy from the Greeks to the Beginnings of Modern Neurology*, 2d ed. (Baltimore: Johns Hopkins University Press, 1971).

11. On bromine and phenobarbital for epilepsy, see Walter Sneader, *Drug Discovery: The Evolution of Modern Medicines* (New York: Wiley, 1985), p. 41.

12. This story is told by Tracy J. Putnam, in Frank J. Ayd, Jr., ed., *Discoveries in Biological Psychiatry* (Philadelphia: Lippincott, 1970), pp. 85–90. The drug at the time was christened diphenylhydantoin.

13. Robert Bing, *Textbook of Nervous Diseases*, trans. Webb Haymaker (St. Louis, 1939), p. 171.

14. *Goodman and Gilman*, p. 475.

15. This account is based on the following sources: telephone interview with Bernard Patten of January 19, 1987; Bernard Patten, "A Personal Tribute to Dr. George C. Cotzias: Clinician and Scientist," *Perspectives in Biology and Medicine* 27 (1983):156–61; George C. Cotzias, ed., *Parkinson's Disease* (New York: Medcom, 1971) (in series "Recent Advances in Therapy"); Lily C. Tang, "A Personal and Scientific Biography of Dr. George C. Cotzias," *NeuroToxicology* 5 (1984):5–12; Lewis Thomas, "George C. Cotzias, 1918–1977," *Transactions of the Association of American Physicians* 91 (1978):23–24; and Benjamin Boshes, "Sinemet and the Treatment of Parkinsonism," *Annals of Internal Medicine* 94 (1981):364–70.

16. See Laura Fermi, *Illustrious Immigrants: The Intellectual Migration from Europe, 1930–41*, 2d ed. (Chicago: University of Chicago Press, 1971), ch. 6.

17. Gregory Zilboorg, *A History of Medical Psychology* (New York, 1941), p. 500.

18. Walter Bromberg, *Psychiatry Between the Wars, 1918–1945: A Recollection* (Westport, Conn.: Greenwood, 1982), p. 147.

19. Reuben Fine, *A History of Psychoanalysis* (New York: Columbia University Press, 1979), p. 572.

20. Mildred Edie Brady, "The Strange Case of Wilhelm Reich," *New Republic* 116 (May 26, 1947):20; Leonard Engel, "Sigmund Freud: Father of Psychoanalysis," *Science Digest* 35 (June 1954):81, 83; Lucy Freeman, *Fight Against Fears* (New York: Crown, 1951); and *Time*'s comment, July 9, 1951, p. 46. For a sampling of *Time*'s numerous other stories on psychoanalysis, see "The Couch Cult," September 11, 1950, p. 58; and "Is Freud Sinful," April

21, 1952, p. 65. *The Saturday Evening Post*'s "little boy" cartoon was reprinted in an adulatory piece by Rollo May, "Medicines of the Mind," The *Saturday Review* 36 (August 15, 1953):17. The "youthful tragedy" cartoon, reprinted from *PM*, ran in *Time*, June 8, 1953, p. 80. Jeffrey M. Masson, *The Assault on Truth: Freud's Suppression of the Seduction Theory* (New York: Farrar, Straus and Giroux, 1984).

21. Joseph Wortis, "More on Psychotherapy," *Biological Psychiatry* 19 (1984): 933.

22. Seymour Fisher and Roger Greenberg, *The Scientific Credibility of Freud's Theories and Therapy* (New York: Basic Books, 1985), p. 395. They discovered, however, that some of Freud's concepts do indeed seem valid.

23. Lester Luborsky et al., "Comparative Studies of Psychotherapies," *Archives of General Psychiatry* 32 (1975), esp. 1002–6. In an end note the authors observe that long-term psychotherapy was not adequately represented in their study. This is mainly because analysts who do such therapy seldom provide any statistics on outcome, to say nothing of control groups.

24. Frank J. Ayd, Jr., "The Impact of Biological Psychiatry," in Ayd, ed., *Discoveries*, pp. 231–32.

25. Quoted in Judith P. Swazey, *Chlorpromazine in Psychiatry: A Study in Therapeutic Innovation* (Cambridge: MIT Press, 1974), p. 217.

26. Statistics on number and rate of psychiatric admissions from U.S. Bureau of the Census, *Historical Statistics of the United States, Colonial Times to 1970, Bicentennial Edition, Part 2* (Washington, D.C.: Government Printing Office, 1975), p. 84. On the probable historic increase in schizophrenia, see E. Fuller Torrey, *Schizophrenia and Civilization* (New York: Jason Aronson, 1980), pp. 21–41; Edward Hare, "Was Insanity on the Increase?" *British Journal of Psychiatry* 142 (1983):439–55; and Edward Hare, "Epidemiological Evidence for a Viral Factor in the Aetiology of the Functional Psychoses," in *Research on the Viral Hypothesis of Mental Disorders,* ed. P. V. Morozov (Basel: Karger, 1983; "Advances in Biological Psychiatry," no. 12), pp. 52–75.

27. Interview of January 30, 1987, at corporate headquarters of the parent company, SmithKline Beckman.

28. John Francis Marion, *The Fine Old House: Smith Kline Corporation's First 150 Years* (Philadelphia: Smith Kline Corporation, 1980), pp. 102–3, 156. The number fifteen thousand is from 1920, but the product line had not changed greatly before 1936.

29. SmithKline Beckman Corporation, "Annual Report," 1985, pp. 23, 31.

30. Quote from Swazey, *Chlorpromazine*, p. 163, who interviewed Grant and the other principals in the chlorpromazine story. The following information in this section relies on her painstaking monograph and on information supplied by John Young.

31. Ibid., p. 196.

32. On this visit, see ibid., pp. 187–88.

33. Ibid., pp. 200–201.

34. *Time*, March 7, 1955, p. 56.

35. Ross J. Baldessarini, *Chemotherapy in Psychiatry: Principles and Practice,* rev. ed. (Cambridge: Harvard University Press, 1985), p. 2; and Swazey, *Chlorpromazine*, p. 161.

36. *Life*, October 15, 1956, p. 149; and *Science Digest* 38 (September 1955):62. I have not told here the story of chlorpromazine's sister drug reserpine. Interested readers may consult Hugo J. Bein, "Biological Research in the Pharmaceutical Industry with Reserpine," in Ayd, ed., *Discoveries*, pp. 142–54.

37. For a historical perspective, see Gerald N. Grob, "Historical Origins of Deinstitu-

tionalization," in *New Directions for Mental Health Services: Deinstitutionalization,* ed. L. Bachrach (San Francisco: Jossey-Bass, 1983), pp. 15–29.

38. *Goodman and Gilman,* pp. 345–46.

39. New York, 1980, now a Bantam paperback.

40. Baldessarini, *Chemotherapy,* p. 236.

41. Leticia Kent, "Leo Sternbach: The Tranquil Chemist," *SciQuest* 53 (December 1980):22. This account of the history of the benzodiazepines is based on an interview with Leo Sternbach, January 29, 1987; Irvin M. Cohen, "The Benzodiazepines," in Ayd, ed., *Discoveries,* pp. 130–41; and "Ich Bin Nicht Stolz Geworden," *Roche Magazin,* no. 28 (November 1986):29–37.

42. Interview of January 29, 1987.

43. See Otto Loewi, "An Autobiographic Sketch," *Perspectives in Biology and Medicine* 4 (1960):20–21. Other details in George B. Koelle, "Reflections on the Pioneers of Neurohumoral Transmission," *Perspectives in Biology and Medicine* 28 (1985):438.

44. Arnold D. Welch, "Reminiscences in Pharmacology: Auld Acquaintance Ne'er Forgot," *Annual Review of Pharmacology and Toxicology* 25 (1985):4.

45. According to Jack Orloff's recollections, interview of February 9, 1987.

46. This account of Axelrod's career from Julius Axelrod, "Biochemical and Pharmacological Approaches in the Study of Sympathetic Nerves," in *The Neurosciences: Paths of Discovery,* ed. Frederic G. Worden et al. (Cambridge: MIT, 1975), pp. 191–208. Robert Kanigel has written a lively account of the sometimes tense relations between Axelrod and his mentor, Brodie, *Apprentice to Genius: The Making of a Scientific Dynasty* (New York: Macmillan, 1986).

47. Solomon H. Snyder, "Drug and Neurotransmitter Receptors in the Brain," *Science* 224 (April 6, 1984):23.

48. A comprehensible account of these mechanisms may be found in David Holzman, "Drug Therapy Picks Up Where Freud Left Off," *Insight* (December 1, 1986): 14–17.

49. See Edward Shorter, "Paralysis: The Rise and Fall of a 'Hysterical' Symptom," *Journal of Social History* 19 (1986):549–82.

50. See Ronald Bayer and Robert L. Spitzer, "Neurosis, Psychodynamics, and *DSM-III,*" *Archives of General Psychiatry* 42 (1985):187–96. On appropriate drug therapy for such physical symptoms of psychological origin as pseudo-seizures, see Alec Roy, "Management of Hysterical Seizures," in *Pseudoseizures,* ed. Terrence L. Riley and Alec Roy (Baltimore: Williams and Wilkins, 1982), pp. 162–63.

51. Peter Tyrer and Angus MacKay, "Schizophrenia: No Longer a Functional Psychosis," *Trends in NeuroSciences* 9 (November-December 1986):537–38.

52. Francis O. Schmitt, "Adventures in Molecular Biology," *Annual Review of Biophysics and Biophysical Chemistry* 14 (1985):19–20.

53. Details from Hounsfield's Nobel prize lecture reprinted in Godfrey Hounsfield, "Computed Medical Imaging," *Journal of Computer Assisted Tomography* 4 (1980):665–74.

54. Paula T. Beall, "A Historical Perspective on Biomedical NMR," *Magnetic Resonance Imaging* 1 (1982):189.

CHAPTER SIX

1. National Center for Health Statistics, *Health, United States, 1985.* DHHS pub. no. (PHS) 86–1232 (Washington, D.C.: Government Printing Office, December 1985), p. 49.

In 1984 death rates for "diseases of the heart" were 37 per 100,000 population for males thirty-five to forty-four, 160 for males forty-five to fifty-four.

2. Data for 1900 and 1963 are taken from U.S. Bureau of the Census, *Historical Statistics of the United States, Colonial Times to 1970, Bicentennial Edition, Part 2* (Washington, D.C.: Government Printing Office, 1975), p. 58; the statistics I cite for 1960 and 1984, which include only heart disease and not the larger spectrum of circulatory and kidney disorders, come from Health Statistics, *Health*, p. 48.

3. Ralph H. Major, *Classic Descriptions of Disease*, 3d ed. (Springfield, Ill.: Charles C Thomas, 1945), pp. 417–18.

4. George Canby Robinson, *The Patient as a Person: A Study of the Social Aspects of Illness* (New York, 1939), pp. 67–69; we lose sight of Mr. Arthur in 1938.

5. Frederick A. Willius and Thomas E. Keys, *Cardiac Classics*, 2 vols. (New York, 1941), vol. 1, p. 223.

6. The TIMI Study Group [Eugene Passamani], "The Thrombolysis in Myocardial Infarction (TIMI) Trial," *NEJM* 312 (April 4, 1985):932.

7. The St. Louis doctor Adam Hammer is generally considered the first to have diagnosed a myocardial infarct in a living patient. He did so in 1878 while living in Vienna, dying himself later that year. See Major, *Medical Classics*, pp. 424–28.

8. James B. Herrick, "An Intimate Account of My Early Experience with Coronary Thrombosis," *American Heart Journal* 27 (1944):5–7, 13–17. For Herrick's original report, see "Clinical Features of Sudden Obstruction of the Coronary Arteries," *JAMA* 59 (December 7, 1912):2015–20.

9. T. Lauder Brunton, "On the Use of Nitrite of Amyl in Angina Pectoris," *Lancet* (July 27, 1867): 97–98.

10. William Murrell, "Nitro-Glycerine as a Remedy for Angina Pectoris," *Lancet*, in four issues beginning January 18, 1879. Quotes from issues of February 1, pp. 151–52, and February 15, pp. 225–27.

11. For a brief account, see Walter Sneader, *Drug Discovery: The Evolution of Modern Medicines* (New York: Wiley, 1985), pp. 112–13.

12. Health Statistics, *Health*, p. 76, table 37. In 1976–80, on an age-adjusted basis, 41.3 percent of the American population twenty-five to seventy-four years old had a systolic blood pressure of at least 140 mm/Hg. and a diastolic pressure of 90 or more, based on a single measurement.

13. Karl H. Beyer, Jr., "Hypertension: From Theory to Therapy," *Trends in Pharmacological Sciences* 1 (1980):115.

14. See Edward Shorter, *Bedside Manners: The Troubled History of Doctors and Patients* (New York: Simon & Schuster, 1985), pp. 89–90, on the measurement of blood pressure in clinical practice earlier in the twentieth century.

15. William Osler, *The Principles and Practice of Medicine*, 6th ed. (New York, 1906), p. 851.

16. Ibid., 8th ed., (1918), p. 842.

17. Henry A. Christian, *The Principles and Practice of Medicine . . . Originally Written by the Late Sir William Osler*, 13th ed. (New York, 1938), p. 1065.

18. Irvine H. Page, "A History of the Council for High Blood Pressure Research," *Hypertension* 6 (March-April 1984):1–208.

19. David Riesman, "High Blood Pressure and Longevity," *JAMA* 96 (April 4, 1931): 1110. When bleeding failed, "I have found leeching from the mastoid process an almost sovereign remedy."

20. Christian, *Principles,* p. 1066. He did suggest nitroglycerin and short courses of phenobarbital, both useless as long-term solutions.

21. On the rice diet, see Walter Kempner's extensive defense of his 1944 proposal, "Treatment of Hypertensive Vascular Disease with Rice Diet," *American Journal of Medicine* 4 (1948):545–77. Also see, "Rice Diet Evaluated," *Science News Letter* 58 (October 28, 1950): 276; and interview with Jerome Green of November 21, 1986.

22. Edward Freis, "Chemotherapy of Hypertension," *JAMA* 218 (November 15, 1971):1010.

23. Merck, Sharp & Dohme Research Laboratories, *By Their Fruits* (Rahway, N.J.: Merck and Co., 1962), insert following p. 23.

24. Julius Comroe, *Retrospectroscope: Insights into Medical Discovery* (distributed, Ithaca: Perinatology Press, 1977), p. 70. Other details in this story from Karl H. Beyer, Jr., "Discovery of the Thiazides: Where Biology and Chemistry Meet," *Perspectives in Biology and Medicine* 20 (1977):410–20; and Beyer, *Trends,* pp. 114–21; and Merck, *Fruits,* pp. 39–41. On the pharmacology of the thiazide diuretics, see *Goodman and Gilman* pp. 785–88. These drugs do not, in fact, inhibit carbonic anhydrase, their formerly postulated mechanism.

25. *Time* tells the heart attack story in issue of October 3, 1955, pp. 15–17, and following weeks.

26. *Time,* October 10, 1955, p. 24.

27. Of course Dr. White was aware of the increasing medical literature incriminating high levels of cholesterol in heart disease. Misunderstood was the dangerousness of even moderate elevations. *Time* quoted John Gofman's work on the atherogenic nature of cholesterol, but then with journalistic evenhandedness informed its readers that "other researchers are not sure that he is right." October 31, 1955, p. 54.

28. *Time,* October 31, 1955, p. 53. Quoting Keys in *Time*'s words.

29. Organization of the Framingham study described in Thomas Royle Dawber, *The Framingham Study: The Epidemiology of Atherosclerotic Disease* (Cambridge: Harvard University Press, 1980), pp. 15–24. Although the first participant was enrolled in 1948, systematic medical examinations began only in the spring of 1950.

30. Ibid., p. 64. Coronary heart disease rates for the twenty-four-year period from tables.

31. Ibid., pp. 55–56.

32. Ibid., p. 181.

33. Public Health Service, *Smoking and Health: Report of the Advisory Committee to the Surgeon General of the Public Health Service,* PHS pub. no. 1103 (Washington, D.C.: Government Printing Office, n.d. [1964]), p. 45.

34. Health Statistics, *Health,* p. 72, table 33. For the 1962 article see J. T. Doyle et al., "Cigarette Smoking and Coronary Heart Disease," *NEJM* 266 (April 19, 1962):796–801.

35. William P. Castelli, "Cardiovascular Disease and Multifactorial Risk: Challenge of the 1980s," *American Heart Journal* 106 (1983):1195.

36. Dawber, *Framingham,* p. 228.

37. Interview with Lenfant on February 9, 1987.

38. Dawber, *Framingham,* p. 99, figs. 6–2, 7–1.

39. National Heart, Lung, and Blood Institute, National Institutes of Health, "Five-Year Findings of the Hypertension Detection and Follow-Up Program," *JAMA* 242 (December 7, 1979): 2562–71.

40. See Eugene Braunwald's praise, "Thirty-Five Years of Progress in Cardiovascular

Research," *Circulation* 70, suppl. 3 (November 1984):111–13. The heart institute's annual report on which Dr. Lenfant drew the X was *Fact Book: Fiscal Year 1985* (Bethesda, Md.: U.S. Department of Health and Human Services, Public Health Service, National Institutes of Health, NHLBI Information Office, October 1985), p. 32.

41. William P. Castelli, "Epidemiology of Coronary Heart Disease: The Framingham Study," *American Journal of Medicine* 76 (1984):11.

42. William P. Castelli, "The Triglyceride Issue: A View from Framingham," *American Heart Journal* 112 (1986):432.

43. Dawber, *Framingham*, p. 134, fig. 8–5.

44. Thomas Dawber et al., "Preliminary Report: The Determinants and Clinical Significance of Serum Cholesterol," *Massachusetts Journal of Medical Technology* 4 (1962): 11–29.

45. Health Statistics, *Health*, p. 78, table 39. High-risk levels of serum cholesterol are defined for the various age groups as follows: twenty to twenty-nine years of age, greater than 220 milligrams per deciliter; thirty to thirty-nine, greater than 240 mg./dl.; over forty, greater than 260 mg./dl.

46. William P. Castelli, "Cardiovascular Disease," p. 1192, table 1.

47. National Institutes of Health, "Consensus Development Conference Statement: Lowering Blood Cholesterol to Prevent Heart Disease," vol. 5, no. 7 (no date), p. 8. Italics in the original.

48. Basil Rifkind, at the heart institute, is deputy director of the Arteriosclerosis, Hypertension and Lipid Metabolism program. Interview of February 9, 1987.

49. See on these Sneader, *Drug Discovery*, pp. 198–99; and on clofibrate, see *Goodman and Gilman*, pp. 835–37.

50. See the Consensus Development Conference Statement. Also the two articles from the "Lipid Research Clinics Program" in *JAMA* 251 (1984):351–64, 365–74.

51. Jesse Huff interview of February 6, 1987. See also *Goodman and Gilman*, pp. 839–41. Merck had earlier sold the license for cholestyramine to the Mead Johnson Laboratories, which marketed the drug as Questran.

52. Donald Fredrickson et al., "Fat Transport in Lipoproteins—An Integrated Approach to Mechanism and Disorders," *NEJM* 276 (January 5, 1967):34–42 and the four following issues.

53. Carl Herman Hoffman et al., "Synthesis of . . . Mevalonic Acid," *Journal of the American Chemical Society* 79 (1957):2316–18.

54. I heard this informally at Merck, but it was repeated in *The Wall Street Journal*, December 23, 1986, p. 16.

55. See the Lovastatin Study Group II, "Therapeutic Response to Lovastatin (Mevinolin) in Nonfamilial Hypercholesterolemia: A Multicenter Study," *JAMA* 256 (November 28, 1986):2829–34; Gloria L. Vega and Scott M. Grundy, "Treatment of Primary Moderate Hypercholesterolemia with Lovastatin (Mevinolin) and Celestipol," *JAMA* 257 (January 2, 1987):33–38.

56. I am grateful to Judy Reemtsma for a transcript of her interview with Brown and Goldstein in January, 1987.

57. Joseph L. Goldstein and Michael S. Brown, "The Low-Density Lipoprotein Pathway and its Relation to Atherosclerosis," *Annual Review of Biochemistry* 46 (1977):897–930.

58. The story is told in their joint Nobel lecture. Michael S. Brown and Joseph L. Goldstein, "A Receptor-Mediated Pathway for Cholesterol Homeostasis," Nobel Foundation, *Les Prix Nobel, 1985* (Stockholm: Almqvist and Wiksell, 1986), pp. 166–206.

59. Spiegel interview of January 9, 1987.

60. Stephen Paget, *Surgery of the Chest* (Bristol, 1896), p. 121.

61. On the historic preconditions that had to be met before open-heart surgery became feasible, see Julius H. Comroe, Jr., and Robert D. Dripps, "Scientific Basis for the Support of Biomedical Science," *Science* 192 (April 9, 1976):106.

62. Elliott C. Cutler, "Cardiotomy and Valvulotomy for Mitral Stenosis," *Boston Medical and Surgical Journal* 188 (June 28, 1923):1023–27.

63. Alfred Blalock and Helen B. Taussig, "The Surgical Treatment of Malformations of the Heart in Which There Is Pulmonary Stenosis or Pulmonary Atresia," *JAMA* 128 (May 19, 1945):189–202. The condition was called the tetralogy of Fallot.

64. John H. Gibbon, Jr., "Development of the Artificial Heart and Lung Extracorporeal Blood Circuit," *JAMA* 206 (November 25, 1968):1983.

65. Eugene Landis told this to Julius Comroe, who was also at Penn in those years. Comroe, *Retrospectroscope*, p. 122.

66. See also on this story, J. Donald Hill, "John H. Gibbon, Jr.: Part I. The Development of the First Successful Heart-Lung Machine," *Annals of Thoracic Surgery* 34 (1982):337; Anthony R. C. Dobell, "John H. Gibbon, Jr.: Part II. Personal Reminiscences," *Annals of Thoracic Surgery* 34 (1982):342–44; Lyman A. Brewer III, "Open Heart Surgery and Myocardial Revascularization: Historical Notes," *American Journal of Surgery* 141 (1981):618–31; and Bernard J. Miller, "The Development of Heart Lung Machines," *Surgery, Gynecology and Obstetrics* 154 (1982):403–14.

67. See the Nobel prize lectures for 1956 of André-Frédéric Cournand, Dickinson W. Richards, Jr., and Werner Forssmann, in *Nobel Lectures in Physiology or Medicine, 1942–62* (Amsterdam: Elsevier, 1964), p. 506ff.

68. Robert S. Litwak, "The Growth of Cardiac Surgery: Historical Notes," *Cardiovascular Clinics* 3 (1971):38.

69. Mason Sones, Jr., and Earl K. Shirey, "Cine Coronary Arteriography," *Modern Concepts of Cardiovascular Disease* 31 (1962):735–38. Improvements in enhancing fluoroscopic images after 1948 contributed as well to making this procedure practical.

70. This account from James Bordley III and A. McGehee Harvey, *Two Centuries of American Medicine, 1776–1976* (Philadelphia: Saunders, 1976), pp. 512–13.

71. H. Edward Garrett, Edward W. Dennis, and Michael E. DeBakey, "Aortocoronary Bypass with Saphenous Vein Graft," *JAMA* 223 (February 12, 1973):792–94. Although the patient was hooked up to a heart-lung machine, it was not actually turned on and the heart beat normally throughout the operation.

72. Nancy Yanes Hoffman, *Change of Heart: The Bypass Experience* (San Diego: Harcourt Brace Jovanovich, 1985), p. 5.

73. Paul M. Zoll, "Resuscitation of the Heart in Ventricular Standstill by External Electric Stimulation," *NEJM* 247 (November 13, 1952):768–71.

74. Administering shocks directly to the heart during operations was pioneered among others by Claude Beck. For details see Stephen L. Johnson, *The History of Cardiac Surgery, 1896–1955* (Baltimore: Johns Hopkins University Press, 1970), pp. 29–34.

75. A brief historical account of the AICD may be found in Roger A. Winkle, "The Implantable Defibrillator in Ventricular Arrhythmias," *Hospital Practice* 18 (1983):149–58. For the first case, see Michel Mirowski et al., "Termination of Malignant Ventricular Arrhythmias with an Implanted Automatic Defibrillator in Human Beings," *NEJM* 303 (August 7, 1980):322.

76. Heart, Lung, and Blood Institute, *Fact Book,* p. 36: "345,000 CHD deaths averted in 1984 due to decline from peak rate in 1963."

CHAPTER SEVEN

1. As told to Leo and Dora S. Rane, "My Daughter Has Leukemia," *Today's Health* 31 (May 1953):36–37, 58, 60. An account of Mary's therapy in Boston continued at length.

2. David Schottenfeld et al., "Recent Trends in Cancer Survival," *Association of Life Insurance Medical Directors of America, 94th Annual Meeting* 69 (1986):66.

3. Leads from the Morbidity and Mortality Weekly Report (MMWR), "Premature Mortality Due to Malignant Neoplasms—United States, 1983," *JAMA* 256 (August 15, 1986):821.

4. Cancer Control Objectives for the Nation: 1985–2000," *NCI Monographs,* no. 2 (1986):3.

5. Robert M. Steckler and Donald P. Shedd, "General Grant: His Physicians and His Cancer," *American Journal of Surgery* 132 (1976):508–14; long quote from p. 511.

6. For statistics, see Edward Shorter, *History of Women's Bodies* (New York: Basic Books, 1982), pp. 242–43.

7. Frederick L. Hoffman, *The Mortality from Cancer Throughout the World* (Newark, 1915), pp. 483–557.

8. Susan S. Devesa and Debra T. Silverman, "Cancer Incidence and Mortality Trends in the United States: 1935–74," *Journal of the National Cancer Institute* 60 (1978):555. Statistics are for whites only; combined figures for blacks and whites are not available before 1950.

9. National Center for Health Statistics, *Health, United States, 1985.* DHHS pub. no. (PHS) 86–1232 (Washington, D.C.: Government Printing Office, 1985), p. 40. "Today" means data for 1984.

10. On major moments in the history of cancer surgery, see Michael B. Shimkin, *Contrary to Nature* (Washington, D.C.: Government Printing Office, 1977).

11. The story is told in Jerome M. Vaeth, "Historical Aspects of Tylectomy [Lumpectomy] and Radiation Therapy in the Treatment of Cancer of the Breast," *Frontiers in Radiation Therapy and Oncology* 17 (1983):2.

12. Frank Adair and Halsey Bagg, "Experimental and Clinical Studies on the Treatment of Cancer by . . . Mustard Gas," *Annals of Surgery* 93 (1931):190–99.

13. This account from Alfred Gilman, "The Initial Clinical Trial of Nitrogen Mustard," *American Journal of Surgery* 105 (1963):574–78; and Louis S. Goodman et al., "Nitrogen Mustard Therapy," *JAMA* 132 (September 21, 1946):126–32. This was the first report of the therapy's success.

14. This account based on Carl Pochedly, "Dr. James A. Wolff II. First Successful Chemotherapy of Acute Leukemia," *American Journal of Pediatric Hematology/Oncology* 6 (1984):449–54; C. Gordon Zubrod, "The Cure of Cancer by Chemotherapy: Reflections on How It Happened," *Medical and Pediatric Oncology* 8 (1980):107–14; and Walter Sneader, *Drug Discovery: The Evolution of Modern Medicines* (New York: Wiley, 1985), pp. 344–47. The derivative of aminopterin called methotrexate in 1972 saved the life of Sneader's own four-year-old son who had been dying of leukemia.

15. On the early history of cancer research in the PHS, see Frank J. Rauscher, Jr., and Michael B. Shimkin, "Viral Oncology," in Stetten, ed., *NIH,* p. 352; C. Gordon Zubrod,

"Origins and Development of Chemotherapy Research at the National Cancer Institute," *Cancer Treatment Reports* 68 (1984):9.

16. Vincent DeVita, Jr., and Abraham Goldin, "Therapeutic Research in the National Cancer Institute," in *NIH: An Account of Research in Its Laboratories and Clinics* ed. DeWitt Stetten, Jr. (New York: Academic Press, 1984), p. 501.

17. Michael B. Shimkin, "As Memory Serves: An Informal History of the National Cancer Institute, 1937–57," *Journal of the National Cancer Institute* 59 (1977):580.

18. Michael B. Shimkin, "In the Middle: 1954–63—Historical Note," 62 (1979):1295.

19. Carter interview of February 5, 1987.

20. Vincent DeVita, Jr., "On Special Initiatives, Critics, and the National Cancer Program," *Cancer Treatment Reports* 68 (1984):1.

21. Robert E. Kohler, *From Medicinal Chemistry to Biochemistry: The Making of a Biomedical Discipline* (Cambridge, Eng.: Cambridge University Press, 1982), p. 218.

22. Shimkin, "Memory Serves," p. 591.

23. Harold P. Rusch, "The Beginnings of Cancer Research Centers in the United States," *Journal of the National Cancer Institute* 74 (1985):395.

24. Zubrod, "Origins," p. 10.

25. Min Chiu Li, "The Historical Background of Successful Chemotherapy for Advanced Gestational Trophoblastic Tumors," *American Journal of Obstetrics and Gynecology* 135 (1979):267–69; and Zubrod, "Origins," p. 13.

26. This account has been assembled from Emil Frei III, "Intramural Therapeutic Research at the National Cancer Institute, Department of Medicine: 1955–1965," *American Journal of Obstetrics and Gynecology* 135 (1979):21–25; Zubrod, "Origins," p. 14; and C. Gordon Zubrod, "The Cure of Cancer by Chemotherapy: Reflections on How It Happened," *Medical and Pediatric Oncology* 8 (1980):113.

27. Schottenfeld, *Association of Life Insurance*, p. 78. In 1976–81, five-year survival for acute lymphocytic leukemia had reached 65 percent in white children; the corresponding survival rate in Hodgkin's disease had risen from 52 percent in 1960–63 to 88 percent in 1976–81. See also Robert W. Miller and Frank W. McKay, "Decline in U.S. Childhood Cancer Mortality: 1950 Through 1980," *JAMA* 251 (March 23, 1984):1570.

28. On the period after 1971 when the War on Cancer began, see Nathaniel I. Berlin, "The Conquest of Cancer," *Perspectives in Biology and Medicine* 22 (1979):511.

29. Sarah Stewart, Bernice Eddy et al., "The Induction of Neoplasms with a Substance Released from Mouse Tumors by Tissue Culture," *Virology* 3 (1957):380–400.

30. Brief accounts of the collaboration between Stewart and Eddy and their role in viral oncology may be found in Frank J. Rauscher, Jr., and Michael B. Shimkin, "Viral Oncology," in Stetten, *NIH,* pp. 356–59; and Thelma B. Dunn, "Intramural Research Pioneers, Personalities, and Programs: The Early Years," *Journal of the National Cancer Institute* 59 (1977):609. For an extensive account of the polyoma virus itself, see Ludwik Gross, *Oncogenic Viruses,* 3d ed., 2 vols. (Oxford: Pergamon Press, 1983), vol. 2, pp. 737–828.

31. Stetten interview of December 6, 1986. Smadel letter to Eddy of October 24, 1960, reprinted in *Consumer Safety Act of 1972. Hearings Before the Subcommittee on Executive Reorganization and Government Research of the Committee on Government Operations, United States, Senate, Ninety-Second Congress, Second Session on Titles I and II of S. 3419* (Washington, D.C.: Government Printing Office, 1972), p. 549.

32. Maurice Hilleman interview of February 6, 1987. Hilleman pointed out, however, that Smadel was "a very brilliant guy."

33. Benjamin H. Sweet and Maurice R. Hilleman, "The Vacuolating Virus, S.V. 40," *Proceedings of the Society for Experimental Biology and Medicine* 105 (November 1960):420-27.

34. See Alan P. Goffe et al., "Poliomyelitis Vaccines," *Lancet* (March 18, 1961):612.

35. The extensive scientific literature on SV 40's potential dangers to the public health was reviewed in Joseph F. Fraumeni, Jr., et al., "An Evaluation of the Carcinogenicity of Simian Virus 40 in Man," *JAMA* 185 (August 31, 1963):713-18.

36. John R. Paul mentions this unpublished memo of June 20, 1961, from Roderick Murray to the Surgeon General in his *History of Poliomyelitis* (New Haven: Yale University Press, 1971), p. 461.

37. Bernice Eddy et al., "Identification of the Oncogenic Substance in Rhesus Monkey Kidney Cell Cultures as Simian Virus 40," *Virology* 17 (1962):65. Similarly, the NIH permitted Eddy's initial observations in 1959-60 of a carcinogenic substance in the monkey kidneys to be published only in 1961, Bernice Eddy et al., "Tumors Induced in Hamsters by Injection of Rhesus Monkey Kidney Cell Extracts," *Proceedings of the Society for Experimental Biology and Medicine* 107 (May 1961):191-97.

38. Perhaps this added nugget was present only because the story, rather than taken from AP wire copy as previously, was written by the *Times'* excellent science reporter, Harold M. Schmeck, Jr., "Studies Identify Virus in Vaccine," New York *Times,* February 7, 1962, p. 27.

39. Sabin interview of December 15, 1986.

40. Kirschstein interview of November 21, 1986. She said, "I think there was a reluctance on the part of some people to bring that whole story out into the public too soon, for fear that we would have another disaster."

41. On this, see Gross, *Viruses,* vol. 2, pp. 853-56.

42. For other sources of the Stewart-Eddy saga, in addition to those listed above, see ch. 3, n. 28.

43. Daniel Greenberg, "What Ever Happened to the War on Cancer," *Discover* (March 1986):51.

44. Richard A. Rettig, *Cancer Crusade: The Story of the National Cancer Act of 1971* (Princeton: Princeton University Press, 1977), p. 79.

45. Benno C. Schmidt, "Five Years into the National Cancer Program: Retrospective Perspectives—The National Cancer Act of 1971," *Journal of the National Cancer Institute* 59 (1977):687.

46. Shimkin, "Memory Serves," pp. 595-96; and Shimkin, "Middle," pp. 1297-99.

47. See Lester Breslow et al., "Cancer Control: Implications from History," *Journal of the National Cancer Institute,* 59 (1977):684; and Umberto Saffiotti, "Carcinogenesis, 1957-77: Notes for a Historical Review," ibid., 59 (1977):620.

48. *NCI Monographs,* no. 2 (1986), pp. 16-17.

49. Ibid., pp. 73-74.

50. Schottenfeld, *Association,* pp. 80, 82. John C. Bailar III and Elaine M. Smith offer a more pessimistic assessment of these statistics, "Progress Against Cancer?" *NEJM* 314 (May 8, 1986):1226-32. Yet the balance tips negatively only when the smoking-related cancers are included. These are notoriously resistant to therapy and still rising as a result of increases in smoking that occurred twenty or thirty years ago.

51. pp. 63-64; whites only. Breast cancer statistics for stages 1 and 2.

52. National Cancer Institute, *National Cancer Program, 1983-84 Director's Report and Annual Plan FY 1986-1990.* U.S. DHEW, Public Health Service, National Institutes of

Health, pub. no. 86–2765 (Bethesda, Md.: National Institutes of Health, November 1985), p. 15. Statistics not for throat cancer in specific but head-and-neck cancer generally.

CHAPTER EIGHT

1. Dr. Myron Miller, who helps run the geriatric medicine program at New York's Mount Sinai Hospital. I am grateful to Mike Jackson for letting me see a transcript of his interview with Dr. Miller of December 5, 1986.

2. This account is based on Martin Gilbert, *Road to Victory: Winston S. Churchill, 1941–1945* (London: Stoddart, 1986), esp. pp. 54, 95, 164, 213–14, 229, 807; and Charles Wilson [Lord Moran], *Churchill Taken from the Diaries of Lord Moran: The Struggle for Survival, 1940–1965* (Boston: Houghton Mifflin, 1966), pp. 19–20, 469, 815, 821.

3. Lord Moran reviews the major problems in Churchill's medical history: a heart attack just after Pearl Harbor, three attacks of pneumonia, and two abdominal operations. None of these resulted in chronic impairment. Then Churchill also suffered recurrently from "senile pruritus" and some kind of conjunctivitis (p. 653). His most salient chronic ailment was his "black dog," or depression, which haunted him for years. But although more frequent in the elderly, depression is by no means distinctive to them.

4. National Institute on Aging, *Normal Human Aging: The Baltimore Longitudinal Study of Aging.* NIH pub. no. 84–2450 (Washington, D.C.: Government Printing Office, November 1984), p. 208.

5. Mike Jackson made available to me the transcript of his interview with Dr. Butler of December 1986.

6. Life expectancy data for the United States as a whole are not available for 1850. Statistics for Massachusetts are found in U.S. Bureau of the Census, *Historical Statistics of the United States, Colonial Times to 1970, Bicentennial Edition, Part 2* (Washington, D.C.: Government Printing Office, 1975), I, p. 56. On the great incidence of infant mortality in the Old World, see Edward Shorter, *The Making of the Modern Family* (New York: Basic Books, 1975), pp. 353–59. In Massachusetts in 1850, one infant in eight died in the first year of life. Ibid., p. 57.

7. Eighteenth-century statistics refer only to white males. Bureau of the Census, *Historical Statistics U.S.*, II, p. 1170. 1870 data for the United States as a whole from ibid., I, p. 15.

8. Michel Dahlin, "Perspectives on the Family Life of the Elderly in 1900," *Gerontologist* 20 (1980):100.

9. See, for example, John Ehrenreich, ed., *The Cultural Crisis of Modern Medicine* (New York: Monthly Review Press, 1978), pp. 10–12.

10. National Center for Health Statistics, *Health, United States, 1985.* DHHS pub. no. (PHS) 86–1232 (Washington, D.C.: Government Printing Office, December 1985), p. 40.

11. Joan Cornoni-Huntley et al., eds., *Established Populations for Epidemiologic Studies of the Elderly: Resource Data Book.* DHEW, Public Health Service, National Institute on Aging, NIH pub. no. 86–2443 (Bethesda: National Institutes of Health, 1986), pp. 60, 66, 80.

12. Mike Jackson interview with Dr. Schneider in November 1986.

13. National Center for Health Statistics, *Current Estimates from the National Health Interview Survey, United States, 1983.* Vital and Health Statistics, series 10, no. 154. DHHS pub. no. (PHS) 86–1582 (Washington, D.C.: Government Printing Office, June 1986), p. 110.

14. "80 percent" cited in Cornoni-Huntley et al., eds., *Established Populations*, p. 95. "Four out of ten" from Center for Health Statistics, *Current Estimates, 1983*, p. 104.

15. Center for Health Statistics, *Current Estimates, 1983,* p. 82.

16. Cornoni-Huntley et al., eds., *Established Populations,* p. 105.

17. Center for Health Statistics, *Current Estimates, 1983,* p. 108.

18. Ibid., p. 112.

19. Alois Alzheimer wrote a preliminary note in the *Neurologisches Zentralblatt* 25 (1906):1134, then described the disease more fully the following year, "Über eine eigenartige Erkrankung der Hirnrinde" ["On a Singular Disease of the Cerebral Cortex"], *Allgemeine Zeitschrift für Psychiatrie* 64 (1907):146–48.

20. The following section is based largely on interviews of Alzheimer's specialists done by Mike Jackson. Mr. Jackson kindly made the following transcripts available to me: interview with Dr. Myron Miller, Mount Sinai Medical Center, December 5, 1986; Linda Nee, social worker at the National Institute for Mental Health, December 9, 1986; Dr. Edward Rall, director of Intramural Research at the National Institute of Arthritis, Metabolic and Digestive Diseases, as well as deputy director of the NIH, December 19, 1986; Dr. Edward Schneider, at the time deputy director of the National Institute on Aging, November 17, 1986; Dr. Trey Sunderland, National Institute of Mental Health, November 17, 1986.

21. See, for example, H. Lauter and J. E. Meyer, "Clinical and Nosological Aspects of Senile Dementia, in *Senile Dementia: Clinical and Therapeutic Aspects* ed. Christian Müller and Luc Ciompi (Bern: Huber, 1968).

22. See the news story by Deborah M. Barnes, "Defect in Alzheimer's Is on Chromosome 21," *Science* 235 (February 20, 1987):846–47; and the reports of original research in the same issue, notably, Peter H. St George-Hyslop et al., "The Genetic Defect Causing Familial Alzheimer's Disease Maps on Chromosome 21," *Science* 235 (February 20, 1987):885–90.

23. *Fourth Annual Report of the Director, National Institute of Arthritis, Diabetes, and Digestive and Kidney Diseases: Improving Health Through Research.* DHEW, Public Health Service, NIH pub. no. 85–2493 (Bethesda: National Institutes of Health, January 1985), p. 29.

24. Center for Health Statistics, *Current Estimates, 1983,* p. 80.

25. Walter Sneader, *Drug Discovery: The Evolution of Modern Medicine* (New York: Wiley, 1985), p. 89.

26. The cost of withdrawing Oraflex alone was $15 million, to say nothing of the cost of developing the drug in the first place and the many later lawsuits, *The Wall Street Journal,* October 19, 1982.

27. William Osler, *Principles and Practice of Medicine* (New York, 1892), p. 371.

28. Center for Health Statistics, *Current Estimates, 1983,* pp. 80, 82. "Elderly" means sixty-five to seventy-four, "middle-aged," forty-five to sixty-four. The rate for women aged sixty-five to seventy-four was 42.7 per 1,000 population.

29. In "Foreword" to *Tagamet (Cimetidine): Ten Years Forward* (Welwyn Garden City: Smith Kline & French Laboratories, 1986), pp. 4–5.

30. Bertram W. Sippy, "Gastric and Duodenal Ulcer: Medical Cure by an Efficient Removal of Gastric Juice Corrosion," *JAMA* 64 (May 15, 1915):1626.

31. See, for example, Henry A. Christian, *The Principles and Practice of Medicine . . . Originally Written by the Late Sir William Osler,* 13th ed. (New York, 1938), pp. 609–10.

32. George Paget's comments in a symposium, *The Discovery of Histamine H2-Receptors and Their Antagonists* (Philadelphia: Smith Kline and French International, 1982), p. 13.

33. This account of the development of cimetidine is based principally on ibid.; see also,

P. Ranganath Nayak and John M. Ketteringham, *Breakthroughs!* (New York: Rawson, 1986), pp. 102–29. Henry Wendt, at the time a Smith Kline vice president, then in 1976 president, told me in an interview of February 12, 1987, what risks moving forward with the County Cork plant entailed. Of course, once the facility was on-line in the spring of 1977, it was just barely able to satisfy world demand for the drug.

34. Cited in Richard L. Grant, "Concepts of Aging: An Historical Review," *Perspectives in Biology and Medicine* 6 (1962–63):468.

CHAPTER NINE

1. The above from the Nobel prize lectures of Nathans and Smith in 1978. See the 1978 volume in the Nobel Foundation's series *Les Prix Nobel.* Awareness of restriction enzymes goes back to Salvador Luria's work in 1952 at the University of Illinois with viruses that invade bacteria. But the mechanism of the bacteria's defense against the virus was a mystery. Then in 1968 at Harvard Matthew Meselson isolated a restriction enzyme. "But no practical use for it had been seen," according to John Lear, *Recombinant DNA: The Untold Story* (New York: Crown, 1978), p. 47.

2. Paul Berg, "Dissections and Reconstructions of Genes and Chromosomes," *Les Prix Nobel* (1980):97–114.

3. This account from Lear, *Untold Story,* pp. 59, 68–70. Additional details also in Stanley N. Cohen, "The Stanford DNA Cloning Patent," in *From Genetic Engineering to Biotechnology —The Critical Transition,* ed. William J. Whelan and Sandra Black (New York: Wiley, 1982), pp. 213–14.

4. Lewis Thomas, *The Lasker Awards: Four Decades of Scientific Medical Progress* (New York: Albert and Mary Lasker Foundation, 1985), p. 25.

5. Story in Nicholas Wade, "The Roles of God and Mammon in Molecular Biology," in Whelan and Black, eds., *Genetic Engineering,* pp. 207–8.

6. Goldstein interview of January 8, 1987.

7. Alick Isaacs and Jean Lindenmann, "Virus Interference. I. The interferon," *Royal Society of London. Proceedings,* 147 (1957):258–67. A historical account was offered in *Time,* March 31, 1980, pp. 47–48. Of the various types of interferon made by different cells and labeled alpha, beta, and gamma, only human alpha interferon is discussed in this chapter.

8. Details from *Time,* March 31, 1980, p. 47.

9. Carter interview of February 5, 1987.

10. DeVita interview of December 16, 1986.

11. *Time,* March 31, 1980, p. 47; DeVita immediately reversed this decision after becoming director of NCI in 1980.

12. New York *Times* story of December 29, 1979; "$3 billion," from Nicholas Wade, "University and Drug Firm Battle Over Billion-Dollar Gene," *Science* 209 (September 26, 1980):1492; Rauscher quote from *Time,* March 31, 1980, p. 47. Spiegel interview of January 9, 1987.

13. Sidney Pestka, "The Purification and Manufacture of Human Interferons," *Scientific American* 249 (August 1983):36–43.

14. This account in Wade, "Battle," pp. 1492–95.

15. This account based on ibid., and on publicity material provided by Hoffmann-La Roche.

16. All interviews with Schering staff except Robert Luciano were conducted on January 9, 1987. I interviewed Luciano on February 27, 1987.

17. Charles Weissmann, "Interferon Trials and Tribulations," in Whelan and Black, eds., *Genetic Engineering*, p. 106.

18. I asked Michael Potter about these events in a telephone interview of March 13, 1987. Potter said Freund seemed to suspect he might have given himself the disease, although Freund said nothing explicit to Potter. Potter asked Freund's personal physician, Emil ("Tom") Frei, what Frei thought, and Frei on different occasions gave contradictory opinions about whether Freund might have caused his own myeloma. Mineral oil certainly can produce pathological changes if it enters the body, and the suggestion is not a far-fetched one.

19. My account vastly simplifies myeloma research at NIH in 1955–60, with its complex cast of characters. See Michael Potter, "Myeloma Proteins," *Experientia* 42 (September 15, 1986):967–70.

20. Some of this information is in Thomas Waldmann, "Immunoglobulin Structure and Genetics," in *NIH: An Account of Research in Its Laboratories and Clinics* ed. DeWitt Stetten, Jr. (Orlando: Academic Press, 1984), p. 159. For an account of Potter's work see his article, "Immunoglobulin-Producing Tumors and Myeloma Proteins of Mice," *Physiological Reviews* 52 (1972):631–719, esp. 636–37.

21. From Milstein's Nobel prize lecture in 1984, p. 191.

22. They reported their original results in "Continuous Cultures of Fused Cells Secreting Antibody of Predefined Specificity," *Nature* 256 (August 7, 1975):495–97. Milstein gave an account of their work in his 1984 Nobel prize lecture. Georges Köhler offered a firsthand version of his experiences in an interview with Nicholas Wade, "Hybridomas: The Making of a Revolution," *Science* 215 (February 26, 1982):1073–75.

23. This story has been reconstructed from interviews with Gideon Goldstein and other Ortho staff on January 8, 1987, and from a telephone interview with Patrick Kung on March 9, 1987. The initial discovery of the OKT series was reported by Patrick C. Kung, Gideon Goldstein et al., "Monoclonal Antibodies Defining Distinctive Human T Cell Surface Antigens," *Science* 206 (October 19, 1979):347–49. Among the many important papers Goldstein later wrote on OKT-3, see Gideon Goldstein, "An Overview of ORTHOCLONE OKT 3," *Transplantation Proceedings* 18 (August 1986):927–30.

24. Sources for this account include the transcript of an interview which Judy Reemtsma did with Burton Sobel in January 1987. Among written sources, Diane Pennica et al. and Désiré Collen, "Cloning and Expression of Human Tissue-Type Plasminogen Activator cDNA in *E. coli,*" *Nature* 301 (January 20, 1983):214–21; Steven R. Bergmann et al., "Clot-Selective Coronary Thrombolysis with Tissue-Type Plasminogen Activator," *Science* 220 (June 10, 1983):1181–83 for the animal experiments; and The TIMI Study Group [John Passamani], "Thrombolysis in Myocardial Infarction (TIMI) Trial," *NEJM* 312 (April 4, 1985):932–36.

25. Berkowitz interview of February 12, 1987.

EPILOGUE

1. Lewis Thomas, *The Lasker Awards: Four Decades of Scientific Medical Progress* (New York: Albert and Mary Lasker Foundation, 1985), p. 34.

2. Alexandra Wyke, "Harder Going," *The Economist* (February 7, 1987): 4, 6.

3. Laubach interview of March 5, 1987.

4. Luciano interview of February 27, 1987.

5. Quoted in Bernard M. Patten, "A Personal Tribute to Dr. George C. Cotzias, Clinician and Scientist," *Perspectives in Biology and Medicine* 27 (1983):159.

6. Michael Heidelberger, "A 'Pure' Organic Chemist's Downward Path," *Annual Review of Microbiology* 31 (1977):6.

7. René J. Dubos, *The Professor, the Institute and DNA* (New York: Rockefeller University Press, 1976), p. 70.

8. Crooke interview of January 30, 1987.

9. Wendt interview of February 12, 1987.

10. Luciano interview of February 27, 1987.

11. Bullock interview of January 9, 1987.

12. This analysis from Wyke, "Harder Going," p. 7.

13. Cited in William H. Gruber, *The Strategic Integration of Corporate Research and Development* (New York: Amacom, 1981), p. 19.

14. Mark Potts and Peter Behr, *The Leading Edge: CEOs Who Turned Their Companies Around: What They Did and How They Did It* (New York: McGraw-Hill, 1987), p. 202.

15. Thomas, *Lasker Awards*, p. 34.

16. Paul interview of December 4, 1986.

17. Schlom interview of December 16, 1986.

18. Fauci interview of December 17, 1986.

19. Thomas, *Lasker Awards*, p. 2.

20. Waldmann interview of December 4, 1986.

CREDITS

P. 8. Ralph Chester Williams, *The United States Public Health Service*, Bethesda, Md: Commissioned Officers Association of the United States Public Health Service, 1951, opposite p. 496.

P. 9. Williams, *Public Health Service*, opposite p. 133.

P. 11. Bess Furman, *A Profile of the United States Public Health Service 1798–1948*, (Washington, D.C.: Government Printing Office, 1973), p. 277.

P. 14. John Francis Marion, *The Fine Old House: SmithKline Corporation's First 150 Years*, Philadelphia: SmithKline Corporation, 1980, p. 81.

P. 15. Marion, *Fine Old House*, p. 81.

P. 15. Marion, *Fine Old House*, p. 81.

P. 24. George W. Corner, *A History of the Rockefeller Institute 1901–1953*, New York: The Rockefeller Institute Press, 1964, opposite p. 33.

P. 27. Arthur Kornberg, ed., *Reflections on Biochemistry*, Oxford: Pergamon Press Ltd., 1976, opposite p. 402.

P. 33. Merck and Company, *Merck Review* 24, no. 1 (Spring 1963):13.

P. 35. Merck, *Merck Review* 43, no. 2 (Fall 1983): 6.

P. 36. Merck and Company, *By Their Fruits*, Rahway, N.J.: Merck and Company, 1962, p. 21.

P. 38. From Gladys L. Hobby, *Penicillin: Meeting the Challenge*, New Haven: Yale University Press, 1985, p. 1.

P. 39. From Gladys L. Hobby, *Penicillin: Meeting the Challenge*, New Haven: Yale University Press, 1985, p. 2.

P. 42. Merck, *By Their Fruits*, insert page opposite clinical case # 1.

P. 44. Photo courtesy Merck and Company.

P. 45. Photo courtesy Merck and Company.

P. 53. Saul J. Farber, "Presentation of the George M. Kober Medal to James A. Shannon," *Transactions of the Association of American Physicians* 95 (1982): cxl.

P. 54. Farber, "Presentation," p. cxlii.

P. 61. From John R. Paul, *A History of Poliomyelitis*, New Haven: Yale University Press, 1971, p. 327.

P. 62. Gene Roehling, "I Live in an Iron Lung," *The Saturday Evening Post* 223 (March 24, 1951): 27.

P. 63. Roehling, "Iron Lung," p. 26.

P. 65. Paul, *Poliomyelitis*, p. 379.

P. 66. National Library of Medicine.

P. 68. Ludwik Gross, *Oncogenic Viruses,* 3d ed., Oxford: Pergamon Press Ltd., 1983, vol. 2, p. 753.

P. 74. Farber, "Presentation," p. *cxlv.*

P. 75. Jack Orloff, "Presentation of the George M. Kober Medal to Robert William Berliner," *Transactions of the Association of American Physicians* 97 (1984): *cliii.*

P. 84. Michael B. Shimkin, "As Memory Serves—An Informal History of the National Cancer Institute, 1937–57," *Journal of the National Cancer Institute* 59, no. 2 (suppl.) (August 1977):575.

P. 98. From Jeffrey Laurence, "The Immune System in AIDS," *Scientific American* 253, no. 6 (December 1985):92.

P. 100. Laurence, "Immune System," p. 86.

P. 105. John F. Fulton, *Harvey Cushing: A Biography,* Springfield, Ill.: Charles C Thomas, 1946, photograph following p. 276.

P. 106. Fulton, *Harvey Cushing,* photograph between pp. 244 and 245.

P. 107. Fulton, *Harvey Cushing,* photograph preceding p. 341.

P. 108. Fulton, *Harvey Cushing,* photograph between pp. 244 and 245.

P. 118. From *Saturday Review* 36 (August 15, 1953): 17 (originally from "The Inside Story," *The Saturday Evening Post*).

P. 119. Cartoon by Ed Nofziger, "Memories Before Birth," *Time* 61 (June 8, 1953): 80 (originally from *PM*).

P. 124. "New Avenues into Sick Minds," *Life* 41 (October 22, 1956):120. Courtesy Hoffmann-La Roche.

P. 128. Leo H. Sternbach, "The Discovery of Librium," *Agents and Actions* 2, no. 4 (June 1972):196.

P. 130. Courtesy Hoffmann-La Roche.

P. 131. Merck, *Merck Review* 43, no. 2 (Fall 1983):7.

P. 138. Courtesy General Electric Co., Medical Systems Group.

P. 139. Courtesy General Electric Co., Medical Systems Group.

p. 140. Courtesy General Electric Co., Medical Systems Group.

P. 145. Squibb Milestones in Cardiovascular History Calendar, 1987.

P. 146. Squibb Milestones in Cardiovascular History Calendar, 1987.

P. 173. Elliott C. Cutler and S. A. Levine, "Cardiotomy and Valvulotomy for Mitral Stenosis," *Boston Medical and Surgical Journal* 188 (June 28, 1923):1026.

P. 176. Lyman A. Brewer, "Open Heart Surgery and Myocardial Revascularization," *The American Journal of Surgery* 141 (June 1981):626.

P. 185. Manuel Lederman, "The Early History of Radiotherapy: 1895–1939," *International Journal of Radiation Oncology/Biology/Physics* 7 (May 1981): 641.

P. 186. Louis S. Goodman, "Nitrogen Mustard Therapy," *Journal of the American Medical Association,* 251, no. 17 (May 4, 1984):2257.

P. 187. Goodman, "Therapy," p. 2258.

P. 189. *Life* 8 (June 17, 1940):35.

P. 194. Merck, *Merck Review* 43, no. 2 (Fall 1983): 51.

P. 197. Gross, *Oncogenic Viruses,* p. 753.

P. 202. Gross, *Oncogenic Viruses,* p. 841.

P. 208. *National Cancer Program 1983–1984 Director's Report and Annual Plan FY 1986–1990,* U.S. Department of Health and Human Services, p. 5.

P. 209. *Director's Report and Annual Plan,* p. 6.

P. 210. National Cancer Institute, *NCI Monographs,* no. 2 (1986): 6.

P. 213. Courtesy Ortho Pharmaceuticals.

P. 221. Bristol-Myers Company Annual Report, 1984, p. 18.

p. 226. Courtesy Pfizer Inc.

P. 236. Daniel Nathans, "Restriction Endonucleases, Simian Virus 40, and the New Genetics," Nobel lecture, December 8, 1978, *Les Prix Nobel 1978,* Stockholm, Sweden: Almqvist & Wiksell International, p. 200.

P. 237. Nathans, "Restriction Endonucleases," p. 201.

P. 242. Harold M. Schmeck, Jr., "Interferon, Virus Foe, Comes of Age," New York *Times,* December 26, 1978, p. III–2.

P. 246. Hoffmann-La Roche, *A Progress Report on Biotechnology,* 2d ed., Nutley, N.J.: 1986, pp. 14–15.

P. 247. "Gene-splicers Brace for a Brawl over Patents," *Business Week,* March 12, 1984, p. 28.

INDEX